Mastering DC

A Newcomer's Guide to Living in the Washington, DC Area

by Kay Killingstad

For information regarding sales of this book, please contact:

Adventures Publishing
PO Box 405
Glen Echo, MD 20812-0405
800-594-1371
301-229-3342 (fax)
e-mail: advpubsdc@aol.com
website: www.masteringdc.com

Published 2000. Fifth edition.

Printed in the United States of America.
Editing: Sheila Donoghue and Dartha Dragnich
Design and Layout: Harris Design, Inc.
Printing: Kirby Lithographic Company, Inc.

Library of Congress Catalog Card Number: 00-132614
ISBN: 0-9631935-4-6

Acknowledgments

Publications like these can only be accomplished with the assistance of a number of people. In my case, I am fortunate to have some highly capable people on my "team." I especially want to thank Dartha Dragnich, who juggled her responsibilities as a wife, mother and teacher to ensure that the fifth edition met its deadline. In addition to functioning as editor of this edition, she wrote and contributed Chapter 10—Young People. Her capable assistance and her commitment to the entire book effort have been immeasurable, and I owe her a debt of gratitude for seeing this through.

My thanks and appreciation also go to Sheila Donoghue for her continued contribution to the Mastering DC production effort. Sheila has provided project management and editorial assistance on each of the editions, and she was instrumental in the planning, development and editing of "To Do" lists, a new feature located at the end of each chapter in this edition. She has also been responsible for the increased focus on promoting environmental sites as evidenced by the feature pages that she contributed.

Kittena (KJ) Hannah was especially helpful to us by providing the fresh eyes for proofreading the updated chapters. She made a number of useful comments and suggestions that helped us with continuity issues and we are especially grateful for her contributions.

Robin Harris of Harris Design, Inc. deserves a particular note of thanks for once again providing the creative design expertise in the layout of both the cover and the text. Her steadiness, patience and flexibility were especially helpful throughout the entire production process.

I owe special thanks to the friends, colleagues and associates who contributed their time to provide review comments, fact checking and input material for the fifth edition. These individuals include Karen Baragona, René Carter, Kate Christen, Nancy Dunn, David Dragnich, Mike Dragnich, Betty Fimiani, Sandra A. Greene, Garnet Tennyson Hadley, Kurt Kehl, Geoff Kieffer, Judith Miernyk, Anand Mishra, Andrew Nicholls, Leslie Enderlin Nicholls, Patricia Powell, Carol Ryder, Anya Schoolman, Blanche Theeman, David Whitehill and Margaret Williams.

Also, my thanks to the staff of Blue Planet Media, Melissa and Todd Christopher and Jason Vick, for their assistance in maintaining the Mastering DC website.

DC	MD	VA
• Adams Morgan	• Bethesda	• Alexandria
• American University Park	• Bowie	• Ballston
• Capitol Hill	• Chevy Chase	• Clarendon
• Cathedral Heights	• College Park	• Court House
• Cleveland Park	• Gaithersburg	• Crystal City
• Dupont Circle	• Germantown	• Fairfax City
• Foggy Bottom	• Greenbelt	• Falls Church
• Friendship Heights	• Hyattsville	• Herndon
• Georgetown	• Largo	• Pentagon City
• Glover Park	• Mitchellville	• Reston
• McLean Gardens	• Mount Rainier	• Rosslyn
• Northeast Washington	• Rockville	
• Shaw and The New U	• Silver Spring	
• 16th Street Corridor	• Takoma Park	
• Southeast/ Anacostia	• Wheaton	
• Southwest and Waterfront		
• Van Ness		
• Woodley Park		

Counties new to this edition:

- Loudoun
- Prince William

Chapter 6 Shopping

Chapter 7 Food And Fun

Chapter 8 Beyond The Job

Chapter 9 Washington Weekends

Chapter 10 Young People

Chapter 11 Resources

A Note to the Reader

Welcome to the fifth edition of Mastering DC, which continues with its original purpose—providing a single resource for information about the Washington, DC area to help new residents get established quickly and easily. Even long-time residents will appreciate the convenience of this one-stop resource guide, and should encounter some new area treasures within its pages.

Washington, DC is more than the site of America's historic past and current seat of power and democracy; it is a city of local neighborhoods and hometown to 554,000 people. When you extend the boundaries to include the entire metro area, there are an amazing 4.4 million people who call this place home. The high-tech industry has pronounced the rustic Virginia countryside the new "Silicon Valley," causing the population to expand and spill from Fairfax County into Loudoun and Prince William Counties. A new section has been added to the Chapter 2, Neighborhoods, to address this new growth.

A quick overview of these 11 chapters and you'll begin to see a pattern emerging; that of a thriving community undergoing new construction and exciting renovation and renewal. We hope the information about this growth makes you more aware of all there really is to master in the DC area.

CHAPTER ONE

Housing

When it comes to finding a place to live in the Washington metropolitan area, the prerogative is yours—from original Victorian-style homes to high-tech high rises. You will probably find that you need to evaluate the choices based on neighborhoods, public transportation and other amenities, and the cost. This chapter clues you into some general rules of thumb for real estate shopping in the DC area and lets you know what you are likely to find and how to make looking a little easier. Also included is information on interim housing options and a list of pointers to help you with the details of moving.

The Local Real Estate Market

The cost of housing in the Washington area varies according to the type of neighborhood, proximity to Downtown and accessibility to the Metro system. Within that framework, the size and quality of the particular home also make a difference. Generally, the farther away from the city you look, the less expensive the housing and the more space for the money.

Housing in Maryland and Northern Virginia is generally less expensive than equivalent accommodations in the District. To get the best bargains, you have to locate close to or just outside the Beltway (Silver Spring, Takoma Park, Greenbelt, Rockville, Herndon, Alexandria south of Old Town and Falls Church). The suburbs offer more public services than the District and a wider variety of convenient shopping. Taxes are also lower.

If you choose to live in the District, having a car can be unnecessary and in many areas actually a nuisance. Having a car in the suburbs, on the other hand, can be a necessity, particularly as you go farther out. Public transportation options in and near the District are terrific, while parking is scarce and often expensive.

Housing Options

Each city has its own terminology to describe apartments and other living arrangements. Washington and its environs have the typical options, but the great number and wide variety of life styles in the city call for additional alternatives. Now more than ever, thanks to new construction in different architectural styles, as well as the periodic renovation of older properties, newcomers have the opportunity to find just the right place to call home. Safety is an important consideration when choosing a place to live. If you are interested in finding out about a particular area, you can call the local police for the latest crime statistics.

RENTING WITH PETS

Pet policies vary throughout the area. Many local companies do not allow pets and those that do may impose a size limit on the animal, require up-front pet deposits in addition to security deposits and charge premium rents. Owners of cats and small dogs often find fewer restrictions than those of large dog owners. However, a number of local property managers, especially in Maryland and Virginia, are beginning to accept large dogs since research shows the size of a dog does not reflect its potential for causing damage. If you have a pet, or think you may want to get one, be certain to ask about pet policies up front to avoid disappointment later.

Rents vary widely throughout the metropolitan DC area depending on proximity to the city and the age of the property. A recent trend in rental property management gives renters more "bang" for their rent "buck." They can sign up and pay for only the amenities they want. The fees are usually not refundable, but the flexibility of choice is appealing. Also, people are negotiating rents more frequently, especially for higher-end rentals and when it is time to renew the lease. Although not encouraged by most property managers, many would rather negotiate than lose a good tenant. Events such as new development can cause rent and housing price fluctuations, therefore it is recommended that you consult a real estate agent and/or current publications regarding specific neighborhood prices. For comparison purposes, typical rental rates are included in this chapter. If you rent, take the time to read your lease and avoid costly surprises down the road.

Efficiencies

These one-room apartments, usually 400 to 600 square feet, generally include a small sleeping alcove and a large closet. The bathroom is small and in many, the kitchen is along one wall of the main room. Efficiencies are normally found in high-rise buildings. You may know them as "studios" elsewhere or as the equivalent of a London "bedsit." Monthly rents range from $700 to $1,300 and up. Some condo buildings also include efficiencies, particularly in the more densely populated neighborhoods.

Junior One-Bedroom Apartments

A junior one-bedroom apartment is basically an efficiency with an extra room—usually the size of a large closet—for a small bed and bureau. Everything is scaled down in size, but the separation of rooms appeals to many. Rents start at about $700 a month and go up to around $1,100.

One-, Two- and Three-Bedroom Apartments

Fairly self-explanatory, these apartments or condos have the specified number of bedrooms, plus living room and dining room (often combined) and a separate kitchen. The number of bathrooms varies and is usually indicated in the ad or description. Depending on location, monthly rent usually falls in the $800 to

$1,900 range for a one-bedroom, and can reach anywhere from $900 to $2,500 and up for a two-bedroom. Three-bedroom apartments are more unusual, with rents from $1,000 to $3,000 depending on location and amenities.

English Basements

This term refers to the ground-floor basement (not underground) of a row house, converted into an apartment. These one- or two-bedroom apartments usually have separate entrances and sometimes a terrace area. In the District, the windows often have bars for safety. Rents tend to be between $950 and $1,200, depending on size and location.

Group Houses

If you already have a large group together or you want to live with several people, you can move into one of the many "group" houses available for rent. Usually each person has a private bedroom and everyone shares the kitchen, bathroom and common rooms. Houses in the suburbs and in the more residential parts of DC also generally have a small lawn and backyard. Rent is most often under

ABBREVIATIONS IN REAL ESTATE ADS

ac or a/c	air conditioned
apt	apartment
avail	available
balc	balcony
bkyd	backyard
bldg	building
br, bdr, bdrm	bedroom
bsmt	basement
b/k	block
CAC	central air conditioning
CATV	cable TV
conv	convenient
cpt	carpeted
dr	dining room
d/w	dishwasher
effic	efficiency
elec	electricity
F	female
flr	floor
fr	from
frpl or fpl	fireplace
gar or grg	garage
hse	house
ht	heat
h/w	hardwood floors
kit	kitchen
lbr	library
lg, lrg	large
loc	location
lr	living room
lux	luxury
lvls	levels
M	male
mo	month
mod	modern
newly ren	newly renovated
nghbrs	neighbors
nr	near
pkg, prkg	parking
prof	professional
pvt	private
rec ctr	recreation center
refs	references
shr	share
TH	townhouse
+ util	plus utilities
w/d	washer and dryer
w/w	wall-to-wall carpeting

GETTING HERE

Moving companies, such as the national chains listed here, will take care of everything from packing to storage to final placement of your belongings. If you are moving locally, you can contact Beltway Movers (301-420-2200; www.beltwaymovers.com), the area's largest local company.

National Moving Companies

Allied Van Lines
800-523-7652

Atlas Van Lines
800-847-6683

Bekins Van Lines
800-545-7817

Starving Students
800-537-7983

United Van Lines
800-325-3870

$500 a person. Group houses can be the best option for newcomers. Living with several people puts you immediately into a social circle and helps ease the anxiety of making the transition to a new city. If you are looking to live in a group house, expect to undergo an interview. Be sure you like the people as much as or more than you like the house—the emphasis in "group house" is on the group. Finally, find out about any "house rules" ahead of time.

Townhouses and Single-Family Homes

Townhouses are a popular choice for couples, small families and singles who want more living space without the responsibility of a large yard. These residential units share at least one exterior wall with other similar units and are designed to create the feel of a block of row houses from earlier days. Many developments are like condo buildings, in that residents share in the upkeep of the common grounds, usually through a management company. Single-family homes range in size and with the wide market for new construction of two-garage, three-story townhouses, you could end up in a single-family home that is smaller than a neighbor's townhouse. The detached house does usually come with a real yard, making it a good choice for families with children. Rental rates for townhouses and single-family homes are largely dependent on size (number of bedrooms and bathrooms) and location, generally in the range of $1,000 to $4,000 for townhouses and $1,400 to $6,000 and up for single-family homes. Townhouses, suitable for a busy and low-maintenance lifestyle, are increasingly popular with empty nesters.

Getting Demographic Data

For housing, tax and demographic data on an area in which you are interested, contact the local **Economic Development Offices**. Call any of these offices for a packet of information.

DC

Greater Washington Board of Trade	202-857-5900

Maryland

Montgomery County	240-777-2000
Prince George's County	301-386-5600

Virginia

Alexandria	703-739-3820
Arlington County	703-358-3571
Fairfax County	703-790-0600

Resources

Once you have decided where you want to live and what kind of housing you are looking for, you have lots of options for resources to help you out. Both companies and individual landlords advertise available space in local newspapers. Real estate and relocation companies, along with specialized services, can help you find your new home. And, increasingly, you can use the Web to shop for a place to live—giving a whole new meaning to the term "home shopping networks." In addition to paid advertisements, you will find lots of housing notices on bulletin boards, both in local community establishments and in the offices of some larger employers.

STORAGE COMPANIES PLUS

Need some space? Not a problem with companies that bring containers to your home for you to pack at your convenience, and then return later to pick them up for safe storage. Check out their websites, which offer one-stop additional services such as truck rentals, relocation guides, packing supplies and self-storage options.

All Boxes Direct
888-ALLBOXES
www.allboxes.com

Public Storage
800-44-STORE
www.publicstorage.com

Shurgard Storage Centers
800-Shurgard
www.shurgard.com

Advertising

Many Washingtonians find their apartments through the *Washington Post.* Fridays, Saturdays and Sundays are the best days to check its classified section for the real estate ads. The *Post* also offers a free Apartments Plus rentals hotline at 202-334-5770 or 888-APT-7800. Their rental consultants will fax or mail you photos, floor plans, maps and more on apartments for rent in DC, Maryland and Virginia. The *Washington Times, City Paper, Current Newspapers, Citizen, InTowner, Hill Rag, Roll Call, Washington Blade, Uptown* and the *Journal Newspapers* also contain classified sections.

Several free guides published by area realtors list available apartments. One of the most extensive listings is the 600-page *Metropolitan Washington Apartment Shoppers Guide.* Free copies can be picked up at CVS Pharmacies, Giant and Safeway stores, and convenience stores. A bi-weekly newspaper, *Apartments for Rent,* is available at most Metro stations, Giants and Safeways. The *Washington Post* publishes *Apartment Showcase,* a comprehensive, full-color reference to apartment homes in the area. This free publication is available in many locations where the *Post* is sold. You can order a free copy by calling 888-245-5818 or via the Internet at www.apartment-showcase.com.

RELOCATION FORMS ONLINE

US Postal Service

MoversNet, through the US Postal Service website at www.usps.gov/moversnet, offers one-stop access to the usual change-of-address forms and moving notices. You can even submit a change-of-address form online. In addition, four checklists are available to help you through the move process: What to Do Before Moving, Packing... From A to Z, Moving Your Pet, and Moving with Kids.

IRS

The IRS provides publications and forms related to your move. Call them at 800-829-3676 or visit them at www.irs.gov to obtain such forms as Moving Expenses, Employee Moving Expense Information, Charitable Contributions, Non-Cash Contributions, and Change of Address.

If you are looking to buy your home, the Washington dailies each have special real estate sections. The *Washington Times* publishes their section on Friday, the *Washington Post* on Saturday. The *Journal Newspapers*, a chain of daily suburban papers, prints a Friday "Home Report" section geared towards the suburban city or county it serves.

Companies

Whether or not the real estate market is booming from an economic standpoint, the transient nature of the local population keeps a number of companies busy helping people find housing, both to rent and to own. The Taxpayer Relief Act of 1997, which virtually eliminates capital gains tax, is expected to increase the demand for apartment living and expand the "renter by choice" segment of the market.

Real Estate Companies

If you are pressed for time during your apartment search, you may want to use a real estate company; their fees are frequently paid by the landlords. And if you are looking to buy, you will need to tap into the expertise of local real estate agents.

The local Bell Atlantic Yellow Pages contains a dozen pages of local and national firms under the heading Real Estate. Most of the national firms list 800 telephone numbers where you can obtain the number of a local area office. A few local companies are listed here.

Arlington Realty Inc.
764 S. 23rd St., Arlington — 703-836-6000
Arlington County

John Formant Company
225 Pennsylvania Ave. SE — 202-544-3900
Capitol Hill

Edward W. Jones Sr. Realty Co.
1229 Pennsylvania Ave. SE — 202-584-4500
DC, Montgomery County, Prince George's County

REAL ESTATE, HOME AND FINANCING INFORMATION

The number of websites featuring real estate services seems almost limitless. A good place to start is the classified section of the *Washington Post* website (www.washingtonpost.com), where you will find links to Apartments.com and NewHomeNetwork.com. Here are some other links to help you with your research.

The Apartment Connection (local)
www.aptconnection.com

Apartment Locators (MD and VA)
www.southernmanagement.com

The Apartment Service (international)
www.theapartmentservice.com

Apartments for Rent Online (national)
www.aptsforrent.com

Cyberhomes
www.cyberhomes.com

Financing Information
www.quicken.com

For Sale By Owner
www.owners.com

Home & Land
www.homes.com

Home Data Base (Mid-Atlantic states)
www.homedatabase.com

Home Scout
www.homescout.com

Loans Online
www.eloan.com
www.IOwn.com

National Association of Home Builders
www.homebuilder.com

National Association of Realtors
www.realtor.com

New Homes Guide
www.homefair.com/nhg

Rates and Calculations
www.bankrate.com

Rent Net (national)
www.rent.net

Long & Foster Realtors
5101 Wisconsin Ave. NW — 202-364-5200
DC and Bethesda

WC & AN Miller Realtors
4910 Massachusetts Ave. NW — 202-362-1300
DC, Bethesda, Gaithersburg

Tutt Real Estate
1755 S St. NW — 202-234-2812
Dupont Circle, Adams Morgan, Georgetown

Weichert Realtors
10201 Main St., Fairfax — 703-691-0555
DC, Maryland, Virginia; residential and corporate relocation

FOR WOMEN ONLY

Women can stay at **Thompson-Markward Hall** (202-546-3255) just across from the Hart Senate Office Building at 235 2nd St. NE. Rooms rent for approximately $147 a week, which includes breakfast and dinner. Each woman has her own room and phone; bathrooms and showers are communal. There is a two-week minimum stay.

The **National Association of Realtors (NARL)** has an Internet service, the Realtor Information Network (www.realtor.com), that lets you comb through the data contained in the Multiple Listing Services (MLS). MLS is an area-wide inventory of homes for sale through member realty companies. The site includes color photos, descriptions, prices, and links with the agents handling the houses.

Relocation Companies

If you are planning to buy a house, you may want to have a relocation service help you find it. Many major real estate agencies either have their own division or a relationship with an independent relocation company. For regional rental information and resources, contact the **National Relocation Service** at 900-420-0040 or www.aptsforrent.com on the Internet.

For people involved in a job-related relocation, the **Employee Relocation Council (ERC)** can provide a range of useful information. ERC (202-857-0857) is an association of organizations concerned with domestic and international employee transfers. The membership includes corporations that relocate their employees as well as companies and individuals from the relocation industries. You can reach them at their office at 1720 N St. NW or at www.erc.org.

Services

In addition to the real estate and relocation companies, a number of real estate services are available to help you with more specific aspects of finding your new home. You can find out more about these services in the free apartment and home sale guides available in local supermarkets and convenience stores.

Finding an Apartment

Apartment Search (800-989-3733; www.apartmentsearch.com) can help you find an apartment in the metropolitan area free of charge. They have offices at 7629 Old Georgetown Rd. in Bethesda, 7500 Leesburg Pike in Falls Church, and 291 S. Van Dorn St. in Alexandria. Each office has access to listings for the whole metropolitan area.

Off-Campus Housing Offices

Universities provide off-campus housing information, often to the public as well as to their students. You can visit the university offices, or, in most instances, visit their website to find links to listings of off-campus housing in the vicinity. You will find many listed below.

American University
Washington, DC
202-885-3270
www.ngen.com/housing/american

Catholic University of America
Washington, DC
202-319-5618
http://housing.cua.edu

George Mason University
Fairfax, VA
703-993-2930
www.gmu.edu/org/focs/index.html

George Washington University
Washington, DC
202-994-7221
www.och.gwu.edu

Georgetown University
Washington, DC
202-687-8467
www.georgetown.edu/student-affairs/life/housing.htm

Howard University
Washington, DC
202-806-5749

University of Maryland
College Park, MD
301-314-3645
www.inform.umd.edu/cacs

Finding Roommates

If you already know some people here, word of mouth is of course the best way to find a roommate. If you do not, you can put an ad in the *Washington Post* or *City Paper*. The *Washington Blade*, a weekly newspaper serving the gay community, also has roommate ads in its classified pages. Or check out the

Roommate Assistant on the Web at www.roommate-assistant.com. If you are having trouble finding a roommate, you can contact Betsy Neal of **Roommates Preferred** at 2262 Hall Place NW (202-547-4666). Betsy will quiz you about your living preferences and habits and then suggest some possibilities. If you decide to pursue them, she will charge you $75. She is easy to work with and has an excellent track record. If you are not happy with your new roommate, Betsy will help you find another at no charge. For more information, visit her website at: www.roommatespreferred.com.

INTERIM ACCOMMODATIONS

For special circumstances, interim housing is a great idea. The demand for extended-stay accommodations—across the country as well as locally—is being fueled by the growing trend toward consultants and temporary employees. Coupled with the rise in the number of people relocating, this means that the demand for interim housing is stronger than ever. An increasing number of organizations are providing services to meet this demand. Students, graduates, and professors on sabbatical often find this approach suits them as well.

Corporate Housing

The Washington area has several firms that specialize in short- and long-term temporary housing. Offering accommodation for stays of 28 days or more, corporate housing has been growing faster than other options, in part because the rates are generally lower and the accommodations larger than a hotel room. You can choose an apartment, a townhouse or a single-family dwelling, with furnishings and services to fit your budget. Most major interim firms can even steer you to pet-friendly buildings and child-friendly communities. Here are a few:

BridgeStreet Accommodations, Inc. 800-278-7337
www.bridgestreet.com

The Corporate Housing Connection 800-340-6242
www.corporatehousing.com

ExecuStay by Marriott 800-735-7829
www.execustay.com

Executive Club Suites 800-535-2582
http://dcexeclub.com

Oakwood Corporate Housing 800-888-0808
www.oakwood.com

Smith Corporate Living 888-234-7829
www.smithliving.com

University Connections

During the summer, many local universities rent dorm rooms by the week to students or recent graduates. Opt for a room with air conditioning; you'll be more comfortable in Washington's high humidity. Below is a list of several university housing offices. Many of these rooms are booked by April, so sign up early.

American University Summer Housing
Rockwood Building
4400 Massachusetts Ave. NW
Washington, DC 20016-8039
202-885-2669

Catholic University Housing
Office of Resident Life, St. Bonaventure Hall
620 Michigan Ave. NE
Washington, DC 20064
202-319-5277

George Washington University Housing
Marvin Center
800 21st St. NW
Washington, DC 20052
202-994-7470

Georgetown University Summer Housing
100 Harbin Hall NW
Washington, DC 20057
202-687-4560

Howard University Office of Residence Life
2401 4th St. NW
Washington, DC 20005
202-806-6131

MOVE ORGANIZER

A Bethesda-based business, **Art of Moving**, has a website packed with relocation information at www.artofmoving.com. The site includes interactive features such as a move checklist and planner, an expense log and a free "yard sale" to advertise items online, plus tips on saving money and time. Many of their online services are free. More extensive services, such as Your Personal Move Organizer, involve fees. For information on their individual and corporate relocation services, contact them at 301-320-0888.

POINTERS FOR MOVING

Planning and Packing

- Decide whether or not to use a commercial mover. Get started early, compare costs and services, and set the schedule.
- Find out what types of insurance coverage the moving company provides; their liability is probably limited. Determine whether your homeowners insurance policy covers household goods in transit; few do.
- Arrange for street parking permits for all vehicles involved. For an apartment complex or condo, coordinate with the property manager and reserve the freight elevator.
- If you do your own packing, get instructions on how to avoid damage to your possessions.
- Number each box and keep a list of the contents.
- Be there to supervise packers and movers; they will be a little more careful if you are close by.
- Plan unloading and unpacking carefully. Avoid paying extra to accommodate last minute changes in where things go.
- Pack an "open-me-first" box with screwdrivers and hammer, scissors, soap and toilet paper, snacks and games, camera, phone numbers of friends back home and other personal items for you and your family. Seal the box so it's easy to open and move it yourself.

Before You Leave

- At least a month ahead, get change-of-address cards from the Post Office (or online at www.usps.gov/moversnet) to officially notify banks, credit card companies, magazine publishers, membership organizations, and any state or federal organizations, such as tax boards or benefit offices. Give your employer your forwarding address so W-2 forms can be mailed to you.
- Schedule shut-down and start-up for utilities and services such as telephone, cable television, trash and newspaper delivery.
- Schedule with someone in your new location to connect appliances, light furnaces or help out with other special details in your new home.
- Arrange for all your legal, medical, military, government and school records to be transferred. Have your lawyer review your will. Ask doctors, dentists and other business and medical suppliers for recommendations about who to contact after you move.
- Check with the local Chamber of Commerce at your destination for information on schools and recreation, places of worship, local laws and taxes, and shopping and transportation.
- Run all your routine errands one last time: dry cleaning, recycling, library books, repairs. Refill prescription medications so you will have a sufficient supply to get you through the move. Get inoculation certificates for your pets.

- Call local charities (Salvation Army, Goodwill, etc.) to pick up items you won't be moving. Consider donating the food in your kitchen to local charities that feed the homeless instead of paying to have it packed and moved. Ask for receipts for tax purposes.
- Close bank accounts. If you have a new account at your destination, you can have the money electronically transferred. If you have a safety deposit box at your bank, empty it and secure the contents to carry with you.
- If you have older children, invite them to help decide how and where they will spend moving day, e.g., helping, or avoiding the chaos by visiting a friend or relative. Consider daycare or a babysitter for small children on the day of your move.
- Make arrangements for the care and handling of pets during the move process. Kennel dogs and cats the day of the move so they do not become overly stressed. If you are flying to your destination, make arrangements with the airline and get a proper pet carrier.

On Moving Day

- Moving day can be hectic. Make sure you have the following with you: auto registration and driver's licenses; cash for tips, checkbook, credit cards, and travelers checks; maps for you and the movers; names and numbers for moving company and real estate agents; local telephone directory; your "open-me-first" box; and a change of clothes for you and your family.
- Be on hand to monitor packing and loading, and stay until the movers are finished. Accompany the driver for an inventory of your items. Read the bill of lading carefully before you sign it. Retain copies of the bill of lading and the inventory until your possessions are delivered, the charges are paid, and any claims are settled.
- If you don't have a cellular phone, keep at least one phone in the house plugged in for emergency use, and take it with you when you leave.
- Remember to turn off programmed systems for the day such as the sprinkler system, the security alarm, etc. And, if you have an automatic garage door, don't forget to take the controls out of your automobiles.

After You Arrive

- Monitor unloading and unpacking. Plug in appliances, etc., and make sure they still work. If there is any damage, notify the movers and complete the appropriate paperwork before they leave.
- Then, get ready to master DC: Take yourself or your family out to eat (chapter 7), pick up something special for your new home (chapter 6), get to know your new neighborhood (chapter 2), or go out and play (chapters 8, 9 and 10).

MASTERING DC: HISTORIC HOUSES

Houses in the greater DC metropolitan area include some fine architectural examples and many distinguish themselves by both their design and their profound sense of history. This listing is merely a sampling of the many notable examples from the past 250 years. Some have seasonal hours so call before visiting.

☐ **Keep Up With the Joneses**: Built in 1818, Federal-era **Decatur House** mansion (748 Jackson Pl. NW; 202-842-0920) was the first private residence built at Lafayette Square, across from the White House.

☐ **Tune in to This Old House:** Constructed in 1765, Georgetown's **Old Stone House** (3501 M St. NW; 202-426-6851), is considered the oldest standing building in Washington. The restored six-room house represents a middle-class dwelling in the late 18th century.

☐ **Get Out to Vote:** The Federal-style **Sewall-Belmont House** (144 Constitution Ave. NE; 202-546-3989) is one of the oldest houses on Capitol Hill. Built in 1799-1800, it is named for original owner Robert Sewall, and for Alva Belmont, whose financial contribution enabled the National Woman's Party to purchase it. The house was home and work place for Alice Paul, founder of the National Woman's Party and author of the Equal Rights Amendment in 1923.

☐ **Call on the Red Cross:** The **Clara Barton National Historic Site**, a three-story Victorian house in Glen Echo (5801 Oxford Rd.; 301-492-6245), was at first a storage site for the American Red Cross. In 1897 it became the organization's first permanent headquarters.

☐ **Keep It All in the Family:** Designed in 1794, by the architect of the US Capitol for Martha Washington's granddaughter, **Tudor Place** (1644 31st St. NW; 202-965-0400) is considered a classic Georgetown mansion. The house remained in the original family until 1983.

☐ **See All the Presidents' Houses:** From Washington DC to Central Virginia... **Woodrow Wilson House** (2430 S St. NW; 202-387-4062), a Neo-Georgian house built in 1915, was this president's home during his retirement. George Washington's **Mount Vernon Estate and Gardens** in Mount Vernon, VA (703-780-2000) is one of the country's oldest ongoing preservation projects. The original portion of **Montpelier Mansion** in Montpelier Station, VA (540-672-2728) was built by James Madison's father in 1760 on a site founded by Madison's grandfather back in 1723. **Monticello**, in Charlottesville, VA (804-984-9822), was designed by Thomas Jefferson and served as home to him and his family for 50 years.

☐ **Go From Colonial to Contemporary:** An example of Georgian-style architecture from 1800, **Woodlawn Plantation** (9000 Richmond Hwy., Alexandria, VA; 703-780-4000) was originally part of the Mount Vernon estate. Frank Lloyd Wright's **Pope-Leighey House**, a 1945 Usonian house, was moved to the Woodlawn grounds in 1965 to prevent it from being destroyed by a highway project.

☐ **Let Freedom Ring:** Known simply as Cedar Hill, the **Frederick Douglass National Historic Site** (1411 W St. SE; 202-426-5960) was the last home of the famous statesman and abolitionist.

☐ **Read 'em Your Rights:** Restored plantation home **Gunston Hall**, in Lorton, VA (10709 Gunston Rd.; 703-550-9220), was built in 1755 by George Mason, framer of the Constitution and father of the Bill of Rights.

CHAPTER TWO

Neighborhoods

Urban neighborhoods of every shape and size; suburban cities and towns steeped in local history; and residential neighborhoods with single-family homes, townhouses, condos and apartment complexes—the Washington area offers a smorgasbord of choices for the newcomer. Many factors influence the decision about where to live. Cost of housing is often the most important and least negotiable issue, but factors relating to transportation time, cost and convenience can also make a difference. Local amenities and the character of the neighborhood often help people choose between otherwise comparable options.

Different life styles are better served by different parts of DC, Maryland and Virginia. Read the general descriptions in the front of the chapter to get an overview of these three areas. Or turn directly to the neighborhood sections for specific information to help you decide what part of the greater Washington area suits you best.

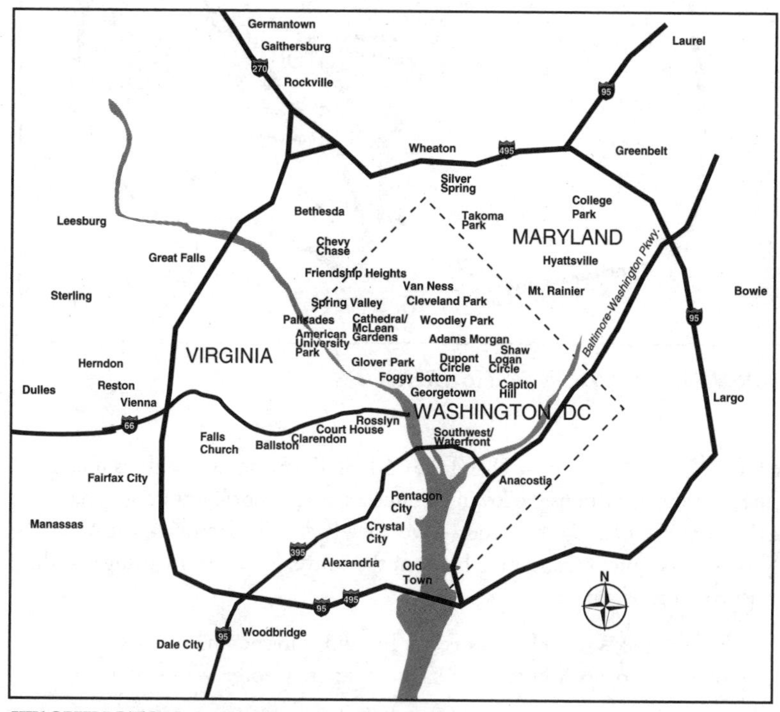

WASHINGTON, DC AREA NEIGHBORHOODS

Washington, DC

The District offers a multitude of neighborhoods, each with its own local character as well as its practical advantages and disadvantages. The Capitol Hill neighborhoods are closer to the seat of national government than any other. Northeast includes many residential neighborhoods, as does Southeast/Anacostia, the last part of the city with land to be developed. Not far away is Southwest, right along the Potomac River Waterfront. In the center of town, Adams Morgan and Dupont Circle offer an ambiance that reminds many of New York's Greenwich Village, with loads of coffee shops, art galleries and ethnic restaurants.

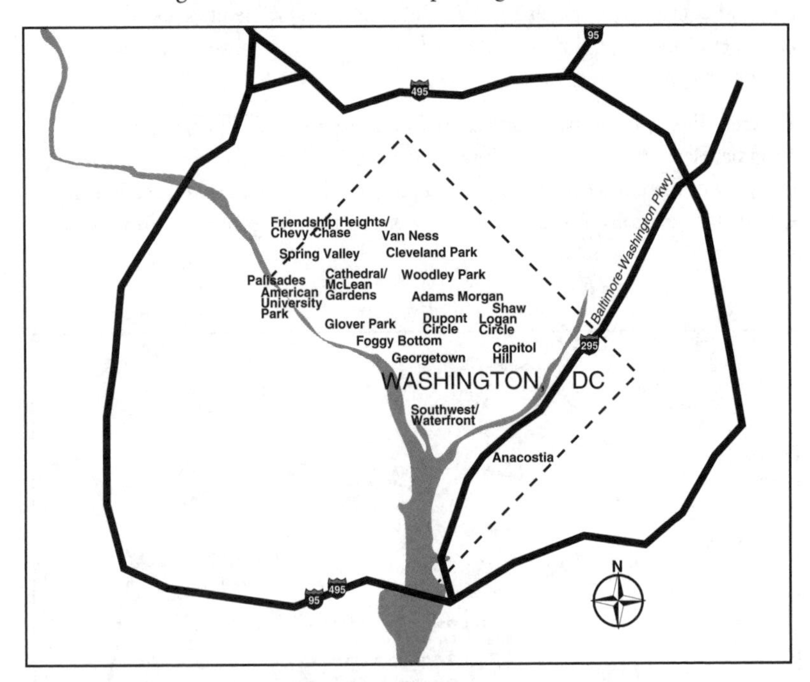

WASHINGTON, DC NEIGHBORHOODS

Close by are Shaw, the New U and the 16th St. Corridor, each with its unique character and attractions. Following Connecticut Ave. north toward Maryland, a series of residential neighborhoods—Woodley Park, Cleveland Park and Van Ness—offers a nice compromise between the conveniences of city living and the quiet comfort of suburban space.

Not far from the White House is Foggy Bottom, a former middle-class neighborhood now best known for its proximity to George Washington

University. At the foot of Wisconsin Ave., along the Potomac River, Georgetown offers a stylish, up-scale life style. The neighborhoods on upper Wisconsin Ave.—Glover Park, Cathedral Heights and McLean Gardens—offer quiet community living and proximity to other parts of the city.

A little farther west, but still in the District, are American University Park, near the campus for which it is named, and Spring Valley, one of DC's most affluent areas. Below that is Palisades, backing up to the C&O Canal National Historical Park. Finally, along the border with Maryland you will find Friendship Heights and the DC side of Chevy Chase, areas known for their concentrations of high-rise buildings.

All five of Metro's subway lines run through Washington, and many city dwellers also make regular use of Metrobus service. Running generally north-south through DC is Rock Creek Parkway—a major transportation route through beautiful Rock Creek Park, the city's pride in public park space. Other major thoroughfares include Connecticut, Wisconsin and Massachusetts Aves. from the center of town out to the west; Route 29 (16th St.) north out to Silver Spring; and Routes 1 and 50 heading out to the Maryland suburbs on the east side of town. The cost of housing varies widely throughout the District, depending on size, location and amenities. For many District residents, location plays a major role, as the character of a neighborhood can change within a few blocks.

Suburban Maryland

Suburban Maryland neatly divides itself into Montgomery County on the west and Prince George's County on the east. Montgomery County is one of the wealthiest counties in the country and a premier location for investing in real estate. With densely populated areas in the more urban parts closer to DC, it still offers large expanses of open land farther out. To the west, the county boasts some of greater Washington's most expensive estates and well-to-do residents. As you make your way eastward, the county offers a more familiar, and more affordable, environment.

As in all the suburbs, residents here depend heavily on their cars to get around. Rockville Pike, the continuation of DC's Wisconsin Ave., runs through the heart of the county to the west and provides much of its shopping opportunities. The many neighborhoods in Montgomery County—Bethesda-Chevy Chase, Rockville, Gaithersburg, Germantown, Silver Spring, Wheaton and Takoma Park—offer a wide range of life styles with something for everyone. The northwestern end of the Metro Red Line extends out to this area, including stops at Friendship Heights, at the border with DC, and at Bethesda, White Flint and Rockville farther out. After dipping down through the center of DC, the Red

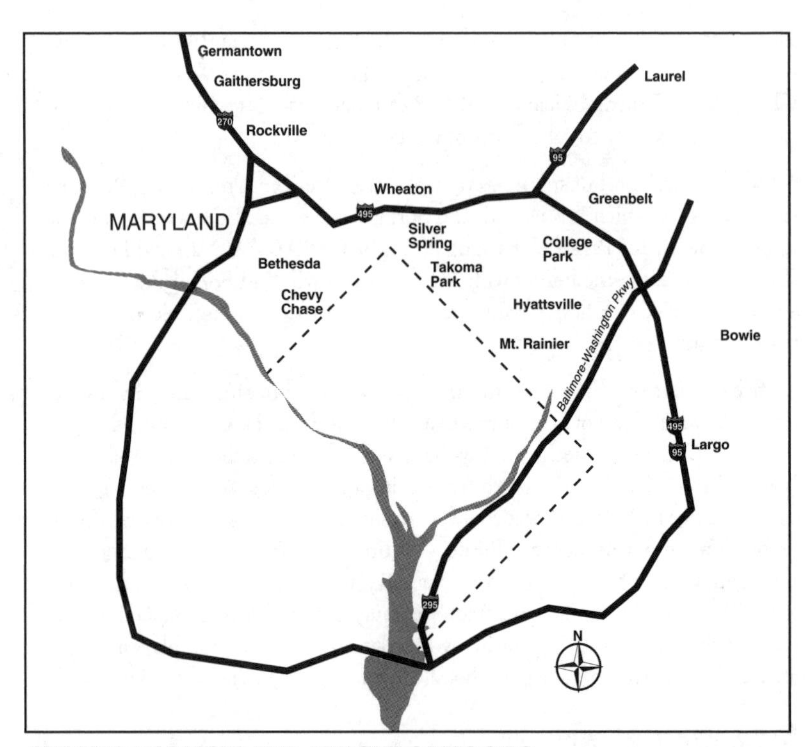

SUBURBAN MARYLAND NEIGHBORHOODS

Line turns back up into Montgomery County, with stops in Takoma Park, Silver Spring and Wheaton on the eastern side of the county.

Prince George's County covers a large area east of DC, from the Potomac River north to Laurel and the state line. Maryland's second-largest county, and the most populous jurisdiction in the Washington area, this county is the nation's wealthiest majority-black suburb. Prince George's County is considered by some to be a diamond in the rough. While it tends to suffer from a lack of upscale restaurants and shopping malls, the county does offer advantages for its residents. Living in Prince George's County, for example in Mount Rainier or Greenbelt, is less expensive than in other parts of Maryland and Virginia, for both buyers and renters. That fact alone can be enough to make a difference for many people. Another big draw is the county's particularly well-established multicultural population and a somewhat more rural atmosphere in its smaller towns. College Park, Hyattsville, Bowie, Largo and Mitchellville are among the better known neighborhoods in the county, offering a variety of life styles and amenities.

The 1996 celebration of the county's 300th anniversary called attention to other local advantages, such as a number of parks and recreational facilities and some small museums. Metro's Green Line extends out to Greenbelt, and Route 1 and the Baltimore-Washington Parkway are the major roads through the area.

NORTHERN VIRGINIA

The closer-in areas of Northern Virginia were once part of the 100-mile square plot of land allocated for the development of the new District of Columbia back in 1791. Arlington and parts of what is now Alexandria were, however, returned to the Commonwealth of Virginia in 1846. As the federal government has grown over the last 50 years, so have the business and residential areas taken up by its many offices, employees and subcontractors, with much of this growth taking place in the Virginia suburbs. Today, DC has virtually reclaimed its own.

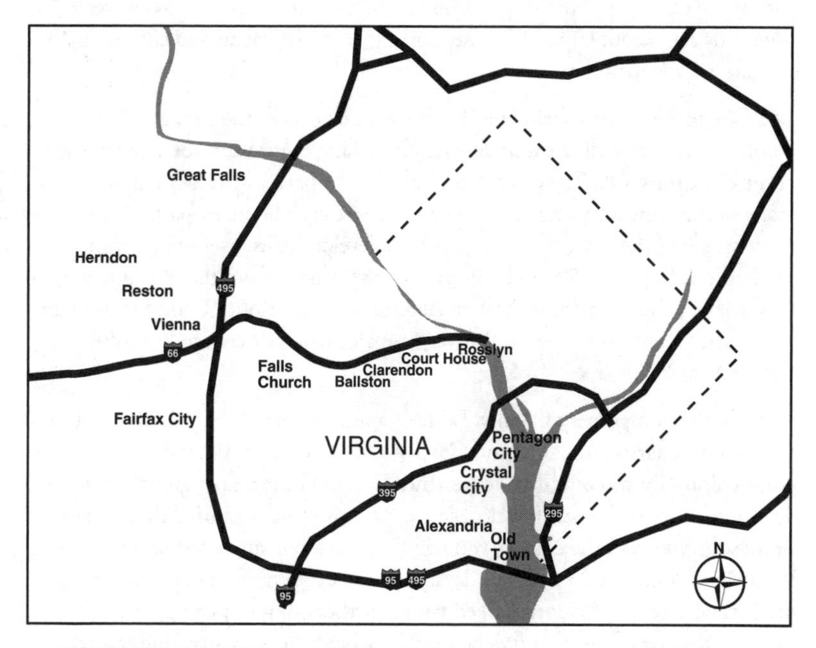

NORTHERN VIRGINIA NEIGHBORHOODS

Virginians from other parts of the state barely consider Northern Virginia, and particularly places like Arlington and Alexandria, to be part of Virginia at all.

Arlington is officially designated as a county and includes no incorporated towns. Rather, it is comprised of many neighborhoods, or districts, such as Rosslyn, Court House, Clarendon, Ballston, Pentagon City and Crystal City.

To meet the demands of its swelling population, Arlington's housing and shopping options have expanded. Many new residential and commercial communities have sprouted up over the last decade along Metro's Blue, Orange and Yellow Lines, all of which run through Arlington. Rental prospects run the gamut from efficiencies to group houses. Condos, houses and townhouses, many small and some large, also abound. Prices for many apartments, especially those in luxury buildings, rival those in the District and Bethesda. Farther out and away from the Metro, prices drop quickly.

Wilson Blvd. and Metro's Orange Line both connect the North Arlington neighborhoods of Rosslyn, Court House, Clarendon and Ballston. The Orange Line's quick access to Downtown makes North Arlington quite popular among commuters. The Pentagon, the world's largest office building, dominates the landscape in South Arlington. Rents here are slightly lower than in the northern part of the county and the neighborhoods are not quite as nice or as convenient. Metrobus travels out Columbia Pike, starting at the Pentagon and continuing on to Baileys Crossroads.

The City of Alexandria includes Old Town Alexandria to the east, along the Potomac River, as well as suburban areas stretching out toward the western edge of the city limits. Old Town is a nice alternative to parts of the District, offering many of the same advantages, but on a smaller scale. The many parts of the western side of the city feature more typical developments, everything from subdivisions from the '50s and '60s to high-rise condos from the '80s and early '90s. Metro's Blue Line runs through Alexandria, as do Route 1 and the southern half of the George Washington Parkway, a major road adjacent to beautiful riverfront space.

Along with Montgomery County, Fairfax County is one of the most affluent in the nation. It surrounds Arlington County and the City of Alexandria. While it is less compactly laid out, it has experienced a significant rate of growth and development over the past few decades, some of it more organized than others. In most locations in the county, you will find proudly maintained remnants of Virginia's Colonial and Civil War days, side-by-side with reminders that DC is not far away. Fairfax County is filled with a plethora of green lawns, tree-lined streets and some of the country's best public schools. It is an area long-settled, quaint and richly historic, with signs everywhere marking important Civil War sites.

Popular parts of the county include Falls Church and the City of Fairfax, closer in, and the planned community of Reston and its sister city, Herndon, farther out. In general, Northern Virginia is known for its large number of high-tech firms and its large, increasingly diverse population. As in all suburbs, residents are heavily dependent on their cars. I-66 runs west through the county while

I-495 crosses from north to south. Metro's Orange Line extends out to this area with stops at Falls Church, Dunn Loring and Vienna. The county-run bus service, the Fairfax Connector, runs between Springfield Plaza and Mt. Vernon. Routes 50 and 29 are also popular avenues, both for transportation and for concentrations of commercial and residential activity.

As its suburban population continues to expand, Fairfax County is spilling over north and west to Loudoun County, and south and west to Prince William County. Once home to mostly farmlands and plantations, scenic Loudoun and Prince William Counties are becoming significant new hubs for business and residential development. Major corporations and businesses are moving away from the traffic and congestion of the city and surrounding suburbs. A new, high-tech frontier is developing in these historic settings of natural rustic beauty.

In Loudoun County, Sterling and Leesburg offer neighborhoods ranging from recreationally enticing to historically restored. Route 7, accessible from I-495 and I-66, is the main highway that connects Loudoun with Fairfax County, and a commuter bus service makes daily runs into Washington, DC.

Prince William County stretches from the Potomac River to the Bull Run Mountains. This county is also experiencing new growth in both residential and business development, but a Land Use Plan is in place to balance this new growth with recreational use. Prince William is accessible by I-66 and I-95, and a commuter rail system provides service both east and west.

Washington, DC Neighborhoods

Capitol Hill

Capitol Hill, known simply as "the Hill," is home to thousands of congressional bureaucrats and staffers. Locals refer to the neighborhoods bordering the Capitol as being on either the "House side," in the Southeast quadrant, or the "Senate side," in the Northeast quadrant. These charming neighborhoods dating back to the early 1800s offer a seemingly endless array of blocks of row houses and lovely, small parks. Back in the 1960s, the Hill underwent a period of gentrification and is now considered one of the city's prime locations. Many people are lured into living here because of its proximity to "the action" as well as by the beautiful Federal and Victorian architecture that lends an enviable charm to the area. One of the nicest aspects of living on the Hill is that some of DC's most famous and most important landmarks are nearby. The Capitol, the Supreme Court, the Library of Congress and the Folger Shakespeare Library are within walking distance. Not much farther away are several of the Smithsonian Institution's many museums as well as the National Gallery of Art, the Botanic Gardens, the Mall and Union Station.

If you decide to live on the Hill, you must keep safety in mind as you consider the choices. Safety conditions vary significantly, sometimes from block to block on the same street; they vary over time as well. Remember that—in general—the closer you live to the Capitol, the safer you are. The area surrounding the Capitol is protected by both DC and Capitol police. Housing costs vary accordingly—you can expect to pay the most for locations within a few blocks of the Capitol. The farther out you go, the lower the cost of housing.

Apartments on Capitol Hill are largely converted homes and schools rather than high-rises, lending more character to both the individual buildings and the neighborhoods. Rental housing can also be found in the many row houses that have been turned into group houses. This housing option is extremely popular, especially among younger Hill staffers. You will also discover an abundance of English basement apartments.

Lying within or just adjacent to Capitol Hill are a number of other interesting neighborhoods—Pennsylvania Quarter, Chinatown, Stanton Park and Lincoln Park.

Pennsylvania Quarter, or Penn Quarter, is a small area between 6th and 9th Sts. NW and Pennsylvania Ave. and H St. It is the result of efforts to rejuvenate the old downtown and stem the tide of middle- and upper-class residential flight to the suburbs. Once a thriving business district, the neighborhood was abandoned back in the 1950s. Market Square, the Pennsylvania and the Lansburgh opened as mixed-use buildings in the 1990s, each offering retail, commercial and residential space all in the same structure. Typical of many thriving downtown living areas, residences here are expensive. For those who can afford it, the amenities are terrific. Art galleries, theaters, restaurants and retail establishments continue to prosper, especially along the 7th St. corridor, and the MCI Center at 7th and F Sts. brings sports-oriented businesses to the area.

Just north of Penn Quarter is Chinatown, bounded by H, I, 6th and 11th Sts. NW. The Chinatown Friendship Arch at 7th and H Sts. NW, one of the largest Chinese arches in the world, marks the entryway to Chinatown. Although this is a small neighborhood, it contains many fine, well-established restaurants and shops. Thanks in large measure to the MCI Center at its southern edge, Chinatown is enjoying a resurgence. On event nights, attendees pour into the surrounding restaurants and coffee shops both before and after games. This influx is changing the character of the neighborhood as redevelopment efforts focus on blending Chinese culture with DC's other urban and suburban cultures.

Set between East Capitol and H Sts., and 2nd and 10th Sts. NE is the Stanton Park neighborhood. Just east of Union Station with its shops, restaurants and Metro stop, the area provides easy access to downtown and the core of Capitol Hill. Marked racial diversity is a hallmark of the community, one cherished by its residents. This area has relatively more affordable 19th-century row houses resembling those in the more pricey Southeast portion of Capitol Hill and in Georgetown and Old Town Alexandria. Affordable rental units have attracted numerous new residents. Group houses are also available here. Many renters are students at Georgetown University Law School or young staffers working in Congress.

Not far away is Lincoln Park, straddling East Capitol St. This neighborhood extends from C St. SE to C St. NE, from 8th to 14th Sts. Many know the area best for its stately park with statues of Abraham Lincoln and Mary McLeod Bethune. Several large homes face the park and many more, of various sizes, can be found on the surrounding streets. Local residents socialize in the park, where many walk their dogs. So many residents own dogs that this has become a selling point for dog owners seeking housing on Capitol Hill.

The entire Capitol Hill area is filled with rather high-priced, mom-and-pop grocery stores. Many residents prefer to shop at **Eastern Market** at 7th St. SE (202-546-2698), Washington's oldest farmers' market. Here you are guaranteed to get fresh produce, flowers and other goods. The blocks surrounding Eastern Market are also full of gourmet shops. Directly across 7th St. from the market you will find Italian delicacies at **Prego** (202-547-8686), and Russian food at **Misha's Place** (202-547-5858). For grocery shopping, you can go either to the **Safeway** at 4th St. and Rhode Island Ave. NE (202-636-8640), or to the one at Kentucky and 14th St. SE (202-547-4333).

On the House side, in Southeast, just above the Library of Congress and the House office buildings, Pennsylvania Ave. has several blocks crowded with commercial activity. Local favorites include **Xando** (202-546-5224), for coffee and light fare, and **Roland's** (202-546-9592), a small neighborhood grocery store. Right around the corner from the Madison Building, **Le Bon Café** at 210 2nd St. SE (202-547-7200), serves pastries, cappuccino, salads and sandwiches. If you have a big appetite and are in the mood for Mexican, there's **Burrito Brothers** (202-543-6835) at 205 Pennsylvania Ave. SE. Other local favorites include **Taverna the Greek Islands** (202-547-8360), **La Lomita Dos** (202-544-0616), the **Tune Inn** (202-543-2725) and **Hawk and Dove** (202-543-3300), a mainstay of many Hill staffers. Farther up Pennsylvania Ave., toward the Eastern Market Metro station, you will find another cluster of restaurants and a **CVS** at 661 Pennsylvania Ave. SE (202-547-9325).

WASHINGTON, DC
Capitol Hill and Northeast Washington

Massachusetts Ave., the main thoroughfare on the Senate side, contains a number of restaurants including **Cafe Berlin** (202-543-7656) and **Two Quail** (202-543-8030). **Capitol Hill Supermarket** at 3rd St. and Massachusetts Ave. NE (202-543-7428) provides the most convenient grocery shopping. Nearby **Union Station** has a nine-screen movie theater, a huge food court and several restaurants and bars, as well as a number of retail shops.

Commute to Downtown 15 minutes by Metro Blue and Orange Lines at Capitol South in SE and Red Line at Union Station in NE

Post Offices National Capitol at 2 Massachusetts Ave. NE (202-523-2628) and Southeast at 600 Pennsylvania Ave. SE (202-523-2173)

Libraries Library of Congress at 1st St. and Independence Ave. SE (202-707-5000), Southeast at 7th and D Sts. SE (202-727-1377), and Northeast at 13th and H Sts. NE (202-727-1347)

Police Stations Fourth District at 415 4th St. SW (202-727-4655) and Fifth District at 1805 Bladensburg Rd. NE (202-727-4510)

Recreational Activities The neighborhood's parks turn into playing fields on warm weekends. The Mall has an exercise circuit at the corner of Independence Ave. and 4th St. SW, as well as huge open spaces for running, walking or biking. There is an indoor public swimming pool at 7th St. and North Carolina Ave. SE.

Northeast

The city of Washington, DC developed toward the west of an off-center center—the Capitol. While this "center" is the point at which DC's four quadrants meet, it is clearly not in the geographic center of the city. Accounts vary as to why the east side of the city was slower to grow; many believe it was due to the commercial and residential advantages offered by the already well-established community of Georgetown lying off to the west. Much slower development in the Northeast quadrant left ideal acreage for large educational institutions and parks. Catholic University, Gallaudet University and Trinity College are all located in this section of the city. The US National Arboretum and the Kenilworth Aquatic Gardens are also to be found here.

The Basilica of the National Shrine of the Immaculate Conception, one of the largest Roman Catholic churches in the United States, sits atop a hill at Michigan Ave. and 4th St. NE (202-526-8300). Its lighted dome adorns the skyline after dark. Like the Washington National Cathedral, the church is built entirely of stone, brick, tile and concrete, and contains no steel skeleton or framework.

Catholic University at 620 Michigan Ave. NE (202-319-5000) is located in Brookland, one of the oldest neighborhoods in the District. Brookland remains an economically and culturally diverse community where residents put down roots and stay. Housing varies in price and design, ranging from row houses near the University to modest detached houses and large Victorians with wraparound porches. Some bungalows and ramblers can also be found here. Although some students rent near the University, most of the housing is owner-occupied.

The Franciscan Monastery at 1400 Quincy St. NE (202-526-6800) is home to monks who raise funds to preserve and restore Christian shrines in the Holy Land. Trinity College at 125 Michigan Ave. NE (202-884-9000) is a top-rated liberal arts college in the United States for women. Gallaudet University at

800 Florida Ave. NE (202-651-5000, TDD 202-651-5104) is the only accredited liberal arts college in the United States for the hearing impaired. The surrounding neighborhood is known as Trinidad.

The North Michigan Park neighborhood was formed out of a part of Brookland after WWII, when many of the area's brick duplexes were built. The affordable, family-sized housing attracted middle-class blacks to an area then populated largely by Irish and Italian Catholics. The new community got its name from its location—just to the north of the older Michigan Park neighborhood. Today this residential area attracts families and younger residents with its reasonable prices and an environment considered safer than many other Northeast neighborhoods. The community's quiet, tree-shaded streets see little traffic, except for South Dakota Ave. Houses range from fixer-uppers to a few detached colonial-style homes.

Commute to Downtown 10-15 minutes by Metro Red Line at Fort Totten, Brookland-CUA or Rhode Island Ave.

Post Offices Brookland Station at 3401 12th St. NE (202-635-5315)

Libraries Langston Branch at Benning Rd. and 26th St. NE (202-724-8665) and Woodbridge Regional Library at Rhode Island Ave. and 18th St. NE (202-727-1401)

Police Stations Fifth District at 1805 Bladensburg Rd. NE (202-727-4510)

Recreational Activities Langston Golf Course at 26th St. and Benning Rd. NE (202-397-8638), the District's only black-owned golf course, sits between the National Arboretum and the Anacostia River.

Southeast/Anacostia

The Anacostia River divides Southeast DC into two sections. The northern section includes the lower eastern portion of Capitol Hill and features several landmarks including Congressional Cemetery, the Washington Navy Yard and RFK Stadium. Congressional Cemetery at 1801 E St. SE (202-543-0539) is the oldest national cemetery in the United States; it contains the graves of some of Washington's greatest historical figures. The Navy Yard sprawls along the waterfront from 1st to 11th Sts. SE, with a main entrance at 9th and M Sts. SE. Once an active naval base, it is now a historic site featuring the Navy Museum (202-433-4882) and the Marine Corps Museum (202-433-3534). Sports events, concerts and trade-shows are all accommodated at RFK Stadium and the DC Armory Hall, which together make up a sports complex called Starplex, at 2001 E St. SE (202-547-9077).

Anacostia is the last section of the city with land to be developed. There is active interest in attracting homeowners to invest in the community and become involved in its economic growth. Developers are demolishing old buildings and developing new townhouses, apartments, and single-family homes, funded through tax credits, federal grants and private loans. Much needed retail outlets and other amenities are planned with the intent of capturing residents who would otherwise cross the District line into Prince George's County and other suburbs. Other improvements include cleaning and restoring the long-neglected Anacostia River, restoring aquatic habitat and wetlands, and reforesting a portion of the stream bank.

Anacostia boasts two institutions with particular relevance to African-American cultural history. The Anacostia Museum is located at 1901 Fort Place SE (202-357-1300), in an area once known as Uniontown, a community settled after the Civil War by freed slaves. The museum focuses on African-American art, culture and history. The Frederick Douglass National Historic Site, known more simply as Cedar Hill, is at 1411 W St. SE (202-426-5960). This was the last home of the famous statesman and abolitionist.

The area is also home to St. Elizabeth's Hospital, commonly referred to as St. E's, at 2700 Martin Luther King Jr. Ave. SE (202-562-4000), and to several Civil War forts preserved as public parks. One of these is Fort Snyder, on the grounds of the hospital. Another is Fort Totten, which remains relatively intact. The surrounding neighborhood, a 12-block residential area west of Fort Totten Park and east of North Capitol St., has numerous apartment buildings, many of which are moderately priced. Here you will find both 40- to 50-year old properties and newer homes with more modern amenities.

Commute to Downtown 15 minutes by Metro Green Line from Anacostia

Post Offices Anacostia Station at 2650 Naylor Rd. SE (202-635-5307) and Southeast Station at 600 Pennsylvania Ave. SE (202-523-2173)

Libraries Anacostia Library at Good Hope Rd. and 18th St. SE (202-698-1190), Francis Gregory Regional Library at Alabama Ave. and 37th St. SE (202-645-4297), and Southeast Branch at 7th and D St. SE (202-727-1377)

Police Stations Seventh District at 2455 Alabama Ave. SE (202-698-1500)

Recreational Activities Anacostia Park (202-472-3873) at Fairlawn Ave. SE, which includes Kenilworth Aquatic Gardens (202-426-6905), offers environmental education programs, exhibitions and a roller skating rink.

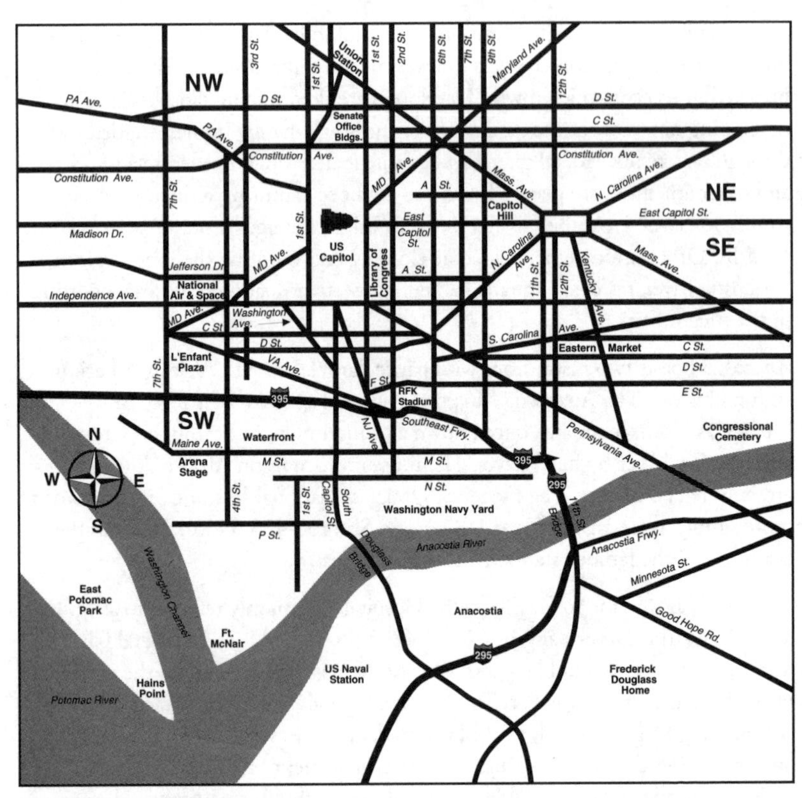

WASHINGTON, DC
Southeast and Southwest Washington

Southwest and Waterfront

While Capitol Hill residents tend to live in row houses, those living in the Southwest and Waterfront area are more likely to be found in a high-rise apartment building, condominium or on a boat. Southwest is home to many government offices, including the Federal Communications Commission, Food and Drug Administration, the Department of Health and Human Services, NASA Headquarters, the Department of Energy and the Department of Transportation. Clearly, convenience makes this an attractive neighborhood for federal workers.

Southwest includes Fort McNair, one of the oldest active military posts in the United States, and the progressive **Arena Stage** (202-488-3300). Located at the corner of 6th St. and Maine Ave., Arena Stage has three threaters and hosts a variety of performances ranging from the classics to cutting-edge drama. In this area you will also find some opportunities for seafood—a row of restaurants line the waterfront, capped by the **Maine Ave. Wharf** at 1100 Maine Ave., a market where you can choose from an enormous selection of fresh seafood. In addition to walking along the river, residents can stroll the short distance to the Waterfront, L'Enfant Plaza and the Smithsonian museums along Independence Ave.

Across the Washington Channel is East Potomac Park which provides a public golf course, tennis courts, swimming pool and picnic tables. Hains Point, at the southern end of East Potomac Park, offers a beautiful view of the waterfront. And at the tip of Hains Point you will find a sculpture titled the Awakening, an aluminum giant rising dramatically out of the earth.

The Tiber Island Co-ops include four mid-rise apartment towers and four clusters of townhouses along M and N Sts., between 4th and 6th Sts. SW. Situated just off the edge of the channel at the southern end of the waterfront, these homes offer an expansive view extending from Reagan National Airport north to Washington National Cathedral, with the city's famous monuments dotting the panoramic vista.

Some of Washington, DC's oldest buildings still stand in Southwest neighborhoods. These include a cluster of residences fashioned in the early Federal style by George Washington's contemporaries in the 1790s: the Thomas Law House (1252 6th St. SW), Wheat Row (1315-1321 4th St. SW) and the Duncanson-Cranch House (468-470 N St. SW). The Edward Simon Lewis House (456 N St. SW), built in 1817, was once home to famous war correspondent Ernie Pyle.

As most of the apartment complexes in Southwest have garages or lots, parking is not a problem for residents. However, you should be prepared to pay an extra monthly fee for parking privileges. The Mall at 4th and M Sts. SW, provides residents with the usual shopping options. At 401 M St. SW, there is both a **Safeway** (202-554-9155) and a **CVS** (202-863-9227).

Unlike the more glamorous areas of the District, Southwest has blocks of high-rises adjacent to public housing areas. Nevertheless, many neighborhood residents enjoy living in the area, so close to the water. Unlike Georgetown, Adams Morgan and Dupont Circle, Southwest shuts down in the evening. Its night life is mostly restricted to the Waterfront restaurants and the area near Arena Stage. Neighborhood activities include the Waterfront Festival and Cherry Blossom Festival in the spring, a festival of lights in December, and free monthly concerts featuring local talent.

Commute to Downtown 10 minutes by Metro Green Line at Waterfront and Green, Yellow, Blue and Orange Lines at L'Enfant Plaza

Post Offices Fort McNair at 300 A St. SW (202-523-2144), L'Enfant Plaza at 458 L'Enfant Plaza SW (202-523-2013), and Southwest at 45 L St. SW (202-635-5302)

Libraries Southwest Branch at Wesley Place and K St. SW (202-724-4752)

Police Stations Fourth District at 415 4th St. SW (202-727-4655)

Recreational Activities Several small parks are in this neighborhood and the Mall is just a brief walk away. There is a major DC-run recreation field and facility at the corner of South Capitol and Eye Sts. SW.

Shaw and The New U

Historically, the Shaw neighborhood was a black social center, with theaters and dinner clubs drawing blacks and whites alike to hear the great jazz musicians and singers of the 1920s and 1930s. The area was home to a number of famous people and institutions, and many notable structures financed, designed and built by and for the black community can still be found in the Shaw and U Street areas of Washington. Notable among them are the Whitelaw Hotel (13th and T Sts. NW) and the old Twelfth Street YMCA—now the Thurgood Marshall Center for Service and Heritage (1816 12th St. NW)—designed by W. Sidney Pittman, son-in-law of Booker T. Washington. The former homes of Clara Barton and Duke Ellington are both located on T St. NW. The historic O Street Market, one of the few surviving DC public marketplaces, is located at the northwest corner of 7th and O Sts. NW. Another historic feature is the Lincoln Theater (202-328-6000), once a popular hangout for African-Americans. After having sat empty for years, it has been renovated and has opened its doors again.

The area has rebounded since the 1960 race riots, a recession, and years of violent crime and drug use. The Metro's Green Line has arrived in the Shaw neighborhood, connecting the area with the rest of the city and stimulating business.

Adjacent to Shaw, running along U St. NW between 12th St. and 17th St. is an area now being called "The New U." This corridor has undergone a remarkable transformation from a run-down collection of boarded up townhouses to new businesses and an active night life. Housing is urban and more affordable than in nearby Adams Morgan. Like Shaw, the New U is an example of how neighborhoods can be rebuilt.

The area offers a variety of eclectic shops. Along U St. there are a number of new and used furniture stores, as well as bookstores, a few art galleries, and an assortment of African clothing boutiques and bars. **Millenium** (202-483-1218) sells 20th century furnishings; **Goodwood** (202-986-3640) has an interesting collection of used furniture from various periods; and **Meeps**

Fashionette (202-265-6546) is a great place for vintage clothing. **Atticus Books and Music** (202-667-8148) includes a collection of African-American literature and **Sisterspace and Books** (202-332-3433) carries a large selection of African-American and lesbian literature.

You'll also find several good restaurants and bars. The **Chi Cha Lounge** at 1624 U St. NW (202-234-8400) is a place where folks can hang out on couches and big comfy chairs; on warm days, the doors at the front of the bar are opened, giving passersby a chance to peek in. **Coppi's** at 1414 U St. NW (202-319-7773) is best known for oven-baked pizzas, but don't miss the Nutella-filled calzones for dessert. **Ben's Chili Bowl** at 1213 U St. NW (202-667-0909) has been around since 1958 and the menu is true to the name; you can order chili dogs, chili half-smokes, chili burgers, chili fries, and, well, chili. **Webbs Southern Fish & Ribs** (202-462-3474) serves southern-style food. At the corner of New Hampshire Ave. and U St., **Julio's** (202-483-8500) has a popular weekend brunch, carryout service and several inexpensive pool tables.

A landmark restaurant in this neighborhood is the **Florida Avenue Grill** at 1100 Florida Ave. NW (202-265-1586) where soul food is the specialty and where historical photos of its patrons are displayed. For added variety, try **Cafe Nema** at 1334 U St. NW (202-667-3215), serving dishes from the Middle East, Somalia, Italy and France.

Revitalization of the Shaw and The New U neighborhoods is destined to continue in one form or another. Investors have shown interest in the area as a result of the development of the MCI Center. A new convention center is under construction at Mount Vernon Square and is scheduled to open in 2003.

16th Street Corridor

The 16th Street Corridor begins just beyond Scott Circle. Bordered on the east by the Shaw and The New U neighborhoods, and on the west by Dupont Circle, Adams Morgan and Mount Pleasant, this area is known for its mix of race and culture. To the west, the neighborhoods are predominantly white and Hispanic; to the east lie the historic black neighborhoods and the adjoining areas of Logan Circle and LeDroit Park. LeDroit Park, one of the city's first planned neighborhoods and now listed on the National Registry of Historic Places, was home to some of the city's leading black citizens early in the century. Just east of LeDroit Park is Howard University (202-806-6100), the most prestigious historically black university in the country.

Several prominent hospitals are located in this part of town. Howard University Hospital is adjacent to the University's campus. East of McMillan Reservoir are Washington Hospital Center, the National Rehabilitation Hospital, Children's National Medical Center and the Veteran's Affairs Medical Center.

As 16th Street heads northward above these neighborhoods, it passes through Columbia Heights. Once a thriving business community hit hard by the 1960 riots, Columbia Heights is currently undergoing a strong rebirth. Planned amenities include a new **Giant**, movie theaters, retailers and restaurants. Located on 16th St. between Florida Ave. and Belmont Rd. is Meridian Hill Park, or Malcolm X Park, known for its terraced waterfalls. Early in the century, the Meridian Hill Park area became prominent for its mansions and apartment buildings, primarily along 16th St. and on Crescent Place. Sixteenth St. continues alongside the neighborhoods of Brightwood and Shepherd Park (named for Boss Shepherd, the legendary and controversial city official back in the 1870s) as well as Walter Reed Army Medical Center before feeding out into the Maryland suburbs.

Commute to Downtown 15 minutes by Metro Green Line at Columbia Heights

Post Offices LeDroit Park at 416 Florida Ave. NW (202-483-5617), Columbia Heights at 1423 Irving St. NW (202-635-5308), and Brightwood at 5921 Georgia Ave. NW (202-523-2392)

Libraries Watha T. Daniel Branch at 8th and Rhode Island Ave. NW (202-672-0212), Juanita E. Thornton-Shepard Park at 7420 Georgia Ave. NW (202-576-7114)

Police Stations Third District at 1620 V St. NW (202-673-6930)

Recreational Activities Nature lovers will find walking trails and biking trails between Rock Creek Park on the west and the National Arboretum and Kenilworth Aquatic Gardens on the east.

Adams Morgan

Quiet by day, crowded at night, Adams Morgan is one of the city's most culturally diverse and vibrant areas. The intersection of Columbia Rd. and 18th St. NW forms the heart of Adams Morgan. Specialty shops, bars and some of Washington's best ethnic restaurants crowd a several block stretch along each of the streets.

Adams Morgan is an area in perpetual transition. Formerly known as Lanier Heights, this area took its current name from two local elementary schools, Adams (attended by white students) and Morgan (attended by black students), when schools were integrated in the 1950s. The neighborhood was largely black until it absorbed an influx of Central American immigrants in the 1980s. It is currently home to a mix of young professionals, working-class families and various ethnic groups.

Real estate investors have begun a campaign to renovate and modernize the neighborhood. Riots in the early 1990s called media and public attention to the disadvantages—and advantages—of living in this area. As in any transitional area, safety conditions can change quickly from one block to the next, and it pays to be a bit "street smart" if you live here. The area between 18th St. and Connecticut Ave., on the west edge of Adams Morgan, is generally considered to be the safest.

Throughout the neighborhood, you will find many beautiful townhouses and brownstones, some of which have been converted to group houses or apartment or condo buildings. There also are a number of elegant, older apartment buildings, some rental and others condo. The variety of housing choices in Adams Morgan is consistent with the neighborhood's eclectic character.

As in many of Washington's more popular neighborhoods, parking is a constant challenge here. Finding a parking spot can be especially tough on weekends, when thousands of Washingtonians and suburbanites invade Adams Morgan for the restaurants and bars. Both a pay parking lot and garage, part of a complex of apartments and shops, are located on 18th St. The closest Metro stations are Dupont Circle and Woodley Park-Zoo/Adams Morgan; a shuttle runs from the latter to the heart of Adams Morgan. Metrobuses run up and down 16th and 18th Sts., providing access to all parts of the city.

The largest supermarket in the neighborhood is the **Safeway** on Columbia Rd., just east of 18th St. (202-667-0774). A better selection of fruits and vegetables can be found at the neighborhood farmers' market on Saturdays, at the intersection of Columbia Rd. and 18th St., right in front of the Crestar Bank.

Corner grocery stores and small ethnic markets fill in the gaps. At 1831 Columbia Rd. NW, **So's Your Mom** (202-462-3666), with its trademark sign of the big kissing lips, sells deli goods. Latin American groceries are sold at **El Gavilan** at 1646 Columbia Rd. NW (202-234-9260). Perhaps the most exotic store in the neighborhood, **Merkato Market** at 2116 18th St. NW (202-483-9499), sells Ethiopian spices and other specialty foods.

Adams Morgan is particularly popular for its many restaurants. You can wander along the couple of blocks near the intersection of 18th St. and Columbia Rd. and end up enjoying cuisine from just about any part of the world. Some of the more popular restaurants are **Cities** (202-328-2100), **I Matti** (202-462-8844), **Perry's** (202-234-6218), **Meskerem** (202-462-4100), **Café Lautrec** (202-265-6436), **Straits of Malaya** (202-483-1483) and **Cashion's Eat Place** at 1819 Columbia Rd. NW (202-797-1819). Several of the more expensive neighborhood restaurants have individual valet parking services, and they work together, parking cars for patrons of each other's restaurants. For dessert, Adams Morgan has a number of after-dinner coffee spots such as **Jolt'n Bolt** (202-232-0077).

Adams Morgan and neighboring Mount Pleasant celebrate local life styles with annual festivals. Adams Morgan Day is one of the city's best annual events. Usually held the second Sunday in September, this huge street fair celebrates the cultural diversity of the neighborhood with an abundance of food and music. The Mount Pleasant Day Festival in June also features art, live music and food from area restaurants.

Mount Pleasant is bounded on the north by Rock Creek Park, on the south by Harvard St., on the west by Adams Mill Rd., and on the east by 16th St. NW. It has long been considered the seat of the District's Latino community. It is also home to many white and black families as well as African and Vietnamese immigrants. Designated a historic district in 1987, this neighborhood is predominantly residential, with a wide range of housing styles. Condominiums, apartment buildings, row houses, detached homes and Victorians sit along tree-lined streets. Most of the homes in the neighborhood are owner-occupied, and the row houses traditionally have been home to recent college graduates or young professionals, in many cases run as group houses.

Complementing the offerings of Adams Morgan, a number of small neighborhood restaurants serve Salvadoran and Mexican dishes, and groceries are available at the **Super Saver Market** at 3162 Mount Pleasant St. NW (202-328-1320).

Commute to Downtown 10 minutes by Metro Red Line at Woodley Park-Zoo/Adams Morgan

Post Offices Kalorama at 2300 18th St. NW (202-523-2904) and Temple Heights at 1921 Florida Ave. NW (202-232-7613)

Libraries Mount Pleasant at 16th and Lamont Sts. NW (202-727-1361)

Police Stations Third District at 1624 V St. NW (202-673-6930)

Recreational Activities Public tennis courts can be found on 18th St. between California and Kalorama Sts. NW. The Marie Reed Recreational Center (202-673-7768) has an indoor swimming pool at 2200 Champlain Ave. NW. There is also a small park at Columbia Rd. and Kalorama St. NW.

Dupont Circle

Originally named Pacific Circle because of its westernmost sector location, Dupont Circle epitomizes city living—busy streets, crowded sidewalks, the rare open parking space, an abundance of row houses and high-rise buildings, movie theaters, distinctive shops, art galleries, bookstores and a multitude of bars and restaurants. It is a vibrant, often hectic area, characterized by a wide diversity of life styles and cultural interests. It is popular with the gay community, professionals and students, especially graduates.

If you plan on living here, you really do not need a car and in fact may be better off without one. Most addresses are a few blocks from one of the two entrances to the Dupont Circle Metro station. You can walk to just about everything, and walking is much easier than driving (and parking) in the evening and on weekends, when people from all over come to partake of the neighborhood's many offerings.

Dupont Circle sits just above Downtown and below Adams Morgan. Technically, this neighborhood spans the area west of 16th St. and east of 24th St., between N St. and Florida Ave., but its high real estate values have led realtors to extend its boundaries to include many other nearby areas, such as Logan Circle and Shaw.

The area on the western side of Connecticut Ave. has several hotels, many embassies and a number of art galleries as well as apartments, condos and private townhouses. The embassies lining Massachusetts Ave., as it travels northwest from Dupont Circle up to Observatory Circle, have helped this part of the avenue earn the name Embassy Row. It can be an excellent route for jogging or taking a long, romantic walk.

The West End section, just off the southwest corner of the heart of Dupont Circle, borders Georgetown to the west and Foggy Bottom to the south. Apartment, condos and townhouses in the West End are mostly luxury residences.

Housing costs in and around Dupont Circle are among the highest in the city, although not quite as high as in Georgetown. The variety of Victorian townhouses and apartment buildings offers a virtually complete selection of housing solutions. Most of the more affordable housing appears on the east side of Connecticut Ave., known as East Dupont. As a result of the relatively high real estate values on both sides of the avenue, you will not find many group houses in Dupont Circle. You should look for them instead on the fringes of the area, to the east of 16th St.

Grocery shopping can be done at the **Safeway** at the corner of 17th and Corcoran Sts. NW (202-667-6825) and at the **Townhouse** at 1800 20th St. NW (202-483-3908). There are also several corner markets that cater to busy city dwellers. You'll find **Metro Market** at 2130 P St. NW (202-833-3720) and **Federal Market** at 1215 23rd St. NW (202-293-0014), which has a thriving noontime business for its terrific sandwiches. Characteristic of markets in urban settings are the cramped aisles and high prices you will find in these stores.

Following Connecticut Ave. north, you can shop at the gourmet market **Lawson's** (202-775-0400) right "on the circle" and at **Viareggio** (1727 Connecticut Ave. NW, 202-332-9100), which has an interesting mix of Italian products and takeout food. The **Freshfarm Market** takes over the block at 20th St. NW between Massachusetts Ave. and Q St. on weekends from May to mid-December, and to complete your meal shopping, stop by **Grape Finds**, a new Dupont Circle shop at 1643 Connecticut Ave. NW (202-387-3146) that organizes wines by category rather than by variety or regions of the world.

The neighborhood is richly populated with coffee shops, including no fewer than three **Starbucks** as well as **Soho Tea and Coffee** (202-463-7646), **Java House** (202-387-6622), and two **Xando** sites (202-296-9341, 202-332-6364), which become bars at night.

Restaurants in Dupont Circle are almost too numerous to count. Food from around the globe and in just about every price range is available. A few highlights are **City Lights of China** at 1731 Connecticut Ave. NW (202-265-6688) for Hunan and Sichuan; **I Ricchi** at 1220 19th St. NW (202-835-0459) for Tuscan cuisine; plus **Levante's** (202-293-3244) for fine eastern Mediterranean food. One of Washington's "power" restaurants, the **Palm** (202-293-9091), is at 1225 19th St. NW, where you can dine among a clientele of high-powered lobbyists and prominent sports figures. The **Tabard Inn Restaurant** at 1739 N St. NW (202-331-8528) is popular for its "New American" food, brick-walled garden, and fireside lounge. **Pan Asian Noodles and Grill** at 2020 P St. NW (202-872-8889) is a trip, this one around the world to sample several Asian cuisines.

Commute to Downtown 5 minutes by Metro Red Line at Dupont Circle

Post Offices Temple Heights at 1921 Florida Ave. NW (202-232-7613) and Farragut at 1800 M St. NW (202-523-2506)

Libraries West End at 1101 24th St. NW (202-724-8707)

Police Stations Third District at 1624 V St. NW (202-673-6930)

Recreational Activities Right in the center of the neighborhood is the actual Dupont Circle, with its large fountain, grassy areas, park benches and lots of people, many with their dogs in tow. This is a popular spot for picnics, reading, skating, meeting up with friends and people-watching. Rock Creek Park has numerous trails for running and biking and a mile-and-a-half-long exercise trail with 18 workout stations, beginning near the Taft Bridge. Avoid running or walking through the park alone or after dark.

WASHINGTON, DC
Shaw, 16th St. Corridor, Adams Morgan, Dupont Circle, Woodley Park, Cleveland Park and Van Ness

Woodley Park

When you spot the large mural of Marilyn Monroe painted on the south side of a Connecticut Ave. townhouse, you know that you have reached Woodley Park, at the north end of the Taft Bridge. This Connecticut Ave. neighborhood is home to a varied population including young and not so young professionals, students, and an interesting "hotel population," for the area is also home to a couple of large convention hotels. Nearby, hundreds of animal species make their home at the National Zoo, a popular spot for tourists and locals alike.

Older high-rise buildings dominate this neighborhood. Many of the apartments are boxy and small, but have a wonderful old-fashioned charm that you won't find in the suburbs. The area's popularity stems from its proximity to Adams Morgan and Downtown and its relative safety. Many residents attribute this safety to the presence of several nearby embassies, each with its own security force. If you are looking for a group house, you should continue up Connecticut Ave. to Cleveland Park as there aren't as many of them in Woodley Park. Street parking can be difficult even with a residential parking sticker, required in all DC neighborhoods with parking restrictions.

Woodley Park's commercial "Main Street" spans a three-block area around the Metro station on Connecticut Ave. The area includes some of Washington's best ethnic restaurants including **Cafe Paradiso** (202-265-8955), **Saigon Gourmet** (202-265-1360), **Woodley Café** (202-332-5773) and the **Lebanese Taverna** (202-265-8681). Around the corner, you will find **New Heights** (202-234-4110) and an Irish bar called **Murphy's** (202-462-7171). For an intimate Italian dinner, try **Petitto's Restaurante d' Italia** at 2653 Connecticut Ave. NW (202-667-5350); go downstairs to **Dolce Finale** for dessert.

You can also find a **CVS** at 2616 Connecticut Ave. NW (202-265-6818) and the **Washington Park Gourmet** at 2331 Calvert St. NW (202-462-5566). There is, however, no major supermarket. Serious grocery shopping requires a trip to one of the bordering neighborhoods—Adams Morgan's **Safeway** (202-667-0774) or Cleveland Park's **Brookville Supermarket** (202-244-9114).

Commute to Downtown 10 minutes by Metro Red Line at Woodley Park-Zoo/Adams Morgan

Post Offices A mini post office is located in the basement of the Sheraton Hotel, 2660 Woodley Rd. NW; the entrance is around back, on Calvert St. NW (202-282-3080)

Libraries Cleveland Park Branch at Connecticut Ave. and Macomb St. NW (202-727-1345)

Police Stations Second District at 3320 Idaho Ave. NW (202-282-0070)

Recreational Activities The running and biking paths in Rock Creek Park are nearby, as is the Park's mile-and-half-long exercise trail, with a series of 18 workout stations that begins just below the Taft Bridge.

Cleveland Park

Cleveland Park was the first Washington neighborhood to be developed outside of Capitol Hill and Georgetown. In the late 19th century, wealthy merchants began building mansions on what was then known as Piedmont Plateau. At the time, the only access to the neighborhood was through Georgetown. President Grover Cleveland sought refuge from the city heat in the 1880s by purchasing a "country house" in this neighborhood, where the temperature was approximately

15 degrees cooler than at the White House. Only when the Taft Bridge opened at the beginning of the century did the neighborhood really begin to develop as part of the city. Today, Cleveland Park offers a growing number of amenities as well as easy access to Downtown and the Hill. A large section of the neighborhood is an official historic district.

Cleveland Park is known for its beautiful, posh houses, but house hunters can also choose from a wide range of apartment buildings lining Connecticut Ave. and many more tucked away on the quieter side streets. Most of the buildings cater to professionals or students and offer efficiencies and one- and two-bedroom apartments. Those searching for a group house will find lots of relatively inexpensive options in the large, older, bungalow-style homes. Street parking is available, if difficult to find during busy times, on side streets on the western side of Connecticut Ave.

As in Woodley Park, most of this area's commercial activity occurs within a three-block radius of the Cleveland Park Metro station. The **Uptown Theatre** at 3426 Connecticut Ave. NW (202-966-5400), one of Washington's best movie houses complete with old-style seating and a balcony, sits in the middle of this activity. In addition to **Brookville Supermarket** at 3427 Connecticut Ave. NW (202-244-9114) and **Magruder's Supermarket** at 3501 Connecticut Ave. NW (202-237-2531), the neighborhood has more than its share of small gourmet stores, including **Vace** (202-363-1999), offering primarily Italian goods, many of which are homemade. Nearby you will find **Uptown Bakers** (202-362-6262), **Quartermaine Coffee Roasters** (202-244-2676), **Starbucks** (202-966-8118) and **Yes! Natural Gourmet** (202-363-1559). You can shop at the **Giant** at Connecticut Ave. and Van Ness St. (202-364-8250), or at Wisconsin Ave. and Newark St. (202-244-5922) or the **Safeway** (202-244-0180) at 4310 Connecticut Ave. NW.

On the east side of the 3500 block of Connecticut Ave. sits a small strip providing even more amenities to the neighborhood, including **Whatsa Bagel** (202-966-8990), **Pizzeria Uno** (202-966-3225) and a **Blockbusters** (202-363-9500) video store.

Several popular local restaurants can be found along Connecticut Ave., including **Spices Asian Restaurant & Sushi Bar** (202-686-3833), **Ireland's Four Provinces** (202-244-0860), **Yanni's Greek Taverna** (202-362-8871), **Palais du Chocolat** (202-363-2462), **Ivy's Place Restaurant** (202-363-7802) for Thai food, and **Greenwood at Cleveland Park** (202-833-6572) for its seasonal California-style menu.

Commute to Downtown 12 to 15 minutes by Metro Red Line at Cleveland Park

Post Offices Cleveland Park Branch at 3430 Connecticut Ave. NW (202-523-2395)

Libraries Cleveland Park Branch at Connecticut Ave. and Macomb St. NW (202-282-3080)

Police Stations Second District at 3320 Idaho Ave. NW (202-282-0070)

Recreational Activities The Cleveland Park Club at 3433 33rd Pl. NW (202-363-0756) has a small swimming pool and offers aerobics classes. There are tennis courts at 45th and Van Ness Sts. NW and next to Hearst School, off Wisconsin Ave. below Sidwell Friends School.

Van Ness

Van Ness is the last Connecticut Ave. neighborhood with access to the Metro. Above Van Ness, the Red Line turns west to Wisconsin Ave. before heading north to Bethesda and other spots in Maryland. In the high-rise apartment and condominium landscape of Connecticut Ave., Van Ness forms an island of commercial activity between Cleveland Park and the rest of upper Connecticut Ave. The presence of Howard University Law School and the University of the District of Columbia (UDC) defines much of the neighborhood's character. Modern apartment buildings provide the bulk of available housing on Connecticut Ave. itself, in the form of efficiencies and one- and two-bedroom apartments. Beyond Connecticut Ave., Van Ness is transformed into a suburban neighborhood of pricey, single-family homes.

Many neighborhood conveniences surround the Van Ness-UDC Metro station. **Giant** (202-364-8250) and a wide variety of other stores can be found within a three-block radius. Van Ness also boasts a handful of fast-food options. Through an entrance on Veazey Terrace, Giant offers free underground parking—a rare treat in the District. On-street parking in Van Ness is limited, especially when the two universities are in session, but there are several underground parking garages. Most apartment buildings offer parking for an additional fee.

Along Connecticut Ave., above Van Ness, blocks of apartment buildings alternate with pockets of commercial activity. There is a small shopping area with several restaurants, gas stations and a **CVS** (202-966-1815) near the intersection of Connecticut and Nebraska Aves. Farther up Connecticut Ave. close to Chevy Chase Circle, you will find several more restaurants, another **Safeway** (202-244-6097), **Magruder's Supermarket** (202-244-7800) and the gourmet bakery **Bread & Chocolate** (202-966-7413). It is about a 20-minute walk from here to the Van Ness-UDC Metro station, and about a 12-minute walk to the Friendship Heights Metro.

Commute to Downtown 15 minutes by Metro Red Line at Van Ness-UDC

Post Offices Friendship at 4005 Wisconsin Ave. NW (202-635-5305) and Chevy Chase at 5910 Connecticut Ave. NW (301-941-2792)

Libraries Cleveland Park Branch at Connecticut Ave. and Macomb St. NW (202-282-3080) and Chevy Chase at 8005 Connecticut Ave. NW (301-986-4313)

Police Stations Second District at 3320 Idaho Ave. NW (202-282-0070)

Recreational Activities UDC has three public tennis courts; UDC students and faculty have first priority.

Foggy Bottom

There are several theories as to the origin of the rather unusual name for this neighborhood. Some say that it is because the neighborhood was built on top of a reclaimed swamp. Others claim that the State Department's murky politics gave rise to the name. Regardless, its proximity to the State Department, the World Bank, the International Monetary Fund (IMF), the Kennedy Center and George Washington University (GWU) makes it an attractive neighborhood for those in the foreign service and for students.

Foggy Bottom is on the National Registry for the architecture of its historic row houses. Over the last century, the area has switched from being the home of thousands of middle-class workers to a neighborhood of students and bureaucrats. A mix of moderate and luxury apartments can be found on Foggy Bottom's residential streets—the most expensive being the Watergate (an establishment known for its class and elegance long before it became a synonym for political corruption). Apartments at the Watergate rent for thousands of dollars a month and sell for millions, but do not despair—more economical housing can be found to the north of Virginia Ave. Buildings closest to the George Washington University campus tend to offer the most reasonable costs. With a little bit of legwork, you should be able to find a wide range of apartment types and get the right deal for you.

Residents buy groceries at the **Safeway** (202-338-3628) in the basement of the Watergate Complex. This is a small, rather exclusive underground shopping mall complete with post office, **CVS** (202-333-5031) and the fabulous **Watergate Pastry Shop** (202-342-1777). In addition, several small mom-and-pop grocery stores catering to students' late-night eating habits dot the area.

Music and movie fans can get their fix at the 2000 Pennsylvania Shopping Mall with **Tower Records** (202-331-2400) at one end and **Tower Video** (202-223-3900) at the other. In the middle, you will find **One Stop News** (202-872-1577) and the **Cone E Island** ice cream shop (202-822-8460) as well as a few restaurants, including **Kinkead's** (202-296-7700) and **Bertucci's Brick Oven Pizzeria** (202-296-2600). Other popular spots include **Foggy Bottom Café** in the River Inn at 924 25th St. NW (202-338-8707); **Aquarelle** (202-298-4455) and **Chen's Watergate** (202-965-4104), both in the Watergate Hotel at 2650 Virginia Ave. NW; the **Kennedy Center's Roof Terrace Restaurant** (202-416-8555); **Zuki Moon** at 824 New Hampshire Ave. NW (202-333-3312); and **Cup'A Cup'A** at 600 New Hampshire Ave. NW (202-466-3677).

Commute to Downtown 5 minutes by Metro Blue and Orange Lines at Foggy Bottom

Post Offices Watergate Complex at 2512 Virginia Ave. NW (202-965-2730)

Libraries West End at 1101 24th St. NW (202-724-8707)

Police Stations Second District at 3320 Idaho Ave. NW (202-282-0070)

Recreational Activities The Mall, with its vast playing fields, is just a few blocks south of the Foggy Bottom Metro station. The Federal Reserve has several tennis courts open to the public; to reserve one, call 202-452-3357.

Georgetown

Georgetown, right on the banks of the Potomac River, started out as a commercial port and remained so until the latter half of the 19th century. This helps explain the layout of this historic quarter. To the west of Wisconsin Ave., you will find some of the neighborhood's nicest homes, where the wealthy merchants used to live. Less prosperous merchants and workers resided to the east of Wisconsin Ave. in a mix of two-story Victorian and clapboard houses. You would hardly be able to guess at the humble origins of much of Georgetown as today it attracts a mostly well-to-do crowd. The neighborhood is filled with historic sites, as noted by plaques placed on the side of many houses.

In addition to being Washington's oldest neighborhood, Georgetown offers its residents urban elegance mixed with an active night life. The intersection of Wisconsin Ave. and M St. forms the business and entertainment hub of the neighborhood best known for its upscale restaurants, fashionable clothing stores, and many popular bars and night spots. Moving away from the hub, you find a beautiful residential neighborhood, full of tree-lined streets and cozy Federal, Georgian and Victorian townhouses. Many young professionals and a large portion of Washington's jet-set have found their niche in this neighborhood, including the exclusive Washington Harbour (yes, they actually spell Harbour with a "u"), right along the banks of the Potomac. While Georgetown does offer a mix of apartments, English basements are probably the most popular choice for students and young professionals in this area.

Street parking in the area around Wisconsin Ave. and M St. is virtually impossible and it is not much easier to find spaces in the residential areas. Of course, apartment residents have the option to pay for private parking, but, as with most things in Georgetown, this amounts to a serious expense.

Georgetown's lack of easy access to the subway prevents many from choosing this neighborhood. The closest Metro station to the eastern half of Georgetown is Foggy Bottom on the Blue and Orange Lines, a 10- to 15-minute walk away. For those nearer to the Georgetown University campus, the Rosslyn Metro station, also on the Blue and Orange Lines, is actually nearer, even though you have to cross Key Bridge to get to it. Fortunately, both Wisconsin Ave. and M St. are on major bus routes.

Well-known retailers have moved into this neighborhood, renovating old buildings and helping renew interest in the upscale area. These businesses are attracted not only to Georgetown's charm and high-income residents, but also to the large number of tourists. Key among Georgetown's wealth of shopping opportunities is **Georgetown Park Mall**, with its nearly 100 shops, boutiques, galleries and cafés. An important feature of this mall is a parking garage for which validation is available. **Washington Harbour**, at 3000 K St. NW, combines commercial and residential space right on the water, with a number of popular bars and restaurants including **Sequoia** (202-944-4200).

Other popular restaurants are **Mr. Smith's of Georgetown** at 3104 M St. NW (202-333-3104) for casual dining and dancing to live entertainment on the weekend; **Aditi** at 3299 M St. NW (202-625-6825) for Indian food; **Filomena Ristorante** at 1063 Wisconsin Ave. NW (202-338-8800) for fine Italian cuisine; and **Vietnam Georgetown** at 2934 M St. NW (202-337-4536).

The **"Social" Safeway** at 1855 Wisconsin Ave. NW (202-333-3223) is the largest supermarket in the area. As its nickname suggests, this Safeway is a popular spot for singles to check each other out while waiting in the checkout lines. Or for the ultimate gourmet market experience, visit **Dean & Deluca** in the Old Market House at 3276 M St. NW (202-342-2500).

Commute to Downtown 25 minutes by foot, 15 minutes by bus

Post Offices Georgetown Branch at 3050 K St. NW (202-523-2405)

Libraries Georgetown Regional at Wisconsin Ave. and R St. NW (202-282-0220)

Police Stations Second District at 3320 Idaho Ave. NW (202-282-0070)

Recreational Activities The C&O Canal Towpath is a great place for walking, running and biking, and ice-skating, under appropriate conditions. You will find

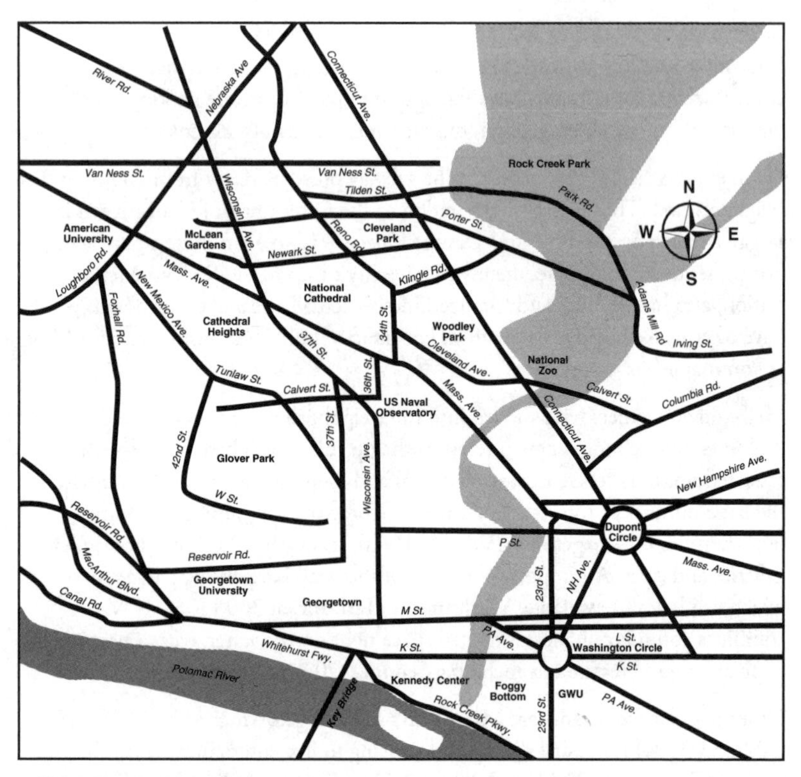

WASHINGTON, DC
Foggy Bottom, Georgetown, Glover Park, Cathedral Heights and McLean Gardens

tennis courts at 30th and R Sts. NW, and at 33rd St. and Volta Place NW. Glover Park, nearby, offers hiking trails through its woods.

Glover Park

Glover Park rests just above Georgetown, bounded by Wisconsin Ave. and Glover and Whitehaven Parks. For an area so convenient to the city, there is a pleasant small-town feel to this neighborhood. The homes here are quaint and charming, a mix of detached single-family homes, townhouses and brownstones, many with front porches where neighbors sit and read, or visit with each other. Young professionals, families, students and long-time residents call this place home. You will find this a popular spot for Georgetown and American University students, due to the variety of group houses and both high-rise and garden-style apartment buildings.

At the edge of Glover-Archbold Park, you will find the neighborhood's Victory Gardens. Begun by President Franklin D. Roosevelt during World War II, the garden plots allow local residents to grow their own vegetables. During war time, the metal that would otherwise have been needed for canning lids was redirected to the war effort. Today there is a waiting list for the 150 or so plots, all bursting with the flowers and vegetables of green-thumbed city dwellers.

Apart from the main retail area on Wisconsin Ave., there are few businesses in Glover Park. A cozy Little League baseball and soccer park at the intersection of Calvert St. and Wisconsin Ave. is surrounded by trees. You can meet your neighbors at Glover Park Day, a neighborhood block party in June. The area has its own monthly paper, the "Glover Park Gazette," and the baby sitting co-op has become a neighborhood institution.

Glover Park's border with Georgetown stirs with commercial activity. In the 2400 block of Wisconsin Ave., you will find **G&G Market** (202-333-5300) and **Pearson's Liquor & Wine Annex** (202-333-6666). The local **Glover Park Market** is at 2411 37th St. NW (202-333-4030) and **Fresh Fields** is at 2323 Wisconsin Ave. NW (202-333-5393). Georgetown's **"Social" Safeway** at 1855 Wisconsin Ave. NW (202-333-3223) is also nearby. Having a car in this neighborhood is less of a challenge than in other areas. Street parking is relatively available and a car makes living here much easier.

Commute to Downtown 15 minutes by bus

Post Offices Calvert Station at 2336 Wisconsin Ave. NW (202-523-5907)

Libraries Georgetown Regional at Wisconsin Ave. and R St. NW (202-282-0220)

Police Stations Second District at 3320 Idaho Ave. NW (202-282-0070)

Recreational Activities The Guy Mason Recreation Center, located at 3600 Calvert St. NW, sponsors art and aerobics classes as well as programs for senior citizens. The neighborhood has several small parks, and tennis courts are nearby at 33rd St. and Volta Place NW. Several trails through the Glover Park woods take you south to Reservoir Rd.

Cathedral Heights and McLean Gardens

Traveling farther up Wisconsin Ave., you reach Cathedral Heights and McLean Gardens, two relatively small, quiet neighborhoods just above Georgetown. Cathedral Heights earns its name from the defining landmark in the area, Washington National Cathedral. Its grounds are a wonderful place to stroll and enjoy a peaceful moment right in the heart of a busy city. When open, the Cathedral's massive towers provide a splendid panoramic view of Washington.

Bounded by Macomb St. on the north, Wisconsin Ave. on the east, Fulton St. on the south, and Glover Archbold Park on the west, Cathedral Heights is a community with both an urban and suburban identity, housing both long- and short-term residents. Most of the neighborhood houses are Tudor and Colonial. Many are owned by residents who have lived there 40 or 50 years. Because it also has a concentration of apartment complexes, it is home to many of the District's short-term residents, including graduate school students and individuals working for an incumbent presidential administration or a foreign embassy. Generally, apartment buildings line Wisconsin Ave. and the side streets to the west. Single-family homes appear on the side streets east of Wisconsin Ave. in the shadow of the Cathedral and bordering on the Cleveland Park neighborhood. Many of these homes are actually in the Cleveland Park Historical District.

Farther up Wisconsin, the former McLean family estate now houses McLean Gardens. The McLean family, one of DC's wealthier families, suffered many misfortunes often blamed on the legendary curse of the Hope Diamond (a famous 45.5-carat blue diamond now on display at the Smithsonian, which so far does not seem to have inherited the curse). In 1941, the federal government bought the estate and built apartment buildings and dormitories to shelter the many people coming to the District to work for the growing War Department. After World War II, private interests took control of the land and turned the buildings into private apartments. Today, McLean Gardens is a large garden apartment and condominium complex and includes a luxury high-rise, the Village Tower.

Just west of here is Wesley Heights, bounded by Nebraska Ave. on the north, New Mexico Ave. to the east, Edmonds St. on the south, and 49th St. to the west. This small residential neighborhood is nestled among three parks—Battery Kemble, Glover-Archbold, and Wesley Heights. Dating back to the 1920s, the homes in Wesley Heights were built around the area's sloping terrain, with old trees and the occasional ravine or running brook gracing the properties. As you might imagine, the area has a reputation as an exclusive and expensive neighborhood.

Most of the commercial activity occurs along Wisconsin Ave. A 24-hour **Giant** (202-244-5922) and a **CVS** (202-966-9268) face each other at the corner of Wisconsin Ave. and Newark St. The first in-town **Fresh Fields** is located at 4530 40th St. NW (202-237-5800) in neighboring Tenleytown. The first **Starbucks Coffee** to open in Washington is at 3430 Wisconsin Ave. NW (202-537-6879). **Cactus Cantina** at 3300 Wisconsin Ave. NW (202-686-7222) offers authentic Mexican food; along with great food, their claim to fame is that there is no can opener in the kitchen.

Commute to Downtown 15 minutes by bus

Post Offices Friendship at 4005 Wisconsin Ave. NW (202-635-5305)

Libraries Tenleytown-Friendship at Wisconsin Ave. and Albemarle St. NW (202-282-3090)

Police Stations Second District at 3320 Idaho Ave. NW (202-282-0070)

Recreational Activities McLean Gardens maintains its own pools, open to residents. Three public tennis courts sit near the corner of Newark and 39th Sts. You can grow your own vegetables and flowers in the public gardens also located at Newark and 39th Sts. NW. To reserve a garden plot, call 202-576-6257.

American University Park

American University Park and Spring Valley are two of the several neighborhoods touching the fringes of American University. Massachusetts Ave., a main DC thoroughfare, runs through these neighborhoods and up in to suburban Maryland. Frequent Metrobuses provide residents with access to Downtown. American University Park is a modest neighborhood, containing reasonable housing options. The suburban feel of this area, combined with affordable starter homes, makes it popular for young families. Apartment housing, though not plentiful, is available; rents tend to reflect the scarcity. Students favor the mammoth apartment buildings just below campus along Massachusetts and New Mexico Aves.

Spring Valley, named after a natural springs that feeds a creek on the land, is known for its quiet, tree-lined streets and convenient location. This affluent section of Washington is one of the few parts of the city to be exempted from the mandatory street grid pattern designed by Washington's original city planner Pierre L'Enfant in the 1790s. (For a discussion of L'Enfant and the street grid layout, see Chapter 3).

For those just beginning to move into houses, leasing a house may be a more practical option. Rental prices here compare to other Northwest neighborhoods. Available rental housing options include attached houses, cluster homes and detached, single-family residences. There are few apartment buildings or complexes in this area.

Palisades, one of the District's oldest residential areas, includes the area west of American University down to MacArthur Blvd. Like American University Park, this neighborhood is family-oriented. Many small apartment buildings are found here along, with brick colonial homes and private yards on tree-lined streets.

Proximity to American University offers residents many entertainment options with university athletic events, performances, movies and museums open to the public. For information about upcoming events, contact the AU Student Confederation at 202-885-6400.

Cafe Deluxe (202-686-2233) at 3228 Wisconsin Ave. NW offers a varied menu and seasonal outdoor dining in a neighborhood atmosphere. **Listrani's** (202-363-0619) at 5100 MacArthur Blvd. NW is a very popular Italian restaurant (offering pizza delivery as well) as is **DeCarlo's** (202-363-4220) at 4822 Yuma St. NW. There is also a **Chicken Out Rotisserie** at 4866 Massachusetts Ave. NW (202-364-8646). **Crate & Barrel** (202-364-6100) and **Starbucks** (202-686-3680) are conveniently located in the 4800 block of Massachusetts Ave. NW.

Grocery shopping can be done at one of two neighborhood Safeway stores—the **Safeway** at 4865 MacArthur Blvd. NW (202-337-5649) or the **"Secret" Safeway** at 4203 Davenport St. NW, just off Wisconsin Ave. (202-364-0290). In nearby Bethesda, just over the Maryland line, there is a **Giant** at 5400 Westbard Ave. (301-652-1484). **Sutton Place Gourmet** at 3210 New Mexico Ave. NW (202-363-5800) satisfies the neighborhood's need for gourmet food and provisions and **Sutton on the Run** (202-966-1740) sits at 4872 Massachusetts Ave. NW.

Commute to Downtown 30 minutes by bus

Post Offices Friendship at 4005 Wisconsin Ave. NW (202-635-5305) and Palisades at 5136 MacArthur Blvd. NW (202-523-2562)

Libraries Palisades at 49th and V Sts. NW (202-727-1369) and Tenley-Friendship at Wisconsin Ave. and Albemarle St. NW (202-282-3090)

Police Stations Second District at 3320 Idaho Ave. NW (202-282-0070)

Recreational Activities The track and indoor pool at Wilson Senior High School, Nebraska Ave. and Chesapeake St. NW (202-282-2216), are open to the public. Turtle Park at Van Ness and 45th Sts. NW hosts organized baseball and soccer teams.

Friendship Heights and Chevy Chase

This tiny, high-rise neighborhood straddles the line between DC and Maryland. Its 32 acres host a variety of upscale stores and mammoth apartment buildings. If you prefer older or cozier neighborhoods, you should look elsewhere. But if you like high-rise living and want to be near upscale amenities and the Metro, this might be just the place for you. Many choose to live here because it has an "urban feel" without the urban taxes—at least on the Maryland side of the line.

Most apartment complexes have swimming pools and relatively inexpensive underground parking. The area's proximity to American University and Downtown, via the Metro Red Line, makes it a convenient location. The **Chevy Chase Shopping Center**, on the east side of Wisconsin Ave., has a **Giant** (301-718-6559) and a **CVS** (301-652-4959). A free shuttle bus service connects all of the major apartment complexes with this shopping center.

The neighborhood is famous for its fashionable shopping district which includes shops such as **Gianni Versace** and **Saks Fifth Avenue**. Two attractive retail malls face each other at the intersection of Wisconsin and Western Aves.—**Mazza Gallerie** and **Chevy Chase Pavilion**. At Mazza Gallerie you will find **Neiman Marcus**; **Williams-Sonoma**; **Saks' Men's Store**; **Harriet Kassman**; the upscale **R Room**; and the **General Cinema at Mazza Gallerie**, the first movie house built in the District in over ten years. Across the street is **Chevy Chase Pavilion** with several specialty stores including **Joan and David**, **Pottery Barn**, **Country Road** and **Talbots**. Shopping choices will only increase with new developments

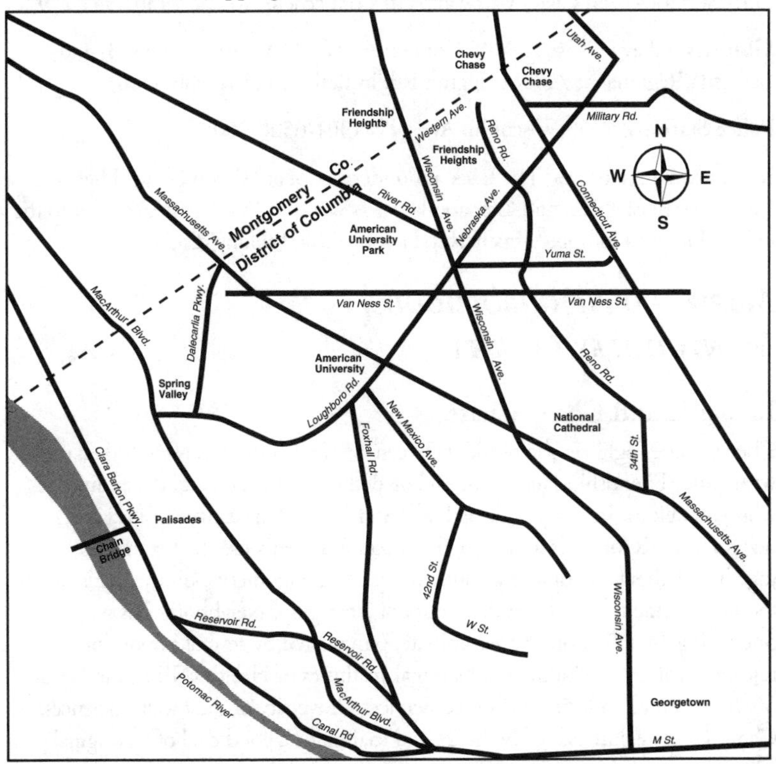

WASHINGTON, DC
American University Park and Friendship Heights/Chevy Chase

on both the District and Maryland sides bringing expanded retail space as well as townhouse and high-rise residences to the area.

Popular restaurants in the area include **TGI Fridays** (202-237-1880) and **Booeymonger** (202-686-5085), both at 5252 Wisconsin Ave. NW; the **Cheesecake Factory** (202-364-0500) in Chevy Chase Pavilion at 5335 Wisconsin Ave. NW; and **Clyde's of Chevy Chase** (301-951-9600) across Western Ave. in the Chevy Chase Shopping Center.

You can contact the Friendship Heights Village Council at 4433 South Park Ave. (301-656-2797) for information on the area. The Village Center, in the same building, provides residents with recreational, educational, cultural and health services.

Commute to Downtown 25 minutes by Metro Red Line at Friendship Heights

Post Offices Main Post Office at 7400 Wisconsin Ave. NW in Bethesda (301-941-2664) and Chevy Chase at 5910 Connecticut Ave. NW (301-941-2792)

Libraries Chevy Chase at 8005 Connectiut Ave. NW (301-986-4313) and Bethesda Regional at 7400 Arlington Rd. in Bethesda (301-986-4300)

Police Stations 7359 Wisconsin Ave. NW (301-652-9200)

Recreational Activities The track and indoor pool at Wilson Senior High School, Nebraska Ave. and Chesapeake St. NW (202-282-2216), are open to the public. Hubert Humphrey Friendship Park is within walking distance.

Maryland Neighborhoods, Montgomery County

Bethesda and Chevy Chase

Chevy Chase, right on the border between city and county, is often linked up with either Friendship Heights in DC or Bethesda in Maryland, depending on who you talk to. In Maryland, Bethesda and Chevy Chase have been sister neighborhoods for years and many local establishments use the two names together. Bethesda occupies the southern tip of Montgomery County and is one of the more affluent suburbs in the metropolitan region. Neighborhoods with pricey single-family homes predominate, punctuated by several important research facilities, including the National Institutes of Health (NIH), the Naval Medical Center and the Uniformed Services University of the Health Sciences. Chevy Chase is just east of Bethesda and maintains a good deal of its original village-like qualities.

While Chevy Chase has its own specific jurisdictional boundaries, as can be seen on any good map, Bethesda is a more sprawling area, with a core of commercial activity surrounding the Metro station that bears its name. There are actually five Metro Red Line stations serving the Bethesda-Chevy Chase neighborhoods—Friendship Heights, Bethesda, Medical Center, Grosvenor and White Flint. This string of stations offers an appealing alternative to driving along the traffic-congested Wisconsin Ave.-Rockville Pike corridor.

Downtown Bethesda demonstrates the recent and rapid expansion this suburb has undergone. Originally a sleepy farm town, Bethesda's development accelerated in the 1970s, spurred on further by the coming of the Metro in 1982. You will find remnants of the old farm town near the Bethesda station, including a weathered old post office and a statue honoring the "Madonna of the Trail," a tribute to Maryland's pioneer women. Next to these, the Rainbow Forest, an aluminum-disc sculpture, and the Hyatt Regency stand as icons of modern-day Bethesda. During the summer, the courtyard by the Metro station rocks to the beat of outdoor concerts; in the winter, it turns into an ice-skating rink. A couple of blocks north is the **Bethesda Theatre Café** (301-656-3337), a popular spot for discount movies and light meals.

Beyond the high-rise buildings characteristic of downtown Bethesda, off to the west of Wisconsin Ave., you will find Woodmont Triangle. Many small shops and some of the area's best ethnic restaurants reside here. Dining options in downtown Bethesda include **Bacchus** (301-657-1722), **Matuba Japanese Restaurant** (301-652-7449), **La Madeleine** (301-215-9139), **Cottonwood Cafe** (301-656-4844), **Montgomery's Grille** (301-654-3595), **Andalucia Restaurante** (301-770-1880), **Positano Ristorante Italiano** (301-654-1717), and **Cafe Bethesda** (301-657-3383).

Because of the increased presence of restaurants and shops in the Woodmont Triangle area, the demand for parking spaces can be intense. Two-hour meters have been installed in the area. Parkers beware—it is against the law to feed the meter beyond the two-hour limit. The fine is steep: At $30, it is $5 more than the fine for expired meters. Watch the posted signs. The city does have numerous parking garages, free on weekends.

Bethesda does not lack for appealing housing, but it does not come cheaply. The newer luxury apartment buildings near the Metro offer all conceivable amenities at top-notch prices. A multitude of older, renovated buildings along Battery Lane, a few blocks away, can be had for slightly less. Kenwood, designed as a planned community, is just south of Bethesda, bordered by Goldsboro Rd., River Rd. and Little Falls Parkway. It features Georgian-style and English Tudor homes. The landscaped and manicured yards contain many cherry trees, whose beautiful spring blossoms draw people to the area. Farther southwest on Goldsboro Rd. sits the small residential community of Glen Echo, with its streets named for major colleges and universities. The Clara Barton National Historic Site (301-492-6245) is also located in Glen Echo, off MacArthur Blvd. at 5801 Oxford Rd.

The Medical Center Metro stop farther up Rockville Pike was built on the campus of the National Institutes of Health and if you exit the Metro at just the right time, you will hear reveille blown from the Naval Medical Center across the street. These institutions border neighborhoods where several homeowners rent out rooms in their homes or in detached apartments, and group houses are also available. Around the Grosvenor Metro station you will find more high-rise condominiums and apartments. Some buildings offer discounts to NIH employees; if you qualify, be sure to ask at the rental office.

In this affluent suburb, grocery stores and supermarkets promise no shortage of fully stocked shelves. Residents can shop at the **Safeway** at 5000 Bradley Blvd. (301-656-8641) or opt for the gourmet **Safeway Marketplace** (301-907-0700) at 7625 Old Georgetown Rd. **Giant**, on its home turf in the suburbs, has a store at Arlington Blvd. and Elm St. (301-718-2470). A **Giant Pharmacy** (301-652-9130) is across the street. **CVS** has one store at 4601 East-West Highway (301-986-9144) and a 24-hour store (301-656-2522) at the corner of Bradley Blvd. and Arlington Rd. In addition, there are several supermarket-sized gourmet stores. **Sutton Place Gourmet** (301-564-3100) has a store in the Wildwood Shopping Center off Old Georgetown Rd. and **Fresh Fields** is at 5225 River Rd. (301-984-4860). There is also the **French Market** (301-986-9661) in the Elizabeth Arcade at 4601 N. Park Ave. On Wednesdays and Saturdays, the **Montgomery Farm Women's Cooperative** hosts a farmers' market selling fruit, flowers and Amish baked goods at 7155 Wisconsin Ave. An outdoor flea market, replete with oriental rugs, furniture and jewelry, takes over this location on Sundays. Bethesda is the place to go for fine crafts.

Free information about the area is available from the Bethesda-Chevy Chase Center (301-986-4325) at 7815 Woodmont Ave.

Commute to Downtown 30 to 35 minutes by Metro Red Line at Friendship Heights, Bethesda, Medical Center, Grovesnor and White Flint

Post Offices Main Office at 7400 Wisconsin Ave. (301-941-2664) and Chevy Chase Branch at 5910 Connecticut Ave. NW (301-941-2792)

Libraries Bethesda Regional at 7400 Arlington Rd. (301-986-4300) and Chevy Chase Branch at 8005 Connecticut Ave. NW (301-986-4313)

Police Stations 7359 Wisconsin Ave. (301-652-9200)

Recreational Activities Cabin John Regional Park (301-299-4555) at 7400 Tuckerman La. has tennis and handball courts, hiking trails and an ice-skating rink. Glen Echo Park at 7500 MacArthur Blvd. in Glen Echo (301-492-6282) is the area's gem, a national park sponsoring hundreds of classes in the arts. Its historic Spanish Ballroom offers a variety of dance classes and four dances per week from April through November. The park also operates a beautiful antique carousel from May through September. A planned 3-year renovation of the entire park began in the fall of 1999.

Rockville, Gaithersburg and Germantown

Rockville has served as the seat of Montgomery County since 1776. It is an area particularly rich in colonial history and it has been neatly transformed over the years into a modern, well-planned city. Efforts to revitalize the downtown Rockville business district are in progress including office buildings, high-rises, and a theater and restaurant pavilion. Many homes are older, detached residences, yet the area offers a great deal of newer construction as well. You will find parks and playgrounds to be an integral part of most Rockville neighborhoods. The city sponsors a popular cultural arts program. Extensive shopping, including **White Flint Mall**, can be found along Rockville Pike. Only 12 miles from DC, Rockville is connected to the District and its closer-in suburbs by excellent commuter access via I-270 as well as Rockville Pike (Route 355) and by the Metro Red Line for those who prefer public transportation.

Going a little farther out either I-270 or Rockville Pike, you come to the City of Gaithersburg, about 20 miles from DC. Incorporated in 1878, Gaithersburg both retains its historic character in the Olde Town district and welcomes the necessary expansion of more recent times. Much of this community's development is due to its proximity to the I-270 corridor, a commercial and business area known for the many corporations that have relocated there. In recent years, a mix of high-tech employers such as IBM and Lockheed Martin Hughes along with a number of biotech firms has led to the area being nicknamed "Biotech Valley" or "Tech Alley." The local population of government workers, scientists and professionals enjoys a diverse mix of life styles.

An ethnically diverse city of approximately 50,000 people, Gaithersburg is one of the fastest growing communities on the east coast. It provides the full range of housing—apartments, townhouses, and both historic and newer single-family homes—as well as many parks and family-oriented recreation centers. Community spirit is evident in such annual events as Olde Town Day and the Labor Day Parade. Geographically in the heart of Gaithersburg is the **Lakeforest Mall** shopping center with over 200 department stores, shops, restaurants and movie theaters. Many other small shopping malls, restaurants and theaters are scattered throughout the city. Revitalization plans for Olde Town Gaithersburg, which will evolve over several years, are expected to include luxury apartments, office buildings, restaurants, shops, entertainment facilities and, thankfully, parking.

The Gaithersburg development called Kentlands, off Route 28, offers its homeowners, condo residents and renters a sense of community much like a "new old-fashioned" traditional neighborhood. As part of the New Urbanist school of architectural thinking, Kentlands offers a small-town lifestyle where neighbors are encouraged to walk everywhere—from their homes to the nearby shopping center, office park, church, school, swimming pool, lakes, and recreation center, all located on Kentland grounds. With mostly brick, stone, brass and other natural building materials, this urban village is truly au natural.

Although not yet an incorporated town, Montgomery Village was given its own designation and zip code on January 1, 1998. It opened in 1967 as a 2,500-acre

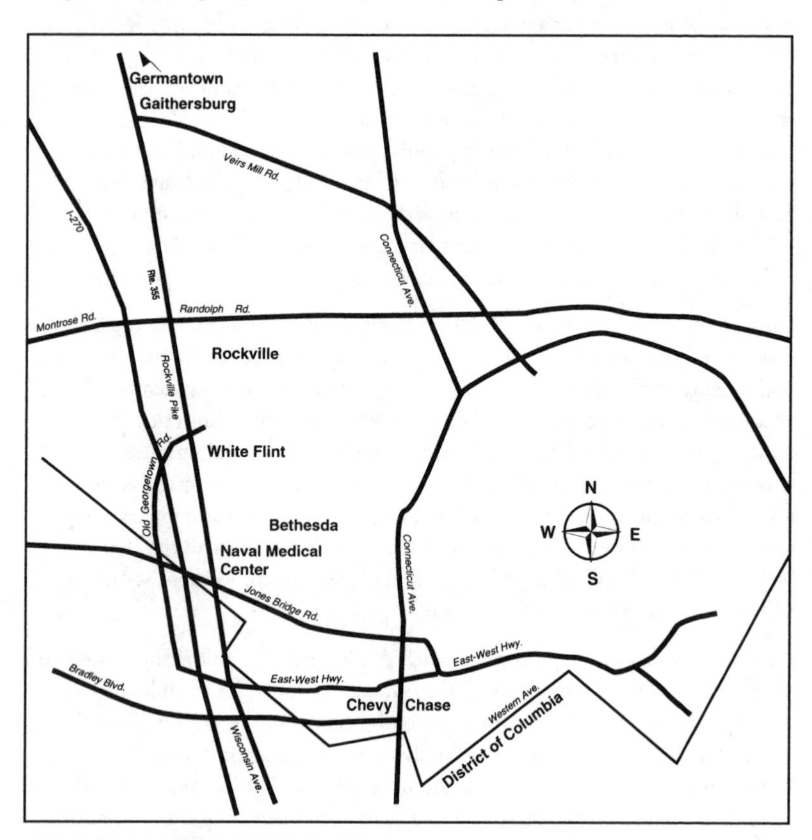

MONTGOMERY COUNTY, MD
Bethesda/Chevy Chase and Rockville/Gaithersburg/Germantown

planned development with individual communities featuring trees, open space, a host of amenities, and easy access to major roads. Today, more than 38,000 people live here and the development continues to expand. Housing includes townhouses, condominiums, detached houses and a senior retirement community. The neighborhoods have community centers, pools and playing fields, tennis courts and lakes. Shopping is available at the nearby Lakeforest Mall. Look for more about this vibrant community at www.montgomeryvillage.com.

About five miles beyond Gaithersburg is Germantown, considered to be Montgomery County's fastest growing area. Germantown is home to several of the county's major employers including the Department of Energy and many high-tech firms along the I-270 corridor. The residential neighborhoods in Germantown offer many older homes as well as a wide variety of new, single-family homes, townhouses, condos and rental apartments. The combination provides for a diverse range of architectural styles. The community is bounded by two streams—Great Seneca to the south and Little Seneca to the north—and by two large parks—Seneca Creek State Park and Black Hill Regional Park. Local bus service to nearby Metrorail stations makes commuting via public transportation available to residents.

Silver Spring and Wheaton

Named for a spring with sparkling bits of mica, Silver Spring is a sprawling area in the easternmost part of Montgomery County. Three Red Line Metro stations are located in the area—Silver Spring, Forest Glen and Wheaton. Downtown Silver Spring is located near the junction of Georgia Ave. and Colesville Rd. (Route 29), and surrounds the busy Silver Spring Metro station. With new or expanding growth in the area by such entities as Discovery Communications, Montgomery College as well as several restaurants, the metropolitan area is springing to life. As part of this revitalization, the American film Institute (AFI) is renovating the historic Silver Theatre. The AFI Silver will be an internationally recognized, state-of-the-art film and video exhibition center.

Single-family homes and clusters of apartment buildings, both high-rise and garden-style, surround each of the three Metro stations serving Silver Spring. Group houses are available around the Forest Glen and Wheaton Metro stations. For those willing to brave the morning commute down Route 29, there are even cheaper options out Colesville Rd., at White Oak and beyond. A boom in new home construction, especially along the Route 29 corridor, is adding to the variety of home styles and ages already available.

The area is served by several large grocery stores. **Snider's** at 1936 Seminary Rd. (301-589-3240) is a local favorite and has a steady following who rave about its meat and wine selections. Larger chains also can be found in downtown Silver

Spring, including **Giant** at 1280 East-West Hwy. (301-585-1670) and **Safeway** at 909 Thayer Ave. (301-565-0686). Another **Giant** (301-949-1458) is located in Wheaton Plaza and there is a **Safeway** (301-949-7690) nearby at 11201 Georgia Ave. A new **Fresh Fields** (301-984-4874) can be found at Fenton and Wayne Sts.

Silver Spring offers a variety of ethnic markets and restaurants to match its varied population. You will find Italian, Ethiopian, Thai, Indian and Latin-American establishments here. Prices are generally better than in other, more up-scale neighborhoods. For ethnic groceries, downtown Silver Spring offers **Italia** at 8662 Colesville Rd. (301-588-6999), **Muskan Fine Indian Grocery** at 956 Thayer Ave. (301-588-0331), the **Thai Market** at 902 Thayer Ave. (301-495-2779) and **Las Americas Ricardo Latino** at 8651 16th St. (301-588-0882). Among the locally favorite eateries are **Mi Rancho** at 8701 Ramsey Ave. (301-588-4744) for Tex Mex; **Kirsten's Café** at 9326 Georgia Ave. (301-495-9686) for coffee and baked goods; and **York Castle Ice Cream** at 9324 Georgia Ave. (301-589-1616), featuring Jamaican ice cream. The **Parkway Deli** at 8317 Grubb Rd. (301-587-1427) has almost everything you could want from a deli.

Farther up Georgia Ave. is Wheaton, a major residential area with moderately priced homes. You can find a number of older detached homes for sale along with several newly constructed condominiums. Wheaton's diversity is reflected in the recent arrival of many ethnic restaurants and small businesses.

The area's largest shopping center, **Westfield Shoppingtown Wheaton** (301-946-3200), lies between Veirs Mill Rd. and University Blvd. Three major Washington department stores, **Hecht's, JC Penney Co.** and **Wards**, anchor this mall.

Commute to Downtown 20 to 30 minutes by Metro Red Line at Silver Spring

Post Offices Main Branch at 8616 2nd Ave. (301-608-1300) and Silver Spring at 8455 Colesville Rd. (301-879-2333)

Libraries Silver Spring at 8901 Colesville Rd. (301-565-7689) and Wheaton Regional at 11701 Georgia Ave. (301-929-5520)

Police Stations 801 Sligo Ave. (301-565-7740)

Recreational Activities The area boasts two great parks. Sligo Creek offers a hiking and biking trail as well as numerous playgrounds and playing fields. Wheaton Regional Park has everything imaginable including horseback riding, hiking trails, a fishing pond, a playground with both carousel and miniature trains, and the beautiful Brookside Gardens.

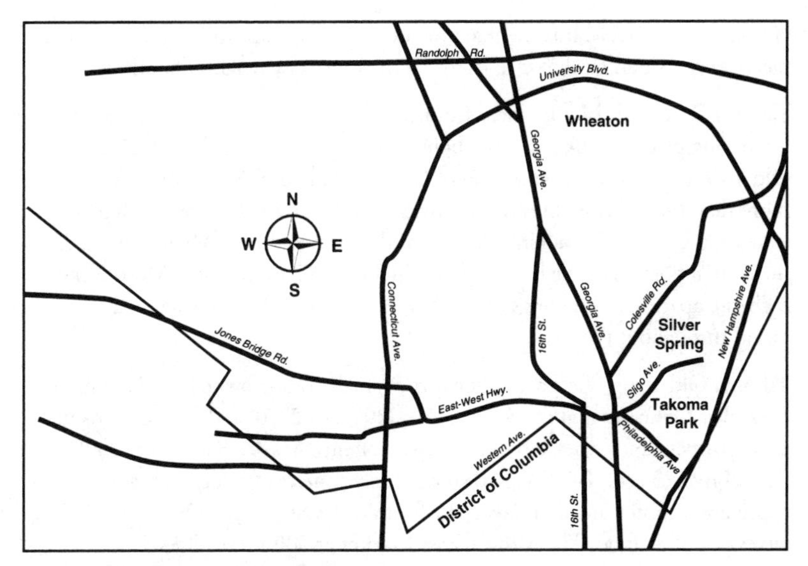

MONTGOMERY COUNTY, MD
Silver Spring, Wheaton and Takoma Park

Takoma Park

The tree-filled neighborhood of Takoma Park rests along the upper northeast boundary of DC. A planned suburban community founded in 1883 along a branch of the B&O railroad, Takoma Park was originally conceived as a healthful clean-water alternative to Washington's malarial swamps. Despite changing times, Takoma Park is still conceived of as an offering outside the mainstream.

A mixture of religion and politics has given shape to the community. From 1904 to 1989, Takoma Park was world headquarters of the Seventh-Day Adventist Church. Two of the church's institutions, Washington Adventist Hospital and Columbia Union College, remain, along with long-standing traditions of family, vegetarianism and temperance. In recent years, signs of the Church's waning influence have begun to appear, including a small bar near the center of town. Takoma Park's population is politically active and has put in place a number of progressive measures such as the declaration of a nuclear-free zone and legal recognition of non-marital partnerships.

Religion and politics aside, Takoma Park is a family-oriented place where neighbors are still neighborly and residents work together to create a safe and nurturing environment for children and adults alike. The local population is an enviably diverse racial mix, representing over 90 countries, without the strained racial tensions that tend to characterize some inner-city neighborhoods.

Takoma Park, with Montgomery County's largest historic district, may be an interesting place to look if you are house hunting. The grand Victorians near Old Town, around the intersection of Carroll and Laurel Aves., will cost much more than those farther out, as will anything that can be described with a straight face as within walking distance of the local Red Line Metro station. A substantial portion of the housing stock in Takoma Park is rental. Most of the high-rise apartment buildings are on Maple Ave., but rental housing may be found throughout the city.

Takoma Old Town offers a quixotic mix of small, locally owned specialty shops. **Everyday Gourmet** is at 6923 Laurel Ave. (301-270-2270) and features take-out or eat-in pastries, sandwiches and other prepared items. **Mark's Kitchen** at 7006 Carroll Ave. (301-270-1884) is a Korean luncheonette offering a semi-vegetarian menu and cappuccino, and **Savory Cafe** at 7071 Carroll Ave. (301-270-2233) serves café-style food. The **Middle East Market** at 7006 Carroll Ave. (301-270-5154) is a great spot for exotic breads, coffee and spices. And from the end of April until mid-December, there is a farmers' market every Sunday in the center of town. While not as big as other area markets, the Takoma Park farmers' market has a loyal following among residents, many of whom consider it a major cultural event.

Eclectic shops offer unique shopping opportunities such as rare books, furniture, and black memorabilia at the **Takoma Underground** (301-270-6380) and American pottery, artwork and antiques at the **Blue Moon** (301-270-6659), next to each other at 7000-B and 7000-C Carroll. You can shop for gifts at **Now & Then** at 6927 Laurel (301-270-2210).

Commute to Downtown 15 minutes by Metro Red Line at Takoma

Post Offices Takoma Park at 6909 Laurel Ave. (301-270-4392) and Langley Park at 1325 Holton La. (301-422-3980)

Libraries Takoma Park, MD Library at 101 Philadelphia Ave. (301-270-1717) and Takoma Park Tool Lending Library at 7500 Maple Ave. behind City Hall, where residents can borrow garden tools, drills and hand tools

Police Stations 7500 Maple Ave. (301-270-1100)

Recreational Activities Takoma Park's best park land includes hiking trails and playing fields on both sides of Sligo Creek, which runs through the eastern part of town. On Sunday, to accommodate bikers, joggers, skateboarders and the like, vehicles are banned from parts of the Takoma Park section of Sligo Creek Parkway.

Maryland Neighborhoods, Prince George's County

College Park and Hyattsville

Old Town College Park is a neighborhood of two personalities. On the one hand, it is steeped in tradition and filled with landmarks. The county is considering bestowing the area with a historic district designation. Most of the homes in Old Town are two-story colonials and bungalow ramblers. Many residences have been maintained or restored in keeping with their late 19th century architecture. On the other hand, Old Town becomes the nightly gathering place for the college crowd. A large portion of the population is transient. Baltimore Ave., the area's main thoroughfare, is lined with strip malls, restaurants and bars. Surrounding Old Town, you will find a variety of typical suburban developments and neighborhoods.

College Park is home to the University of Maryland (301-405-1000), and College Park Airport Museum (301-864-6029) with its memorabilia from the time when the Wright brothers brought their plane to the airfield in the early part of the century. Located nearby is the Department of Agriculture's Beltsville Research Center (301-504-5193).

Just south of the University's College Park campus is a residential community called University Park. This community is home to just under a thousand families and is one of the area's best buys for housing. Here you'll find red-brick colonials built in the 1920s and 1930s and some 1950s ramblers. Prices can be significantly less than those for comparable homes in Montgomery County neighborhoods. While University Park has official restrictions prohibiting commercial development in the town, there are plenty of recreational facilities, parks and tennis courts reserved for its residents. Residents here appreciate the small town feel and are active in preserving it, socially, environmentally and culturally.

The nearby community of Hyattsville, established in 1742 and incorporated in 1854, was once a major port on the Anacostia River. Houses in this area tend to be older, single-family residences, and it is one of many suburbs that has recently attracted the attention of people who want to renovate and refurbish this type of home. Many of the people who live in Hyattsville work for the federal government, as the town is only five miles from DC. Many others work at the University of Maryland.

Commute to Downtown 20 to 25 minutes by Metro Green Line at West Hyattsville Metro, Prince George's Plaza or College Park-U of MD

Post Offices North College Park Station at 9591 Baltimore Blvd. (301-345-1714) and Main Post Office at 4325 Galatin St., Hyattsville (301-209-8900)

Libraries Prince George Memorial Library at 6532 Adelphi Rd. (301-699-3500) and Hyattsville Library at 6530 Adelphi Rd. (301-984-4690)

Police Stations University Park Police Department, 6724 Baltimore Ave., Hyattsville (301-277-0050)

Recreational Activities The University of Maryland at College Park offers visual and performing arts programs. Prince George's Plaza Community Center at 6600 Adelphi Rd. in Hyattsville (301-454-1400) offers recreational programs for all ages. Several parks are located in the area including Greenbelt Park, Sligo Creek Park, and Magruder Park.

Mount Rainier

Barely more than a mile square, Mount Rainier is an early 20th century "streetcar suburb," situated along Washington's northeast border, at the gateway to Prince George's County. It has become known for its eclectic combination of businesses, reflecting the diversity of the entire Prince George's County community. Located along the Route 1 corridor (Rhode Island Ave.), Mount Rainier is barely five miles from the center of DC, and Metro's Green Line at West Hyattsville has made it an even more convenient spot. It is one of the last places inside the Beltway where you can still find single-family detached homes selling for under six figures and is reputed to have one of the area's most compatible racial and ethnic mixtures.

As Mount Rainier is primarily residential, most of the housing stock consists of small, owner-occupied, pre-war bungalows and other modest house styles, including numerous Thirties-era Sears mail-order homes with spacious rooms and hardwood floors. A few larger Victorians can be found in the blocks just north of Rhode Island Ave., many of which are being renovated. Once predominantly white, Mount Rainier now boasts a multicultural population. There are many young black families and a growing Hispanic population, in addition to a solid enclave of senior citizens. Rental apartment complexes are located along Eastern Ave. at the DC-Maryland border and at Queens Chapel Rd. on the city's northern edge, close to the West Hyattsville Metro station.

Some consider Mount Rainier to be a smaller, more blue-collar version of nearby Takoma Park. Both communities are known for their wonderful old houses, progressive local governments and diverse populations. Both neighborhoods have a long tradition of providing group housing to college students from the University of Maryland. And both neighborhoods teetered on the borderline between decline and revitalization before becoming gentrified. The history and architectural value of the homes was recognized in 1990 when two-thirds of the city was listed in the National Register of Historic Places.

Downtown Mount Rainier shopping can be characterized as serviceable at best. The main draw is the **Glut Food Co-op** at 4005 34th St. (301-779-1978), the Washington area's oldest surviving food co-op and a great place to stock up on inexpensive grains, spices, whole wheat bread, fresh fruit and vegetables. One other notable downtown store is discount-minded **Party Times Liquors** at 3307 Rhode Island Ave. (301-927-3037). The nearest major grocery store is the **Giant** (301-699-0501) in **Queens Town Shopping Center** in Hyattsville.

Commute to Downtown 20 to 30 minutes by Metro Green Line at West Hyattsville or by Metrobus to the Red Line at Rhode Island Ave.

Post Offices Mount Rainier Branch at 3709 Rhode Island Ave. (301-699-8856)

Libraries Mount Rainier Branch at 3409 Rhode Island Ave. (301-864-8937)

Police Stations 3409 Rhode Island Ave. (301-985-6590)

Recreational Activities Mount Rainier has a number of neighborhood parks scattered throughout the town, including a nature and recreation center (301-927-2163) at 4701 31st St.

Greenbelt

This suburban Maryland planned community was created in the mid-1930s by the federal government as part of the New Deal. Greenbelt provided needed jobs for people in the area during the Depression, and its row houses and apartment buildings gave them an inexpensive place to live. The government sold all of the property in 1953. The tenants of the more than 1,600 row houses formed a co-op and purchased the property; the co-op functions to this day. Much of the original landscaping is still intact, with many paths connecting little parks to the shopping center, ballfields, a 1938 movie theater, and a lake. Today, the city has a high concentration of academics, scientists and engineers, many of whom work at the NASA/Goddard Space Flight Center or the University of Maryland in nearby College Park. NASA/Goddard Visitors Center (301-286-8981) is just off I-95 exit 22A. Greenbelt is the home of many community activists, clubs and co-operatives, including the grocery store, nursery school, weekly newspaper, and weekend café hosting local talent.

The town of Greenbelt sits at the intersection of five major roads, making it ideal for people commuting in all directions. The Baltimore-Washington Parkway, the Capital Beltway, I-95, Kenilworth Ave. and Route 1 all go through

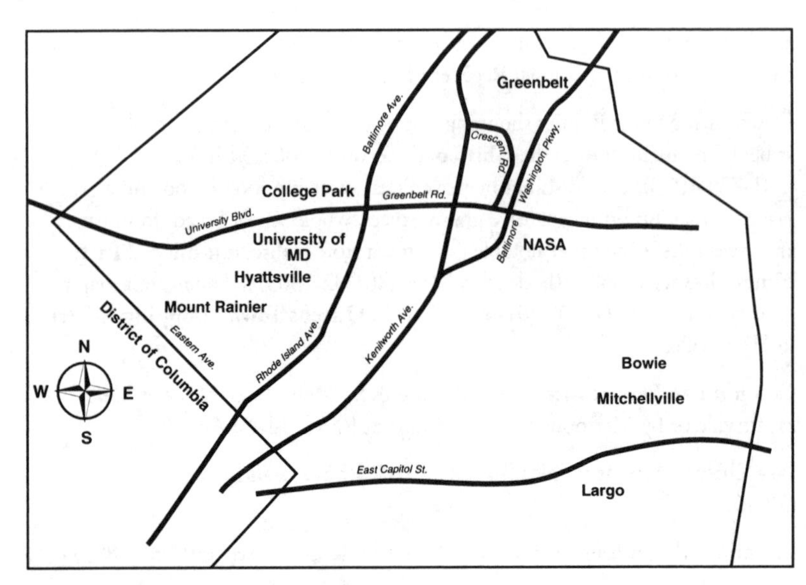

PRINCE GEORGE'S COUNTY, MD
College Park and Hyattsville, Mount Rainier, Greenbelt, Bowie, Largo and Mitchellville

or around Greenbelt. Downtown DC is only about 15 miles away and Baltimore only 25. The Green Line's Greenbelt Metro station is available for those who prefer to metro.

The original section, known as "Old Greenbelt," follows the original city plan and is essentially the same as it was when it first opened in 1937. The long apartment buildings, with their utilitarian lines and art-deco accents, are reminiscent of the 1930s. Over the years, some single-family homes have been incorporated into the community plan and today they line several quiet streets in the west side of town. The newer parts of Greenbelt extend in either direction along Route 193 (Greenbelt Rd.), with modern townhouse communities taking up much of the real estate to the east. For renters, Greenbelt is home to one of the largest apartment complexes in the area, Springhill Lake (301-474-1600), with close to 3,000 units and its own public recreation center.

Many of the town's amenities, including the Community Center, library, municipal building, pools and fitness center, post office, community stage, and **Co-op Supermarket & Pharmacy** (301-474-0522) at 121 Centerway, are located within a hundred yards of each other in the middle of Old Greenbelt. Farther out, you will find **Giant** at 6000 Greenbelt Rd. (301-982-5482), **Safeway** at 7595 Greenbelt Rd. (301-345-0150), and **CVS** at 7573 Greenbelt Rd. (301-513-5965).

The main event of the year in Greenbelt is the Labor Day Festival and Parade—three days of pageants, carnivals, music, an art show, and a variety of other activities.

Commute to Downtown 30 minutes by Metro Green Line at Greenbelt

Post Offices Greenbelt Branch at 119 Centerway (301-345-1721)

Libraries 11 Crescent Rd. (301-345-5800). Greenbelt's wonderful library also serves as a popular community center

Police Stations 550 Crescent Rd. (301-474-7200)

Recreational Activities The Community Center at 15 Crescent Rd. (301-397-2208), housed in the renovated 1937 elementary school, offers classrooms, a senior center, gym, art studios and other community services. Greenbelt Park at 6565 Greenbelt Rd. (301-344-3948) has walking trails and areas for camping and picnicking. Just east of Greenbelt Park, along Hanover Parkway, is Schrom Hills Community Park (301-552-2004). The entire northern edge of Old Greenbelt is bordered by the Department of Agriculture's Beltsville Research Center, a huge tract of government farmland criss-crossed by rarely traveled two-lane country roads, great for biking and running.

Bowie, Largo and Mitchellville

Bowie and the areas surrounding it are about halfway between Washington, DC and Annapolis, MD on Route 50. Housing in Bowie generally consists of single-family homes built in the 1960s. Newer construction includes moderate and higher priced single-family homes as well as townhouses. In **Bowie Town Center** you will find apartments, townhouses, offices and a popular shopping mall.

The area is home to Bowie State University (301-464-6600; www. bowiestate.edu), which plays a role in the social and cultural life of the area. The former Bowie Race Track is now an equestrian training facility, rather appropriately, for it is considered the birthplace of American thoroughbred racing. For horse racing, fans travel farther north to Laurel, along Route 1.

The neighboring town of Largo is experiencing an expansion in the housing market, spurred by commercial development in the area. Here you will find single-family homes, townhouses, condominiums and apartments. **Landover Mall**, achored by **JC Penney Co.** and **Sears**, draws shoppers from several parts of the county. Another highlight in the area is **BET Sound Stage** (301-883-9500), Black Entertainment's first theme restaurant and entertainment complex. The restaurant has over 500 seats and features Southern, Caribbean and Mexican food and wine from California, Europe and South Africa. The entertainment theme changes daily, and the Sunday brunch is accompanied by gospel music videos. **Radio One** (301-306-1111), the nation's largest African-American-owned radio company, is located in neighboring Lanham.

Prince George's County is the wealthiest predominantly African-American jurisdiction in the United States. Lake Arbor, near Largo, is one of the wealthiest areas in the county, white or black. A planned development made up of neighborhoods of single-family homes and townhouses, man-made lakes and rolling hills, most of Lake Arbor was built in the mid- to late 1980s. The community's borders are Rt. 202, Central Ave., Lottsford Rd. and the Western Branch stream.

Handsome, expanding communities such as Mitchellville and wealthy subdivisions such as Woodmore have re-created Prince George's County over the last decade as a showcase of African-American affluence. In Mitchellville, you'll find spacious houses that rival the embassies in downtown Washington. The homes are larger and sited on larger lots, but for less money than you would pay for the same property in Montgomery County. In this relatively undeveloped part of Prince George's County, you can still find and enjoy open spaces, woodlands and country roads. Woodmore, known for its up-scale townhouses, also has single-family homes and a beautiful country club and golf course. Watkins Park is well known for its beautiful and festive holiday light show during the Christmas season.

Commute to Downtown 30 minutes by Metro Orange Line from Landover

Post Offices Main Post Office at 6710 Laurel Bowie Rd. (301-464-0707), West Bowie Station at 13030 9th St. (301-464-1611), and Mitchellville-South Bowie Branch at 1500 Pointer Ridge Place (301-249-2511)

Libraries Bowie Branch at 15210 Annapolis Rd. (301-262-7000) and Largo-Kettering Branch at 9601 Capital Lane, Largo (301-336-4044)

Police Stations Bowie Police Station at 601 Crain Hwy., Bowie (301-390-2100)

Recreational Activities Greenbelt Park at 6565 Greenbelt Rd. (301-344-3948) offers bridle paths, hiking trails and picnic grounds. Also in Landover, you will find FedEx Field (301-276-6000), the home of the Washington Redskins.

Virginia Neighborhoods, Arlington County

Rosslyn

When you look across the Potomac River from Washington, DC to Rosslyn, Virginia, be prepared for an architectural altitude adjustment. High-rise office buildings, forbidden by height restrictions in the District, dominate the skyline of this close-in suburb. What Rosslyn lacks in aesthetic appeal, though, it makes up for in convenience, sitting directly across Key Bridge from Georgetown and across Roosevelt Bridge from the Mall. Metro's Orange and Blue Lines both stop here on their way out to other Virginia suburbs. The Rossyln Metro station is known for its incredibly steep and long escalator ride.

The main thoroughfare, five-laned Wilson Blvd., climbs up from Key Bridge and heads out to the west beyond Rosslyn. Several sky-walks were built as part of the original planning concept for Rosslyn, to separate automobile and pedestrian traffic. In reality, these ramps are confusing and many seem to lead nowhere. Fortunately, Arlington County has a long-range plan for enhancing the central business area, and renovation of some of the 30-year-old buildings has already begun.

During the day, countless workers toil away in Rosslyn's many office towers but at night the local streets are typically deserted. This lack of night-time activity should not dissuade new residents. According to the Arlington police department, Rosslyn is quite safe. One night of the year, however, the area is particularly busy, as some of the best views of the Fourth of July fireworks on the Mall can be had from the rooftops of Rosslyn's towering buildings.

Despite Rosslyn's less than charming appearance, many young professionals and students, especially from George Washington University, find the neighborhood a fine place to live. Rosslyn offers a surprising array of garden and high-rise apartments, some right on the Potomac. Generally, housing costs are slightly below those of the Northwest's most popular neighborhoods. Those looking for group houses should explore the streets north of Wilson Blvd. toward I-66.

Rosslyn is home to the Newseum, an interactive museum of news, at 1101 Wilson Blvd. (703-284-3700), and the adjacent Freedom Park which sits atop a section of elevated highway that was never completed.

Both Rosslyn and Court House, the next neighborhood out Wilson Blvd., have wonderful Southeast Asian restaurants, including Vietnamese, Cambodian, Thai and Korean. You'll find lots of menu choices along the major streets not far from the Metro station, including **Santa Fe Cafe** (703-276-0361). The usual neighborhood conveniences are concentrated at or around the intersection of Wilson Blvd. and North Lynn St. You will find several dry cleaners, **CVS** (703-243-4993) and **Tivoli Gourmet** (703-524-8904). Residents do their grocery shopping at **Safeway** (703-276-9315) at 1525 Wilson Blvd. A 30-foot-tall sculpture called "Anna and David" marks the spot for this underground grocery store, making it easy to find.

Commute to Downtown Seven minutes by Metro Blue and Orange Lines at Rosslyn

Post Offices Rosslyn Station at 1101 Wilson Blvd. (703-525-4336)

Libraries Central Library at 1015 North Quincy St. (703-228-5990)

Police Stations 2100 North 15th St. (703-558-2222)

Recreational Activities Two tennis courts are at Lyon Village Park at the intersection of 20th Rd. and North Highland St.

Court House

It will come as no surprise that the Arlington County Courthouse is the focal point of this neighborhood. While you may not initially think that living near a courthouse is a plus, it does make handling official business less complicated.

Relatively new luxury apartment buildings and a shopping complex can be found around the Courthouse and out along Clarendon Blvd. These buildings offer a selection of one- and two-bedroom apartments. There are several older, smaller and less expensive apartment buildings on the side streets, supplying an even wider range of apartment options. A number of large-scale developments have also been built south of Clarendon Blvd. toward Route 50.

The plaza adjoining the Courthouse contains a convenience store called the **Metro Market** (703-841-3530), several restaurants, gourmet food shops and an eight-screen **AMC movie theater** (703-998-4AMC). There are several supermarkets nearby—the **Safeway** in Rosslyn (703-276-9315) and another about a mile away at 3713 Lee Highway (703-841-1155) as well as two **Giants**, one at 3115 Lee Highway (703-527-9453) and another near the Virginia Square Metro, at 3450 North Washington Blvd. (703-358-9343). There is a **CVS** (703-524-2617) at the corner of 10th St. and Washington Blvd.

A weekly farmers' market takes place near the Courthouse on Saturday mornings from May to October. Farmers sell their fresh produce on 14th St. between North Courthouse Rd. and North Veitch St., just past the police station.

In addition to a wide variety of restaurants offering Southeast Asian cuisine, you'll find **Village Bistro** (703-522-0284), **Pizza de Résistance** (703-351-5680) and **RT's Seafood Kitchen** (703-841-0100) in this area.

Commute to Downtown 10 minutes by Metro Orange Line at Court House

Post Offices Courthouse Station at 2043 Wilson Blvd. (703-525-4441)

Libraries Central Library at 1015 North Quincy St. (703-228-5990)

Police Stations 2100 North 15th St. (703-558-2222)

Recreational Activities There are two tennis courts at Lyon Village Park at 20th Rd. and North Highland St.

Clarendon

Clarendon, just up Wilson Blvd. from Court House, has not yet been subjected to the high-rise building boom enjoyed (or suffered) by its neighbors. It remains a mostly quiet, low-key neighborhood, full of ethnic restaurants and older single-family homes. The abundance of older houses makes Clarendon a great area for group houses. The area will be seeing increased development for mixed-use facilities with office, retail and residential space. Even so, it will not be seeing the same high rises as some of its neighbors, due to strict zoning regulations that limit the height of office buildings.

The square at the Clarendon Metro station is the hub of the neighborhood and reflects the changes taking place there. In the middle of the square, a World War I monument stands in stark contrast to the sleek, modern high-rise building that dominates the spot from its location on Clarendon Blvd. But across Wilson Blvd., you're back to older, storefronts that today are full of small shops and restaurants. The changing cultural nature of the area is evidenced by the large number of Asian establishments nearby, including some of Washington's best Vietnamese restaurants. Some of the most popular restaurants in this area are **Queen Bee Restaurant** (703-527-3444), **Hard Times Cafe** (703-528-2233), the **Clarendon Grill** (703-524-7455), **Mister Days Sports Rock Café** (703-527-1600), and **Red, Hot & Blue** (703-276-7427).

If you are planning to live here, you will need a car as most conveniences are not easily reached on foot. There are several large supermarkets to choose from, including the Safeways and Giants mentioned in the section on the Court House area. **Fresh Fields** has a store (703-527-6596) at 2700 Wilson Blvd., two blocks east of the Clarendon Metro station.

Commute to Downtown 15 minutes by Metro Orange Line at Clarendon

Post Offices Arlington Main Office at 3118 North Washington Blvd. (703-525-4838)

Libraries Central Library at 1015 North Quincy St. (703-358-5990)

Police Stations 2100 North 15th St. (703-558-2222)

Recreational Activities Washington-Lee High School at 1300 North Quincy St. (703-358-6262) has a public swimming pool and a track. Six public tennis courts are across the street at Quincy Park.

Ballston

Like Rosslyn, Ballston is a suburb with many high-rise buildings situated within a few blocks of the Metro station that bears its name.

Housing can be found in any one of the many apartment buildings or townhouses on the side streets off Fairfax Dr., Washington Blvd. and Glebe Rd. High-rise apartment buildings generally offer one-, two- and three-bedroom apartments, but not many efficiencies.

The blue-roofed **International House of Pancakes** (703-522-3118), known as IHOP, stands as an old-time landmark on Fairfax Dr., having weathered the many years of changes to the neighborhood. It stays open round the clock and is a great spot for midnight meals and Sunday morning breakfasts. In addition, the area has a large shopping mall, **Ballston Common. Giant** (703-358-9343) is at the corner of Washington Blvd. and Lincoln St., a short walk from the Virginia Square Metro and George Mason Law School. If you have a car, you can shop at **Harris Teeter Grocery** in Hyde Park Plaza (703-526-9100) at 600 North Glebe Rd. **Tivoli Gourmet** (703-528-5201), right at the Metro station, is the neighborhood's only gourmet shop. **Rio Grand Cafe** (703-528-3131) and **Memphis Bar-B-Q** (703-875-9883) are some of the area's most popular restaurants.

Commute to Downtown 20 minutes by Metro Orange Line at Ballston

Post Offices Buckingham at 235 North Glebe Rd. (703-525-4170)

Libraries Central Library at 1015 North Quincy St. (703-228-5990)

Police Stations 2100 North 15th St. (703-558-2222)

Recreational Activities Washington-Lee High School at 1300 North Quincy St. (703-358-6262) has a public swimming pool and a track. Six public tennis courts are across the street at Quincy Park.

Pentagon City

This quiet community off Army-Navy Dr. is just south of the Pentagon. Many single-family homes and several massive apartment buildings congregate in the area. This is a working class neighborhood where housing is available at lower prices than in nearby Crystal City or North Arlington. A wide selection of group houses occupies the streets behind the Virginia Highlands Park off South Ives St. Whether you live in an apartment building or a house, parking never seems to be a problem.

This neighborhood is home to a major mall, the **Fashion Centre at Pentagon City**, which is anchored by one of the area's several **Nordstrom** stores and a large

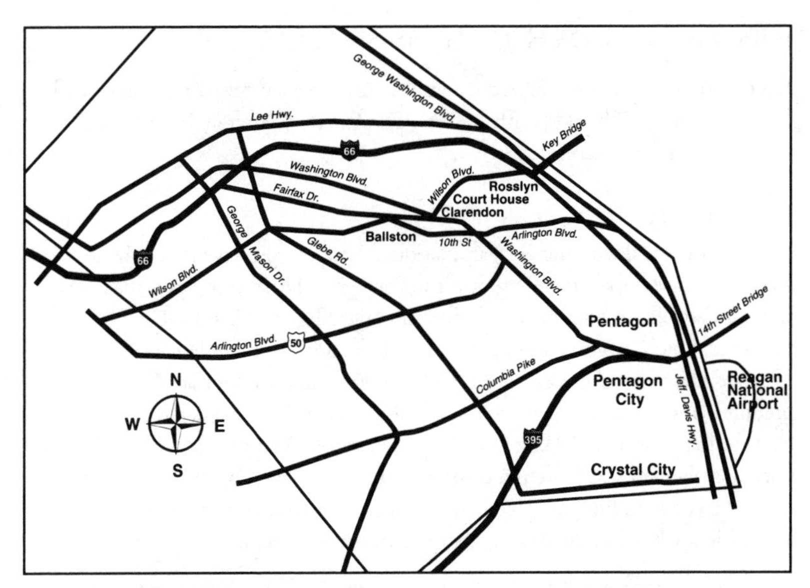

ARLINGTON COUNTY, VA
Rosslyn, Court House, Clarendon, Ballston, Pentagon City and Crystal City

Macy's. Residents particularly enjoy the mall's six-screen movie theater and huge food-court. The Pentagon City Metro, on the Blue and Yellow Lines, has an exit leading directly into the mall, which also has its own large parking garage.

Pentagon City has a variety of restaurants including **Chevy's Mexican Restaurant** (703-413-8700), **California Pizza Kitchen** (703-412-4900), and **Woo Lae Oak** (703-521-3706) for Korean cuisine.

While the neighborhood does not have a large grocery store, there is a convenience store in the basement of River House I at 1111 Army Navy Dr. Also, a huge **Costco Wholesale Club** (703-413-2324) is available across the street from the fashion mall in the city's "other center"—**Pentagon Centre**. The nearest **Safeway** is in Crystal City at 2129 Crystal Plaza Dr. (703-415-0422), just a Metro stop away. If you have a car, you can go to the **Safeway** at 2303 Columbia Pike (703-920-2909) or the **Giant** at either 2515 Columbia Pike (703-685-7050) or 1303 South Glebe Rd. (703-836-0245).

Commute to Downtown 20 to 30 minutes by Metro Blue and Yellow Lines at Pentagon City

Post Offices Eads at 1720 Eads St. (703-979-2108)

Libraries Aurora Hills at 735 South 18th St. (703-228-5715)

Police Stations 2100 North 15th St. (703-558-2222)

Recreational Activities Six public tennis courts are at Virginia Highlands Park, at the corner of 17th and South Ives Sts. The Carver Center at 1415 South Queen St. has three tennis courts.

Crystal City

If you have ever flown into Reagan National Airport, you have probably noticed a crowd of skyscrapers towering near the Pentagon. These complexes make up Crystal City, lining both sides of Jefferson Davis Highway (Route 1) with a mix of offices, hotels, condos, and apartments. The Patent and Trademark Office, followed closely by the Navy and then by various support contractors, is the predominant tenant in the Crystal City area; some private firms have located here for that reason and to be near Reagan National Airport. The core of Crystal City was planned and built as a unit and originally owned by one developer. Over the years, additional construction has only intensified the density of the area which, while lacking charm, abounds in conveniences.

This area's gigantic apartment and condominium buildings offer a variety of choices. You will easily find everything there from efficiencies to three-bedrooms at prices lower than those in North Arlington. Some older single-family homes, perfect for group houses, can be found on the west side of Jefferson Davis Hwy.

If you live in Crystal City, especially in one of the central high-rises, you could go for months on end without ever venturing out of doors as most of Crystal City is connected by miles of underground passages. Here, all "roads" lead to the **Crystal City Underground Shopping Center**, with every imaginable amenity, including a post office, several small gourmet shops, restaurants and a **Safeway** (703-415-0422). Even the Crystal City Metro station feeds into this underground mall, giving you access to all parts of the metropolitan area through connections from the Blue and Yellow Lines.

A word of caution—because of Crystal City's proximity to Reagan National Airport, airplane traffic can be heard throughout the day. The noise gets particularly loud during the early evening hours and can be a serious problem in residences facing east toward the airport. Flight departures are restricted after 10:00 p.m.; however, planes under a certain noise level are allowed to land after that hour. If you are looking for an apartment or house here, be sure to ask about the noise and then drop by at night or early in the morning to gauge it for yourself.

Crystal City's 23rd St. South is famous for streets lined with restaurants including **Portofino** (703-979-8200), **Crystal City Sports Pub** (703-521-8215), and **Saigon Crystal** (703-920-3663).

Commute to Downtown 25 minutes by Metro Blue and Yellow Lines at Crystal City

Post Offices Crystal City Station at 1735 Crystal Dr. (703-413-9267)

Libraries Aurora Hills at 735 South 18th St. (703-228-5715)

Police Stations 2100 North 15th St. (703-558-2222)

Recreational Activities Six public tennis courts are available at Virginia Highlands Park at the corner of 17th and South Ives Sts.

VIRGINIA NEIGHBORHOODS, CITY OF ALEXANDRIA

Originally Virginia's center for commerce and culture, the 16-square-mile City of Alexandria, bordering the Potomac River, today includes one of the country's most historic communities. At the far east end of Alexandria is Old Town, the city's best known neighborhood, looking almost too good to be true. Strict zoning regulations protect its freshly painted Georgian houses, cobblestone streets and clean sidewalks. The historic quarter begins right along the waterfront and continues west along King St. and the many other quaint streets in the orderly, colonial part of town—a great place for walking tours. As you might expect, housing costs are highest here.

While greater Alexandria has five Metro stops—Braddock Rd., King St., Eisenhower Ave. and Huntington on the Yellow Line and Van Dorn St. on the Blue Line—none of them serves Old Town directly. It is quite a walk from the center of Old Town to the nearest station, Braddock Rd. Fortunately, there are a number of Metrobus routes as well as DASH, the local bus system, linking the many parts of Alexandria to each other and to the District. DASH runs six bus routes through Alexandria. Frequent air travelers may want to consider living in Alexandria, as it is less than a 10-minute commute to Reagan National Airport.

As you leave Old Town and travel south down Washington St. toward Mt. Vernon, you will find several apartment complexes that try to capitalize on their proximity to Old Town. You will find more of the same type of housing out along Route 1 South. Farther to the west and southwest, there are even more high-rise and garden-style buildings along Beauregard and Duke Sts. and in the part of town known as Alexandria's West End. The West End is not far from the Van Dorn Metro station and the densely populated area offers housing in just about every price range. The northwest end of the city, near the Braddock St. Metro and the airport, contains a mix of up-scale condos and low-rent housing. There is a lovely, quaint area along Russell Rd., in the shadow of the Masonic Temple, a visual and historic landmark close to Old Town.

Since colonial days, space has been set aside in Old Town Alexandria's town square for a farmers' market. Today, the tradition of selling fresh produce, meats and baked goods continues at the weekly Saturday morning market on the south plaza of the City Hall at 301 King St. This market is for early birds—it closes at 9:00 a.m.! More typical shopping can be done at **Giant** at 530 1st St. (703-739-0751) at the north end of Old Town, about seven blocks from the Braddock Rd. Metro station, at **Safeway** (703-836-0380) at 500 South Royal St., at the south end; and at **Fresh Fields** at 6548 Little River Turnpike (703-914-0040). **Sutton Place Gourmet** at 600 Franklin St. (703-549-6611), **Starbucks** at 532 King St. (703-836-2236), and **Magruder's Supermarket** at 4641 Duke St. (703-461-0533) are among the popular and convenient spots in the area. The number of grocery stores and shopping centers in greater Alexandria is too high to count; wherever you are in the area, one is bound to be nearby, especially along the more important through-streets such as King St., Seminary Rd. and Duke St. (Route 236), which turns into Little River Tpk. farther west after crossing I-395.

A new complex of retail shops, restaurants and a megaplex, modeled after Reston's Town Center, can be found along Eisenhower Ave. **Landmark Mall** in Alexandria includes **Sears** and **Hecht's** under its roof. While Landmark is not near a Metro line, you can get there using public transportation (Metro Blue Line to Van Dorn then DASH bus to the mall). Driving is much quicker; take I-395 to Duke St. East. **Potomac Yard Center**, a massive new shopping center, is located just south of Reagan National Airport on old railroad yards. Anchored by **Target**, the center provides a unique retail opportunity for people living inside the Beltway.

Commute to Downtown 30 to 45 minutes by Metro Yellow Line at Braddock Rd., King St., Eisenhower Ave. and Huntington, or Blue Line at Van Dorn

Post Offices Main Branch at 1100 Wythe St. (703-549-4201), George Mason at 126 South Washington St. (703-549-0813), Park Fairfax at 3682 King St. (703-379-6017), Trade Center at 340 South Pickett St. (703-823-0968), and Jefferson Manor at 5834 North King's Hwy. (703-960-4440)

Libraries Dedicated in early 2000, the Charles E. Beatley Jr. Library at Duke and Pickett Sts. (703-519-5900) is Alexandria's new central library. The Local History Library (703-838-4577) and Barrett Library (703-838-4555) are both located at 717 Queen St. James Duncan Library is found at 2501 Commonwealth Ave. (703-838-4566).

Police Stations 2003 Mill Rd. (703-838-4444)

Recreational Activities Chinquapin Park (703-931-1127) at 3210 King St. has an indoor pool, fitness room, racquetball courts, tennis courts, picnic areas and a nature trail. Cameron Run Regional Park at 4001 Eisenhower Ave. (703-960-0767) has a wave pool, miniature golf course (a tough one—no windmills and dog houses here), and batting cages.

Virginia Neighborhoods, Fairfax County

Falls Church

Falls Church was originally the name of a local Anglican church built in 1733. The town that grew around the small wooden (now brick) church adopted the name; the church and its cemetery remain as historic landmarks. While the actual City of Falls Church spans only two square miles, the area Washingtonians refer to as Falls Church is much larger. Much of the area between northern Arlington and the posh community of McLean has a Falls Church mailing address.

East Falls Church encompasses the area between Arlington Blvd. at the **Seven Corners Shopping Center** and the East Falls Church Metro station. Rents here are relatively low for the Washington metropolitan area. The high-rise and garden apartment complexes located along commercial Leesburg Pike (Route 7) supply an abundance of efficiencies and one-bedroom apartments. In general, locations closer to the East Falls Church Metro are more convenient, although slightly more expensive. Group houses can be found in and around the Washington Blvd. area.

West Falls Church, by contrast, has fewer choices for apartment seekers and more for those looking to buy. The exceptions here are the few high-rise apartment complexes between the West Falls Church Metro station and Tysons Corner.

Falls Church is a shopper's paradise. In East Falls Church, there is **Seven Corners Shopping Center**, which houses one of the area's super-sized **Barnes & Noble** bookstores and **Starbucks**. West Falls Church sits in the backyard of up-scale shopping at **Tysons Corner Center** and **Tysons Galleria**, featuring **Bloomingdale's, Macy's, Neiman Marcus, Nordstrom** and **Saks Fifth Avenue**.

The only way to reach one of the best supermarkets in the area, the **Giant** (703-845-0446) at Baileys Crossroads, is by car. This Giant has everything. If you choose to shop here, go during the week; the supermarket and surrounding mall are extremely popular on the weekends and the parking lot is occasionally full and often chaotic. Another **Giant** (703-237-9609) is at the corner of West Broad St. and Haycock Rd., within walking distance of the West Falls Church Metro station. You will find **Safeways** at 6118 Arlington Blvd. (703-241-4131) and 7397 Lee Hwy. (703-573-2057) and **Magruder's Supermarket** (703-280-0440) on Graham Rd. **Fresh Fields**, at 7511 Leesburg Pike (703-448-1600), between I-66 and Tysons Corner, offers a large selection of organically grown produce.

Commute to Downtown 30 to 45 minutes by Metro Yellow Line at East Falls Church and West Falls Church—VT/UVA

Post Offices Main Office at 301 West Broad St. (703-532-8822) and Bailey's Crossroads at 6021 Leesburg Pike (703-671-0221)

Libraries Thomas Jefferson at 7415 Arlington Blvd. (703-573-1060) and Mary Riley Styles at 120 North Virginia Ave. (703-248-5030)

Police Stations 300 Park Ave. (703-248-5054)

Recreational Activities The Falls Church Community Center at 223 Little Falls St. (703-241-5077) sponsors a variety of sports activities and offers classes in cooking and dancing. The Washington & Old Dominion bike trail whisks bikers and joggers all the way east to the border between Arlington and Alexandria and as far west as Purcellville.

Fairfax City

Fairfax City dates back to the pre-Revolutionary War era and retains the charm of its colonial roots, particularly in its Historic District where many original homes and buildings can be found. However, the 12 miles separating it from downtown Washington, DC have not shielded it from the rapid growth of the metropolitan area in recent decades. Downtown Fairfax City remains village-like, with small houses and restaurants. Beyond that, however, you will find many strip malls and housing developments. The area known as Fairfax now extends well beyond its official boundaries; large sections of the outlying county are considered part of the city, complete with Fairfax addresses.

Fairfax is home to George Mason University (GMU), one of the largest schools in the Virginia state system. The Fairfax Symphony Orchestra and the Virginia Opera perform at GMU's Center for the Arts. The Patriot Center is a venue for both concerts and sports events.

All types of housing are available for purchase and rental. Apartments and townhouses in the Fairfax Circle area are most convenient to the Metro, some within walking distance of the Vienna/Fairfax-GMU station. From other areas, rail commuters must use the CUE bus, the city's own mini-bus system, or drive to the Metro station. Several apartment and townhouse communities are located along Blake La. going northwest to Fairfax Circle. There are others along Main St. (Route 236) between downtown and Pickett Rd. Rents in Fairfax follow the

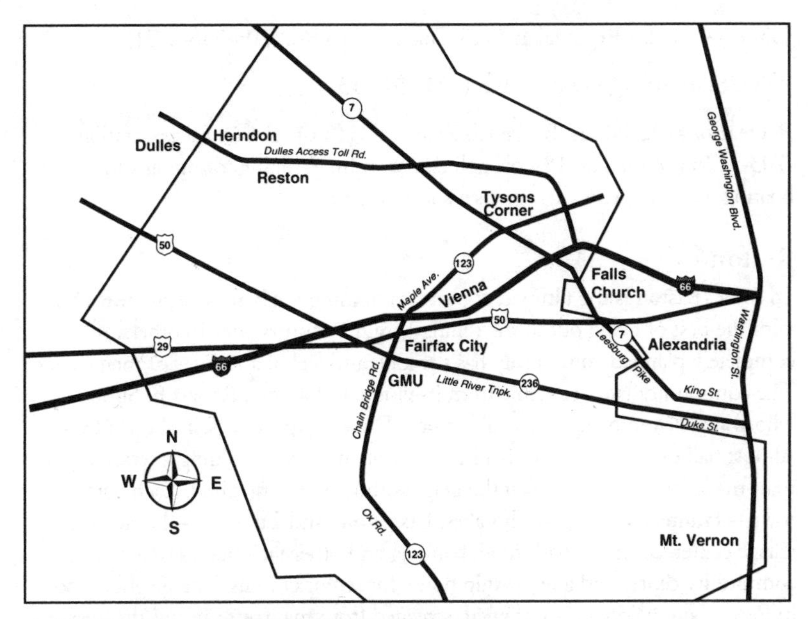

ALEXANDRIA AND FAIRFAX COUNTY, VA
Alexandria, Falls Church, Fairfax City, Reston and Herndon

Washington area rule—the more accessible the area is to DC, the more you pay to live there.

There are numerous smaller shops in downtown Fairfax and several convenient shopping centers. But for serious shopping, area residents head for nearby malls, including **Fair Oaks** at the intersection of Route 50 and I-66, anchored by **Hecht's, Sears** and **JC Penney Co.**

Victoria's Cakery at 10430 Main St. (703-273-0800) is tucked away in one of the funky Victorian houses in downtown Fairfax and is guaranteed to satisfy any sweet tooth. **Safeway** has locations at the Courthouse Plaza Shopping Center (703-591-8473) and at 3043 Nutley St. in the Pan Am Shopping Center near Fairfax Circle (703-560-6696). **Giant** is at 11054 Lee Highway (703-273-0147), 9570 Main St. (703-323-9108) and 12997 Lee Jackson Memorial Highway (703-803-7732). Fairfax also has its own **Costco Wholesale Club** at 4725 West Ox Rd. (703-802-1223) for buying in bulk.

Commute to Downtown 45 to 60 minutes by Metro at Vienna/Fairfax-GMU

Post Offices Main at 3951 Chain Bridge Rd. (703-273-5571), Turnpike at 3601 Pickett Rd. (703-239-2900), Fairfax at 5616 Ox Rd. (703-250-9188), and Chantilly at 4410 Brookfield Corporate Dr. (703-968-7272)

Libraries Fairfax Regional at 3915 Chain Bridge Rd. (703-246-2281)

Police Stations 10600 Page Ave. (703-691-2131)

Recreational Activities Burke Lake Park at 7315 Ox Rd. in Fairfax Station (703-323-6600) has an 18-hole golf course, fishing, hiking, camping and boating. Children enjoy its carousel and miniature train.

Reston

To some, Reston is the ultimate suburb, combining the best of being near DC with the best of living out in the rolling Virginia countryside. To others, this completely planned community has the look and feel of a residential theme park. The community takes its name from its visionary founder, Robert E. Simon, who willed it into being on farmland near Dulles Airport back in the 1960s. Almost half of Reston is park land or other open space, including a series of four man-made lakes around which the neighborhoods are organized. Each part of town—Hunters Woods, South Lakes, Lake Anne and Tall Oaks—has its own village center, complete with food, banking and other facilities, as well as a community center and a fellowship house for senior citizens. The neighborhoods in Reston are mainly self-contained, screened from major streets and the busy Dulles Toll Rd. by dense groves of trees. In the past few years, Reston and other communities have been home to a blitz of development. Office buildings lining the Dulles Toll Rd. house high-tech businesses in this part of the state.

Reston Town Center at 11911 Freedom Dr. is a mall and gathering place that looms up out of the landscape and is a focal point for the area's nightlife. In the middle of Town Center is an outdoor pavilion with seating for some of the restaurants. Concerts are held here during the summer, and in the winter the pavilion is converted into an ice-skating rink. Aside from dozens of shops, Town Center houses a number of restaurants and the **Reston Town Center Multiplex Cinema** (703-318-1800). Some of Georgetown's dining landmarks have made their way out to Reston's Town Center which now includes **Clyde's** (703-787-6601) and **Paolo's** (703-318-8920). **Rio Grande Cafe** (703-904-0703) serves delicious fajitas and the **Market Street Bar & Grill** (703-709-6262) offers a good brunch and a bit of culture with live jazz Friday, Saturday and Sunday nights. A couple of other popular spots in the area are **Romano's Macaroni Grill** (703-471-4474) and **On the Border** (703-904-1240).

The Reston Visitor's Center (703-471-7030) at 11450 Baron Cameron Ave. provides detailed information and directions to all areas. Rental rates and housing prices vary depending on the size of the unit and proximity to the neighborhood lake.

In Reston you can do your grocery shopping at the **Giant** in North Point Village (703-437-0031) or the one in Tall Oaks Village (703-478-6718). There are **Safeways** at 11130 South Lakes Drive (703-620-3400) and at 2304 Hunters Wood Plaza (703-716-4193). A **Fresh Fields** is at 11660 Plaza America (703-736-0600). For gourmet groceries, you'll find **Sutton Place Gourmet** at 11860 Spectrum Center (703-787-4888). Reston also has a **CVS** at 11160 South Lake Dr. (703-620-6691).

Commute to Downtown No Metro. The Fairfax connector provides access to the West Falls Church-VT/UVA Metro station during rush hours. Non-rush-hour service is provided by the Reston Internal Bus System (RIBS).

Post Offices Reston Post Office at 11110 Sunset Hills Rd. (703-437-6677) and one at 1860 Michael Faraday Dr. (703-437-7822).

Libraries Reston Regional at 11925 Bowman Towne Dr. (703-689-2700)

Police Stations 12000 Bowman Towne Dr. (703-478-0904)

Recreational Activities Reston has lots of public swimming pools and tennis courts for its residents. In addition, there are footpaths and bike trails all over town, linking together the area's many neighborhoods.

Herndon

Herndon, Reston's next door neighbor, is quite different. Herndon developed over time and along very different lines. Once a small village railroad stop, Herndon got caught up in the regional growth that accompanied the construction of the Dulles Toll Rd. High-tech, defense-oriented and service businesses, attracted by the convenience of the airport, have created a commercial nexus known as the Dulles Corridor. Herndon has absorbed much of the influx of businesses, residents and related activity.

You can still sense something of Herndon's history as you travel along the historic, restored town center. The town still has the look and feel of the small village it was not long ago. The tiny, old railroad station, once the focal point of Herndon, still sits proudly in the center of town. Renovating late Victorian houses has become trendy here, but recent townhouse and apartment construction has begun to change the area's old-fashioned look. Renovated older homes and townhouses tend to be located close to the village center with newer accommodations on the outskirts, although in a town of just over four square miles, that does not require going very far. On average, for roughly similar housing, Herndon's prices are below those in Reston.

Downtown Herndon is home to the **Ice House Cafe and Oyster Bar** at 760 Elden St. (703-471-4256). The small, dark jazz club has been a local institution for years. Also on Elden St. are the **Hard Times Cafe** at #428 (703-318-8941), **Anita's Mexican Food** at #701 (703-481-1441) and **Outback Steakhouse** (703-318-0999) at #150, as well as a discount movie theater showing almost-current flicks. A **Loew's Cinemas** (703-318-9290) can be found near Exit 2 of the Dulles Toll Rd., in the **Worldgate Plaza**, also home to several shops and the **Worldgate Athletic Club** (703-709-9100), a popular health club with great facilities.

Residents do their grocery shopping at a gourmet **Giant Marketplace** at 1228 Elden St. (703-437-3162) or out at the Worldgate Plaza's **Shoppers Food Warehouse** at 2425 Centerville Rd. (703-713-1227). For breads and other baked goods, try **Great Harvest Bakery** at 785 Station St. (703-471-4031). In the center of town you will find a **CVS** at 1062 Elden St. (703-471-9478) and **Rite Aid** at The Pines Shopping Center (703-471-7440).

Commute to Downtown 45 to 60 minutes via the Fairfax Connector to the West Falls Church-VT/UVA Metro station. An express bus runs during rush hour. Local bus routes are available at other times.

Post Offices Herndon Post Office at 590 Grove St. (703-437-3740)

Libraries Herndon Fortnightly Library at 768 Center St. (703-437-8855). The original Herndon library was formed by the Ladies Fortnightly Club, and today the library—open on a more regular schedule—retains the name as part of the area's local history. The library has meeting rooms available for community group activities and sponsors children's story times.

Police Stations 1481 Sterling Rd. (703-435-6846)

Recreational Activities The Washington & Old Dominion Railroad Regional Park (703-729-0596) has trails for running, bicycling, horseback riding and hiking.

Virginia Neighborhoods
Loudoun County and Prince William County

As suburban populations continue to expand, they stretch and grow across county lines. It's happened again. This time, Fairfax County is spilling over north and west to Loudoun County, and south and west to Prince William County. Once home to mostly farmlands and plantations, scenic Loudoun and Prince William Counties are becoming significant new hubs for business and residential development. Major corporations and businesses are sounding the charge to "Go West," away from the traffic and congestion of the city and surrounding suburbs. Both newcomers and locals alike are heeding the call and moving to the new, high-tech frontier developing in this historic setting of natural rustic beauty.

Loudoun County

Nestled in the foothills of the Blue Ridge Mountains, Loudoun is currently the third fastest growing county in the nation. Loudoun's traditions and history have blended with its high-tech future to produce an appealing community, with attractive business and living opportunities, valued by its residents.

With the completion of Dulles International Airport, the new Dulles Town Center and office parks, the most eastern section of the county has come into its own. Companies including America On Line, MCI WorldCom and UUNet Technologies have set up shop joining other high-tech companies along the Dulles corridor. Continued residential development is planned for extensive stretches of land near the airport and Dulles corridor. Several affordable apartment complexes are located here and residential hotels can be found to accommodate the ever-increasing number of business travelers.

Loudoun County's seven incorporated towns and six planned residential communities offer their residents country living with built-in convenience. Just off Route 7, the town of Sterling is home to several suburban communities. The Sterling Commuter Bus Service makes daily runs into DC, about 25 miles away. Sterling Park, built by US Steel Corporation, features 70 acres of land for recreational use.

Backing up to the 500-acre Algonkian Regional Park are two new planned communities, Cascades and neighboring Countryside. They are located on the north side of the Route 7 corridor with commuter service offered by the Sterling bus line. These communities are self-contained with schools; parks; offices and retail space; shopping plazas; and sports, recreational and leisure-time activities.

On the south side of the Route 7 corridor sit the two new adjoining planned communities of Ashburn Farms and Village/Broad Run. Enticing accoutrements of community living include a 32,000 square-foot Sports Pavilion in Ashburn Village along with miles of jogging paths, bike trails, baseball and soccer fields, lighted tennis courts, and a lake with a marina. For shopping, Countryside Towncenter is handily located to the east and the historic city of Leesburg is minutes away to the west. Many of Leesburg's residents commute the 35-mile trip into Washington, DC, using Route 7. Leesburg's Historic District has many beautifully restored 18th and 19th century buildings and homes in the Victorian style.

A considerable assortment of styles, ages and prices make up Loudoun County's real estate market. It's all here to choose from, including colonials, farmhouses, small carriage houses, older Victorian-style homes, condominiums and new single-family detached houses. Generally, Loudoun County's housing prices and real estate taxes are lower than those of closer-in suburbs. The county's easternmost section offers new master-planned communities with golf courses, walking paths and recreation centers.

Private bus service is available and Route 7 is the main highway that connects Loudon commuters eastward into Fairfax County. Several convenient shopping centers include Loudoun Valley Shopping Center, Tysons Corner, Fair Oaks and Dulles Town Center Mall.

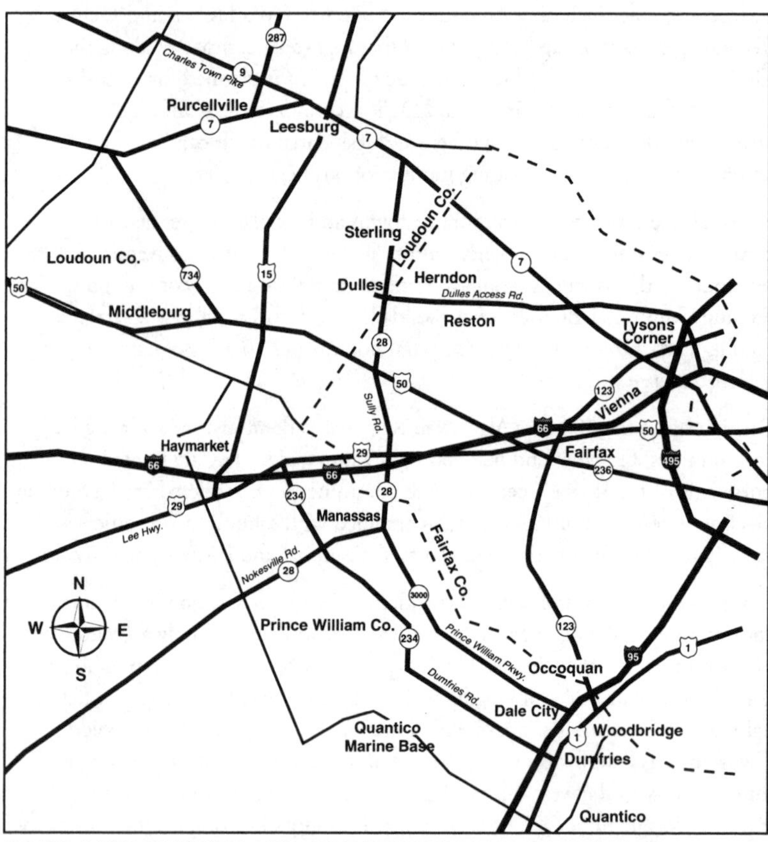

LOUDOUN COUNTY AND PRINCE WILLIAM COUNTY, VA
Dulles, Sterling, Leesburg, Manassas and Dale City

Almost 45 miles of the Washington and Old Dominion Railroad Regional Park are located here, offering hiking, biking, and bridle trails. Algonkian Regional Park, located along the Potomac River, features an 18-hole golf course and a swimming pool. Locals and tourists alike enjoy historical sites such as Morven Park, Waterford, and Oak Hill.

Prince William County

Stretching from the Potomac River to the Bull Run Mountains is naturally beautiful Prince William County. Named for King George II's youngest son, the country originated in 1731 and was the site of both the first and second Battles of Manassas. The battlefield is now a national park. Popular with tourists for years, even the locals enjoy spending mini-vacations in the county's Old Town Manassas. Successful community efforts have preserved the county's old plantations and farmlands. Once ranked the "fastest growing county in the nation" in the 1960s, its population had slowed, and then remained stable. However, America On Line is constructing an immense data facility in the county which has once again put it on the fast track for growth, with predictions that Prince William is the next "place to be" for technology companies.

Prince William County is home to the Quantico Marine Base and the FBI Academy. Many corporations are relocating here including IBM, which has a large facility in Manassas. A Land Use Plan is in effect that protects and preserves the area for both growth and recreation. Interstate Highways I-66 and I-95 serve the area, and a commuter rail system offers service both east and west.

Potomac Mills Mall, located at I-95 and the Dale City Interchange, provides a shopper's paradise with over 200 stores. Many other shopping districts are scattered throughout the county. With its high quality of life, employment opportunities, and a wide range of housing choices—from older homes to townhouses to new planned communities—Prince William County is an appealing place for the area newcomer.

MASTERING DC: INTERNATIONAL ARCHITECTURE

More than a city of government buildings and monuments, Washington is rich in hidden architectural treasures. If you want to see beyond the picture postcards, grab a map and visit places that will transport you around the world and across time.

☐ **Value the Jewel of Islam:** The **Islamic Mosque and Cultural Center** (2551 Massachusetts Ave. NW) is a captivating example of the architecture found in the **Muslim** culture. With a 160-foot minaret, this impressive building, on Embassy Row, is the religious and cultural center for the Washington area's Islamic community. With proper attire (covered legs, arms and, for women, heads) you are welcome to visit.

☐ **Consider Captivating Cairo:** Built in 1894, the **Cairo** (1615 Q St. NW) is a 12-story, steel-framed, **Romanesque**-style apartment, a style prevalent in Europe in the 9th-12th centuries. Look for the gargoyles that appear to keep this towering structure standing.

☐ **Experience a Place of Peace: Luther Place Memorial Church**, at Thomas Circle, features the medieval **Gothic-Revival** style common in Western Europe in the 12th-15th centuries. Built after the Civil War, it serves as a memorial to the end of slavery and the return of peace.

☐ **Wander Around the Wonder:** The breathtaking **Scottish Rite Temple** (1733 16th St. NW) is of **Art-Moderne** design, inspired by the architecture of the Mausoleum of Halicarnassus—one of the Seven Wonders of the World. Tour the elegant inner sanctum and the reference library containing eclectic collections dating to the 16th century.

☐ **Feast Your Eyes on Federalist Finds:** The **Tudor Place House Museum and Gardens** (1644 31st St. NW) is a preeminent example of **Federal-era** mansions in the United States. The **Lillian and Albert Small Jewish Museum** (703 3rd St. NW), is both home to the Jewish Historical Society of Greater Washington and the oldest standing synagogue in the city.

☐ **Admire the Asian Archway:** Ornamented in the art of the **Ming and Ch'ing dynasties**, the sparkling **Freedom Archway** is an enchanting entrance to Chinatown (H St. at 7th St. NW). The bejeweled arch was built jointly by the DC and Beijing governments in 1986 for $1 million.

☐ **Be Dazzled by Deco:** Washington is bedecked with **Art Deco** buildings, a style born of the 1925 Paris Exposition. Outstanding examples include the **Uptown Theatre** (3426 Connecticut Ave. NW), and the Aztec Art-Deco **Kennedy-Warren** apartments (3133 Connecticut Ave. NW).

☐ **Appreciate Beau Washington:** Washington became the nation's model for the City Beautiful (**Beaux-Arts**) movement inspired by the World's Colombian Exposition in 1893. The city is rich in this architectural style, easily identified by its magnificent public spaces. **The McCormick**—now the **National Trust for Historic Preservation** (1785 Massachusetts Ave. NW)—is still considered the finest apartment building ever constructed in Washington.

☐ **Expect a Miracle:** The **Franciscan Monastery** (1400 Quincy St. NE) is gloriously decorated in the **Byzantine** style with round arches, large domes and intricate spires. It is surrounded by gardens and replicas of religious shrines in the Holy Land and the grotto at Lourdes.

CHAPTER THREE

Getting Around

The best approach to mastering transportation in the Washington area is to take the time to learn the layout of the city and its major suburbs. With a good map and a few insider tips, getting around the area is relatively easy. Many Washingtonians will assure you that this is because the city's grid-like layout is simple to learn. While this is certainly true in theory, the picture becomes more complex once you take into account the many special features of DC's layout and the constantly evolving nature of the Maryland and Virginia suburbs.

This chapter provides a brief overview of the area and introduces the major streets, roads and circles in DC, as well as the major arteries in adjoining suburban Maryland and Northern Virginia. Modes of transportation for getting into, around and out of the area are also covered.

The metropolitan Washington area is comprised of the small, compact city of Washington, DC—only about 10 miles across—and the bordering counties in Maryland and Virginia. The boundaries with Maryland are designated by Western, Eastern and Southern Aves. The Potomac River serves as the boundary between DC and Virginia, with five bridges connecting the two. Each bridge is named in honor of a person or place important to local or national history, and most are best known by a somewhat unofficial name. Following the flow of the Potomac from the northwest to the southeast, the bridges are Chain Bridge, (Francis Scott) Key Bridge, (Theodore) Roosevelt (Memorial) Bridge, (Arlington) Memorial Bridge, and a complex of spans collectively known as the 14th St. Bridge.

The original boundaries for Washington, DC formed a 100-square-mile area often referred to as a diamond. The diamond encompassed all of what is now DC as well as what is now Arlington County and a small piece of the City of Alexandria in Virginia. While the federal government returned the Virginia property in 1846, many maps continue to show an outline of the original diamond shape.

DRIVING

Thousands of motorists drive into the city each weekday. Most of these people work in the city; some are visitors, others are tourists. Most know where they are going, or at least think they do; many do not. This results in congestion, confusion and chaos just about every day. The more you know about the area, the more successful you will be in handling the challenges.

AREA MAP WITH ORIGINAL DC BOUNDARY

Streets, Roads and Circles

Many of the streets and roads within DC continue out into the surrounding suburbs. Some change names along the way and are so designated in this section, where appropriate. In the metropolitan area, traffic circles are unique to DC; however, city planners are considering their potential use for handling increasing growth in certain suburbs.

DC

To understand Washington's streets, it helps to understand their history. In 1791, Major Pierre Charles L'Enfant, a French engineer-architect and former American Revolutionary soldier, was commissioned to draw up plans to build the nation's capital. L'Enfant patterned elements of his design after his native city, Paris,

France. Much still survives of his original concept which, once learned, can help orient you as you travel in and around DC.

The basic grid is the relatively orderly and logical part of the layout. The city is divided into four quadrants—Northwest (NW), Northeast (NE), Southeast (SE) and Southwest (SW), with the Capitol at the point where the quadrants meet. The boundaries for these quadrants are the streets radiating out from the Capitol—North Capitol, South Capitol and East Capitol Sts.—and the Mall, which is what would have been West Capitol St. The streets running parallel to North and South Capitol Sts. are numbered, with numbers going up as you go farther away from the Capitol, either to the east or to the west. This means that there are two 14th Sts.—one 14 blocks east of the Capitol building and one 14 blocks west of it.

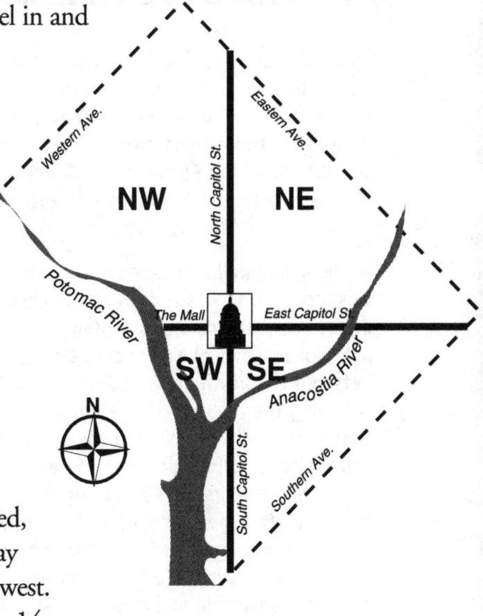

DC QUADRANTS

The streets running parallel to East Capitol St. and the Mall are arranged alphabetically, starting at the Capitol and moving out to the north and south. Close in, the alphabet is used for street names such as C St. and K St. As with numbered streets, there can be two streets with the same name, such as one C St. three blocks north of the Capitol and another three blocks south. In the Mall area, no streets are named A or B. The east-west streets closest to the Mall are named for Presidents Jefferson and Madison. One block farther out, you'll find Constitution and Independence Aves.

No matter how hard you look, you will not find J St. The official explanation is that "J" was eliminated from the plans to avoid confusion with I St., as the Roman letter "I" was once written in the same way. A more colorful explanation—popular in DC for its political undertones—is that L'Enfant disliked Chief Justice John Jay and deliberately left out J St. to slight him. You will find I St. commonly spelled "Eye" to avoid confusion with 1st St. (There goes the official J St. explanation!) Unfortunately, no official explanation exists for the absence of streets named X, Y and Z. One possibility is that W St. was the border of the original settled area and there was no need for the other letters.

WASHINGTON, DC: PART HISTORY, PART LEGEND

In 1790, Congress decided it needed a new home and gave President George Washington the authority to oversee the project. He chose a location at the confluence of the Potomac and Anacostia Rivers, a largely rural territory referred to by many as "Wilderness City."

Washington had his reasons for picking this location. It was midway in the chain of seaboard states and provided a political solution to early economic conflict between the North and the South, following the ravages of the War of Independence. It provided easy access for trade with its strategic location near rivers, bay and ocean. It was largely protected from potential opposing forces by the natural land barrier of the Eastern Shore. And, it was close to his beloved Virginia countryside and Mount Vernon estate.

The original plot of land was a square, 10 miles on each side, with corners pointing north, south, east and west. Washington hired Andrew Ellicott as the city's first surveyor; Ellicott brought with him Benjamin Banneker, a highly respected African-American mathematician and astronomer from Philadelphia.

In 1791-92, Ellicott and Banneker used handmade astronomical devices to survey the land, placing large stones, weighing several hundred pounds each, as mile markers along the boundaries of the original 100 square miles of the city. One of the remaining markers can be seen near the Friendship Heights metro station, on the west side of Wisconsin Ave. In the mid-1990s, the accuracy of the original survey work was verified using today's "modern" technology; the study proved that Ellicott and Banneker did more work in less time, with simpler tools and greater accuracy, than most surveyors today can imagine possible.

LEGEND: The City of Washington was built out of a swamp.

In fact, the land includes four geographical areas, none of which are swampland. There is a low river terrace to the southwest and southeast, a high rounded hill toward the east, irregular terraces rising toward the northwest, and the upper Tiber Valley along the northeast edge.

Close to 100 years after the city was established, engineers brought Hains Point out of the river, along with the land around where the Lincoln Memorial stands. This is perhaps one of the reasons why this legend exists. Another reason may be the way that Pierre L'Enfant, who would be called on to design the city, described his arrival as amidst "heavy rain, thick mist, mud and swamps."

LEGEND: Washington, DC, also called the District of Columbia, was made up out of land from Maryland and Virginia.

The two states did cede the land, including two existing port cities—Georgetown, MD and Alexandria, VA. But the commissioners overseeing the project had decided to call

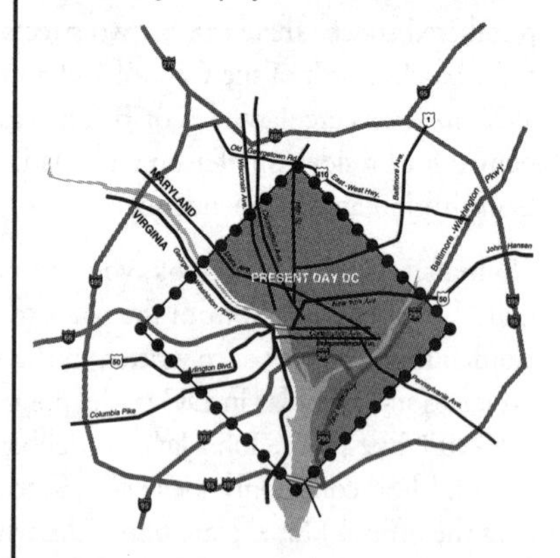

the Federal District "The Territory of Columbia" with the Federal City within its boundaries to be named "The City of Washington." Georgetown, Alexandria and Washington were to function as incorporated cities within the District.

Things didn't turn out exactly as planned. The land ceded by Virginia was returned in 1846. Some say it was because the federal government decided it would not need it. Other stories tell of near riots in the streets of Alexandria as residents fought to get their land back. It is also said that Georgetown tried to secede but Maryland did not want it back.

LEGEND: Washington, DC was designed by Pierre L'Enfant.

French engineer-architect Pierre Charles L'Enfant was hired by Washington to design the new federal city. L'Enfant was known to the leaders of the nation at the time, for he had redesigned Federal Hall in New York City when it was the seat of the federal government. And he had served under George Washington during the American Revolution. With this experience, he was no stranger to the ideals of the new nation: freedom, openness, space, and community.

L'Enfant's goal was to create a design at once practical and aesthetic, a symbolic representation of the entire country. The original plan, known as L'Enfant City, was based on a "federal triangle" made up of Congress House on Jenkins Hill (the Capitol Building on Capitol Hill), President's House (the White House), and a waterfront equestrian statue of George Washington (where the Washington Monument now stands). Grand Avenue (now the Mall) would connect the statue and Congress House. Broad avenues, named for the states, would radiate out from both Congress House and President's House. An organized grid of north/south and east/west streets would underlie the plan of circles, parks and radial avenues.

LEGEND: L'Enfant alone designed the entire city.

The general impression is that L'Enfant designed what today is Washington, DC. In fact, his plan included only the area south of today's Florida Ave. (then called Boundary St.) and east of Georgetown. L'Enfant's project was not spared the influences of controversy and local politics. It quickly became a tumultuous and explosive situation.

L'Enfant was a man of great vision, great enthusiasm, and great ego, which would prove to be his downfall. He came to be seen as stubborn, truculent, and obstinate, as well as unable to stay within a budget and unwilling to submit to the authority of the project's commissioners. Within a year, he was fired from the project. Some say that when he left, he took his plans with him.

Within six months, Jefferson hired Andrew Ellicott to produce engraved plans for the city, based on L'Enfant's design. One story says it was actually Benjamin Banneker who recreated L'Enfant's plans, entirely from memory. In any case, Washington and Jefferson promoted these plans, published without any recognition of L'Enfant, as official maps of the city. This led to the impression that Ellicott was the city's designer.

LEGEND: L'Enfant was the creative genius behind it all.

Any changes made by Ellicott and/or Banneker were not dramatic, and in 1901, a park commission was charged with rejuvenating L'Enfant's original plan. So perhaps there is a great deal of justice in the impression held today that we owe it all to him.

Unfortunately, L'Enfant met the fate of many famous artists and died in poverty. He is buried in Arlington National Cemetery, in a tomb bearing the words, "Engineer—Artist—Soldier." One of the most impressive views of the city is from his grave site, perhaps the ultimate tribute to the man who created so much and received so little for his efforts and his gifts.

-Sheila Donoghue

WHERE TO OBTAIN MAPS

ADC The Map People puts out a comprehensive series of maps and atlases for both DC and the surrounding counties. You can find them at bookstores, drugstores, convenience stores, supermarkets, fine newsstands and office products stores. Contact them at 800-ADC-MAPS, on-line at www.adcmap.com, or visit their downtown store listed below.

ADC Map & Travel Center
1636 Eye St. NW
202-628-1608

This Washington, DC landmark, formerly known as the Map Store, maintains a solid reputation and a loyal clientele. In addition to maps, they also stock travel guidebooks and globes.

Other sources for maps include:

Rand McNally Map & Travel Stores
Montgomery Mall, MD 301-365-6277
Tysons Corner, VA 703-556-8688

Thomas Bros. Maps
888-936-2732
www.thomas.com

Travel Books & Language Center
4437 Wisconsin Ave. NW, DC
202-237-1322

Maps On-Line
Door-to-door driving directions and customized maps are available on the Web. Capabilities vary, so do a little testing to determine which system best fits your needs. One popular site is:

MapQuest
www.mapquest.com

The alphabet system continues as you travel farther away from the Capitol, particularly into the Northwest and Northeast quadrants. Following the first alphabet of C-W Sts., a second alphabet carries two-syllable names and a third uses three syllables. In the most northern tip of DC, close to the Maryland border, a few streets are named for trees and flowers, again in alphabetical order. All addresses in DC include the designation of the quadrant where they are located. Addresses are logically numbered within the grid system in hundreds; for example, addresses on K St. between 17th and 18th Sts. form the 1700 block of K St.

Larger streets crossing the city at angles are called avenues and are named after states. The proximity of each avenue to the Capitol is based on when the state entered the Union, with New Jersey, Delaware and Pennsylvania Aves. intersecting the Capitol grounds, and Alaska and Hawaii Aves. practically in Maryland. Washington Ave. was missing for awhile, mostly to avoid confusion between the city on the East Coast and the state on the West Coast. But finally, in 1989, Washington State was honored by being given a small stretch of asphalt near the Capitol.

And now, for a few good complications. Freeways, parkways and roads meander through the District creating havoc out of the basic grid. Some streets are affected by traffic patterns that change twice a day to accommodate the dominant rush-hour traffic into and out of the city. (Refer to the section on Surviving Rush Hour for more specifics.) Street signs can be hard to read and even missing in places, and there isn't an honest local who won't admit to having turned the wrong way down one of DC's many one-way streets. Take these factors into account and you begin to see where confusion arises.

To complicate matters further, Washington is full of traffic circles, originally introduced as a way of compensating for the intersection of north-south and east-west streets with diagonal avenues while providing public space in the middle. With today's heavy traffic flows, circles can be difficult to negotiate. Often you have to be in a specific lane of the circle to exit onto a particular street. Unfortunately, these lanes are not always marked. Congestion is alleviated somewhat at several circles by routing the major road through a tunnel underneath the circle. In spite of the challenges of the traffic circles, the avenues are a good way to expedite getting across town. Mastering DC involves getting to know these major routes through, into and out of the city; a little experience and a lot of patience go a long way.

RED LIGHT RUNNING

Red-light cameras are installed at various intersections in DC, and in parts of suburban Maryland and Northern Virginia. Owners of cars caught on camera illegally running a red light will be sent a fine in the mail, and may be assessed points on their driving record. The amount of the fine and number of points vary by jurisdiction.

Massachusetts Ave. is the most convenient and potentially the most confusing street in Washington. It is the quickest way to go from Capitol Hill to Dupont Circle, on to Washington National Cathedral, and out to the west side of Bethesda in Maryland. However, it does not follow a straight line and the unwary driver can quickly get sidetracked around one of the several traffic circles it goes through. The route gets particularly tricky as it jogs around Mount Vernon Place at 7th, 9th and K Sts. NW. Watch carefully for signs and follow them—on faith. After a few side turns, you actually do end up back on track.

During evening rush hour, if you are going north to Bethesda, Chevy Chase or Rockville, the quickest route is Connecticut Ave. Coming from Georgetown, you can also use Wisconsin Ave. to go north to Chevy Chase and Bethesda. Running roughly parallel to 16th St., Georgia Ave. travels up through town and out to Silver Spring.

Stately Pennsylvania Ave. no longer follows a direct route across town, as it once did. Today, its path begins in Georgetown, jogs around the White House on its way to the Capitol, and continues east through the District and on into Prince George's County in Maryland. Security precautions in the vicinity of the White House have complicated traffic patterns further by blocking off portions of the avenue.

Finally, you should familiarize yourself with Rock Creek Parkway. The beautiful road winds through Northwest DC with only one light to slow the flow of traffic, making it an excellent north-south route. The major entrances are on K St. near the Kennedy Center, P St. in Georgetown and Massachusetts Ave. near Embassy Row. Along several portions of its route, Rock Creek Parkway has

SmarTraveler®

The Washington, DC metropolitan region is the nation's second most congested area, following on the heels of Los Angeles. The region also has the second longest commute time; area residents spend an average of 76 hours a year stuck in traffic. Over the next 25 years, traffic in the region is expected to increase by 70%, while currently planned projects will only increase highway capacity by 20%.

A public-private partnership of 39 agencies and businesses, called Partners in Motion, has brought a state-of-the-art traveler information network to the metropolitan Washington, DC area. Their first product, called the SmarTraveler® Information System or SmarTraveler®, provides on-demand, real-time and route-specific information on all modes of travel (i.e., highway, bus and rail). You can access up-to-the-minute information regarding highway and transit conditions, as well as construction, weather and special event information. This new system helps travelers make informed decisions on the most efficient means of reaching their destinations, attending local sporting and entertainment events, or plotting alternate routes and modes of travel for morning, daytime and evening commutes.

SmarTraveler® is free and there are three easy ways to access it:

Phone	202-863-1313
Mobile Phone	#211
Internet	www.smartraveler.com

Partners in Motion continues to introduce additional ways of obtaining traveler information. SmarTraveler® TV, which covers traffic, transit and weather, is now available through Jones Communications and Cox Cable in Virginia, with DC and Maryland likely to follow. Future possibilities include in-vehicle navigation devices, personal pagers, and kiosks at major sporting, shopping and employment areas.

no dividers to separate the two lanes of traffic traveling in opposite directions. This can be disconcerting, even dangerous; so can driving there at night, particularly on weekends. Parts of the parkway are restricted to pedestrian and bicycle traffic on weekends and holidays, creating new traffic patterns.

Maryland

In Montgomery County, there are four predominant north-south routes leading into and out of the District. On the western side of the county, Wisconsin Ave. (which becomes Rockville Pike north of Bethesda) is the major route. This road originates at the Potomac River in Georgetown and when you have time for a long, beautiful country drive, you can follow it all the way to the state of

Pennsylvania. In central Montgomery County, Connecticut Ave. and 16th St., which merge into Georgia Ave., are options for heading north. On the east side of the county, New Hampshire Ave. is a straight shot out of town. For rush-hour commuting, Connecticut and Georgia Aves. change from three lanes in each direction to four lanes in the direction of commuter traffic and two the other way.

All four of these routes intersect with the Beltway for moving east and west through the county. Just inside the Beltway, another intersecting thoroughfare is East-West Hwy. (Route 410). This road runs from Bethesda on the west to the Baltimore-Washington Parkway (officially named Gladys Spellman Parkway) in Prince George's County on the east, intersecting all the north-south avenues mentioned above.

Once you have made your way to the Beltway, several major highways provide access to the more suburban communities. To head northwest, Route 270 is the predominant route, reaching the communities of Rockville, Gaithersburg and Germantown. While traffic can be slow to merge onto 270 from the Beltway, this highway quickly expands to as many as seven lanes in each direction. In the northeast direction, toward Baltimore, you can take either I-95 or the Baltimore-Washington Parkway. These routes lead to the suburban communities of Greenbelt, Beltsville and Laurel.

The highway that leads directly east out of the District is Route 50. This takes you to Annapolis, the capital of Maryland, and farther east to the Maryland and Delaware shores on the Atlantic Ocean. To go south out of the District on the Maryland side of the Potomac, take I-295 then continue onto Indian Head Highway. These routes lead you through or near Suitland, Oxon Hill and Fort Washington.

Virginia

Traffic patterns in the Virginia suburbs closest to DC vary by location, due in part to the way the area developed over the years. Of particular interest are the streets and roads in Arlington and Alexandria.

Newcomers are lucky they do not have to master the pre-1934 Arlington street plan. Back then, residents had to find their way around a hodgepodge of streets, many with identical names. There once were, for example, 10 different streets named Arlington and 11 named Washington. Today, Arlington's streets and roads are still somewhat confusing but much easier to navigate. Arlington's main east-west thoroughfares are Lee Highway, I-66, Wilson Blvd., Arlington Blvd. (Route 50), Columbia Pike and I-395. Lee Highway runs roughly parallel to I-66 all the way out to Falls Church where the two cross. Lee Highway turns into Washington St. in Falls Church before it heads farther out into Virginia.

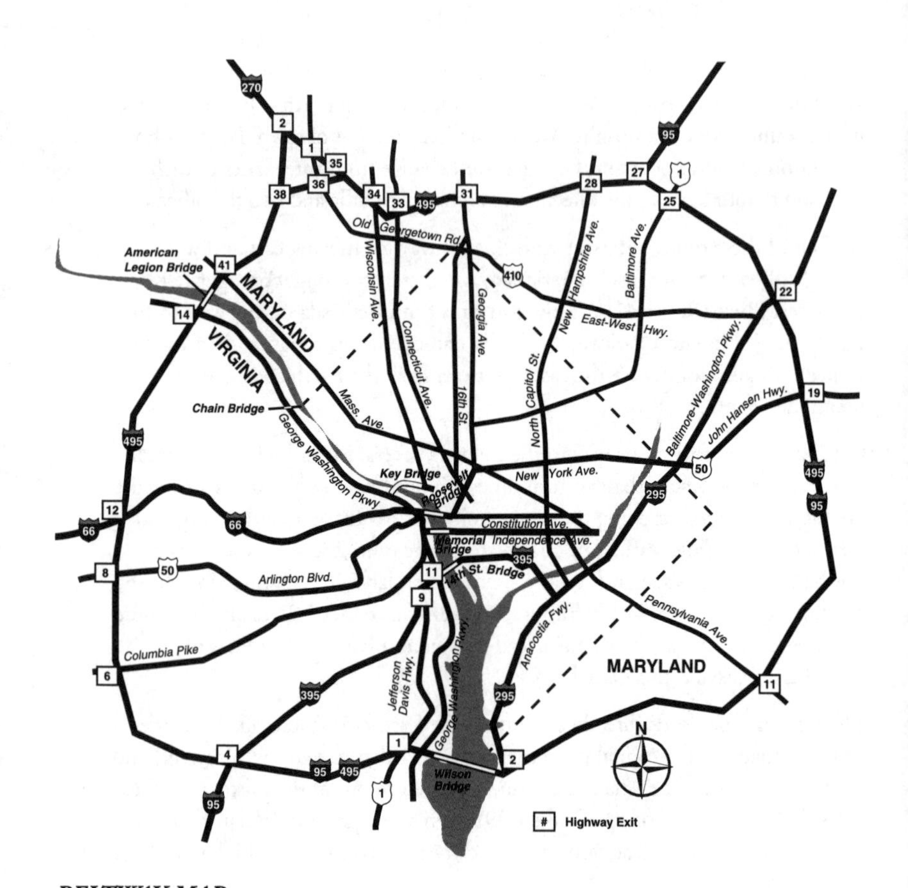

BELTWAY MAP

Wilson Blvd. begins in Rosslyn and travels west through North Arlington. Wilson becomes one-way (heading west) for about two miles through the Court House and Clarendon sections of Arlington. During this stretch, Clarendon Blvd. provides a parallel route going east.

In Arlington, named streets are ordered alphabetically and run north-south, beginning at the Potomac River and extending westward. Street names start with one-syllable names, Ball to Wayne Sts., and progress to two- and three-syllable names and one lonely four-syllable name (Arizona). Numbered streets and boulevards named after historic figures run parallel to Arlington Blvd. in an east-west direction.

One of the most complex interchanges in the area is on the Virginia side of the Arlington Memorial Bridge. In a seemingly random and confusing pattern, this interchange connects several major highways including the George Washington

Memorial Parkway and Routes 27 and 110 as well as major access lanes for Arlington Blvd. and I-395. To make matters worse, cars travel through the area at top speed. Keep a sharp eye out for the small signs to direct you and do not get too frustrated if you end up on the wrong road the first couple of times. This one takes a while to learn; practice during non-rush-hour times is strongly recommended.

Following the shores of the Potomac River, the scenic George Washington Memorial Parkway starts at Mount Vernon, south of DC, crosses the southern side of the Beltway, continues past Alexandria and Reagan National Airport, and ends up at the northwestern side of the Beltway at the Virginia-Maryland border. Glebe Rd. is the main thoroughfare in western Arlington. Jefferson Davis Highway (Route 1) splits off from I-395 at the Pentagon and carries traffic through Crystal City and on into Alexandria.

The major thoroughfare in Alexandria is Washington St. This street runs parallel to the Potomac River and is the "in-town" stretch of the George Washington Memorial Parkway, running north to the District and south to Mount Vernon. King and Duke Sts. are popular east-west routes. These are Old Town's main streets, forming a neat backbone for the grid pattern of the historic center of Alexandria.

FIXING THE MIXING BOWL

The Springfield Interchange, where I-95, I-395 and I-495 come together, is aptly referred to as the "Mixing Bowl," and is one of the most dangerous spots in the area. Numerous accidents occur because motorists are required to cross several lanes in a short distance when entering or exiting the highway. A massive rebuilding project is under way to improve the interchange and make it safer. The effort is anticipated to take at least eight years, during which time traffic delays could add significant time to daily commutes. All travel lanes are expected to remain open during rush hours; however, lane closures at other times can be expected. For daily updates, call the project's hotline at 703-383-VDOT, or log on to www.springfieldinterchange.com. You can visit the Information Center at Springfield Mall for personalized answers to your questions about the project.

Route 1 cuts through Alexandria and splits into two one-way streets in Old Town Alexandria: Patrick St. (Route 1 North) and Henry St. (Route 1 South). During morning rush hour, Patrick St.'s three lanes frequently become grid-locked.

The Beltway and Highways

Washington's most famous highway, the Beltway (I-495/I-95), takes 67 miles to circumnavigate the city and many of its suburbs. Rush-hour traffic reports often refer to the Beltway's "inner" and "outer" loops. The inner loop is the set of clockwise-traveling lanes circling the city; the outer loop carries traffic in the opposite direction, counterclockwise, outside the inner loop. All highways

RIDESHARING

Tap in to DC's carpool network by calling one of the numbers listed here.

DC
202-783-POOL

Maryland
301-593-9291

Montgomery County
301-770-POOL

Virginia
703-783-POOL

Fairfax County
703-324-1111

coming into the area either intersect with or end at the Beltway, which has interchanges approximately every two miles and provides access to all major roads leading to the downtown area. The major interstates connecting DC, Maryland and Virginia with the Beltway are I-270, I-95, I-66 and I-395. Inside the District, interstate and highway routes retain their route markings. Maryland and Virginia highway routes stop at the DC border, so be attentive to street names once inside the District line. Note that there is no direct freeway access to the downtown area from the north.

A bit of local history can help you master these highways. When first built, the entire Beltway was called I-495, all the way around the city. It was intersected by I-95, coming up from the south, terminating in the center of DC and picking back up on the north side of the Beltway. Many years later, to make I-95 a contiguous highway through the area, what had been the eastern half of I-495 was renamed I-95. The east side of the Beltway is marked with both route numbers. The portion of I-95 inside the Beltway took the name I-395. Exit numbers were rearranged along with route numbers, and the orderly logic of the Beltway, originally advertised as the area's first "circumferential highway" became little more than a fond memory among long-term residents. If this bit of bureaucratic history doesn't help you get around on these highways, perhaps it will at least keep you more amused than confused. Still, signage for the Beltway can be quite confusing. It is helpful to refer to a map in advance, so that you have an idea of where your destination lies (east, west, north or south).

Route I-270, one of Montgomery County's main highways, runs north off the Beltway a few miles from the American Legion Bridge (formerly Cabin John Bridge) at the border between Virginia and Maryland, providing direct access to Rockville and Germantown and to the City of Frederick, farther out.

Straight south of DC, the Woodrow Wilson Bridge carries I-95 over the Potomac River, connecting Prince George's County on the east with Alexandria on the west. One word sums up the problem with this route—drawbridge. To accommodate rush-hour traffic, the Coast Guard prohibits openings from 4:00 to 9:00 a.m. and from 2:00 to 7:00 p.m. The bridge opens on average once a day, causing lengthy traffic delays and occasional serious accidents. Most radio stations keep listeners apprised of scheduled drawbridge activity.

Often the first choice of Virginia commuters on the west side of DC, I-66 stretches 70 miles from Arlington to Front Royal. During morning rush hour, cars traveling eastbound between the Beltway and the District must have at least two people in them; the same is true in the opposite direction during evening rush hour. Shirley Highway (I-395) runs through Arlington County from the Potomac River to I-95, providing one of the most direct routes from the District to Crystal City and Alexandria. Three lanes travel in each direction, with a two-lane rush-hour road down the center that changes direction to accommodate the predominant traffic flow.

Virginia is home to the Washington area's two toll roads. The first, the Washington Dulles Access and Toll Road, runs between Exit 12 of the Beltway and Dulles International Airport. The other, the Dulles Greenway, is a privately owned, 14.5-mile toll road that runs between the airport and Leesburg, as an alternative to traffic-choked Routes 7 and 50. Commuters may want to consider using Smart Tag, an electronic toll collection system that lets you pre-pay tolls. As you travel through the tollgates, the amount of the toll is subtracted from your prepaid Smart Tag account via a device mounted on your windshield. Smart Tag-only lanes are open at selected plazas on both toll roads to eliminate congestion. To learn more about this service, call 877-SMARTAG or visit www.fastoll.com.

GUARANTEED RIDE HOME PROGRAM

Thanks to the Metropolitan Washington Council of Governments, DC, Maryland and Virginia have joined forces to offer the **Guaranteed Ride Home Program**, which assists commuters stranded by problems with public and group transportation. Commuters can count on a free taxicab ride (excluding the tip), a free Metro ride, or a rental car if they have to go home quickly because of illness or family emergency, or if they miss a van or car pool due to unscheduled overtime. To qualify for the program, commuters must take some form of alternative transit (bus, rail, ride share, walking or biking) at least twice a week. It also applies to people who take local bus services and those riding MARC and VRE trains. You must have used some form of transit on the day you request assistance.

The program runs from 6:00 a.m. to 10:00 p.m. weekdays, excluding holidays (and likely some inclement weather days as well). To obtain information on requirements for participation, or to register in the program, call 800-745-RIDE or visit www.mwcog.org.

Surviving Rush Hour

If you are from Los Angeles, Boston or New York, rush-hour traffic in the DC area will not only look familiar, it may be even worse. The entire Washington metropolitan area grew more quickly in the 1980s and 1990s than the road system could readily accommodate. And rush hour is no longer just about getting into and out of DC. As the suburbs have grown, rush-hour traffic within local areas has become more of a challenge. To compensate, some traffic rules

ROAD EMERGENCIES

Mobile Phone
DC Police; MD or VA State Police
#77

DC Police
202-727-1010

MD State Police
410-653-4200 or
410-486-3101

VA State Police
703-345-4500

change during rush hour on several of the more well-traveled streets. Rush hour is generally from 6:30 to 9:00 in the morning and from 4:00 to 6:30 in the evening. If you commute to, from or within the suburbs, you should become familiar with the High Occupancy Vehicle (HOV) lanes in effect on many of the interstates during the morning and evening rush hours. Where posted, you must have a minimum of two (HOV-2) or three (HOV-3) passengers in your vehicle. Take these restrictions seriously. The police do, and fines are steep.

In Northwest DC, from Woodley Park almost to the Maryland border, Connecticut Ave. switches from three lanes in each direction to four in the direction of commuter traffic and two the other way. A good portion of Rock Creek Parkway becomes one-way during each rush hour, as does Canal Road, running parallel to the Potomac River on the DC side. Once a day, 17th St. (in the morning) and 15th St. (in the evening) between Massachusetts Ave. and Eye St. become one-way. All the way from the Maryland border to Adams Morgan, 16th St. has altered traffic patterns. Georgia Ave. between 16th St. and Forest Glen has a middle lane that changes direction during each rush hour.

Like Connecticut Ave. in the District, Colesville Rd. and Georgia Ave. in Maryland change from three lanes in each direction to four lanes going in the prevailing direction of commuter traffic.

Maryland's first HOV lanes are in operation on I-270, one of the region's most congested highways. HOV-2 restrictions are in effect southbound from 6:00 to 9:00 a.m., and northbound from 3:30 to 6:30 p.m.

During morning rush hour, the three lanes of Patrick St. in Old Town Alexandria (Route 1 North) become grid-locked. One lane is set aside from 6:30 to 9:00 a.m. as an HOV-2 lane. In the afternoon, Henry St. (Route 1 South) supports homebound commuter traffic as an HOV-2 lane from 3:00 to 7:00 p.m. Southbound Route 1 provides access to I-95 South, while northbound Route 1 continues up through Crystal City and branches off to I-395 North.

In Arlington, Columbia Pike switches some of its four lanes to accommodate the flow of traffic. Three lanes carry traffic toward the District in the morning; in the afternoon, three lanes transport cars back out to the suburbs.

HOV restrictions for Interstates 66, 395 and 95, and the Dulles Toll Road vary depending on direction and time of day, as shown in the following table.

HOV Restrictions on Virginia Highways

Highway	Eastbound (a.m.)	Westbound (p.m.)	Restrictions
I-66, inside Beltway	6:30 to 9:00 a.m.	4:00 to 6:30 p.m.	HOV-2
I-66, outside Beltway	5:30 to 9:30 a.m.	3:00 to 7:00 p.m.	HOV-2
I-395	6:00 to 9:00 a.m.	3:30 to 6:00 p.m.	HOV-3
I-95	6:00 to 9:00 a.m.	3:30 to 6:00 p.m.	HOV-3
Dulles Toll Road	6:30 to 9:00 a.m.	4:00 to 6:30 p.m.	HOV-2

Washingtonians are pretty good about sharing their commuting time and expenses with others. **Commuter Connections** (800-745-RIDE) helps arrange car pools all over the metropolitan area. An informal car pool system, known succinctly as "slugging," has developed in the Virginia suburbs to take advantage of the HOV lanes on I-95 and I-395. For example, commuters head to the Springfield Plaza parking lot to meet up with drivers willing to take on passengers. At the end of the day, many of these same commuters can be found lined up in the slug line along 14th St. NW at the Mall, looking to help drivers meet the southbound HOV restrictions.

In fact, the art of slugging has become so popular that there's a website devoted to the subject: www.slugvirginia.com. Here you will find lots of useful information, including maps showing the location of slug assembly areas, particularly in Prince William and Fairfax counties. The book, *Slugging - The Commuting Alternative for Washington, DC*, by David E. LeBlanc, provides everything you need to know and everywhere you can go in the metro area to find fellow sluggers.

Slugging may be of particular importance to some in the near term when several major construction projects will impact traffic patterns through area Interstate highway interchanges.

FARECARD ADVICE

The maximum amount of change from any Farecard machine is $4.95 and it is returned only in quarters and nickels. Unless you intend to buy a large-value farecard, plan to carry smaller denomination bills and change. There are no bill changers in the subway stations and the attendants are not permitted to supply change.

Farecard machines can be quite finicky. Veteran riders know never to go to the machine closest to the entrance. It always gets the most use and its bill sensors suffer the greatest wear and tear. Luckily, the newer machines are increasingly less sensitive to ragged-edged bills.

Farecard machines may reject a card that is creased, dog-eared, scratched or demagnetized. Metro's plastic Farecard holders can help maintain your card in good condition. They are available at Metro Center, or by calling Metro at 202-637-1328.

Parking and Parking Tickets

Drivers face a dual challenge when it comes to parking in the city. Not only do you have to find a space, you have to make sure it is a legal one. Do not take this task lightly. You will quickly learn that the DC traffic enforcement officers spare neither speed nor ink in writing tickets for every possible infraction of the parking laws. They issue over two million expensive parking tickets each year. If you do find a bright-pink ticket prominently displayed on your windshield, it is best to respond as stated on the ticket. Diplomatic status does not exempt you, nor does having out-of-state license plates. If you disregard parking tickets, you may end up having your car booted. If this happens, call the **DC Booted Vehicle Office** at 202-727-5000. In addition, **Dorsey & Associates Inc.** (202-434-8189; www.parkingviolations.com) helps individuals and businesses handle parking tickets and moving violations in the District. Their fee is $20 per ticket, $50 per moving violation, and $75 if an accident is involved. The amount you save usually exceeds the fee.

The trick here is to recognize that DC has overlapping parking controls and you have to be on the lookout for all of them. On some blocks, parking is free but limited to two hours, unless you are a DC resident and have a current Residential Parking Permit for the particular neighborhood or zone. In other, more commercial blocks, there is metered parking, with most meters accepting only quarters. If you are going to be in one of these neighborhoods for an entire weekday, consider taking the Metro. Or leave your car in an all-day parking garage for around $12 a day. Street parking downtown is illegal in many places during rush hour, no matter how many quarters or parking permits you have. A final layer of parking restrictions allows for street cleaning of various blocks on a rotating schedule.

Downtown, Dupont Circle, Georgetown, Adams Morgan, Southwest and Capitol Hill are some of the District's most difficult areas for parking. The trend to more and more parking restrictions—and ticketing—is spreading out into the suburbs as the whole area becomes more densely populated. For example, parking in Old Town Alexandria, VA and Bethesda, MD can at times be as difficult as it is in DC.

Public Transportation

Metropolitan DC area residents have numerous public transportation options. The Metro system, run by the Washington Metropolitan Area Transit Authority (WMATA), connects neighboring communities with the DC business district. Commuter lines bring people in from suburbs farther out. And taxicab service is available throughout the area.

Metrorail and Metrobus

Washingtonians use the term "Metro" to describe both the overall regional transportation system and the rail service that is part of it. Metro—the system—links DC and the Maryland and Virginia suburbs by rapid rail and bus routes. Metrobuses provide feeder service to the Metrorail stations and offer routes and connections in areas where there is no subway (rail) service. While a few of the rail stations open today are above ground, the first ones to open were all underground, and the rail system is still sometimes referred to as "the subway."

Each system—bus and rail—has its own operating hours, schedules and fares. These change from time to time and you can keep abreast with information provided at the rail station kiosks. If you don't see the information you need prominently displayed outside the kiosk, ask the attendants. They keep selected brochures and guides on hand. You can reach Metro by phone at 202-637-7000 or on the Web at www.wmata.com. You can view timetables on screen and print them, along with the subway map, fares, and other station information.

Metro has a host of fare options for each of its systems. There are large-denomination farecards with discounts, various types of passes for the Metrobus,

CONTACT METRO

Metrorail/Metrobus Information
Monday-Friday
6:00 a.m. - 10:30 p.m.
Saturday-Sunday
8:00 a.m. - 10:30 p.m.
202-637-7000
202-638-3780 TDD

Bus or Rail Timetables
via 24-Hour Return Fax
202-962-1420

Events Hotline (Recording)
202-783-1070

Consumer Assistance
Weekdays, 8:30 a.m.– 4:00 p.m.
202-637-1328
202-638-3780 TDD

On-Call Metrobus Service
202-962-1825

Metro ID Cards for Riders with Disabilities
202-962-1245
202-628-8973 TDD

MetroAccess
301-588-8184
301-588-8186 TDD

Lost and Found
202-962-1195

Bicycle Lockers
202-962-1116

Metro Transit Police (Emergencies)
202-962-2121

SAVING MONEY ON METRO

$5 One-Day Pass
Metro's $5 One-Day Pass allows you to ride Metrorail as frequently as you want after 9:30 a.m. on weekdays, weekends or federal holidays. The one-day period begins when the card is passed through the faregate and ends at midnight the same day. You can purchase these passes in advance and keep them handy for future use. One-Day Passes are available at the Passes/Farecards machines in many stations, at the various Metro Sales offices and transit commuter centers, and at participating grocery stores. Call 202-637-7000 to find the sales location nearest to you.

Kids Ride Free
Up to two young children, under five years of age, can ride free when accompanied by a paying adult.

Reduced Fares
Reduced fares are available for Medicare card holders, qualifying senior citizens and riders with disabilities who have Metro ID cards.

special fares for senior citizens and riders with disabilities, and a special workplace transit benefit program called Metrochek, and the permanent rechargeable SmarTrip card. Information on these and other options is available from Metro.

Metrorail

At the heart of Washington's public transportation system, Metrorail (Metro) serves as a model for subway systems in other cities. It is safe, clean, convenient and efficient. There are five Metrorail lines, each marked with its own color. (See the map on the inside back cover.) The Red Line starts in the Shady Grove/Rockville area to the northwest, travels south through Bethesda, loops down through Northwest and Downtown DC, then turns north up to Silver Spring and ends at Glenmont. The Blue Line runs from Franconia-Springfield through DC and out to Addison Rd. in Prince George's County. The Orange Line parallels the Blue Line through the District with end points in Vienna, VA and New Carrollton, MD. The Yellow Line travels northbound from Alexandria through Chinatown to Mt. Vernon Square and the University of the District of Columbia's downtown campus. The Green Line currently reaches from Anacostia to Greenbelt. The final five Green Line stations—Congress Heights in DC, and Southern Avenue, Naylor Road, Suitland and Branch Avenue in Prince Georges County, MD—are scheduled to open in 2001.

There are several central transfer points where you can switch lines. The Red, Blue and Orange Lines all converge at Metro Center, the system's busiest station. The Blue, Orange, Green and Yellow Lines meet at another busy station, L'Enfant Plaza. The Red, Green and Yellow lines meet at Gallery Place/Chinatown. Between the Rosslyn and Stadium-Armory stations, the Blue and Orange Lines run on the same track and transfers can be made at any of the shared stations.

Street entrances to the subway stations are easily identified by the brown pylons capped with the letter M. The horizontal stripes near the top show the color of the lines serving that station. Inside every station, there are large system-wide rail route maps as well as detailed neighborhood street maps; tall posts on the platform level list the stations on the routes followed by the arriving trains. The key to successful travel on this system is to know the color and endpoint of the particular line you need, as each line has trains running in opposite directions. Watch out for the Red Line trains—they do not all go to the last station on the map. Before you board any train, check the display above the train's front and side windows.

Many of the Metro stations are equipped with elevators, making access possible for the disabled and those with baby strollers.

Metro starts operating at 5:30 a.m. on weekdays, and 8:00 a.m. on Saturdays and Sundays. Although midnight is the official closing time during the week, an eight-month pilot program—begun November 1, 1999—extends Metro's closing time to 1:00 a.m. on both Friday and Saturday nights. An insider's word of advice: be sure to check the time that the last train will be leaving a station, as final departure times do vary.

On weekends and holidays, the trains and buses run less frequently. For travel on these days, be sure to consult a schedule, especially if you plan to transfer from Metrorail to Metrobus, which also runs less frequently.

M

Unless you plan carefully, rarely will you use up the value of a farecard exactly. If you find yourself with a drawer full of low-value cards, here are a few options.

Insert your old card into the **Used Farecard Trade-in** slot in one of the Farecard machines at the station entrance (not the Exitfare machines at the exit). Insert the amount you wish to add and press the **Push for Farecard** button. You receive a replacement farecard in the new amount.

To cash in several farecards at once, obtain an envelope at a station kiosk and mail the farecards into Metro headquarters to receive a replacement card.

You can also donate low-value farecards or employer-provided Metrochek cards to help homeless veterans get to and from interviews and the job site until they receive their first paycheck. Metro consolidates the low-value cards into ones of $20 or more and the Veterans Administration distributes them. For further information, call the Veterans Administration Medical Center at 202-745-8313.

The DC Metro is included in an interactive database of subway systems in cities around the world. You can find it at www.metropla.net on the Internet.

Fares and Farecards Fares are based on the time of day (peak or off-peak hours) and distance traveled. Currently, one-way fares during peak weekday hours (5:30 to 9:30 a.m. and 3:00 to 7:00 p.m.) range from $1.10 to $3.25, compared with non-peak fares of $1.10 to $2.10.

Farecards, the admission tickets in and out of the Metro system, are sold through machines at the stations. You can buy a farecard for the exact amount to get to your destination by first checking the posted fares. Or, buy a higher-value farecard good for several trips.

Metro offers two kinds of vending machines in all its station locations. Standard machines, marked Farecards, sell single cards and accept cash only. The second type, marked Passes/Farecards, sells single or multiple farecards and passes; you can also add value to SmarTrip cards. These machines accept cash and credit cards. A talking feature can be activated by pushing the Audio button.

Procedures for Farecard machines:

- Insert bills or coins into the appropriate slot—the amount you deposit appears in the lighted display above the words Select Farecard Value.
- To adjust the value of the farecard, use the "-" and "+" buttons.
- Once you have the display set to the fare you need, press the Push for Farecard button to receive the farecard and any change.

Procedures for Passes/Farecard machines:

- Follow the prompts, and use the A, B and C buttons located on the left of the screen.
- Select A to buy passes, Select B for a single farecard, or C for multiple farecards.
- Make your selections for value and insert money and/or farecard.
- To pay by credit card, press B, insert and quickly remove your credit card.
- To receive a receipt, press B when prompted; to decline, press C.
- Remove your farecard or passes and any receipt and change.

To add value to a SmarTrip card:

- Touch your SmarTrip card to the circular target and follow the prompts.
- Insert money, a used farecard or Metrochek worth less than $7, or an unused Metrochek or farecard of any value. Each one requires a separate transaction.
- Follow the prompts for value and payment selection (for credit card purchases, the default amount is $20).
- When finished, touch the SmarTrip card to the circular target a final time. This updates the card and shows the new balance including bonus (if applicable).
- Remove the receipt from the tray if you requested one.

- When using SmarTrip cards, pass through the faregates with the appropriate target affixed.
- Simply touch your card to the target and the fare will be deducted from your card.

To enter the train platforms, insert your farecard into the pass-through gate with the green light and white arrow. The machine records time and location information on the magnetic strip and returns the card to you as the gate opens to let you through. Be sure to take the card with you; you will need it to exit the system. When you reach your destination, follow the same procedure. As you pass through the exit gate, the machine automatically deducts the cost of the trip and prints the remaining value, if any, on your card. When the card value reaches zero, the machine keeps the card.

If you have insufficient fare to exit the system at your destination, you will need to use the Exitfare machine near the exit gate. Insert your card as instructed on the machine and deposit the amount of change indicated in the display. If you do not realize ahead of time that your farecard is "short," it will be rejected as you try to pass through the exit gate. This happens even to the most veteran rider, and during rush-hour congestion, getting back to the Exitfare machine can remind you of salmon swimming upstream.

Special Features and Transfers Many Metro stations, especially those in the suburbs, have a Kiss & Ride area for dropping off and picking up passengers. Another special feature at many of the suburban stations is Park & Ride. Fees and restrictions vary by lot, although parking in all of the Metro-operated lots is free on weekends and federal holidays. In many of them, weekday parking is free, if you leave the lot before 3:00 p.m. Some lots adjacent to Metro stations are privately owned and do not offer free parking, so be sure to check the rate schedule.

Free bus transfers, available at Metrorail stations, get you a discounted rate on Metrobus travel in DC and Virginia. You still pay some for the bus ride, but less than the normal fare because you started your trip on Metrorail. Bus transfers are available from machines usually placed next to the escalators or stairs leading to the train platforms. You must get your transfer at the station where you entered the system for your transfer to be valid. There are no transfers from Metrobuses to Metrorail and in Maryland, rail transfers are not valid toward bus fares.

Metrobus

The Metrobus system complements Metrorail, extending into the far reaches of the area's neighborhoods with almost 400 routes and some 13,000 bus stops. The buses also link parts of the city and suburbs not served by the rail system.

The flat rate fare is $1.10 and buses accept only exact change. There are no peak and off-peak fares, transfer charges, or zone or state crossing charges. The exception is a $2 charge on express routes connecting points outside the Beltway with Downtown DC or the Pentagon. Bus-to-bus transfers are free. They are valid for up to two hours, and there are no limits on route, stop or direction. The standard rail-to-bus transfer charge is $.25, and $1.15 on express routes.

The weekly Bus/Rail Fast Pass (good from Sunday to Saturday) allows you to pay a single fee for unlimited rides on all Metrobus routes and Metrorail. Depending on the type of pass you buy, you also get a predetermined amount of Metrorail value. Weekday commuters make only a small amount of money on the deal, benefiting more from the convenience offered. But for those who also use the bus for other reasons, Fast Pass savings really pile up. Fast Passes can be purchased from the Metro kiosk at the Metro Center Sales Office and at participating Giant, Safeway and Super Fresh stores.

The Metro system has some wheelchair accessible buses. For such a bus or to check on availability at a particular station, call 202-296-1825 or 202-628-8973 TDD for On-Call Metrobus Service, or 202-296-1245 for Metro ID Cards for Riders with Disabilities.

After 9:00 p.m., riders may request that the Metrobus driver let them off the bus at any safe location along the route that is more convenient to their destination than the bus stop. This service, called **Request-A-Stop**, is available on all Prince George's County and Montgomery County Metrobuses, including Ride-On, and on selected routes in the District and Virginia.

MetroAccess

MetroAccess provides curb-to-curb service for persons with disabilities who cannot use regular public transportation and have been certified eligible to use paratransit service. It is sponsored by WMATA, local governments and local fixed-route transportation operators. The many sponsors include Montgomery County Ride-On, Prince George's County The Bus, Laurel Connect-A-Ride, Fairfax County Connector, Reston Internal Bus System, Tysons Shuttle, City of Fairfax CUE, City of Alexandria DASH and Arlington County Trolley. People eligible to use MetroAccess are those who (a) are unable, as a result of physical or mental impairments, to get on, ride or get off any vehicle on the transit system; (b) need the assistance of a wheelchair lift or other boarding device to get on, ride or get off an accessible vehicle but find that such a vehicle is not available on the route when they want to travel; or (c) have specific impairment-related conditions which prevent travel to or from a bus stop or rail station. If you or someone you know may qualify for this service, contact MetroAccess at 301-588-8184 or 301-588-8186 TDD.

Commuter Lines

To ease the commute from the farthest suburbs, the states of Maryland and Virginia, as well as some local jurisdictions, sponsor special commuter bus and train lines to and from the District.

The **Maryland Rail Commuter System (MARC)** (800-325-7245; www.mtamaryland.com/marc) shuttles nearly 20,000 passengers daily along the three Amtrak lines from as far to the northeast as Baltimore and as far to the west as Harper's Ferry and Martinsburg in West Virginia. The MARC lines intersect with Metrorail stations at various points and all lines terminate at Union Station, which is also the District's Metro and Amtrak station near Capitol Hill. MARC tickets may be purchased on a daily, weekly or monthly basis.

Montgomery County's **Ride-On** (240-777-7433 or 240-777-2222 TDD) is an extensive bus service, making connections throughout the county at MARC, Metrorail and Metrobus stops. The fare for the Ride-On service is $1.10 for rush hour and $0.90 at other times. Be sure to check out the transfer options as a MARC train ticket provides you with free Ride-On service, and transfers may be used between Metrobus and Ride-On. Log on to the Montgomery County Department of Public Works and Transportation Website at www.dpwt.com for a full range of in-transit services, routes and schedules.

The Bus (800-486-9797), in Prince George's County, connects Upper Marlboro County with the Addison Rd. and New Carrollton Metro stations. It runs from 6:00 a.m. until 7:15 p.m. Fares are $0.75 all day, $0.35 for disabled individuals. Transfers to the Metrorail and Ride-On connector service are available for $2.50 during rush hour and $1.50 during non-rush-hour periods.

In Virginia, several options for commuter travel are available as well. **The Virginia Railway Express (VRE)** (703-684-1001; www.vre.org) uses the Amtrak lines to ferry passengers from Manassas on the west and Fredericksburg to the south. These lines also intersect the Metrorail system, providing optional routes for getting to and from work. Both 10-trip and monthly tickets may be purchased at reduced prices. Or purchase a Transit Link Card, good for unlimited travel on MARC, VRE and Metrorail for a full month.

For bus lines, the **Fairfax Connector** (703-339-7200) operates in the regions between Springfield Plaza and Mt. Vernon, dropping passengers off at the Huntington, Pentagon and Dunn Loring Metro stations. It also connects Reston with the West Falls Church Metro during rush hour; non-rush-hour service is provided by the **Reston Internal Bus System (RIBS)**. The **Tysons Shuttle** connects the West Falls Church area with Metro during rush-hour periods only. Alexandria's **DASH** (703-370-DASH) connects passengers with Metrobus,

DC

Capitol Cab	202-546-2400
Clean Air Cab	202-667-7000
Diamond Cab	202-387-6200
Yellow Cab	202-544-1212

Maryland

Tri-County Cab	301-248-2073

Montgomery County

Barwood Cab	301-984-1900
Checker Cab	301-816-0066
Yellow Cab	301-984-1900

Prince George's County

Checker Cab	301-270-6000
Yellow Cab	301-864-7700

Virginia

Red Top Cab	703-522-3333

Yellow Cab

Alexandria	703-549-2500
Arlington	703-522-2222
Fairfax	703-941-4000

To/From Dulles Airport

Washington Flyer	703-528-4440
	www.flyertaxi.com

Metrorail and the Fairfax Connector. The **Fairfax CUE** (703-385-7859) connects most of the city proper to the Vienna Metro station on a daily basis. The fare is $0.50; for seniors and students it is $0.25.

For commuters traveling between Montgomery County and Tysons Corner, there is Metro's **SmartMover**, Montgomery-Tysons Beltway Express. WMATA uses HOV lanes and Beltway shoulders during both a.m. and p.m. rush hours. The fare is $1.10 each way; all Metrobus, MARC and VRE passes are accepted. Complete information may be obtained by calling 202-962-2575, 202-638-3780 TDD; or on-line at www.wmata.com.

Taxicabs in DC and the Suburbs

For the past 60-some years, DC taxicabs have run on a rather complicated zone system originally designed to keep legislators' fares cheap. In the 1930s, the DC Public Utilities Commission wanted to replace the traditional ad-hoc method of setting cab fares. The plan was to initiate a metered system, but the federal government had another idea. Cleverly designed by Congress, the new zone system was based on concentric circles radiating out from the Capitol. Any time you travel to or from the Capitol area, a taxi ride seems like a true bargain and you see for yourself the original motivation for the zone system.

According to the *Washington Post*, from 1933 to 1986, each DC appropriations bill included language requiring the continuance of the congressionally designed zone system. Originally scheduled to be implemented in 1998, the conversion of DC cabs to a metered system is still being discussed.

In the meantime, the zone system continues to be one of the challenges of getting around town. The District is divided into five zones, each with as many as eight subzones. The price of your ride is determined by the number of zones and subzones you cross on the way to your destination. A one-dollar surcharge is added to all trips originating in the District during the morning (7:00 to 9:30 a.m.) and evening (4:00 to 6:30 p.m.) rush hours. Get to know the zone map (usually displayed behind the driver's seat) and the correct rates for trips you take on a regular basis. As you become familiar with the city's geography and the zone map, you will find that sometimes a two- or three-block walk can shave $1.50 off your fare. The lowest in-town rate is $4.00. Because the rates are fixed in the zone system, you can ask the driver what the total fare will be before getting in the cab. If the amount doesn't sound right to you, the problem just might be with the driver and not the system.

DC cab drivers are allowed to pick up additional passengers en route to your destination and to charge them full fare. They are also allowed to double their fares during a declared snow emergency. If DC-licensed cabs are taking you out of the District, they determine fares by using their odometers—currently $2 for the first mile and $0.60 for each additional half-mile. It is a good idea to ask first what the fare is likely to be.

Individuals interested in supporting environmentally friendly ventures will be pleased to know about a local cab company whose vehicles run only on natural gas. As an added attraction, they accept credit cards. **Clean Air Cab Company** provides service throughout the metro area. Call 202-667-7000 to reach their 24-hour dispatch service.

Cab companies in the suburbs are metered. Under a reciprocity agreement with the District, suburban cab drivers are allowed to pick up fares in the District after discharging passengers or as part of pre-arranged trips, as long as those cabs are also licensed in the District.

Other Modes of Local Transportation

Washington is not just for people with cars, farecards, and bus and cab fare. In fact, you'll find increasing numbers of local residents who get around on either two wheels or two feet. Some of them won't have it any other way—for work and for play.

Bicycling

Some 480 miles of marked bike routes and 670 miles of paved, off-road bike paths make the Washington area a cyclist's dream. Statistics confirm that biking to and from work in our area continues to grow in popularity, especially as more downtown office buildings are outfitted with showers, changing rooms, and bike racks or indoor bike storage rooms. Rock Creek Parkway gives cyclists a quick route from the Connecticut Ave. neighborhoods to Downtown. To get across the Potomac River from Virginia, both Key Bridge and the 14th St. Bridge have wide sidewalks that also make for great bike paths.

The paths along the Chesapeake & Ohio Canal provide an excellent car-free route in from Maryland towns. Remnants of the flooding caused by the blizzard of 1996 are still evident along the canal and towpath, although much of the repair work has been done. The effects of Mother Nature and public use cause constant erosion, resulting in an ongoing need for volunteers to assist with indoor and outdoor projects. Volunteer work sessions meet in the spring and fall (March, April, and May, and September, October and November). Dedicated bikers, hikers and other nature lovers can get involved by contacting the General Volunteer Coordinator (301-714-2233). The independent Rebuild the Towpath Foundation (202-785-4500) continues actively to raise funds to support the effort.

During rush hour, you should avoid the major avenues in town, particularly North Capitol St. and Massachusetts, Pennsylvania, Connecticut and Wisconsin Aves. Commuters often exceed the speed limit and bikers can easily find themselves in gutters—or worse. Beach Drive, a main part of Rock Creek Parkway, should also be avoided during commuter hours. On weekends and holidays, however, certain sections of Beach Drive are reserved for biking, hiking and in-line roller-skating, making it one of the most popular weekend spots for active Washingtonians.

The Metropolitan Branch Trail, serving both commuters and recreational riders, runs eight miles from Union Station to Silver Spring. It will eventually connect with the popular Capital Crescent Trail (which runs from Georgetown to Silver Spring) and bike paths along the Mall to form a 25-mile "Bicycle Beltway within the Beltway."

Bicycles are permitted on Metrorail weekdays between 10:00 a.m. and 2:00 p.m. and after 7:00 p.m., and on weekends and holidays, with the exception of the Fourth of July. Bikes are to be boarded on the last car of the train and are limited to two per train on weekdays and four on weekends and most holidays. Bicycle lockers are available at many Metro stations for 6- or 12-month rental periods. Bicycles are not permitted on Metrobuses.

Montgomery County Ride-On buses are equipped with bike racks on their front bumpers. Each rack accommodates two bicycles. Riders load and unload their own equipment, but do not have to have permits or pay any extra fees.

Walking

The local lifestyle in many parts of DC and in some suburban neighborhoods does not necessarily depend on access to car, train, bus or subway. If you live in one of the more central parts of the District or just across the Potomac River in Rosslyn, Crystal City or Pentagon City—and you love to walk—you can get to many interesting and important locations on your own steam. In these areas, getting to work, shopping, running errands, and meeting up with friends and colleagues can all be done on foot. With a scarcity of affordable parking, the benefits of having a car in many DC neighborhoods can often be outweighed by the cost and aggravation. Many Washingtonians can afford to live where they do because they have no car payments, insurance costs, or parking and gas expenses. And the flexibility of walking can't be beat. Farther out in Virginia and suburban Maryland, getting around without a car becomes increasingly difficult, even if you live close to a Metro station or bus line. This is one of the many trade-offs offered by the wide variety of approaches to living in and mastering DC.

Inter-City Transportation

Washington and its suburbs constitute a major hub of activity on the East Coast and a major location with regard to the entire nation—if not the world. Accordingly, the area is not lacking in effective means for inter-city transportation. Metropolitan Washington boasts three major airports as well as Amtrak train and Greyhound and Peter Pan Trailways bus service.

Airports

The three major airports serving the metropolitan DC area are Ronald Reagan Washington National Airport on the banks of the Potomac River in Arlington, Washington Dulles International Airport in the far-western suburbs of Virginia, and Baltimore-Washington International Airport in Maryland. Massive renovations and expansions at both Reagan National and Dulles and the addition of a new international terminal at Baltimore-Washington were all completed in 1997.

Reagan National

Reagan National Airport, in common parlance, Reagan National, is a blessing for residents of the District and northern Virginia. Opened for business in 1941, Reagan National serves as a "short-haul" airport. It offers non-stop service only to destinations within 1,250 miles of Washington. For destinations farther away, travelers must book connecting flights or use one of the other two major airports.

July 1997 marked the opening of Reagan National's new terminal, following a decade-long renovation. The quarter-mile-long glass and steel structure welcomes travelers with a 65-foot domed ceiling, a panoramic view of the Mall monuments and the Capitol with the Potomac River in the foreground, and original art adorning both the walls and floors. Airport visitors have a choice of two dozen restaurants and can shop in numerous stores scattered throughout the airport. Next on the construction schedule is the renovation of Terminal A, the original structure from the 1940s.

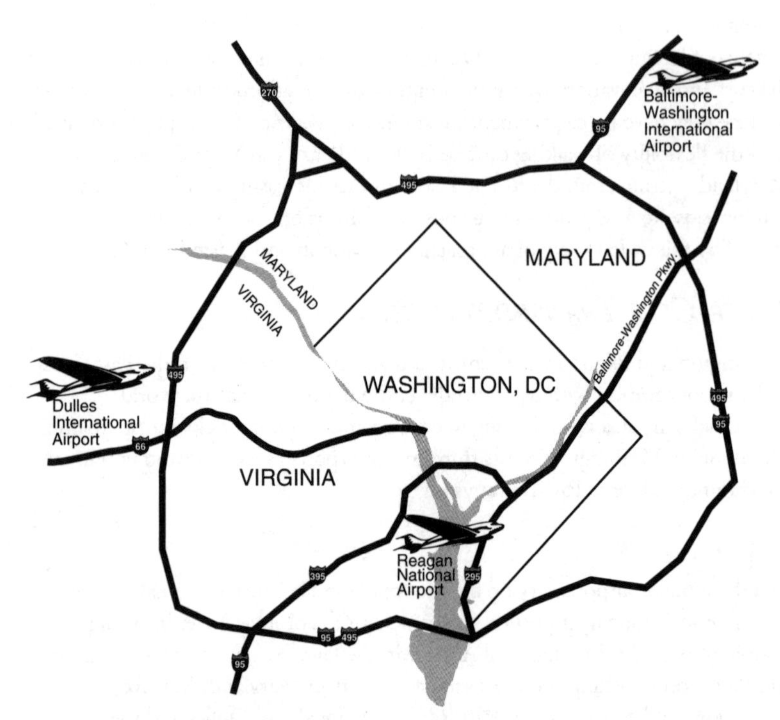

WASHINGTON AREA AIRPORTS

Reagan National can be as close as a 15-minute drive from most locations in the District, Arlington and Alexandria, under the very best of traffic conditions. As the only predictable thing about area traffic is its unpredictability, you should test the trip ahead of time so you are well prepared, know where you are going, and have an alternate route in mind.

Metro's Yellow and Blue Lines go to Reagan National. Two covered bridges connect the Metro station to Terminals B and C, and a shuttle bus connects to Terminal A. Cabs from Downtown DC cost $9 to $12. The Washington Flyer (800-WASHFLY) offers shuttle bus service from the airport. The $8 shuttle bus originates at New York Ave. and 11th St. NW and makes stops at many of the big downtown hotels. To drive from DC, the quickest route is to take 14th St. (south) over the 14th St. Bridge and follow the Airport signs. From McLean, Arlington or Alexandria, the George Washington Memorial Parkway is the best option. Travelers from Montgomery County can either cut through DC and take 14th St. or take the Beltway to the George Washington Memorial Parkway. The main number for Reagan National Airport is 703-685-8000; the website is www.metwashairports.com/national.

Dulles

For cross-country and international flights there is Washington Dulles International Airport in northern Virginia. Dulles was all the rage when it opened in the mid-1960s, with its Eero Saarinen design. Much larger than Reagan National and much farther from DC (26 miles from Downtown), Dulles offers non-stop flights to a long list of domestic and foreign destinations.

A major expansion project, completed in 1997, doubled the size of the Main Terminal, adding an award-winning observation deck and the lovely, new Chesapeake Garden. The new Concourse B is the first of three planned midfield buildings. Mobile lounges, known as People Movers, continue to shuttle passengers to the original Midfield Concourse and now to Concourse B. Passengers departing from these two concourses will continue to check in at the Main Terminal and ride the mobile lounges out to the midfield locations. Plans call for construction of a tunnel linking Concourse B with the Main Terminal. Equipped with moving sidewalks, the tunnel will replace the mobile lounges.

Because Dulles is so far from most of the metropolitan region, taxicabs in either direction cost approximately $44. The Washington Flyer taxis go to Dulles; their buses go to both Dulles and Reagan National. The one-way fare for the bus service from New York Ave. and 11th St. NW is $16. It takes approximately an hour to get to the airport and stops at a number of downtown hotels as well as Union Station. You can also take the Orange Line to the West Falls Church station. From there, the Washington Flyer Dulles Express bus provides direct service to the airport every half-hour for $8. For more information, call 800-WASHFLY. If you are driving, take I-66 west to the 17-mile Dulles Access Road. No matter how you get there, remember to budget the extra 10 to 15 minutes it takes on the People Mover to actually reach your airplane. General information about Dulles is available at 703-661-2700 or on the Web at www.metwashairports.com/dulles.

The Dulles Access Road has been designated one of 10 national sites for a federal demonstration program on bus transit. The project is a possible precursor to a light-rail network from the inner suburbs to the airport. Watch for bus stations to be located in eastern Loudoun County, at the airport, Reston-Herndon, Tysons Corner and the West Falls Church Metrorail station.

BWI

The Baltimore-Washington International Airport (BWI), 28 miles from Downtown, has long been considered the area's number three airport. Massive renovations have been completed in the last couple of years to extend runways, enlarge concourses, add passenger gates and build a new parking garage. The new international terminal, completed in 1997, is a steel and glass building with a 90-foot atrium, white walls and gray terrazzo floor. It has twice the original space available for international flights, and now rivals Dulles for international and longer-distance domestic flights. If you are driving, take I-95 or the Baltimore-Washington Parkway to I-195 and follow the signs to BWI. While the Metro system has no direct service to BWI, Amtrak (800-USA-RAIL) provides travelers with access to and from the airport through Union Station in Northeast DC. There is a free shuttle bus from the train station to the airport. You can also get to BWI via the MARC-Penn Line (800-325-RAIL), which connects to Metro's Red Line at Union Station and Orange Line at New Carrollton. In addition, Airport Connection (301-261-1091) runs a shuttle between BWI and downtown DC every 90 minutes from 7:00 a.m. to 8:30 p.m. One-way fares cost $14. A new light rail station provides airport users with the first direct link to Penn Station in downtown Baltimore. BWI's main number is 301-261-1000. The BWI Website is www.baltwashintlairport.com.

Of note, BWI is the only commercial airport in the country with a trail winding around its perimeter. The final phase of the trail was completed in late Spring of 1999. Most of the trail is asphalt and is great for bikers, skaters, walkers and joggers. The trail is maintained by the Anne Arundel County Department of Recreation and Parks, the State Highway Administration and the BWI Neighbors Committee, made up of community organizations that deal with various airport issues.

Trains

Amtrak (800-USA-RAIL) provides nationwide passenger service running in and out of Union Station at 50 Massachusetts Ave. NE. Amtrak also links with the Metrorail system, providing access to Washington, DC and the Maryland and Virginia suburbs. For an unusual East Coast voyage, consider taking friends, family and your car on Amtrak's daily non-stop auto train from Virginia to Florida. You must accompany your car on this journey. One-way off-peak and peak season rates range from $93 to $182 and $142 to $230 per person.

Amtrak welcomes you to its official web "station" at www.amtrak.com. You can make reservations and buy tickets on-line, as well as peruse schedules, route maps and special offerings. The reservations page may be accessed directly at http://reservations.amtrak.com.

Buses

In addition to Metrobus service, the Washington area is served by Greyhound (800-231-2222; in Spanish 800-531-5332). The line serves Washington and Baltimore from main terminals downtown to satellite terminals in the suburbs. It also provides nationwide and some commuter service from several passenger stations. In addition to the District terminal at 1005 1st St. NE (202-289-5160), stations are located in Silver Spring at 8100 Fenton St. and Sligo Ave. (301-588-5110), Arlington at 3860 South Four Mile Run Dr. (703-998-6312), Fairfax County at 4103 Rust Rd. off Lee Hwy. (703-273-7770), and Springfield at 6583 Backlick Rd. off Old Keane Mill Rd. (703-451 5800). Greyhound's website is www.greyhound.com.

Peter Pan Trailways, the largest privately owned bus company in the country, also serves the area with daily service throughout the Northeast and New England. They utilize the Greyhound Bus facilities at 1005 1st St. NE in the District, and at 8100 Fenton St. and Sligo Ave. (301-588-5110) in Silver Spring. For schedules and fares, contact them at 800-343-9999, or visit their website at www.peterpan-bus.com

MASTERING DC: THE C&O CANAL

In 1954, Supreme Court Associate Justice William O. Douglas made a now legendary 185-mile walk along the towpath of the Chesapeake & Ohio Canal, from Cumberland, MD to Georgetown. He wasn't just out for a stroll: he was fighting to save the canal area from development. Today, residents of the greater Washington area continue in his footsteps, enjoying the sights and working to preserve the local and national treasure that is the C&O Canal National Historical Park.

☐ **Paddle the Potomac:** Put your **canoe or kayak** in the river near Violettes Lock (mi. 22). Paddle across and downstream, through the old Seneca Canal on the Virginia side, back across to the Maryland side, and on up the canal.

☐ **Follow the Mule:** Take a tour on a **mule-drawn barge** and learn about local life in the canal years, 1850-1924. April to November, depart from Great Falls Tavern (mi. 14.4; 301-299-3613) and travel through woodlands, or visit the historic district from Georgetown (202-653-5190).

☐ **Ferry 'Cross the River:** Whites Ferry (mi. 35.5) is the only remaining ferry, popular as a regular commute or a country drive. A boat ramp and parking lot mark the site of the former **Edwards Ferry** (mi. 30.9). Near **Whites Ferry**, check out the **Monocacy Aqueduct** (mi. 42.2) or, closer to DC, **Seneca Aqueduct** (mi. 22.7).

☐ **Take a Walk in the Dark:** Venture through the 3,118-foot **Paw Paw Tunnel** (mi. 155.2). Take along a flashlight to guide you through this dark passage—one of the most distinctive spots in the canal.

☐ **Go Fish:** Drop a line below Little Falls near Chain Bridge (mi. 4.2), at **Whites Ford** (mi. 38.7), at **Botelors Dam** (mi. 71.4), or in the canal itself… and bring along your Maryland state fishing license.

☐ **Hike and Ski but Don't Skate:** Hike the towpath or go rock climbing at **Carderock** (mi. 11.1) and **Great Falls Gorge**. Camp at the many sites located every four to eight miles along the towpath. Go cross-country skiing—but heed the signs against skating; it can be quite risky.

☐ **Ride the Rails:** Amtrak's **Capitol Limited** (800-USA-RAIL) runs along the historic Baltimore & Ohio route between Harpers Ferry, WV and Cumberland, MD. From Cumberland, take the **Western Maryland Scenic Railroad** (800-TRAIN-50) steam train to Frostburg and back, wending your way through scenic mountains and valleys.

☐ **Watch Out for That Bird:** Visit some of the islands and wildlife sanctuaries along the way for outstanding **birdwatching**. Highlights are Fletcher's Boathouse (mi. 3.2), the Dierssen Waterfowl Sanctuary (mi. 20), and the McKee-Besher Wildlife Management Area (mi. 27.2).

☐ **Unlock the Mystery:** The 74 **lift locks** on the canal formed the backbone of the system used to move boats and barges. In Georgetown and at Great Falls, see locks in action and at Four Locks (mi. 108.8), visit the restored wait house, lock house and mule barn.

☐ **Join the Club:** Contact the **C&O Canal Association** (301-983-0825) about hiking trips, including ones to commemorate Douglas' landmark walk. Subscribe to the Park's newsletter, *Kiosk*, or visit www.nps.gov/choh.

Note: Mile markers start in Georgetown

CHAPTER FOUR

Dealing with the Local Bureaucracy

After looking for an apartment, buying furniture, setting up house and getting to know the place you now call home, it's time to begin navigating the bureaucratic labyrinths towards establishing residency. This chapter helps you plan your route as you deal with car ownership—drivers' licenses, registration, and insurance—and income and property taxes, as well as establishing bank accounts. Also included are pointers on making sure your four-footed friends are legal residents of the metropolitan Washington area.

The Responsibility of Car Ownership

While some local residents simplify things by living life as pedestrians, most people in the area do own and regularly use a car to get around. For those people, the bureaucratic responsibilities of car ownership must be taken seriously. No matter where you live in the area, you need to acquire a local driver's license, register your vehicle and be sure that it is adequately insured. Traditionally, these activities have consumed the most time and inspired the best stories about dealing with local bureaucracies. In recent years, however, a concerted effort has been made to make these types of services more accessible and efficient. While improvements have been made, the District still lags behind the suburban cities and counties. If you don't relish the thought of dealing with these kinds of details, contact the local company, **United States Vehicle Registration Service**, at 202-342-2558. For $65 in the District and $100 in Virginia and Maryland, they will obtain a title, registration and parking permit for your car. For an additional $75, you can get your car inspected as well. Check their website for their full range of services and associated costs: www.usvrs.com.

DRIVER'S LICENSE FEES

	Driver's License	Learner's Permit
District of Columbia	$20	$15
Maryland	$30	$45*
Virginia	$12*	$3

*Average rate.

Getting Your Driver's License

Regardless of where you live, bring your checkbook, your current license (if you have one) and your social security card (if you can find it). You must also bring one other form of identification bearing your name and birth date. Birth certificates, passports, and employer and school IDs are all acceptable, but only the original documents; photocopies will get you nowhere. Take these

BIKE OWNERSHIP

For those of you who prefer self-propelled transportation, you will be relieved to know that registering a bicycle in the District is much easier than registering a car. Just take your bike to any District police or fire station. Your bike must be equipped with a night light and a horn. Registration costs just $1 for five years, and proof of ownership is required. For more information, call 202-576-6768. In Maryland, you can simply register your bike for only $1 at any police station. Bicycles in Arlington must be registered at 2100 North 15th St. (703-228-4252). Bring the serial number and $0.50. Alexandria cyclists must also register their bikes and can do so at the Police Department at 2003 Mill Rd., not far from the Metro's Yellow Line Eisenhower Station. As in Arlington, the fee is only $0.50; the police will record your bike's serial number and give you a decal. Fairfax County does not require a bike permit. They do, however, recommend that you etch your social security number on your bike so that you can identify it in the event of loss or theft.

materials—as well as patience and a sense of humor—to the closest full-service motor vehicle office. (See section titled Registering Your Car for specific information on locations and hours.)

Current out-of-state license holders have a 30-day grace period to get a local driver's license and license plates. If you surrender a valid driver's license from another US state or territory, you do not need to take a driving test. Vision tests are mandatory in all jurisdictions. District residents must take a 20-question written test and score 75% or better to pass. Virginia and Maryland both waive written requirements for current license holders.

If you have never had a driver's license, you must first apply for a learner's permit and take a written exam. Once you pass, you can sign up for a road test.

Foreign license holders must bring a green card or social security card along with a current passport and proof of a foreign license. Without proof of a foreign license, you will have to apply for a license from scratch—learner's permit and all. Non-US citizens must pass both vision and written tests. These tests are usually given the same day, so come prepared. The decision to require a road test is handled on an individual basis. If you do have to take it, you will need to make an appointment once you pass the written test.

Graduated Driver's License (GDL) systems, generally targeted toward teenage drivers, are being introduced throughout the area. The District has passed legislation which, if approved by the DC Financial Control Board and Congress, will be implemented in September 2000. It will raise the minimum age for obtaining a permanent driver's license from 16 to 18, and will require a three-step process to receive an unrestricted license. Maryland's restrictive "Rookie Driver" program, in effect since July 1999, pertains to all applicants, regardless of age, who have never held a license in Maryland or any other state or country or who have held their out-of-state license for less than 18 months. Virginia has not yet instituted a GDL system.

Registering Your Car

Regardless of where you live in the area, you will need to bring the following items when registering your car—a copy of the title of the car, out-of-state registration (if applicable), proof of auto insurance, proof of address and your checkbook. Other details vary by jurisdiction.

DC

Newcomers should know that before doing anything else through the District's Department of Motor Vehicles (DMV), you must first have a valid DC driver's license. For **licenses and car registration**, go to the Central Office of the DMV at 301 C St. NW. The hours of operation are weekdays from 8:15 a.m. to 4:00 p.m., with extended hours to 8:00 p.m. on Wednesday. Parking in the neighborhood can be quite difficult, and it is much easier to take the Metro Red Line to Judiciary Square. The building is just across the street from the Metro station.

District residents have been known to spend countless hours at the DMV offices. Efforts have been made to make the system more efficient and, while the bureau is much more user-friendly than it used to be, the wait can be lengthy. DMV suggests visiting early in the day to ensure that all your transactions can be completed the same day.

Room 1157 is the single most important room you need to visit. Upon entering, stop at the information desk for a number and the application paperwork. You can complete the Application for Certificate of Title for a Motor Vehicle or Trailer, and any other paperwork, while waiting for your assigned number to be called. Expect to pay $20 for the certificate of title, $15 for each recorded lien on your car and a registration fee based on the car's weigh. For cars under 3,500 pounds the fee is $65; for heavier cars it is $98. These two fees already include the $10 inspection fee. The District also charges **excise taxes** based on the fair market ("blue book") value of the vehicle—currently 6% for a small car and 7% for a large one. There are a few exceptions; unless they apply to your situation, be prepared to pay the taxes on the spot.

In addition to the main office at Judiciary Square, there is a DMV adjunct office in the Community Services Center at 616 H St. NE. This office provides services for registration renewals, residential parking permits, driver's license renewals and non-driver identification cards. The hours are 11:00 a.m. to 7:00 p.m. on weekdays and 8:15 a.m. to 4:00 p.m. on Saturday. No tests are given at this site.

PET LICENSING

The District requires that residents register their dogs with the local animal control officer. First-time licensees are required to have certificates of neutering or spaying, as well as distemper and rabies vaccinations. Fees are $10 for neutered males and $35 for females and non-neutered males. For information, call 202-442-4509.

The state of Maryland requires that residents register their dogs and cats with the local animal control officer. New residents have 30 days to register their animals. A rabies certificate from a licensed veterinarian is required. For further information, call Montgomery County at 301-279-1095 or Prince George's County at 301-499-8300.

In most of Northern Virginia, dogs six months of age and older must be licensed each year;in Fairfax County, the age is four months. A rabies certificate from a licensed veterinarian is required. Except in Alexandria, cats do not have to be licensed. They are, however, required by law to be inoculated for rabies by four months of age. For information, call Alexandria at 703-838-4775, Arlington County at 703-228-3057 or Fairfax County at 703-222-8234.

Residential parking permits, required on blocks with residential parking restrictions, are essential in the District. For just $10 per year, the permit allows you to park your car on your neighborhood street during times when parking is limited to two hours for non-residents. To obtain a parking permit, you must present a valid DC vehicle registration along with proof of insurance and residence. You can show proof of residence by bringing along a signed lease, a notarized statement from your landlord or a utility bill.

Full-time students, temporary residents (those living in the District fewer than 180 days), congressional staff and military personnel can keep their home state license plates by applying for a reciprocity sticker. Students must show proof of full-time status (at least nine credit hours) and proof of residence in the District. If you live on a street that has residential parking, you must still pay the $10 parking permit fee.

If you are seeking a **handicapped parking permit,** you should go to Room 1033 to file your application. If you are issued handicapped tags, you will not need a residential parking permit.

Once you leave the DMV, your car still has to be inspected. **Safety and emissions inspections** must be done within 30 days of receipt of your DC registration, and all first-time inspections must be done at 1001 Half St. SW (between Eye and M Sts.). If the lines are short, your inspection experience can be over in less than 15 minutes. Try to avoid visiting near the end of the month, when lines tend to be longest. Vehicle inspection station hours are from 6:00 a.m. to 8:00 p.m. on weekdays and 7:00 a.m. to 3:00 p.m. on Saturday. You will have already paid the $10 fee for the inspection when you registered your car. After the first year, the District will mail you paperwork for renewing your registration. You still have to have the car inspected, now on a two-year cycle, but the rest of the renewal process can be handled by mail.

If your car fails the inspection, you can go to a District- or a private-licensed facility for re-inspection. A list of all approved inspection stations is available at the District's Half St. site. Private inspection stations will charge a fee for repairs. These places are licensed to give inspection stickers once the car passes re-inspection.

If you have any questions, you can call the DMV's automated information system (202-727-5000). If the series of recorded messages does not answer your questions, stay on the line and an operator will eventually answer.

Washington, DC Department of Motor Vehicles (DMV)

Information	202-727-5000
Central Office	301 C St. NW
Hours	Monday, Tuesday, Thursday and Friday, 8:15 a.m. to 4:00 p.m. Wednesday, 8:15 a.m. to 8:00 p.m.
Adjunct Office	616 H St. NE
Hours	Monday through Friday, 11:00 a.m. to 7:00 p.m. Saturday, 8:15 a.m. to 4:00 p.m.

DMV website: www.dmv.dcgov.org

Maryland

Before you even set foot in a Maryland Motor Vehicle Administration (MVA) office, you should go to an authorized service station for **inspection**. Vehicles must have been inspected within the 90-day period preceding registration and titling, and proof of passing inspection must accompany the application for title. The inspections are thorough and can take up to two hours. Prices generally range from $40 to $50.

Once your car has passed the safety inspection, you will need to bring your current title, certificate of inspection and all insurance information (company, policy and agent) to a full-service MVA office. MVA charges $20 for **titling**, $70 for **registration** (good for two years) and $20 to record each lien (if your car is financed). Marylanders must also pay a **one-time excise tax** amounting to 5% of the fair market value of the car. If you have paid sales tax on your car in another state, bring your original bill of sale; the previously paid tax will be credited towards the current tax. Maryland has a minimum payment of $100 and although this one-time tax may seem high, Marylanders should consider themselves lucky not to be hit with the annual personal property taxes paid by Virginians.

Most Maryland counties also require **vehicle inspections** and **emissions testing**. For locations and contact information on inspections, check the Yellow Pages under Automobile Inspection Stations. The Vehicle Emissions Inspection Program (VEIP) is handled separately. Emissions testing is required every two years and costs $12. New vehicles are exempt for two years from the date of titling. There are 19 VEIP sites in the state. You can find out more by calling the automated information system at 800-638-8347, or by visiting the MVA website, which includes a map and addresses for the VEIP stations.

The MVA has installed self-serve kiosks at various local shopping malls, including but not limited to Columbia Mall, Beltway Plaza Mall in Greenbelt, Martin's Food in Hagerstown and Laurel Center. You can renew vehicle registrations at the kiosks as long as you have a renewal form and a valid automobile insurance form. Long-term plans call for expanding the service to include renewing driver's licenses and, ultimately, paying taxes.

Under the Driver Privacy Protection Act, Marylanders can request that their driver and vehicle record information be kept confidential. Unless you specifically request this, your records will remain available to the public. To do this, call the toll-free service at 888-682-3772, download privacy request forms from the MVA website (see below) or call the Fax on Demand service at 410-424-3050 (TDD 800-492-4575).

Maryland Motor Vehicle Administration (MVA)

Full-Service Offices

Information	301-948-3177
Hours	Monday through Friday, 8:30 a.m. to 4:30 p.m. Saturday, 8:30 a.m. to 12:00 p.m. (drivers' licenses only)
Beltsville	11760 Baltimore Ave. (MD Route 1)
Frederick	1601 Bowman's Farm Rd. (Exit 56 off I-70)
Gaithersburg	15 Metropolitan Grove Rd. (off Clopper Rd.)

MVA Customer Service Center

Information	800-950-1682
Hours	Monday through Friday, 8:00 a.m. to 8:00 p.m. Saturday, 8:00 a.m. to 1:00 p.m.
MVA Website	www.mva.state.md.us

Virginia

Virginians should be prepared for a scavenger hunt and for handling both state and local bureaucracies. First, you have to find a state-registered service station to have your car inspected. Your car must undergo two inspections—for safety and for emissions. The **safety inspection** is done annually and the **emissions inspection** is done every other year. Not all places are licensed to perform both tests. Signs at gas stations indicate which tests can be performed there.

With your approved emissions and safety documents in hand, your next stop is a full-service Division of Motor Vehicle (DMV) office to register your car. Blue signs with the letters "DMV" in white let you know you are closing in on one of them. In return for a $10 titling fee plus 3% sales and usage tax based on the sale price of the vehicle (minimum of $35), you will receive a Virginia **title**, a **registration card**, **license plates**, and current **plate decals**. Registration cards and decals are valid for one year. Those who have moved to Virginia for the long haul may want to opt for the two-year registration plan—double the registration fee and save yourself some effort next year.

Inspection fees total $30 (emissions $20 and safety $10). Like doctors who examine their patients from head to toe, inspectors check everything. So, if you are aware of needed repairs, be sure to have the work done before getting the car inspected. If the car fails inspection, don't expect to have the fee refunded. For a current list of inspection stations near you, check the Yellow Pages under Automobile Inspection Stations or call 703-583-3900.

RENTERS' INSURANCE

Most homeowners have already dealt with the issue of insuring their property. But many renters don't realize that similar protection is available for their belongings. If you have an expensive stereo system, computer, large wardrobe or other valuable personal property, you should consider buying renters' insurance. Renters' insurance is usually pretty cheap, relative to the cost of replacing your possessions. A $10,000 policy can cost as little as $100 a year. If you are interested in renters' insurance, ask your car insurance agent for a quote first. You can often obtain a discount if you buy more than one type of insurance from the same agent.

The final stop after getting the safety inspection decal, the registration and the license plates is the local city hall or county courthouse to register for the local **personal property tax** and to get the **license decal for the city** or **county**.

Alexandria Alexandrians must register to pay the **personal property tax** in Room 1410 in City Hall at 301 King St. (703-838-4560). Lines here, even during lunch hour, are not that long. The registration office is open weekdays from 8:00 a.m. to 5:00 p.m. and Saturday from 9:00 a.m. until noon. You need to bring your driver's license and one of the following—your state vehicle title, state vehicle registration card or bill of sale. The city bills you in August for payment by October 5. If you register your car in Alexandria after October 5, you are given a 30-day grace period to pay your personal property taxes. City stickers, required for on-street parking, cost $25 annually, with residents in zoned areas paying an additional $15.

Arlington County In Arlington County, the Courthouse at 2100 Clarendon Blvd. marks the final stop on your bureaucratic journey. Here you can **register** your car and while you are at it, register to vote and pick up newcomers' information at the desk right by the main entrance. There is a convenient, inexpensive parking garage on site or you can take the Metro Orange Line to the Court House station.

The Office of Personal Property Tax in Suite 218 (703-358-3135) is where you file your **personal property tax** forms and pay the Arlington County processing fee. The county charges just under 5% of the current "blue book" value of the car. A wave of relief sweeps over most Arlington residents when they learn that they do not have to pay these taxes on the spot. This tax can amount to a few hundred dollars a year for newer cars. If you register between December 16 and June 15, taxes are due September 15. For those registering between June 16 and December 15, the deadline is March 15.

Fairfax County Fairfax County residents must bring their Virginia registration card to any county office in order to **register** a vehicle and purchase **county tags**. Call 703-222-8234 to find the county office closest to you. Tags cost $25 for cars and trucks. The process for paying **personal property tax** is simple. Just fill out the proper form and you will be billed in late September for payment by December 5. Tax rates are just over 4.5% of the current trading value of your car. Fairfax does prorate its property tax, which is good news if you move to the area halfway through the year.

Virginia Division of Motor Vehicles (DMV)

Full Service Offices

Information	703-761-4655
Hours:	Monday through Friday, 8:30 a.m. to 5:30 p.m. Saturday, 8:30 a.m. to 12:30 p.m.
Alexandria	2681 Mill Rd.
Arlington	4150 South Four Mile Run Dr.
Franconia	6306 Grovedale Dr.
Vienna	(Tysons Corner) 1968 Gallows Rd.
DMV Website	www.dmv.state.va.us

Insuring Your Car

Car insurance is a necessity, regardless of where you live. Insurance rates are determined by factors that are often out of your control—such as neighborhood (people in the city pay more), age (older is better than younger), gender (women have lower rates) and marital status (married drivers are preferred). Virginians tend to have the lowest auto insurance rates. Residents of the District have the highest and Marylanders generally fall somewhere between the two, depending on the specific location.

For buying insurance, you have three options—mail-order, company agents or independent agents. Groups or organizations such as AAA offer insurance by mail. Company agents represent the large insurance companies like Allstate or State Farm. Independent agents sell insurance from various companies and tend to be a little more expensive. Often, the independent agents tend to have close ties with one or two companies and try to push their products. So make sure you call around to a few independent agents and compare their prices and products. Phone book listings of insurance agents and companies tend to be confusing. When calling, you may want to ask if you are talking to a company agent or an independent agent. Or contact the **Insurance Helpline** at 800-942-4242 for assistance.

For the best rates, shop around and ask lots of questions, even if you think the answers are obvious. When you call insurance agents for price quotes, be sure to give each the same information so that you can make accurate comparisons. When applying, honesty is definitely the best policy; the truth comes out eventually, even if it doesn't come from you.

DEALING WITH YOUR TAXES

Everyone knows the line about death and taxes—and the situation is no different in the Washington area. Federal income tax has to be dealt with no matter where you live, and local jurisdictions levy their own income tax as well as personal and real property taxes.

Federal Income Tax

If you do not find the form you need in your mail, at your post office or at other places offering them, you can call the **Internal Revenue Service** (IRS) at 800-829-3676. Federal tax information and assistance is available at 800-829-1040. For those who like to browse the Net, the IRS has a website at www.irs.gov featuring tax forms, publications, news on recent developments and other related information. Locally, the *Washington Post* prints a tax guide every February summarizing all of the federal and state tax regulations in the area.

State and Local Income Tax

The District takes the gold medal for the highest income tax rates in the area. Maryland gets the silver and Virginia, the bronze. Before you begin this annual ritual, consult the state instruction booklets for information about filing requirements. Unless you arrived on New Year's Day, you should pay special

DC HOMEBUYER TAX CREDIT

The Taxpayer Relief Act of 1997 provides a tax credit of up to $5,000 for DC homebuyers who close on a principal residence after August 5, 1997 and prior to December 31, 2001, and who satisfy two criteria. First, you must not have owned a primary residence in the District for the previous 12 months prior to closing. Second, your adjusted gross income generally must be less than $70,000 for single filers and $110,000 for joint filers. You will need to submit tax Form 8859 "DC Homebuyer" which you can obtain from the IRS at 800-TAX-FORM, or you can download it from the IRS web site at www.irs.gov. The best source of current information about this issue is the office of DC Delegate Eleanor Holmes Norton,at 202-225-8050, or her web page at www.house.gov/norton, which spells out eligibility and income limits.

attention to information for part-year residents and non-residents. If you need extra help, each jurisdiction offers assistance.

DC

District of Columbia residents are required to file returns by April 15. Tax rates are progressive and currently range from 6% to 9.5% on taxable income. Exemptions include a personal exemption of $1,370 for an individual, if single; $2,740 for married filing jointly; and $2,740 for head of family. An additional $1,370 exemption is allowed for taxpayers over age 65 and taxpayers who are blind.

The Income Tax Help office, in Room 550 at 441 4th St. NW, will answer questions about District taxes; you can call them at 202-727-6130. This office keeps extended hours during tax season, January to April. In addition, District residents can pick up tax forms at several locations including the District Building at 1350 Pennsylvania Ave. NW, the Recorder of Deeds Office at 515 D St. NW, Martin Luther King Library at 901 G St. NW, the Potomac Building at 614 H St. NW or the Reeves Center at 2000 14th St. NW. DC tax forms can be found on the Web at www.dccfo.com; if you would like to have tax forms mailed to you, call 202-727-6170.

Maryland

Maryland imposes a graduated income tax at the current rates of 2% to 6% on taxable income, generally defined as the same as federal income taxes. Returns must be filed by April 15. Maryland income tax information and forms can be found on the Web at www.comp.state.md.us.

In addition, the Maryland counties may levy a local "piggy-back" income tax, varying from 50% to 60% of the state tax liability, which is withheld and collected on the same form as the Maryland state income tax.

Maryland income tax forms are available weekdays between 8:00 a.m. and 5:00 p.m. at 11510 Georgia Ave. in Wheaton (301-949-6030) or can be obtained by mail. If you have any questions while you are preparing your return, try talking to someone in the state tax office at 800-638-2937.

Virginia

The Commonwealth of Virginia imposes a graduated income tax at the current rate of from 2% to 5.75% on taxable income, generally defined as the same as federal income taxes. Virginia returns must be filed by May 1.

In Alexandria, forms are available at City Hall at 301 King St. (703-838-4570). Arlington residents can pick up their state income tax forms on the second floor of the Courthouse at 2100 Clarendon Blvd. (703-358-3055) or at any of the seven county public libraries. If you would like forms mailed to you, call the Richmond Center at 804-367-8205. Virginia tax forms can be found on the Web at www.tax.state.va.us.

Personal Property Tax

Neither the District of Columbia nor the state of Maryland levies a personal property tax on individuals. In Virginia, such taxes are controlled by the local governments. Counties set a base rate for all unincorporated areas, towns may elect to add a town rate to the county's base rate and cities set a rate that is paid in lieu of the county tax. Automobiles, boats, mobile homes, motorcycles and business personal property are all subject to tax. Personal effects, household goods, money and securities are not taxed.

Real Property Tax

In DC, all real property is subject to taxation and is assessed at 100% of the estimated market value. Real property tax rates are set in June by the Council of the District of Columbia. There is a $30,000 homestead exemption on owner-occupied residential units; the exemption reduces the assessed value prior to taxing. Application must be made for this exemption, and once granted, is good for five years.

Maryland assesses real property at approximately 40% of fair market value. The state tax rate is $0.21 per $100 of the assessed value. Maryland property is assessed every three years; increases are proportioned over the subsequent three years. More information on Maryland property taxes is available on the Web at www.dat.state.md.us. Each county, city and district may levy additional taxes that will need to be factored into your planning.

In Virginia, real estate taxes are levied by local governments and not by the state.

Contact one of the following for further information on assessments and taxation.

District of Columbia 202-727-6460

Maryland

Montgomery County 240-777-8950

Prince George's County 301-952-2500

Virginia

Alexandria	703-838-4646
Arlington County	703-228-3090
Fairfax City	703-385-7883
Fairfax County	703-222-8234
Falls Church	703-241-5022

BANKING

The Washington, DC area has many banks and financial institutions offering a wide variety of services. As you shop around, keep in mind that most banks offer similar general banking products—checking, savings and money market accounts; consumer loans and mortgages; banking by mail; automated teller machines (ATMs) and safe deposit boxes. Watch for an increasing number of products being offered through ATM machines. Among the products already being offered are stamps and pre-paid phone cards. Other options being explored are concert and travel tickets, money orders and bill paying. To make your best choice among the many available, you'll probably need to investigate other factors such as branch locations and hours, fees and interest rates, PC banking options, network connections for the ATMs, direct deposit of paychecks, rates and policies for mortgages and home equity loans, investment services, and credit cards. Deciding what really matters to you before you approach the bank can simplify things. You can state what you need and then ask what additional services the bank representative would recommend.

If you are relocating from outside the area, consider establishing a relationship with a bank here prior to your move. The process for this varies from bank to bank. Some will allow you to open an account through the mail or even over the telephone. One common denominator, however, whether you handle this before or after your move, will be the need to present some form of personal identification. This could include your driver's license number, Social Security number or proof of residence, items that the bank will use to establish your credit rating. Some banks may want to verify your employment and income, in which case a letter from your employer on company letterhead may be requested.

To assist you in your effort to select a new bank, find out where your employer banks, or ask colleagues, friends, relatives or neighbors for personal recommendations. Keep in mind that the banking industry continues to be in a state of flux, and that one bank may be about to buy out another one. The best sources for this kind of information are the local papers, neighbors and the bank staff. Following is a list of some of the major banks in the area for your convenience. A complete listing can be found in your area telephone directory.

The Adams National Bank	202-466-4090 www.adamsbank.com
Chevy Chase Bank	301-598-7100 www.chevychasebank.com
Citibank	800-926-1067 www.citibank.com
Citizens Bank	301-206-6000 www.citizensbank.com
Crestar Bank	800-273-7827 www.crestar.com
First National Bank of MD	800-441-8455 www.firstmd.com
First Union	800-801-0714 www.firstunion.com
George Mason Bank	703-219-4800 www.georgemasonbank.com
Nations Bank	800-337-2324 www.nationsbank.com
Riggs Bank	301-887-6000 www.riggsbank.com
Signet Bank	800-955-1500 www.signet.com

Registering to Vote

Thanks to the National Voter Registration Act (popularly known as Motor/Voter), residents of all three jurisdictions in the metropolitan area can register to vote at local departments of motor vehicles. While in line to register your vehicle or take care of other business, you can fill out the voter registration form and drop it off before you leave.

You can also obtain forms in other ways. In the District, call the city's 24-hour line at 202-727-2525 to have the forms mailed to you, or pick them up at public libraries, police stations, or fire stations. Maryland residents can call the Montgomery County 24-hour service at 301-217-8683 or the Prince George's County service at 301-627-2814. If you live in Virginia, visit the State Board of Elections' website at www.sbe.state.va.us for a complete listing of addresses and phone numbers for city and county voter registration offices. Or check the government listings in the Blue Pages of the telephone book.

FEDERAL GOVERNMENT WEBSITES

One of the benefits of living in the Washington, DC area is being within arm's reach of the wealth of information available through the federal government. You can obtain information on virtually any subject through agency public information offices as well as from those federal research libraries that grant public access. You can also obtain information through the Internet without having to leave your home or office. Listed here is a sampling of websites available for some of the major government offices. Watch local publications for announcements of new websites and check around on the Internet using some of the general addresses listed below.

General Government Information:

FedWorld Information Network .... www.fedworld.gov
Government Information .... www.yahoo.com/government
Federal Information Exchange, Inc. .... http://ecs.rams.com/wwwlinks
4anything Network www.4government.com

The White House .... www.whitehouse.gov

The Cabinet:

Department of Agriculture .... www.usda.gov
Department of Commerce .... www.doc.gov
Department of Defense .... www.dod.gov
Department of Education .... www.ed.gov
Department of Energy .... www.doe.gov
Department of Health and Human Services .... www.dhhs.gov
Department of Housing and Urban Development .... www.dhud.gov
Department of the Interior .... www.doi.gov
Department of Justice .... www.doj.gov
Department of Labor .... www.dol.gov
Department of State .... www.state.gov
Department of Transportation .... www.dot.gov
Department of Treasury .... www.ustreas.gov
Department of Veterans Affairs .... www.va.gov

Selected Agencies:

Census Bureau .... www.census.gov
Central Intelligence Agency .... www.cia.gov
Commission on Civil Rights .... www.usccr.gov
Consumer Product Safety Commission .... www.cpsc.gov
Environmental Protection Agency .... www.epa.gov
Equal Employment Opportunity Commission .... www.eeoc.gov
Federal Aviation Administration .... www.faa.gov
Federal Bureau of Investigation .... www.fbi.gov

Federal Communications Commission	www.fcc.gov
Federal Elections Commission	www.fec.gov
Federal Emergency Management Administration	www.fema.gov
Federal Highway Administration	www.fhwa.dot.gov
Federal Judicial Center	www.fjc.gov
Federal Reserve System	www.bog.frb.fed.us
Federal Trade Commission	www.ftc.gov
Food and Drug Administration	www.fda.gov
General Accounting Office	www.gao.gov
General Services Administration	www.gsa.gov
Government Printing Office	www.gpo.gov
Health Care Financing Administration	www.hcfa.gov
Immigration and Naturalization Service	www.ins.usdoj.gov
Internal Revenue Service	www.irs.gov
International Trade Commission	www.usitc.gov
Library of Congress	www.loc.gov
National Aeronautics and Space Administration	www.nasa.gov
National Endowment for the Arts	http://arts.endow.gov
National Institutes of Health	www.nih.gov
National Park Service	www.nps.gov
National Science Foundation	www.nsf.gov
National Transportation Safety Board	www.ntsb.gov
Occupational Safety and Health Administration	www.osha.gov
Office of Personnel Management	www.opm.gov
Securities and Exchange Commission	www.sec.gov
Small Business Administration	www.sba.gov
Social Security Administration	www.ssa.gov
US Customs Service	www.customs.ustreas.gov
US Fish and Wildlife Service	www.fws.gov
US House of Representatives	www.house.gov
US Postal Service	www.usps.gov
US Senate	www.senate.gov

Congressional Information Websites:

Congressional Record	www.access.gpo.gov/su_docs/
Federal Register	www.nara.gov/fedreg/
Thomas	http://thomas.loc.gov
US House Committee Schedule	http://thomas.loc.gov/home/hcomso.html
US Senate Calendar of Business	www.access.gpo.gov/congress/cong004.html

MASTERING DC: THE FEDERAL GOVERNMENT

You've seen the Washington Monument, the White House and the Smithsonian. But have you seen behind the scenes? Our federal government locally employs more than 300,000 people. Take the opportunity to observe some of these people hard at work for you.

☐ **Tell Nothing but the Truth:** Especially when you visit the **Supreme Court** (1st St. and Maryland Ave. NE; 202-479-3000) on Thursdays and Fridays when in session. Join one of two lines to view justice at work—one for a quick peek, the other for a lengthier look. On weekdays when Court is not in session, tours and public lectures are conducted in the courtroom.

☐ **Find a Philatelist:** The stamp collector in your family will enjoy visiting the **US Postal Service Headquarters** located at 475 L'Enfant Promenade SW (202-268-4910). Past and current commemorative stamps are displayed and on sale.

☐ **Organize Those Old Files:** Call to reserve a time to drop in and take a look at our national documents at the **National Archives and Records Administration** (700 Pennsylvania Ave. NW; 202-501-5400), including Watergate Trial tapes and JFK assassination materials. The opportunities for in-depth research are extensive and the records are the real McCoy.

☐ **Dig a Little Deeper:** Reserve a seat in the user-friendly workshop on research at the **Library of Congress** (Madison Building, 101 Independence Ave. SE; 202-707-3370) to learn about navigating this extraordinary accumulation of knowledge.

☐ **Breathe Easier:** Since 1970, the **Environmental Protection Agency** has been protecting human health and safeguarding our air, water and land. Its History Office at 401 M St. SW (202-260-2675) offers its historical document collection to researchers and the general public; call ahead to reserve a date and time to stop in.

☐ **Stand at Attention:** Travel across the 14th St. Bridge to Virginia (I-395) and follow the signs to the **Pentagon** (202-695-1776). Public tours, every half-hour from 9:00 a.m. to 3:30 p.m., include the Hall of Heroes and the Flag Corridor.

☐ **Search the Stars:** Just ask for help from the staff at the **United States Naval Observatory**. A free 90-minute tour of its facilities is given every Monday night at 8:30 p.m. Learn about the Master Clock, observe the stars through telescopes, and talk with astronomers about UFOs. No reservations are required.

☐ **Be Diplomatic:** During the work week, the **State Department** (2201 C St. NW; 202-647-3241) offers three tours a day of its exclusive Diplomatic Reception Rooms. Plan ahead...up to a month...these tours are popular and reservations are required.

☐ **Get Rich Quick:** Reservations are required but admission is free for the 90-minute Saturday morning tour of the **Treasury Department** (15th St. between F and G Sts. NW; 202-622-0896). Don't miss the chance to see a burglar-proof vault dating back to 1864.

☐ **Get Richer Quicker:** At least make million-dollar plans as you tour this land o'green called the **Bureau of Engraving and Printing** (14th and C St. SW; 202-874-3188). A highlight of this tour—a stack of one million dollar bills piled high.

CHAPTER FIVE

Getting Connected

A big part of getting settled in, no matter where you live, is getting connected to local services. This chapter tells you how to get wired in to the basic utilities and services you need to run your home—telephone, cable television, natural gas, electricity, trash and recycling, and water and sewer—in the various jurisdictions within the DC metropolitan area. It also helps you connect to the other major outlets of information—the other type of power on which Washington runs. Local papers, magazines, newsstands, broadcast media and websites are covered, as well as phone numbers for access to the Internet.

Wiring In

There is nothing particularly unusual about the utilities available in the Washington area—other than, perhaps, the fact that setting them up may seem more bureaucratic than elsewhere. The best advice is to know what you want done and to call early to make the arrangements. Installation of many services tends to be on an "8 to 12" or "1 to 5" schedule and you will most likely have to be at home at least half a day. The companies are working hard to meet customer requirements, but with the area's dense and transient population, there is usually more than enough for them to do.

Telephone Service

To set up residential phone service, call your local **Bell Atlantic** office. If you do not have a credit history, you will be asked to give a deposit. The phone company will generally connect your service within a few business days. Phone numbers for English and Spanish are listed here. You can also reach Bell Atlantic through its website at www.bell-atl.com.

District of Columbia	202-965-6263	(English)
	202-954-6250	(Spanish)
Maryland	301-954-6260	(English)
	301-954-6250	(Spanish)
Virginia	703-954-6222	(in state)

LOCAL AREA CODES

Although Washington (202), Northern Virginia (703 and 571) and neighboring parts of Maryland (240 and 301) have different area codes, all calls within a 30-mile radius of the Washington Monument are local. You do not have to dial "1," but you do have to use the area code to call across jurisdictions and for all local calls in Maryland and Northern Virginia, even within the same area code. Calls to the rest of the states of Maryland (410 and 443) and Virginia (757 and 804 to the east and 540 to the west) are long distance.

A number of other companies are providing residential telephone service to area customers as a result of deregulation. If you are interested in an alternative to Bell Atlantic, you'll have choices among such providers as **Connectiv Communications** (888-850-4600), **e.spire Communications** (888-637-7473), **MCI** (800-950-5555) and **Starpower** (877-STARPOWER). Check your local telephone directory for other options. Many of these providers serve selected areas as opposed to the entire metropolitan Washington, DC area.

Cable Television

A number of companies, listed here, provide local cable television service. With the recent changes in legislation governing the telecommunications industry, there could be lots more in the near future.

DC

District Cablevision — 202-635-5100 (English)
202-635-5110 (Spanish)

Maryland

Montgomery County
Cable TV Montgomery — 301-424-4400 (English)
301-424-6999 (Spanish)

Prince George's County
Jones Communications
Northern PG County — 301-731-4260
Southern PG County — 301-499-1980

Virginia

Alexandria
Jones Communications — 703-823-3000

Arlington County
Cable TV Arlington — 703-841-7700

Fairfax County
Cox Communications — 703-378-8411

Reston
Jones Communications — 703-716-9701

Satellite Television

Many local residents are turning to the satellite dish for expanded viewing options. The two large satellite television companies are **DirectTV** (800-445-2190; www.directv.com) and **Dish Network** (800-333-3474; www.dishnetwork.com).

Natural Gas

If your apartment or house needs gas service turned on or off, call **Washington Gas** at 703-750-1000. The gas company serves all three area jurisdictions. For customer service outside the metropolitan area, call 800-752-7520. Information on the gas company and its services is available at www.washgas.com. Consider joining the new Washington Gas Customer Choice Pilot Program (WGCCPP). Washington Gas will still deliver the gas, but you will have the freedom to choose the supplier. This choice could lower your gas bill. Participating suppliers can provide you with details and you can find more information on the program—available in the District, Maryland and Virginia—on the Washington Gas website.

Electricity

To turn on the electricity, residents in the District and Maryland turn to **Potomac Electric Company (PEPCO)** at 202-833-7500, or at www.pepco.com. Northern Virginia residents can contact **Virginia Power** at 888-667-3000, or at www.vapower.com.

Trash

Each jurisdiction handles trash pick-up differently for the homes of its residents. In most apartment and condo buildings, trash pick-up is handled on a building-wide basis, so check with the management company to find out if you have to do anything on your own.

District of Columbia	202-442-8000
Maryland	
Montgomery County	240-777-6410
Prince George's County	301-952-7630
Virginia	
Alexandria	703-751-5130
Arlington County	703-228-6570
Fairfax City	703-385-7995
Fairfax County	703-550-3481

Recycling

In most of the Washington area, local governments arrange for recycling. This is the best way to dispose of newspapers, aluminum cans, and plastic and glass containers. The specifics vary by jurisdiction, so call the appropriate number from the list below to find out what is available in your part of town. In condo and apartment buildings, the management company usually arranges for recycling, but there are a number of local residents who—being more "green" than others—go the extra mile and deliver their recyclables to centralized drop-off points.

District of Columbia	202-727-1000
Maryland	
Montgomery County	240-777-6400
Prince George's County	301-952-7630
Virginia	
Alexandria	703-751-5872
Arlington County	703-358-6570
Fairfax City	703-385-7995
Fairfax County	703-324-5052

Water and Sewer

If you live in a private home, you will have to make arrangements to set up the connection to water and sewer services. The list here will get you started. Again, for condo and apartment buildings, you probably won't have to make your own arrangements.

District of Columbia	202-757-5240
Maryland	
Montgomery County	301-206-4001
Prince George's County	301-206-8000
Virginia	
Alexandria	703-751-5130
Arlington County	703-228-3636
Fairfax City	703-385-7915
Fairfax County	703-698-5800

Staying Informed

Living in or near Washington, DC—the nation's capital and a major international city— you'll find there is no shortage of sources for news and information. The major "local" papers have a global scope and one of them, the *Washington Post,* is considered one of the country's major national dailies. On television, it is sometimes hard to tell the local news from the networks' national broadcasts out of New York. In addition to the major print and broadcast media, the number—and quality—of local newspapers, magazines, and television and radio stations is increasing. Finally, Washington media and information sources cater to the area's international population, with a number of newsstands that sell local, national and international publications. There also are a number of international television and radio programs—in just about every language and for just about every culture.

Newspapers

In the Washington area there are two major dailies—the *Washington Post* and the *Washington Times*—in addition to a number of regional and specialized newspapers.

The Washington Post

The *Washington Post* is the area's major newspaper and one of the best in the country. It offers readers a broad perspective on current events both inside and outside the Beltway and has a well-deserved reputation for both national and political coverage. Its Federal Page covers the latest news—and scandals—from the Hill. Many area residents rely on Friday's Weekend section for its listings of the city's social, cultural and entertainment events. Saturday's Real Estate section includes a feature called Where We Live, which focuses weekly on individual neighborhoods. The Metro section brings news about neighborhoods in and around DC, on a daily basis. You may also want to consider a local daily or weekly to keep tabs on your community. Subscription rates for the *Post* run approximately $12 a month. To arrange for home delivery, call the paper at 202-334-6100. The *Post* is available on-line at www.washingtonpost.com.

The Washington Times

The Rev. Sun Myung Moon's Unification Church funds this newspaper, although most people feel that the paper reflects extreme political conservatism rather than the Rev. Moon's theology. Its layout is flashier than its better-known rival (the *Post*) and it offers good coverage of local politics and sports. The yearly subscription rate is $117; call 202-636-3333 for home delivery. For further information, check out the *Times* Website at www.washtimes.com.

USA Today

The national newspaper, *USA Today*, is published Monday through Friday by Gannett Co., Inc., headquartered in Arlington, VA. The paper covers news from

LIBRARIES

American University, Bender Library
202-885-3200

Catholic University, Mullen Memorial Library
202-319-5077

George Washington University, Gelman Library
202-994-6558

Georgetown University, Lauinger Library
202-687-7452

Historical Society of Washington
202-785-2068

Library of Congress
202-707-5000

Martin Luther King Memorial Library
202-727-1111

National Archives
202-501-5400

National Geographic Society Library
202-857-7783

LOCAL NEWS ON-LINE

Maryland
Montgomery, Frederick, Prince George's Counties
www.gazette.net

Howard County
www.lifegoeson.com

Virginia
Fauquier, Loudoun, Fairfax Counties
www.timespapers.com

Washington Area Military Installations
www.dcmilitary.com

across the nation in capsule form and in full color. Subscriptions cost about $13 a month. The annual subscription rate is $119. Subscription and general information is available at 800-USA-1000 or www.usatoday.com.

The Journal Newspapers

The Journal Newspapers, Inc. publishes six county-wide papers in Maryland and Virginia—*Alexandria Journal, Arlington Journal, Fairfax Journal, Montgomery Journal, Prince George's Journal* and *Prince William Journal.* The full-color papers are published Monday through Friday. The minimum three-month subscription costs $21. Call for home delivery at 703-560-4000. You can reach the Journal Newspapers' website at www.jrnl.com.

Specialized Newspapers

In an attempt to satisfy the information needs of various constituencies within the local population, a number of independent, specialized newspapers are available throughout the area.

Washington's weekly *City Paper* (202-332-2100; www.washingtoncitypaper.com) does an excellent job covering local news and cultural events, particularly the arts. Well-known for its candid features on Washington phenomena and personalities, the *City Paper* has a steady following. You can pick up the latest *City Paper* on Thursdays at Metro stations and many District stores and less formal restaurants, such as coffee shops and carry outs. Best of all, it is free, a rare example of getting much more than you pay for!

On the Hill, *Roll Call* helps congressional staffers keep up with the latest news. This biweekly newspaper (appearing on Monday and Thursday) covers Congress on much the same level that other community papers cover their neighborhoods. A year's subscription costs $240. You can reach this newspaper's website at www.rollcall.com.

The *Washington Business Journal*, published every Friday by American City Business Journals, Inc., covers the local business community. Small and large businesses in nearly every local industry have come to rely on this informative publication. The *Washington Business Journal* has become particularly well-known for its weekly feature, The List, which ranks the top companies in key area industries and provides basic information on them. Once a year, these lists are compiled into the Book of Lists, available in print or on disk. The annual subscription rate for the newspaper is $73. You can reach the newspaper at 703-875-2200 or on its website at www.amcity.com/washington.

The *Washington Blade*, another free weekly, is the newspaper of Washington's gay and lesbian community. This paper is especially helpful to interested newcomers with its directory of gay professionals and community resources. The *Blade* is available in a number of area shops and restaurants; for more information, call 202-797-7000.

There are many free neighborhood newspapers around to keep residents in touch with community news and issues. Examples include the *Georgetowner, Hill Rag, InTowner, Uptown Citizen, Common Denominator, Current Newspapers, McLean Providence Journal* and *Arlington Courier.* Check the local phone book for phone numbers and keep an eye out for copies in local shops and restaurants.

Many specialized papers cater to Washington's various ethnic and religious groups. The *Washington Afro-American* (202-332-0080) and *Washington Informer* (202-561-4100) cover news and topics of interest to the African-American community. Washington's sizable Hispanic community is chronicled in the pages of *Tiempo Latino* (703-527-7860) and *El Progonero* (301-853-4504). The *Washington Jewish Week* (301-230-2222) follows the area's Jewish community and the *Korean Times* (202-723-6100) provides news to a growing Korean population.

Recreation News (301-474-4600) is a monthly publication devoted to providing government employees with the facts on Washington weekend entertainment and road trips. Copies are available at any government building.

Other Print Media

In addition to the national, regional and specialized newspapers, Washington has no shortage of other options for interesting and informative print media. The city is covered in its own city magazines, the *Washingtonian, Capital Style* and *Regardie's Power.* These and other magazines—on virtually every topic imaginable—are available at newsstands all over town.

Washingtonian

Washingtonian, a glossy monthly magazine, contains feature articles and in-depth interviews with Washington's movers and shakers as well as restaurant reviews, Washington trivia, the occasional exposé and a gossip column. *Washingtonian* is known for its frequent lists of the area's best restaurants and entertainment. Subscription information is available at 202-331-0715. You can reach *Washingtonian Online,* "the electronic magazine Washington lives by," at www.washingtonian.com.

WASHINGTON WEBSITES

There are a number of interesting Internet resources available to give you more information about the Washington area. Listed here are some highlights.

Washington, DC has its own official website at www.dchomepage.net

Celebrate "The American Experience" with the official tourism website, brought to you by the Washington Convention and Visitors Association at www.washington.org

Keep abreast of development in the downtown Business Improvement District (BID) at www.downtowndc.org

A commercial service provides access to another DC—Digital City: www.digitalcity.com

Other sites serve as launch pads to see what else is out there in DC cyberspace:
www.dcpages.com
www.dcregistry.com
http://washington.sidewalk.com

Follow DC life, government and politics through an on-line magazine at www.dcwatch.com. On their site you can subscribe to *themail*, an e-mail discussion forum and a great place to go to find out what your neighbors are thinking about current issues facing the city. It carries event listings and classified ads.

Capital Style

Published by Roll Call, Inc., this magazine covers "the art of political living" in Washington, DC through feature articles and columns. Subscriptions are $16.95 for 10 issues per year. To subscribe, call 800-289-9331, or visit their website at www.capstyle.com.

Regardie's Power

The most recent magazine to cover local Washington life is Regardie's Power. Published bi-monthly, this magazine covers "the business of greater Washington." Subscriptions are $50 for 12 issues per year. For additional information, contact them by phone at 202-332-9200 or on the Internet at www.regardies.com.

Area Newsstands

If you are in the mood to read something new, you don't have to go far to satisfy the desire. Newsstands can be found in convenience and grocery stores and pharmacies, and even in some of the area's coffee shops. While these smaller newsstands don't offer as much breadth as the real newsstands, they are certainly readily available.

When you want the real thing, turn to one of the area's larger bookstores, such as **Borders**, and **Barnes & Noble**. For a special treat, you can go to one of the major area newsstands offering a wide range of domestic and international newspapers and periodicals. The **Newsroom** (202-332-1489) is the best of its kind. You will find it at 1803 Connecticut Ave. NW, just north of Dupont Circle. The store offers an array of national and international newspapers as well as magazines, scholarly journals, foreign language textbooks and bilingual dictionaries. There is also the **American International Newsstand** at 1825 Eye St. NW (202-223-2526) and **One Stop News** (202-872-1577) at the corner of Pennsylvania Ave. and 20th St. NW. **Trover Books**, on the Hill at 21 Pennsylvania Ave. SE (202-547-2665), carries a wide selection of domestic newspapers.

Broadcast Media

The Washington area is well-connected to national networks and to international sources of information; the local broadcast media seems limitless. Listed here you will find a sampling of the television channels and radio stations available. Tune in to your local papers and flip channels and stations to see what else is around.

Channel 4	WRC	NBC
Channel 5	WTTG	FOX
Channel 7	WJLA	ABC
Channel 9	WUSA	CBS
Channel 20	WBDC	WB

Television

In addition to the national networks and Public Broadcasting Service stations, listed below for easy reference, there is a world of programming available through cable television service providers. Refer to the section on Cable Television earlier in this chapter.

Channel 22	WMPT	PBS
Channel 26	WETA	PBS
Channel 32	WHUT	PBS
Channel 48	WMDO	Univision
Channel 56	WNVC	(International Programming)

Radio

Washington area radio stations have something for every listening taste. Mergers, acquisitions and general format changes cause stations to revise their programming over time. A sampling of stations is given below; however, a more complete, up-to-the-minute listing can be found in the *Washington Post* Style section.

AM Stations

570	WWRC	All Business
630	WMAL	News, Talk
980	WTEM	Sports, Talk
1120	WUST	New World Radio, International
1450	WOL	Black Talk
1500	WTOP	All News, Live Oriole's game broadcasts
1540	WMDO	Latin

FM Stations

88.5	WAMU	National Public Radio News, Talk, American Genre Music
90.9	WETA	Classical, National Public Radio, American Public Radio
96.3	WHUR	Urban Adult
98.7	WMZQ	Country
103.5	WGMS	Classical
105.9	WJZW	Smooth Jazz
106.7	WJFK	Talk, Sports
107.3	WRQX	Adult Contemporary

The Information Highway

Washingtonians are increasingly well-connected and well-informed electronically as well as through print and broadcast media. A recent survey ranked the DC area first in the nation in the number of adults online, surpassing even the San Francisco/Silicon Valley area. The survey cites the reasons: a booming technology industry; the presence of federal government headquarters; and the number of professionals in fields that rely heavily on research, such as lawyers, policy makers and journalists. To help you get connected, or reconnected, here are several names and numbers for the major service providers.

On-Line Services

Several companies offer commercial on-line information services, typically including access to the Internet.

America Online www.aol.com
800-827-6364

CompuServe www.compuserve.com
800-848-8990

Microsoft Network www.msn.com
800-376-3676

Prodigy www.prodigy.com
800-825-5667

Internet Service Providers

In addition to using an on-line service to gain access to the Internet, you can travel a more direct route by connecting through an Internet service provider. With the proliferation of ISPs, there are numerous services from which you can choose. Listed below is a sampling.

AT&T WorldNet	www.att.com/worldnet/wis/ 800-WORLDNET
CAIS Internet	www.cais.com 703-715-1300
EarthLink Network	www.earthlink.net 800-395-8425
Erol's Internet Services	www.erols.com 888-GO-EROLS
GTE Internet Solutions	www.gte.net 800-927-3000
IDT Internet Services	www.idt.net 800-245-8000
MCI Worldcom	www.wcom.com 800-444-3333
MindSpring Enterprises	www.mindspring.com 800-677-7464

Wireless

The Washington area has one of the country's highest rates of cell-phone use. Contact one of these service providers for assistance with data, voice and messaging services.

AT&T Digital PCS	800-462-4463 www.att.com/wireless
Bell Atlantic Mobile	800-922-0204 www.bam.com
Cable & Wireless	800-486-8686 www.cwusa.com
Cellular One	800-235-5663 www.getcellone.com
Nextel	800-639-6111 www.nextel.com
Sprint PCS	800-480-4727 www.sprintpcs.com

FOR INTERNATIONAL NEWCOMERS

Relocating is an anxiety-producing endeavor, as just about anyone who's ever been transferred will tell you. International newcomers have the extra challenge of making the transition to an entirely new country, often with significant language and cultural differences. Being the major world capital that it is, Washington, DC has a vast international community and a wealth of international resources. As a newcomer to the area, the key to a smooth transition is finding the appropriate resources as quickly as you can. For starters, skip ahead in this book to Chapter 11, Resources. You will find a comprehensive listing of foreign embassies as well as contact information for some of the area's ethnic and cultural organizations. Also, throughout *Mastering DC*, foreign language phone numbers are included whenever available. Finally, a variety of services and publications are listed below to help the international newcomer master DC.

Hello! America, Inc.
5310 Connecticut Ave. NW #18
Washington, DC 20015
202-966-9385
www.hellousa.com

This multilingual firm provides personal orientation services for international newcomers. Judy Priven, author and publisher, understands the unique requirements of international relocation. She can provide information on both public and private resources to assist with housing, transportation, shopping, schools, English instruction, medical care, money matters and much more. Her handbook, *Hello! USA*, is available from bookstores, by calling her office or by visiting her website.

The Interchange Institute
11 Hawes Street
Brookline, MA 02146
617-566-2227
www.interchangeinstitute.org

A nonprofit organization, The Interchange Institute focuses on the needs of families and individuals who are in the process of moving from one country to another. Their publications, books and seminars by cross-cultural specialists assist the newcomer in making a smooth transition. Their monthly newsletter, *Newcomer's Almanac*, features information, advice and cultural interpretation for international families, couples and singles. A sampling of topics includes practical tips and thoughtful analysis of American cultures; how cross-cultural transitions affect women, men, children, and families; idioms and language oddities; and what to expect, and what not to expect, from schools and teachers.

The National Council for International Visitors (NCIV)
202-842-1414
www.nciv.org

The NCIV is a national network of program agencies and community-based, nonprofit organizations. They provide professional programs, cultural activities and home hospitality opportunities for foreign leaders, specialists and international scholars. They may be of assistance to international visitors in meeting others with similar professional interests.

Internet Networking
www.expatexchange.com

Expatriates can also find assistance through a community of networks on the Internet. Here you will find a wealth of information and resources on topics such as moving, taxes and finances, jobs postings, doing business abroad and repatriation issues. The website above includes a library of articles and direct links to other useful sources.

Multilingual Services

From maps to tours to everything in between, multilingual services are available to help the international newcomer become familiar with the city of Washington, DC. The Washington Metropolitan Transit Authority publishes Metro Pocket Guides in French, Italian, Spanish, German and Japanese, available at the kiosks in Metro stations. A multi-language visitor map, published by ADC The Map People, comes with text in French, German, Spanish and Japanese. Many attractions such as the White House, Smithsonian Institution, Kennedy Center and Library of Congress offer brochures in several languages. The Smithsonian Institution provides multilingual information at the Visitor Center in the Castle building. The National Gallery of Art offers scheduled museum tours in several languages. And Meridian International Center offers multilingual services at its information desk at Dulles International Airport, plus a telephone language bank. For details call Meridian International Center at 202-667-6800.

Newsworthy Resources

The Washington Diplomat
301-933-3552
www.washingtondiplomat.com

This must-see publication for the international newcomer can be delivered monthly to your home or office at a cost of $25/year (or free at several area bookstores). It is a treasure-trove of news and entertainment information featuring the goings-on about town, all from the multicultural viewpoint—from restaurants and movie reviews to arts, music and the theater.

A number of other resources are available to help you keep abreast of local, national and international news and events. City dailies, national and international newspapers, and magazines are available at various bookstores and newsstands throughout the area. Radio, television and cable networks all have international programming.

Final Note

A good suggestion for international newcomers is to make friends soon; find someone who will serve as your "cultural informant," who will take you shopping and help you learn the subtleties of mastering daily life in the Washington metropolitan area. Many people choose to live in the Washington area because of its international nature, so you are sure to find a willing neighbor or coworker to help you out.

MASTERING DC: CIVIL WAR SITES

The Civil War comes to life at the famous battlefields of Maryland, Virginia, West Virginia and Pennsylvania, where crucial clashes were waged between Union and Confederate forces in the years 1861-65. Much of the historic landscape is now preserved and visitors can drive, walk or bike through history on these hallowed grounds.

☐ **Visit the Battles of Maryland, West Virginia and Pennsylvania:** Begin at **Monocacy, MD** (301-662-3515), the battle that saved Washington, DC; then it's on to **Harpers Ferry, WV** (304-535-6223), site of the surrender of the largest number of US troops, and **Antietam, MD** (301-432-5124), the bloodiest single-day battle in American history. End the drive in **Gettysburg, PA** (717-334-1124), known for more casualties than any other battle in North America.

☐ **See Virginia's Civil War History:** Begin in Fredericksburg, where the battles of **Fredericksburg, Chancellorsville, Wilderness** and **Spotsylvania Courthouse** are commemorated (540-371-0802). On to the capital of the Confederacy, **Richmond** (804-226-1981), which ultimately fell to the Union. End up at **Petersburg** (804-732-3531), where Confederacy forces were trapped for 10 months and **Appomattox Court House** (804-352-8987), where they finally surrendered. Closer to home, visit National Battlefield Park in **Manassas** (703-361-1339), where the Confederates won major victories in 1861 and 1862.

☐ **Follow a Campaign:** Virginia has driving tours marked by road signs, each following a major campaign in the war, with exhibits along the way. Call the **Virginia Civil War Trails** (888-CIVILWAR) for brochures detailing the routes.

☐ **Experience DC's Civil War:** Take a walking tour of 14 downtown sites and 6 in residential areas. Annotated maps are available from the Chamber of Commerce Visitor Information Center (1300 Pennsylvania Ave. NW; 202-638-DCCC).

☐ **Tour a Museum:** At the **National Museum of the Civil War Soldier** at Pamplin Historical Park (Petersburg, VA; 877-PAMPLIN), take an audio-visual tour and walk the historic Breakthrough Trail. While in Pamplin, tour nearby **Tudor Hall**, an 1812 plantation house that served as a Confederate brigade headquarters during the 1864-65 Petersburg Campaign. In Frederick, MD visit the **Museum of Civil War Medicine** (301-695-1864).

☐ **Go for the Great Escape:** With information from the National Park Service, you can trace the legendary Underground Railroad that helped thousands of slaves escape from the South before and during the Civil War. The Washington area has 22 designated sites, including the **Metropolitan AME Church** (1518 M St. NW), a railroad "station," and the cemetery at **Mount Zion United Methodist Church** (2600 Q St. NW), where fleeing slaves were reportedly hidden in a burial vault.

☐ **Remember the Sacrifice:** Visit Civil War cemeteries such as **Soldiers & Airmen's Home National Cemetery** (21 Harewood Rd. NW), **Monocacy Cemetery** (Rtes. 28 and 109, Beallsville, MD), the smallest of all the national cemeteries at less than one acre; and **Ball's Bluff Cemetery** (Rt. 15 north of Leesburg, VA), the second smallest national cemetery in the country, where only Union soldiers are buried.

CHAPTER SIX

Shopping

Notwithstanding the emphasis on e-commerce and virtual shopping, the Washington area affords a myriad of shopping opportunities to fit any budget. This chapter clues you into the local shopping scene—with information about everything from buying groceries for tonight's dinner to finding a specialized nut or bolt at an old-fashioned hardware store. In between, you will find details on gourmet and specialty food markets—including ones representing a wide range of international cuisines—as well as outlets for furniture, housewares, and new and used books. Special features of Washington shopping are also described, from the freshest piece of fish to the finest 18th century mahogany bureau. From Frugal Fannies to Neiman Marcus, major clothing stores and their key locations are also listed.

Grocery, Gourmet and Specialty Food Stores

As you would expect in any large metropolitan area, Washington and the Virginia and Maryland suburbs have all kinds of places for groceries and both gourmet and specialty food items. You can shop at any of a number of major chains, as well as at discount grocery stores. Beyond the main stores, there are several gourmet and specialty chains competing for the attention of local residents along with a surprising number of bakeries. Several neighborhoods have food co-ops, usually offering natural foods at reasonable prices and often trading discounts for time spent working in the store. Finally, in keeping with the international flair of the Washington area, there is no shortage of small international markets—representing cuisines from literally all over the world.

Major Grocery Store Chains

For typical everyday groceries and staples for the home, you can turn to the two major grocery store chains, Giant and Safeway. Virtually every suburban community has at least one or the other and most have both. In the District, Safeway is more prominent than Giant, but you can find either one if you look. In addition, there are some "discount" grocery stores, such as Shoppers Food Warehouse and Food Lion. To compete with these somewhat lower-priced stores, the main chains frequently run sales and in-store specials. With good planning, you can save lots on your monthly grocery bill, without having to run around town for the lowest price on each item.

Giant

Giant, one of the two largest grocery chains serving the area, caters mostly to suburbanites. However, there appears to be a renewed interest in the city by major grocery chains, and Giant Food Inc. is among the chains looking to increase its presence in the District. On the horizon is a new site with a large underground parking facility north of the Washington National Cathedral at the Friendship Heights border. The new site is expected to open sometime in 2001.

The Gourmet Giants offer a somewhat greater number of specialty items, although at Giant, "gourmet" usually means bigger, not necessarily better. Giant's Someplace Special, in McLean at 1445 Chain Bridge Rd. (703-448-0800), is truly "gourmet." Every Giant has a salad bar and an ATM. Most of the newer stores also have in-store bakeries, pharmacies and seafood departments. "Special Discount" aisles offer bulk items at low prices.

Safeway

Safeway, which has maintained a major presence in the city, also is looking to expand its operations. Several stores are located in the city and many more can be found in the suburbs. The Safeway in Georgetown at 1855 Wisconsin Ave. NW (202-333-3223), known as a place to meet people and hence called the "Social Safeway," boasts the largest sales volume of any Safeway in the country. The "Secret Safeway" hides away just off upper Wisconsin Ave. at 4203 Davenport St. NW (202-364-0290). Like Giant, all stores offer check cashing and ATMs. There is also a Townhouse store in Dupont Circle at 20th and S Sts. NW (202-483-3908).

LIQUOR LAWS

Each of the surrounding jurisdictions has its own regulations with regard to the sale of liquor. Here is a brief summary.

DC
Privately owned liquor stores; beer and wine available in some grocery stores.

Maryland
Montgomery County: County-owned and operated liquor stores; beer and wine not available in grocery stores. Montgomery is the only county in the entire country that controls the sale of liquor.

Prince George's County: Privately owned liquor stores; beer and wine not available in grocery stores.

Virginia
State-owned and operated liquor stores (ABC liquor stores); beer and wine available in grocery stores.

Gourmet and Specialty Chains

If you are looking for something special and can't find it at either Giant or Safeway, you have lots of other choices. The Washington area offers a large number of specialty shops, including several gourmet and specialty chains. Each of these chains has its own claim to fame, and you will find that many of them foster a great deal of loyalty among their regular shoppers.

Dean & DeLuca

The New York institution, Dean & DeLuca (D&D), has migrated south to Washington. Its flagship location is the Georgetown Market House at 3276 M St. NW (202-342-2500), a historically preserved building that has endured several failed incarnations in years past. Its overwhelming popularity should ensure that D&D will make a little history of its own, with its great selection of gourmet meats and cheeses, fresh vegetables and bakery items. The 30-minute free parking offered to any customer making over $10 in purchases (not a difficult task) makes D&D especially appreciated in parking-scarce Georgetown. D&D has opened two other cafés in DC, in the Warner Theatre building at 1299 Pennsylvania Ave. NW (202-628-8155) and at 1919 Pennsylvania Ave. NW (202-296-4327).

Fresh Fields Whole Foods Market

One of the area's fastest growing chains, Fresh Fields' supermarkets sell "good-for-you foods." The good-for-you list includes organic produce as well as meat, seafood, dairy products, gourmet and vegetarian prepared foods, natural health care products and environment-friendly household goods. Prices lower than at other gourmet supermarkets will please your wallet. In early 1996, Fresh Fields opened its first DC store in Tenleytown at 4530 40th St. NW (202-237-5800), where one-hour parking validation is available. There is another DC location, in Georgetown at 2323 Wisconsin Ave. NW (202-333-5393), and plans include a store at 1440 P St. NW in 2000 with other sites to follow. In Maryland there are stores in Rockville at 1649 Rockville Pike (301-984-4880) and Bethesda at 5225 River Rd. (301-984-4860). In Virginia, you will find Fresh Fields in Tysons Corner at 7511 Leesburg Pike (703-448-1600), Springfield at 8402 Old Keene Mill Rd. (703-644-2500), Annandale at 6548 Little River Tpk. (703-914-0040), Vienna at 143 E. Maple Ave. (703-319-2000), Arlington at 2700 Wilson Blvd. (703-527-6596) and in Reston's Plaza America at 1160 Plaza America Dr. (703-736-0600). Plans are in the works to add even more Fresh Fields markets around the metropolitan area.

Sutton Place Gourmet

Sutton Place Gourmet specializes in the exotic and the esoteric. This chain flies in produce daily from all over the world. While only the very well-off can afford to buy all of their groceries here, Sutton Place is great for picking up special ingredients, coffees, cheeses, meats and fish. Sutton Place has two stores in Northwest DC, at 3201 New Mexico Ave. (202-363-5800) and at 4872 Massachusetts Ave. (202-966-1740). There is one in Bethesda at 10323 Old Georgetown Rd. (301-564-3100); and three in Virginia, in Old Town Alexandria at 600 Franklin St. (703-549-6611), in McLean at 6655 Old Dominion Dr. (703-448-3828) and in Reston at 11860 Spectrum Center (703-787-4888).

Trader Joe's

Trader Joe's, a California-based gourmet food store and relative newcomer to the area, features unique foods and beverages at affordable prices. Stores are located

ETHNIC FOOD STORES

Americana Market (Latin American)
8541 Piney Branch Rd., Silver Spring
301-495-0864
6128-30 Columbia Pike, Falls Church
703-671-9625

Asian Foods (Thai)
2301 University Blvd. E., Wheaton
301-933-6071

Daruma (Japanese)
Talbot Center, 1049 Rockville Pike, Rockville
301-738-1042
6931 Arlington Rd., Bethesda
301-654-8832

Eden Supermarket (Vietnamese)
6763 Wilson Blvd., Falls Church
703-532-4950

Eko Food Market (West African)
6507 Annapolis Road, Landover Hills
301-341-5050

German Gourmet
7185 Lee Hwy., Falls Church
703-534-1908

Indian Spices and Gifts
3901 Wilson Blvd., Arlington
703-522-0149

Litteri's Italian Grocery
517 Morse St. NE
202-544-0183

Lucky World (Korean)
3109 Graham Rd., Falls Church
703-641-8585

Maxim (Chinese)
460 Hungerford Dr., Rockville
301-279-0110
640 University Blvd. E., Silver Spring
301-439-0110

Mediterranean Bakery (Middle Eastern)
352 S. Pickett St., Alexandria
703-751-1702

Merkato Market (Ethiopian)
2116 18th St. NW
202-483-9499

Red Apple Market (West Indian)
7645 New Hampshire Ave., Langley Park
301-434-1810

Russian Gourmet
1396 Chain Bridge Rd., McLean
703-760-0680

Yekta Market (Persian)
1488-A Rockville Pike, Rockville
301-984-1190

in Maryland at 12268H Rockville Pike (301-468-6656) and 6831 Wisconsin Ave. in Bethesda (to open in 2000). Virginia locations include Bailey's Crossroads, 5847 Leesburg Pike (703-379-5883); Fairfax, 9464 Main St. (703-764-8550); and 7514 Leesburg Turnpike (703-288-0566). You can learn more about the store, its additional sites as it expands in the area, and its products at www.traderjoes.com.

Bakeries

Many Washingtonians get their daily bread—and pastries, muffins, cakes and pies—at one of the many relatively new bakeries in the area. Some of the bakeries also offer fresh-brewed coffee and café tables where you can gather with friends for a delicious break.

Breads Unlimited

The owner of Breads Unlimited at 6914 Arlington Rd. in Bethesda (301-656-2340) oversees the making of his sourdough bread like a brew master caring for his beers. In addition, all the two dozen different breads baked there are fat and cholesterol free. A second location, called the New Yorker Bakery at 8313 Grubb Rd. in Silver Spring (301-585-8585), makes its fresh bagels in front of an appreciative audience.

Corner Bakery

The Corner Bakery, a bistro-style bakery and café chain, has bakeries throughout the area. The original site, located at Tysons Galleria at 2001 International Drive, shares an entrance with Maggiano's Little Italy restaurant. It offers more than 20 European-style hearth-baked breads. In addition, it has a cafeteria with salads, soups, sandwiches, hot pasta dishes, pizza and desserts. Additional sites are located at Union Station, 50 Massachusetts Ave. NE (202-371-8811); the National Press Building at 14th and F Sts. NW (202-662-7400); 5331 Wisconsin Ave. NW (202-237-2200); and Montgomery Mall, Bethesda (301-469-0600). More stores are planned for the metro area, so watch for openings near you.

Firehook Bakery and Coffee House

In keeping with the traditional feel of its Old Town Alexandria neighborhood, the Firehook Bakery and Coffee House at 106 North Lee St. (703-519-8020) bakes its breads in a 17-foot-diameter wood-burning oven. The bread is baked with a thick crust much like bread was made 100 years ago. Other special features include twice-monthly poetry readings and complete breakfasts on weekends with quiche, French toast, fresh juice and Italian sodas. The original Old Town location is complemented by three shops in DC, at 1909 Q St. NW in Dupont Circle (202-588-9296), 912 17th St. NW (202-429-2253) and 3411 Connecticut Ave. NW (202-362-2253).

Heidelberg Pastry Shop

Located at the intersection of Lee Hwy. and N. Culpeper St., Arlington (703-527-8394), this popular spot specializes in German baked goods. Regular bakery offerings include delicious strudels, and pastry made with marzipan; seasonal items include Christmas stollen, hot cross buns and Easter bread. An added attraction is the deli section which carries German meats, cheeses and sausages.

WHERE TO BUY FISH

Fresh fish is available at the Maine Avenue Wharf, down along the Waterfront at 1100 Maine Ave. SW. You can stroll around the market and view the dozens of different fish literally at your feet—most of the stalls are built into large boats on the water and the trays of fish float just a few inches from the sidewalk. At night, this fish market resembles a carnival or small fair, with bright lights illuminating the rows of open stalls as groups of people stroll around and the fish sellers call out to get their attention. The Wharf is open everyday from 7:30 a.m. to 9:30 p.m.

If you can not get down to the wharf, you can find excellent fresh fish and seafood at other area markets. Try Canon Seafood at 1065 31st St. NW (202-337-8366) and 762-A Walker Rd. in Great Falls (703-759-4950) or Pruitt Seafood, 11th and Maine Ave. SW (202-554-2669). Dean & DeLuca, Fresh Fields and Sutton Place Gourmet, all mentioned elsewhere in this chapter, also have great selections.

Reeves

You only need to know two words about Reeves Restaurant & Bakery—strawberry pie. This Downtown bakery at 1306 G St. NW (202-628-6350) has operated for more than a century and is famous for many products beyond its delicious pies. Reeves also offers a selection of pastries and other baked goods and its two-floor restaurant serves sandwiches and other light fare.

Uptown Bakers

Cleveland Park residents are fortunate to have this bread bakery right in their own neighborhood. From its prolific ovens, Uptown Bakers at 3313 Connecticut Ave. NW (202-362-6262) offers 17 types of bread, including sourdough ficelle, killer toast (perfect for breakfast) and olive bread. They also feature no-fat breads which are excellent.

Food Co-ops—Food for People, Not for Profit

Co-ops are cooperatively owned food stores. In theory, they are owned by their customers, thereby taking away the incentive for profit. While few co-ops in today's economy are truly cooperatively owned, these stores generally do offer lower prices on organic products and bulk foods such as nuts, grains, beans, pasta and flour.

Bethesda Co-op

The Bethesda Co-op at 6500 Seven Locks Rd. (301-320-2530) sells organic and commercial produce, bulk foods, shampoos and household cleaners. Six hours of work at the co-op each month entitles you to a 20% discount. To get there by Metro, take the Red Line to Bethesda and change to a Ride-On bus.

Glut Food Co-op

For over 20 years, the Glut Food Co-op at 4005 34th St. in Mt. Rainier (301-779-1978) has been providing natural food in a not-for-profit setting. On most days, they also have baked breads. To reach the co-op, take the Metro Red Line to Rhode Island Ave. and change to one of several local buses.

Takoma Park-Silver Spring Food Co-op

Takoma Park-Silver Spring Food Co-op at 201 Ethan Allen Ave., Takoma Park (301-891-2667), packs plenty of products into a small space. Discounts are available in exchange for volunteer work. The closest Metro is Takoma Park station, and it's a few minutes' walk from there to the shop.

Uncommon Market

The Uncommon Market at 1041 S. Edgewood St. in Arlington (703-521-2667), a co-op in the true sense of the word, is owned by its 3,900 members. You can also become a part-owner for an investment of $200. Owners receive a 5% discount on their groceries, and a 15% discount on case lots. If you work at the co-op, you can get a further discount—three hours a month translates into an additional 15% off.

FURNITURE

Setting up a new home in the Washington area is easy, thanks to the many choices available for furniture and housewares. You can choose the lower-cost option of buying furniture that you have to put together yourself, or you can buy ready-made furniture in just about any price range. You also have other options, such as selecting from local collections of used furniture, shopping the area and the surrounding countryside for fine antiques, and even renting furniture if you don't want to buy it. In addition to furniture stores, Washington offers a virtually unlimited number of places to shop for housewares and decorative items.

Some Assembly Required

If you are looking to economize on your furniture budget, the "you buy/you build" approach may be just for you. In general, the furniture is relatively simple to assemble and can make for a fun weekend project, especially if you have someone on hand to help out. The largest choices of unassembled furniture are found at Ikea, although you will find other places in the phone book.

Ikea

Most everyone will recommend the warehouse-sized Ikea in Potomac Mills at Exit 156 off I-95, south of Washington. Ikea (800-254-IKEA; www.ikea.com) sells a wide range of home furnishings and is best known for its put-it-together-yourself, Scandinavian-style furniture. If you live in the Maryland suburbs, a more convenient Ikea location for you may be the one at White Marsh Mall (410-931-5400) north of Baltimore at I-95 Exit 67B. Ikea receives accolades for prices, not quality or service. If long-term durability is a concern for you, consider looking elsewhere.

Saah Unfinished Furniture

A long-term fixture on the local landscape is Saah, a great place to shop for solid wood furniture. While you are there, pick up the stains or paints you will need to give your new pieces a custom look. You will find Saah at 811 Hungerford Drive, Rockville (301-424-6911; www.saahfurniture.com); and in Virginia at 5641-F S. General Washington Dr., Alexandria (703-256-5314); 2330 Columbia Pike, Arlington (703-920-1500) and 14348 Jefferson Davis Hwy., Woodbridge (703-494-4167).

Ready Made

For those who want to buy furniture already assembled, many traditional stores can meet your needs. Naturally, major department stores have furniture departments where you can expect to find quality furniture at higher prices. Unless you come across a good sale, though, bargains can be few and far between. If you can afford the time, shop around and watch the newspapers and Sunday circulars for specials.

Scan

While Scan Contemporary Furniture seems to many to be an upscale Ikea, it has in fact been around quite a bit longer. Scan sells some assembly-required furniture at prices competitive with Ikea's, but most of Scan's furniture is well-made, pre-assembled and priced to match. Scan's largest store is in Loehmann's Plaza at 7311 Arlington Blvd (703-573-0100). There is another Virginia store in Springfield (703-644-0500) and Maryland stores in Columbia (410-730-1060), Bethesda (301-656-2900) and Rockville (301-230-9339). Peruse their on-line catalog at www.scanfurniture.com.

Marlo

Marlo boasts that it sells more furniture in the area than anyone else. They simplify their maze-like showroom by organizing each aisle according to style (traditional, contemporary, Italian, etc.). Beware of their expensive delivery and set-up charges—as much as 7% of the total cost of the furniture, before tax. The District store, at 901 Seventh St. NW (202-842-0100), is within walking distance of the Gallery Pl.-Chinatown Metro. Suburban Maryland stores are located in Laurel at 13450 Baltimore Ave. (301-419-3400), in Forestville at 3300 Marlo Lane (301-735-2000) and in Rockville at 725 Rockville Pike (301-738-9000). The Virginia store is in Alexandria at Edsall Rd. and I-395 (703-941-0800). Visit them on-line at www.marlofurniture.com.

RoomStore

The RoomStore has many locations in the Maryland and Virginia suburbs. These furniture centers carry contemporary and traditional styles for living, dining and bedroom areas. Check the *Washington Post* for their frequent advertisements. In Maryland, the RoomStore is at 4350 Branch Ave. in Marlow Heights (301-423-5464), at 7970 Annapolis Rd. in New Carrollton (301-577-9500) and at 1150 Rockville Pike in Rockville (301-762-6164). Virginia residents can shop at 7031 Columbia Pike in Annandale (703-941-1800).

Other Options

A popular housewares store in the area, **Crate & Barrel**, features bedroom, dining and living room furniture on the second level of their store at 4820 Massachusetts Ave. NW (202-364-6500 for its Furniture Dept.). The **Container Store** specializes in home office furniture, as well as storage systems for the entire home including the kitchen and closets. Stores are located at 1601 Rockville Pike (301-770-4800) in Rockville and at 8508 Leesburg Pike (703-883-2122) near Tysons Corner.

Antique Shops

Antiques are one of the many hidden treasures of the Washington area. Collected from all over the mid-Atlantic states and the Carolinas, beautiful antique furniture and collectibles can be found in local shops. The best buys are traditional, early American style furniture and mahogany pieces from the 1930s and 1940s. You can also find solid oak, cherry or mahogany items—such as bureaus, tables and desks—that have become even more attractive with age. Most antiques are competitively priced, especially when compared to newer, often less-well-made pieces.

Getting the best deals requires time and effort. Be prepared to negotiate, and always turn down the first offered price. Antique shops in the immediate area are generally more expensive than those in the Maryland or Virginia countryside. The farther out you travel, the better the deal. Consider combining antique shopping with a leisurely day trip in the country.

ANTIQUES

Antiques in the Maryland Suburbs

Antique Row
Five city blocks on Howard Ave. in Old Town Kensington
301-949-2318

Olney Antique Village
16650 Georgia Ave., Olney
301-570-9370

Antique Crossroads
Hagerstown, MD
301-739-0858

Emporium Antiques
112 E. Patrick St., Frederick
301-662-7099

Columbia, Maryland Sunday Antique Market
Under the parking deck adjacent to Columbia Mall
410-329-2188

Antiques in the Virginia Suburbs

Thieves Market
8101 Richmond Hwy., Alexandria
703-360-4200

Fairfax Antique Mall
10334 Main St., Fairfax City
703-591-8883

Shops at Laws
7208 and 7217 Centreville Rd., Manassas
703-330-9282

DAY TRIPPING FOR ANTIQUES

New Market, MD
More than 30 individual antique shops within easy walking distance of each other.
301-865-3450

Main Street in Ellicott City, MD
410-461-8700

Savage Mill, MD
301-369-4650

Weaver's Antiques Mall
Sinking Spring, PA
215-777-8535

If you are willing to go as far as some of the small towns in North Carolina or West Virginia, you stand an even greater chance of finding a good piece of furniture at an excellent price—that is where the antique dealers themselves go to shop.

Closer in, you will find that the metropolitan DC area is rich in antiques with both numerous individual shops and several antique malls. In Northwest DC, antique shops can be found on 18th St. in Adams Morgan, along M St. and Wisconsin Ave. in Georgetown, and on Connecticut Ave. starting at Dupont Circle and going north to the Van Ness area. In Maryland, concentrations of antique shops can be found in Kensington, Olney, Hagerstown, Frederick and Columbia. In Virginia, you will find them in Alexandria, Fairfax and Leesburg. Check the Yellow Pages for specific listings. You will also find directories of local antique dealers and announcements about upcoming expositions, fairs, shows and conventions at many shops.

Watch local newspapers for special antique shows at fairgrounds, convention centers, shopping malls, high schools, hotels, armories and churches. The Gaithersburg Fair Grounds in Maryland is noted for its many expositions throughout the year, featuring antiques, furniture, toys and dolls, glassware and other collectibles. Antiques can also be bought at estate or house sales. Check the *Washington Post* Home section on Thursdays or the daily classified ads.

Listed in this chapter are some of the unique antique villages located in historical settings, both nearby and just far enough away to make a memorable day trip. Call ahead to check hours of operation.

Other Options

If you like the low cost aspect of shopping at Ikea but don't want to spend your free time assembling furniture, do not despair. There are several other options for furnishing your home in the Washington area. You can find used furniture at thrift shops and floor samples or previously rented items at clearance centers. This type of shopping can be very entertaining, and with a commitment of time and patience, you will be surprised at what you can end up with. In addition, you can rent just about anything, if that approach suits you better than buying.

Thrift Shops

Thrift shops are another great alternative for the truly budget-minded furniture shopper. The selection can be somewhat erratic and it may take time to find the right bargains. It helps to have a car on these shopping expeditions, because many of these shops do not deliver. Since so many people move in and out of the Washington area, the used-furniture market is large and constantly replenished. Thrift shops near military bases can be a particularly good starting point.

Thrift Shops for Furniture Items

AMVETS
5944 George Palmer Hwy., Landover — 301-925-4668

Columbia Pike Thrift Shop
4101 Columbia Pike, Arlington — 703-521-3110

Fort Myer Thrift Shop
224 Forest Cir., Arlington — 703-527-0664

Goodwill Industries
2200 South Dakota Ave. NE — 202-636-4233

Prevention of Blindness Thrift Shop
900 King St., Alexandria — 703-683-2558

Salvation Army
6528 Little River Tpk., Alexandria — 703-642-9270

St. Coletta Thrift Store
2919 Columbia Pike, Arlington — 703-486-2362

Clearance Centers

Clearance centers provide another option, especially for those on tight budgets. Clearance centers sell discontinued furniture and housewares. **Hecht's Clearance Center** (703-354-1900) in Landmark Plaza, just off I-395 at the Duke St. West Exit, sells furniture, televisions and other housewares. All prices are 20% to 50% below retail. Hecht's has an automatic price reduction policy where prices are reduced 5% every 30 days.

You can purchase used rental furniture at various clearance centers in the suburbs. For the best buys, head over to **Cort's Clearance Centers** at 3135 Pennsy Dr. in Landover, MD (301-773-3369); in Rockville at 11711 Parklawn Dr. (301-468-6443); in Alexandria at 5710 A General Washington Dr. (703-354-2600) and 14130 Sullyfield Cir. in Chantilly, VA (703-818-2678).

Furniture, rugs, and accessories can also be obtained at **Storehouse Furniture Clearance Center**, at 5898A Leesburg Pike, Falls Church (703-379-5327), and **Pier 1 Clearance Store**, 3045 Columbia Pike, Arlington (703-486-8164).

Furniture Rentals

If you know that your stay in Washington will be brief, you may want to consider renting your furniture. Renting prevents many hassles, including what to do with your furniture when you move on. Most furniture rental stores have showrooms. Their salespeople can show you samples and discuss the availability of "packages" and what they might include, and details of price, length of lease, delivery and insurance. Renting furniture creates a pile of paperwork, including a credit application, a lease and insurance papers. Most rental companies require one month's rent as a security deposit and will deliver your furniture within three to five business days. Many places offer student discounts.

Although renting furniture can be enticing, be aware of the pitfalls. Get a quote for the entire price. Unlike rent for an apartment or house, furniture rentals are subject to tax. In addition to this, rental companies often charge for a fire damage waiver. Be sure to include these extras in your budget. If you already have renters' insurance, you do not need to pay the damage waiver fee—just ask your insurance agent to supply you with a certificate of coverage for the full value of the furniture.

Furniture Rental Outlets

Aaron Rents Furniture
5720 General Washington Dr., Alexandria 703-941-7195

Cort Furniture Rental
1100 New York Ave. NW 202-223-9241
2101 L St. NW 202-293-9400
5710 A General Washington Dr., Alexandria 703-354-2600

Beds and Futons

Its many outlets and aggressive advertising make **Mattress Discounters** easy to find. This local chain gained its prominence not just through advertising, but from its relatively low prices. They offset their $35 delivery charges by including a free frame with each purchase of a king or queen mattress and box spring. Certain purchases include free delivery within a 20-mile radius of the store. Call (800-666-2344) to find the store nearest you.

Several stores have the same prices as Mattress Discounters, but since they cannot afford the large advertising budgets, they often get overlooked. Salespeople at these stores are always willing to make a deal. The **Market** at 3229 M St. NW (202-333-1234) in Georgetown sells mattresses, futons and carpeting.

Getting a futon rather than a bed can add much-needed room, particularly in an efficiency. Futons come in all sizes and you can purchase the mattresses alone or with a variety of adjustable frames. Washington has several futon dealers with very competitive prices. One of the most popular in the suburbs is **Atlantic Futon** in Tysons Corner (703-893-9125), Sterling (703-709-0075) and Chantilly (703-968-9416). **Ginza** in Dupont Circle at 1721 Connecticut Ave. NW (202-331-7991) sells Japanese-style futons that simply roll out on the floor, without frames. In general, prices at Ginza tend to be slightly higher than the rest, but they do run frequent sales and have the advantage of being in the District close to a Metro station. While in the District, check out **Futons by Z** at 2130 P St. NW (202-833-3717).

Discount Department Stores

Wards (formerly Montgomery Ward) is changing its strategy and offering trendy apparel and home furnishings, and renovating many of its stores nationwide—including several locally. While they do not have a store in the District, there is one in Wheaton at 11160 Veirs Mill Rd. (301-468-5300), and others in Falls Church at 6100 Arlington Blvd. (703-241-8700) and in Springfield Mall (703-922-3500). For a full list of their sites, consult the telephone directory or visit their website at www.wards.com.

Wal-Mart made its grand entrance into the Washington area in 1992. Since the opening of the first Wal-Mart in Easton, MD at 8155 Elliot Rd. (410-819-0140), many stores have opened around the area including ones in Waldorf at 11930 Acton Lane (301-705-7070), Hagerstown at 1650 Wesel Blvd. (301-714-1373), Fairfax at 13059 Fair Lakes Blvd. (703-631-9450), Manassas at 7412 Stream Walk Lane (703-330-5253), Leesburg at 950 Edwards Ferry Rd. (703-779-0102) and Woodbridge at 14000 Worth Ave. (703-497-2590).

Housewares

Bed, Bath & Beyond in Bailey's Crossroads at Rt. 7 and Columbia Pike (703-578-3374) sells everything you could want for your kitchen, bathroom and bedroom at reasonable prices. The quality of their merchandise is also superb. The Metro does not stop anywhere nearby, so you will need to get there by car or Metrobus. Marylanders can shop at their location at 1519 Rockville Pike (301-770-4330).

Crate & Barrel carries well-designed and colorful housewares, plus lots of kitchen gadgets. You will find them in DC at 4820 Massachusetts Ave. NW (202-264-6100) and in Bethesda at 7101 Democracy Blvd. (301-365-2600). In Virginia, Crate & Barrel has locations at 1100 Hayes St. in Arlington (703-418-1010) and in Tysons Corner Center in McLean (703-847-8555).

Pier 1 Imports sells housewares primarily, but they do carry some furniture items. In particular they feature dining room furniture, and you will find a number of wicker and rattan items as well. Pier 1 has numerous stores throughout the area so check your telephone directories for the location most convenient to you. A few of their addresses include 4477 Connecticut Ave. NW in the District (202-537-5053), 6801 Wisconsin Ave. in Chevy Chase (301-657-9196) and 7253 Arlington Blvd. in Falls Church (703-573-1931).

Potomac Mills Outlet Mall (800-VA-MILLS) in Woodbridge, VA was designed to resemble a main street scene with over 200 stores from which to choose. There are over 25 stores in the home furnishing category alone.

G Street Fabrics at 11854 Rockville Pike (301-231-8998) won't disappoint if you are in the market for home furnishing fabrics and books on decorating.

Hardware and Appliance Stores

Once the furniture is in place, a trip to the hardware store is often the next step in making your home—whether house or apartment—more livable. Hardware stores are few and far between in DC, but are readily available in the suburbs. In the Metropolitan area, you have major chains as well as neighborhood independent stores—some of which are fine reminders of simpler times gone by.

The Big Chains

After 88 years in business, the Largo-based chain, Hechinger, closed its doors in 1999, leaving Home Depot and Lowe's as the two major chains in the area. Both offer wide selections of hardware and appliances as well as lumber, and in some cases, even things like kitchen and bathroom cabinets and lawn furniture. Other popular national chain stores, such as Circuit City and Best Buys, can be found in shopping centers throughout the area. Read here about the bigger chains and check the Yellow Pages for locations and other options near you.

Home Depot

District residents must travel to either Maryland or Virginia to shop at a Home Depot. In Maryland, stores can be found in Gaithersburg at 15740 Shady Grove Rd. (301-330-4900), in Oxon Hill at 6003 Oxon Hill Rd. (301-839-9600) and in Silver Spring at 2330 Broadbirch Dr. (301-680-3500). Virginia Home Depots are found in Alexandria at 400 Pickett St. (703-823-1900), in Fairfax at 12275 Price Club Plaza (703-266-9800), in Merryfield at 2815 Merrilee Dr. (703-205-1245) and in Sterling at 46261 Cranston Way (703-444-2900).
As planned expansion continues, Home Depot stores are moving into some of the former Hechinger sites. Check the phone book for additional sites.

Lowe's

Like Home Depot, Lowe's Home Improvement stores are located in the outlying areas and are less convenient to DC residents. The near-in stores are at 205 Kentlands Blvd. in Gaithersburg, MD (301-208-0400), and at 6750 Richmond Hwy. in Alexandria, VA (703-765-8011). Addresses of other sites in Maryland and Virginia can be located at their website at www.lowes.com.

The Independents

In addition to the chains and discount stores, there are many small, independent hardware stores. Typically, these stores have smaller collections than the much larger stores, but the independents can surprise you with their compact storage and knowledgeable staff. If you live near one of these, be sure to stop by to see for yourself.

Bray and Scarff

If you are looking for appliances, contact Bray and Scarff. They can assist you with kitchen appliances, washers, dryers and air conditioners from major manufacturers. You'll find them in Maryland at 7924 Wisconsin Ave., Bethesda (301-654-4150); 831 Rockville Pike (301-251-6150) and 11950 Baltimore Ave., Beltsville (301-470-0065). In Virginia, stores are located at 11015 Lee Hwy., Fairfax (703-385-6713); 8486 Tyco Rd., Vienna (703-734-8780); 5715 Lee Hwy., Arlington (703-534-2800); and at 6733 Richmond Hwy. and 5601 General Washington Dr. in Alexandria (703-941-7320).

Candey Hardware at 1210 18th St. NW (202-659-5650) has been dispensing its goods since the beginning of the 20th century and retains the original musty charm just to prove the point. This store's location is ideal for those working in and near Dupont Circle and Downtown. **Frager's Hardware** at 1115 Pennsylvania Ave. SE (202-543-6157) serves the Hill.

Strosnider's Hardware, in Bethesda at 6930 Arlington Rd.(301-654-5688) and in Potomac at 10110 River Rd. (301-299-6333), offers all the usual items, from lawn and garden to electrical and housewares. There is also a **Strosnider's Kemp Mill Paint and Hardware** in Silver Spring at 1386 Lamberton Dr. (301-593-5353), but it is unrelated to the one in Bethesda. **Zimmerman and Sons Hardware** is located at 8860 Brookville Rd. (301-585-5200) in Silver Spring and at 3801 Sandy Spring Rd. (301-421-1900) in Burtonsville.

Restoration Hardware, a combination hardware store and Crate & Barrel, provides a unique shopping experience for both men and women. You are as likely to find traditional tools and gadgets from your father's hardware store as books, herbs and flowers for your bath, and even gourmet ginger ale. Items are cleverly labeled with witty descriptions created by the store's founder. Restoration

Hardware can be found at 1222 Wisconsin Ave. NW (202-652-2771; www.restorationhardware.com), at 614 King St. in Alexandria (703-299-6220) and at 1961 Chain Bridge Rd. in McLean (703-821-9655).

Residents of Arlington can visit their own **Virginia Hardware** at 2915 Wilson Blvd. (703-522-3366), within sight of the Clarendon Metro. In Alexandria, **Smitty's Servistar** at 8457 Richmond Hwy. (703-780-7800) houses a huge lumber yard and will deliver.

Computer and Electronic Equipment

Many newcomers don't consider themselves moved in until the computer is turned on and the stereo system is tuned in. Major chains and independent retailers in the area will help you get your life back, or at least get you plugged back in.

Computer Equipment

Computers; they aren't just for geeks anymore. Make your way to one of the multitude of high-tech stores in the area where everyone from grandparents to toddlers are checking out the latest in computer technology. And don't let inexperience stop you—many stores offer technical services and training classes to speed up your learning curve. For the computer-literate newcomer, consider yourself pointed in the right direction.

Best Buy

In Maryland, stores are at 15750 Shady Grove Rd., Gaithersburg (301-990-8839); 14160 Balto Ave., Laurel (301-497-1890) and 1200 Rockville Pike, Rockville (301-984-1479). Virginia locations are at 1201 S. Hayes St., Arlington (703-414-7090); 13058 Fairlakes Pkwy, Fairfax (703-631-3332); 6201 Arlington Blvd., Falls Church (703-538-1190); 1861 Fountain Dr., Reston (703-787-3760) and 6555 Frontier Dr., Springfield (703-922-4980).

CompUSA

You'll find Maryland locations at 500 Perry Pkwy. in Gaithersburg (301-947-0001) and 1776 E Jefferson in Rockville (301-816-8963); and Virginia locations at 5901 Stevenson Ave. in Alexandria (703-212-6610), 8357 Leesburg Pike in Vienna (703-821-7700) and 14427 Potomac Mills Rd. in Woodbridge (703-492-6262).

Erol's TV & PC

Erol's stores are at 15813 S. Frederick Ave. in Rockville (301-548-9800) and at 7921 Woodruff Court in Springfield (703-321-8000).

Micro Center

Micro Center is located at 3089 Nutley St. in Fairfax (703-204-8400).

Stereo Equipment

Circuit City and Myer-Emco are the two biggest chains in the area. They are prepared to take care of your complete audio needs, from woofers and tweeters to tuners and receivers, and more.

Circuit City

Maryland stores are at 11011 Balto Ave. in Beltsville (301-595-0166), Wheaton Plaza in Wheaton (301-946-1580), 845 Rockville Pike in Rockville (301-881-4581) and 2009 Brightstar Rd. in Landover (301-386-5020). Virginia locations include 7039 Old Keene Mill Rd. in Springfield (703-912-9105), Circuit City Express at 2001 International Dr. at Galleria Tysons II (703-893-4664) and Circuit City Super Store at 7039 Old Keene Mill Rd. (703-912-9105).

Myer-Emco

Myer-Emco has one store in the District at 2241 Wisconsin Ave., NW in Georgetown (202-342-9200). In Maryland, stores can be found at 11611 Old Georgetown Rd. in Rockville (301-468-2000), 2-B Bureau Dr. in Gaithersburg (301-208-2100) and 11000 Balto Ave. in Beltsville (301-595-7900). Virginia locations are at 3511 Carlin Springs Rd. in Bailey's Crossroads (703-379-8800), 8138 Watson St. in McLean (703-893-0700) and 12300 Price Club Plaza Dr. in Fairfax (703-803-9400).

BOOKSTORES

In recent years, a kind of 'literature and latté' culture has taken root in the Washington area, centered around a growing number of quality bookstores both large and small. You will find the new breed of giant booksellers, including Barnes & Noble, Borders and Super Crown, many of which also offer coffee bars and music departments. Smaller bookstores, often featuring specialized collections, and a number of used book outlets are also popular spots for shopping, idle browsing and meeting up with friends. In addition, you can almost always find a book signing or reading to attend. Such events are publicized twice a month in the Sunday Book World section of the *Washington Post.*

Barnes & Noble has many superstores in the area. The one at the corner of M and Jefferson Sts. in Georgetown (202-965-9880) is a three-story facility complete with cathedral ceiling, 220,000 volumes and an espresso coffee bar featuring Starbucks coffee. Other stores are located at 4801 Bethesda Ave. in Bethesda (301-986-1761), at 6201 Arlington Blvd. (703-536-0774) in Seven

Corners, at 3651 Jefferson-Davis Hwy. (703-299-9124) in Alexandria and at 1851 Fountain Dr. in Reston (703-437-9490). You can shop at Barnes and Noble on the Web at www.bn.com.

Borders Books and Music attracts the serious reader and music lover, with a tremendous selection of more esoteric titles, while still providing all the broadly popular items found elsewhere. Borders shops also have cafés in which to sit and enjoy your recent purchases. Their Downtown store is at 1801 L St. NW (202-466-4999). The Rockville store (301-816-1067) is in White Flint Mall; other Maryland stores include Gaithersburg Square (301-921-0990), in Columbia at 9501 Snowden Square (410-290-0062) and in Bowie at 4420 Mitchellville Rd. (301-352-5560). Northern Virginia residents are served by stores in Arlington at 1201 Hayes St. (703-418-0166); Baileys Crossroads, where Rt. 7 and Columbia Pike meet (703-998-0404); and Borders Books in Vienna is at 8311Leesburg Pike (703-556-7766). The Borders Website is at www.borders.com.

A subsidiary of Barnes and Noble, **B. Dalton** is the nation's number one mall-based bookseller. You will also find **Waldenbooks** stores, operated by Borders, located in many shopping malls. Each has numerous sites throughout the area and, to a lesser degree, so do **Crown** and **Super Crown** (www.crownbooks.com). Check the phone book for the location most convenient to you.

Olsson's Books and Records, a smaller local chain, sells books and music side by side in each store. Olssons has seven locations—Georgetown at 1239 Wisconsin Ave. NW (202-338-9544), Dupont Circle at 1307 19th St. NW (202-785-1133), Downtown at 1200 F St. NW (202-347-3686) and 418 7th St. NW (202-638-7610); Bethesda at 7647 Old Georgetown Rd. (301-652-3336); and 2111 Wilson Blvd. (703-525-4227) and Old Town Alexandria at 106 S. Union St. (703-684-0077). They also have a mail order department (202-337-8084).

At 221 Pennsylvania Ave. SE, on Capitol Hill, **Trover Books** (202-547-2665) carries a complete line of Penguin titles and a terrific variety of magazines. Other Trover locations are at 1031 Connecticut Ave. NW (202-659-8138) and at 1706 G St. NW (202-789-2290).

Chapters Literary Bookstore at 1512 K St. NW (202-347-5495) emphasizes personal service to the serious reader. You won't find coffee drinks, CDs or mass-market commercial titles here. What you will find, however, is serious literary work—some of the best written books in all fields. They will order any book you want and have become one of the main stops for visiting authors, with readings several times each week.

Not far away, at 1911 Eye St. NW, **Franz Bader Bookstore** (202-337-5440) offers an impressive collection of books on art—everything from fine art to graphic and industrial art, and architecture.

VIDEOS

The area has no shortage of places to rent videotapes and discs. **Blockbuster** (www.blockbuster.com) is, of course, the largest and most well known, and **Hollywood Video** (www.hollywoodvideo.com) is another popular spot. You'll find them both in the Yellow Pages, or locate a store near you through their websites. Increasingly, the independent ("indie") and foreign filmmakers are catering to the local video rental crowd. Film aficionados craving something other than the latest Hollywood releases may want to visit some of the area's specialized stores. The owners and managers are often veteran movie lovers, with a more-than-passing interest in film. Not surprisingly, they have something special to offer people with the same interests. Here are a few:

Independent
Potomac Video
3418 Connecticut Ave. NW
202-362-6695

Video Americaine
6925 Laurel Ave.,
Takoma Park
301-270-4464

Video Vault
323 Washington St.,
Alexandria
703-549-8848
www.videovault.com

African and African-American
Sankofa Video and Book Store
2714 Georgia Ave. NW
202-234-4755

Asian
Lucky Laurel Video Shop
14222 Cherry Lane Ct.,
Laurel
301-470-3656

See Man Din Inc.
4316 Markham St.,
Annandale
703-256-7037

Thai-Asian Tape
2318 Price Ave.,
Wheaton
301-942-4433

French
Version Français
4822 Saint Elmo Ave.,
Bethesda
301-654-2224
www.francevision.com

Indian
The Bombay Store
7033 Brookfield Plaza,
Springfield
703-569-5777

Subzi Mandi
757 Hungerford Dr.,
Rockville
301-424-8220

Spanish
Estrella Del Sur Spanish Video
3339 Glen Carlyn Dr.,
Falls Church
703-931-9051

Luna and Children Video
3064 Mount Pleasant St. NW
202-588-5862

Book lovers will want to check out **Politics and Prose** at 5015 Connecticut Ave. NW (202-364-1919; politics-prose.com). This unique bookstore and coffee house presents a new guest author for free-of-charge book readings and signings, almost on a nightly basis.

Dupont Circle's top bookstore is **Kramerbooks & Afterwords** at 1517 Connecticut Ave. NW (202-387-1400). Kramerbooks is a good, all-purpose bookstore with strong selections in the current and paperback fiction sections. Just as attractive is the two-tier café located in the rear, and the newer bar and small art gallery in the recent addition. Offering everything from coffee, tea and drinks to sandwiches, full dinners and brunch, Kramer's sunny atrium seating and outdoor area provide a relaxed setting to start enjoying your books.

Lambda Rising at 1625 Connecticut Ave. NW (202-462-6969) specializes in gay books and literature. **Lammas**, at 1607 17th St. NW (202-775-8218), focuses on feminist and lesbian literature.

The **Travel Books and Language Center** at 4437 Wisconsin Ave. NW (202-237-1322) fills its shelves with thousands of language books, guidebooks, atlases and history books for the well-informed traveler. Downtown, the **ADC Map & Travel Center** at 1636 Eye St. NW (202-628-2608) stocks up on the obvious, maps—and also has a sizable selection of travel and guidebooks.

Mystery lovers will not want to miss the **Mystery Bookshop** in Bethesda at 7700 Old Georgetown Rd. (301-657-2665) and **MysteryBooks** at 1715 Connecticut Ave. NW (202-483-1600). In addition to wide selections and well-read staff, these stores offer books on tape, games, and other mystery-related items for the aficionado.

Finally, if you prefer to do your book shopping electronically from the comfort of your home or office, log on to **Amazon.com Books** at www.amazon.com. Place your order and watch for its arrival in the mail. While some booklovers are unwilling to sacrifice the intimate, personal bookstore experience by shopping this way, for others, it is a virtual pleasure. The prices are competitive, the selection is outstanding, and the convenience can not be beat.

Used Books

You can economize on books, and sometimes on music, at some of the local used bookstores. These are also great locations for selling books, whether you are moving or just cleaning out your own overstocked bookshelves.

Cheap books and a broad selection mark the **Lantern Bryn Mawr Bookshop** at 3241 P St. NW (202-333-3222). Several features make this store unique and less expensive than most other used bookstores. Most of the books are donated and the store is run entirely by volunteers. "The Lantern," as it is known by its regulars, is a great place to browse, and you can justify all those book purchases as charity—net proceeds support scholarships at Bryn Mawr College.

Capitol Hill Books at 657 C St. SE (202-544-1621) and **Yesterday's Books** at 4702 Wisconsin Ave. NW (202-363-0581) are two of the area's best used bookstores. **Second Story Books and Antiques** features antiques, international art, and used records, cassettes and CDs in addition to used books at its three locations—at 2000 P St. NW in Dupont Circle (202-659-8884), at 4836 Bethesda Ave. in Bethesda (301-656-0170) and at 12160 Parklawn Dr. in Rockville (301-770-0477).

In Wheaton, **Bonifant Books** at 11240 Georgia Ave. (301-946-1526) is a good, general stock used bookstore. An added benefit for bookworms without wheels is its proximity to Wheaton Metro station. **Atticus Books and Music**, at 1508 U St. NW (202-667-8148), is another well-known shop.

Shopping

Shopping and Outlet Malls

While the predominance of shopping centers and malls is in the suburbs, the District has several spots of note. Many of the DC and suburban malls are accessible by Metro. A number of major outlet malls are within reasonable driving distance of the Washington area. Combining a nice drive with a good deal attracts many Washington shoppers. For directions and other information, call the main numbers listed here.

Several area malls are undergoing renovation and expansion, adding new retailers and incorporating such features as state-of-the-art movie theaters and theme restaurants to broaden customer appeal. New mall construction is proceeding at a slower pace, with the most recent addition, Arundel Mills mall, scheduled to open in November 2000. A megamall, Arundel Mills, near the Baltimore Washington Parkway and Route 100 in Anne Arundel County, will be a sister mall to Potomac Mills, which has become Virginia's top tourist attraction since it opened in 1985.

Shopping Centers and Malls

District of Columbia

The Shops at Chevy Chase Pavilion
5335 Wisconsin Ave. NW — 202-686-5335
Metro: Friendship Heights

The Shops at Georgetown Park
3222 M St. NW — 202-298-5577

Mazza Gallerie
5300 Wisconsin Ave. NW — 202-686-9515
Metro: Friendship Heights

The Shops at National Place
1331 Pennsylvania Ave. NW, Suite 1331N — 202-662-1250
Metro: Metro Center

Union Station Shops
50 Massachusetts Ave. NW — 202-371-9441
Metro: Union Station

Maryland

City Place Mall
8661 Colesville Rd., Silver Spring 301-589-1091
Metro: Silver Spring

Lakeforest Mall
701 Russell Ave., Gaithersburg 301-840-5840

Landover Mall
2103 Brightseat Rd., Landover 301-341-3200

The Mall in Columbia
10300 Little Patuxent Pkwy. 410-730-3300
www.themallincolumbia.com

Prince George's Plaza
3500 East West Hwy., Hyattsville 301-559-8383
Metro: Prince George's Plaza

Westfield Shoppingtown Montgomery Mall
7101 Democracy Blvd., Bethesda 301-469-6000
www.montgomerymall.shoppingtown.com

Westfield Shoppingtown Wheaton Plaza Shopping Center
11160 Veirs Mill Rd., Wheaton 301-946-3200
www.wheaton.shoppingtown.com
Metro: Wheaton

White Flint Mall
11301 Rockville Pike, Rockville 301-468-5777
Metro: 1/2 mi. from White Flint, take shuttle to mall

Virginia

Ballston Common
4238 Wilson Blvd., Arlington 703-243-8088
Metro: Ballston

Dulles Town Center
21100 Dulles Town Circle 703-404-7120
www.shopdullestowncenter.com

Fair Oaks Mall
US Hwy 50 and I-66 703-359-8300

Fashion Centre at Pentagon City
1100 Hayes St., Arlington — 703-415-2400
Metro: Pentagon City

Landmark Mall
5801 Duke St., Alexandria — 703-941-2582

Springfield Mall Shopping Center
I-95 (Exit 69-Franconia), Springfield — 703-971-3000
Metro: 1/4 mi. from Springfield, take Fairfax Connector to mall
www.springfieldmall.com

Tysons Corner Center
Rts. 7 and 123, McLean — 703-893-9400
www.shoptysons.com

Tysons Galleria
2001 International Dr., McLean — 703-827-7730

Outlet Malls

Blue Ridge Outlet Center
315 West Stephen St., Martinsburg, WV — 800-445-3993

Chesapeake Village Outlet Center
Rt. 50 and 301 East of the Bay Bridge, MD — 410-827-8699

Potomac Mills
I-95 (Exit 156-Dale City), Woodbridge, VA — 800-VA-MILLS
www.potomacmills.com

Department Stores

Many of the well-known national chains are represented in the area. Listed below is a selection of department stores featuring clothing, and the major malls in which they are located. The listing is not all inclusive, but it will give you some starting points.

Department Stores

Bloomingdale's
Tysons Corner Center — 703-556-4600
White Flint Mall — 301-984-4600

JC Penney Co.
Ballston Common — 703-524-1300
Dulles Town Center — 703-421-6572
Lakeforest Mall — 301-840-0010

Prince George's Plaza	301-270-3400
Springfield Mall	703-971-8850
Tysons Corner Center	703-488-9111
Wheaton Plaza	301-929-5100
Lord & Taylor	
Dulles Town Center	703-430-2800
Friendship Heights	202-362-9600
Tysons Corner Center	703-506-1156
White Flint Mall Shopping Center	301-770-9000
Macy's	
Pentagon City	703-418-4488
Springfield Mall	703-719-6100
Tysons Galleria	703-556-0000
Neiman Marcus	
Mazza Gallerie	202-966-9700
Tysons Galleria	703-761-1600
Nordstrom	
The Mall in Columbia	410-715-2222
Montgomery Mall	301-365-4111
Pentagon City	703-415-1121
Tysons Corner Center	703-761-1121

Discount Apparel

Annie Sez	
Falls Church: 3512 S. Jefferson St.	703-931-6544
Rockville: 12268 Rockville Pike	301-816-2100
Silver Spring: 13875 Outlet Dr.	301-890-3663
Frugal Fannie's Fashion Warehouse	
Herndon: 2445 Centreville Rd.	703-713-6000
Springfield: 5265 Port Royal Rd.	703-321-4800
Nordstrom Rack	
Silver Spring: 8661 Colesville Rd.	301-608-8118
Woodbridge: 2700 Potomac Mills Circle	703-490-1440
Syms	
Falls Church: 1000 E. Broad St.	703-241-8500
Rockville: 11840 Rockville Pike	301-984-3335
Woodbridge: 2700 Potomac Mills Circle	703-497-7332

Membership Clubs

The Washington suburbs offer two super discount membership clubs, Costco Wholesale Club and Sam's Club. These stores are well suited to large families or group houses. The attractive bulk prices can lead shoppers to over-buy: Watch out for temptation and false economies. Membership usually costs about $35.

Costco Wholesale Club

In Maryland, Costco Wholesale Clubs, formerly Price Clubs, can be found in Beltsville at the intersection of Route 1 and Powder Mill Rd. (301-595-3400), in Marlow Heights at 4501 Auth Pl. (301-423-6303) and in Gaithersburg at 880 Russell Ave. (301-417-1520). Virginia is served by facilities in Fairfax at 4725 West Ox Rd. (703-802-1223), in Pentagon City/Arlington at 1200 S. Fern St. (703-413-2324), in Springfield at 7373 Austin Blvd. (703-912-1200) and in Sterling at 21398 Price Cascades Plaza (703-406-7000). Check your phone book for other sites near you.

Sam's Club

Sam's Club has two Maryland locations, one in Gaithersburg at 610 North Frederick Ave. (301-216-2550), the other in Landover at 8511 Landover Rd. (301-386-5577). In Virginia, there is a Sam's Club in Woodbridge at 14045 Worth Ave. (703-491-2662).

GARDENS, PLANTS AND HERBS

City dwellers with window boxes and container gardens, individuals with outdoor ground gardens, and indoor gardeners will all need sources for plants and gardening supplies. You will find a number of such places throughout the area, including the following which have knowledgeable staff who can serve as valuable resources.

American Plant Food
5258 River Rd. Bethesda (Main Store)
301-656-3311
7405 River Rd., Bethesda (Beltway)
301-469-7690

DeBaggio Herbs
43494 Mountain View Dr., Chantilly
703-327-6976

J. Byron Nursery
9034 Leesburg Pike, Vienna
703-759-7350

Johnson's Flower and Garden Centers
4200 Wisconsin Ave., NW
202-244-6100
10313 Kensington Pkwy., Kensington
301-946-6700
12201 Darnstown Rd., Gaithersburg
301-948-5650
5011 Olney-Laytonsville Rd., Olney
301-987-1940

The Third Day, Inc.
2001 P St. NW
202-785-0107

WEEKEND FARMING: MARKETS, FARMS & ORCHARDS

Looking for fresh fruits and vegetables, cheese, or eggs? Need to get away from the city scene or out of the weekend routine? Want to enjoy the out-of-doors and the bounty of the local harvest? Then farmers markets and "u-pick" orchards are the way to go. Throughout the city and suburbs, loads of neighborhoods have their own markets. Most of the ones listed here feature local produce or produce sold by the farmers who produced it. Good for you—and good for the local farming communities. Go one step further and reap your own harvest. Plan a great friends-and-family outing, or a solitary sojourn, at a local farm or orchard where you can pick the goods yourself. The locations listed here welcome visitors and customers alike.

Weekend Farmers Markets

Washington, DC

Adams-Morgan Farmers Market
Columbia Rd. & 18th St. NW
Saturday, 7:30 am to 1:00 pm
Starts in early June

Eastern Market Outdoor Farmers Market
225 7th St. SE
Saturday & Sunday, 9:00 am to 4:00 pm
All year

Freshfarm Market
20th St. & Massachusetts Ave. NW
Sunday, 9:00 am to 1:00 pm
From early May to mid-December

New Morning Farm Markets
35th & Newark Sts. NW
Saturday, 11:15 am to 1:30 pm
Both begin in early June

Maryland

Bowie Mainstreet Farmers Market
15200 Annapolis Rd.
Sunday, 9:00 am to noon
From late May to late October

Kensington Farmers Market
At the train station on Howard Ave.
Saturday, 8:00 am to noon
From mid-May to late October

Montgomery Farm Women's Co-op Market
7155 Wisconsin Ave., Bethesda
Saturday, 7:00 am to 3:00 pm
All year

Rockville Farmers' Market
Rockville Town Center
Saturday, 9:00 am to 1:00 pm
From early June to late October

Silver Spring Farmers Market
Fenton St. & Silver Spring Ave.
Saturday, 7:00 am to 1:00 pm
From mid-May to late October

Takoma Park Farmers Market
Laurel Ave. between Carroll & Eastern Aves.
Sunday, 10:00 am to 2:00 pm
From mid-April to mid-December

Wheaton Farmers Market
Blueridge Ave. & Elkin St.
Sunday, 8:00 am to 1:30 pm
From mid-June to late October

Virginia

Burke Centre Farmers Market
Roberts Rd. & Burke Center Pkwy.
Saturday, 8:00 am to noon
From early May to late October

Columbia Pike Farmers Market
Edgewood St. & Columbia Pike, Arlington
Sunday, 10:00 am to 2:00 pm
From early May to early November

Del Ray Farmers Market
Mt.Vernon & Oxford Aves., Alexandria
Saturday, 8:00 am to noon
From late May to late November

Old Town Fairfax Farmers Market
Crestar Bank parking lot, between 4029 Chain Bridge Rd. & 4020 University Dr.
Saturday, 8:00 am to 1:00 pm
From early May to late October

Reston Farmers Market
Lake Anne Plaza, N. Shore Dr.
Saturday, 8:00 am to noon
From late May to early November

Farms & Orchards

Apples, peaches, pears. Berries of just about every kind and color. Vegetables full of farm-fresh goodness. That's what awaits you at these farms and orchards. Ripening dates and availability vary according to the crop and recent local weather. Call ahead to find out what is ready, and enjoy the trip as much as the produce.

Maryland

Becraft's Farm
14722 New Hampshire Ave., Silver Spring
301-236-4545

Butler's Orchard
22200 Davis Mill Rd., Germantown
301-972-3299

Catoctin Mountain Orchard
US Rte. 15 & N. Franklinville Rd., Thurmont
301-271-2737

Darrow Berry Farm
Bell Station Rd., Glenn Dale
301-390-6611

Due-Berry Acres
4319 Norrisville Rd., White Hall
410-692-6251

Homestead Farm
15600 Sugarland Rd., Poolesville
301-977-3761

Johnson's Berry Farm
17000 Swanson Rd., Upper Marlboro
301-627-8316

Larriland Farm
2415 Woodbine Rd., Rte. 94, near Lisbon
301-854-6110

Miller Farms
10140 Piscataway Rd., Clinton
301-297-9370

Rock Hill Orchard
28600 Ridge Rd., Mount Airy
301-831-7427

Virginia

Belvedere Plantation
Route 17, 7 miles SE of Fredericksburg
540-373-4478

Crooked Run Orchard
Business Rte. 7 & Rte. 287 between Purcellville & Hamilton
540-338-6642

Linden Vineyards & Orchards
3708 Harrels Corner, Linden
540-364-1997

Mt. Olympus Farm
US Rte. 1, north of I-95, Exit 104, Carmel Church
804-448-0395

Potomac Vegetable Farms
9627 Leesburg Pike, just west of Tysons Corner
703-759-2119

-Sheila Donoghue

MASTERING DC: THE CHESAPEAKE BAY

Some 200 miles long, with 2,300 square miles of surface area over 15 trillion gallons of water, the Chesapeake Bay is the largest estuary in North America. It is also the most biologically productive, with more than 350 species of fish, shellfish and waterfowl and 2,700 species of plants. The bay starts at Hampton Roads, where Atlantic Ocean salt water mixes with fresh river water from a watershed stretching through Virginia, Maryland, West Virginia, Pennsylvania, Delaware and New York, home to some 15 million people. Get to know the bay, and you'll want to be part of the movement to save it—for future visits and future generations.

☐ **Look for the Light:** See examples of the distinctive architecture of Chesapeake Bay lighthouses in **Havre de Grace, Solomons, St. Michaels** and **Virginia Beach**.

☐ **Live Life on the Water:** Fishing, crabbing, cruising, sailing—for sport or work—it's all about the water. See it in **Annapolis, St. Michaels** or any of the smaller fishing villages.

☐ **Take to the Islands:** Soft-shell crab capital of the world, **Tangier Island** in Virginia's side of the bay is home to a fishing community known for a distinctive accent reminiscent of Elizabethan forefathers. Just across the state line is **Smith Island**, named for Captain John Smith and populated by descendants of the original colonists.

☐ **Get to Know Hampton Roads:** This area includes **Virginia Beach**, the state's largest city with 38 miles of Atlantic Ocean and Chesapeake Bay beaches...**Norfolk**, the second largest city and home to the world's largest Navy base...**Portsmouth**, with the largest collection of historic homes between Alexandria, VA and Charleston, SC...**Suffolk**, peanut capital of the world...and **Chesapeake**, the area's latest boom-town, not far from **Great Dismal Swamp National Wildlife Refuge**.

☐ **Live the Legend:** Visit **Gloucester County, VA**, a land of fields, farms and blue waters, and the place where legend says Pocahontas saved the life of Captain John Smith.

☐ **Tour the Towns:** The Eastern Shores of Maryland and Virginia are key to the history and lifestyle of the bay. Visit **Easton, MD, Cambridge, MD,** or **Chincoteague, VA** to see what life is like on the other side.

☐ **Follow the Fleet:** Once upon a time, a fleet of close to 1,000 Skipjacks dredged oysters under sail in the bay. Fewer than 20 remain, with only 10 still operating. These wooden-hulled, single-masted, shallow-draft vessels, symbol of the bay, are a bittersweet reminder of the days when local oysters were abundant and the health of the bay was taken for granted.

☐ **Visit the Watermen:** Among the many places where the real life of the bay continues are the Eastern Shore Watermen's villages of **Deal Island, Chance, Wenona** and **Tilghman Island**.

☐ **Go Over and Under:** Marking the north and south edges of the bay are **Bay Bridge**, from Sandy Point to Kent Island, and **Chesapeake Bay Bridge-Tunnel,** from Virginia Beach to the Eastern Shore. Each spring, Bay Bridge is closed for the one-day Bay Bridge Walk.

☐ **Become a BaySaver®:** Contact the Chesapeake Bay Foundation (888-SAVEBAY; www.cbf.org) to find out what you can do—at home and on the bay—to protect this critical natural resource.

CHAPTER SEVEN

Food and Fun

*A*s befits an international city filled with residents, visitors and diplomats from around the world, Washington offers a stunning diversity of dining and drink options. One recent assessment found the area's ethnic restaurants represent more than 50 cultures—from soft-shell crabs, ribs and jambalaya to Ethiopian injera, Thai lemon grass soup, Vietnamese Bò-Dun and Jamaican jerk chicken. Of course, wine, beer and mixed drinks are available in many restaurants and all the bars, and beer is also available at the local microbreweries that dot the area. And the opportunity to savor coffee or catch tea time seems to be growing exponentially.

This chapter introduces you to the variety of dining and drink options available—but in the end, it is up to you to explore some of the more than 1,500 restaurants and bars in the greater metropolitan area and to develop your own list of favorites.

RESTAURANTS

Washington's restaurants run the gamut of type of food, style of dining and expense. The restaurants listed here are classified by type of food and represent some of the more popular and better known ones in each category.

American

American food can mean anything from chili to salads to ribs to burgers, and there are several notable eateries specializing in various types of American dining.

Named after President Nixon's noteworthy yacht, the view from the water is just as picturesque at **Sequoia** restaurant, right on the Potomac River at 3000 K St. NW (202-944-4200) in Georgetown's Harbour Place. The menu is varied, and the outdoor seating area is spacious and sublime.

The **Cheesecake Factory** is an outpost of a popular Los Angeles chain, with sites at 5335 Wisconsin Ave. NW (202-364-0500) in Friendship Heights and 11301 Rockville Pike in the White Flint Mall in Bethesda (301-770-0999). Since the Cheesecake Factory does not accept reservations, you should be prepared for a sometimes lengthy wait on a busy night. Be sure to save room for dessert—there are over 30 types of cheesecake available.

Mendocino Grille and Wine Bar at 2917 M St. NW (202-333-2912) has a cooking style and wine list centered around California, as the name suggests.

Hard Times Cafe at 3028 Wilson Blvd. in Arlington (703-528-2233) serves three types of chili—Vegetarian, Cincinnati and Texas—from huge vats behind the bar, as well as a terrific selection of beer. Before you order, ask for a chili sampler so you can choose your favorite. Five-way Cincinnati chili and onion rings flavored with chili oil are two special treats. Hard Times has three other locations—in Alexandria at 1404 King St.(703-683-5340), in Rockville at 1117 Nelson St. (301-294-9720), and in Herndon at 428 Elden St. (703-318-8941).

At **Lulu's**, on the corner of 22nd and M Sts. NW (202-861-LULU), you can choose from a variety of New Orleans fare including po'boys, jambalaya, creole and gumbo. Lulu's is connected to Deja Vu, a popular nightclub and dance spot, so happy hour draws a fairly large crowd. Expect lines on Friday evenings.

American Pub Food

Food experts might dispute the existence of American pub food as an official classification, but it effectively describes a typically American style of eating and drinking establishment. These restaurants are essentially up-scale beer and burger joints and Washington is full of them. While they do not offer much in the way of individuality, they do offer the hungry eater a no-surprises, solid meal at generally reasonable prices. The typical menu includes a wide selection of beer and several different types of salads and sandwiches to go with the variously topped, six- to nine-ounce burgers.

Scattered all across town with clusters in Dupont Circle, Georgetown, Capitol Hill and Alexandria, these restaurants are great places for meeting friends after work. In Dupont Circle, your choices include the **Front Page** at 1333 New Hampshire Ave. NW (202-296-6500) and **Timberlake's** at 1726 Connecticut Ave. NW (202-483-2266). Together in the 1800 block of M St. are the **Sign of the Whale** at #1825 (202-785-1110) and the **Madhatter** at #1831 (202-833-1495). These places are particularly popular for happy hour.

More American pub restaurants can be found in Georgetown. Burgers and daiquiris have put **Mr. Smith's** (202-333-3104) on the map, at 3104 M St. NW. A second location is at 8369 Leesburg Pike, Vienna (703-893-5500). Also on M St. you will find the **Guards** at #2915 (202-965-2350), which looks expensive but is not; **Garrett's** at #3003 (202-333-1033), with good seafood chowder; and **J. Paul's** at #3218 (202-333-3450), which has its own house beer and terrific crab cakes. The **Tombs** at 1226 36th St. NW (202-337-6668), full of crew memorabilia, is a favorite spot for Georgetown students.

A couple of Georgetown establishments have spread out into the suburbs. **Houston's**, in DC at 1065 Wisconsin Ave. NW (202-338-7760), in Bethesda at 7715 Woodmont Ave. (301-656-9755) and in Rockville at 12256 Rockville Pike (301-468-3535), has great ribs. **Clyde's** is just plain popular with locations in DC at 3236 M St. NW (202-333-9180), in Chevy Chase at 70 Wisconsin Cir.

(301-951-9600), in Tysons Corner at 8332 Leesburg Pike (703-734-1900), and in Reston at 11905 Market St. (703-787-6601). Other locations include 1700 N. Beauregard St., Alexandria (703-820-8300) and in Columbia at 10221 Wincopin Circle (410-730-2828).

In the U St. corridor, at 1342 U St. NW, **Polly's Cafe** (202-265-8385) is a neighborhood bar with great food. This small restaurant has some café seating outside, a casual room with tables, and a bar below street level. Polly's offers a selection of sandwiches, burgers, excellent specials and a tasty weekend brunch.

The **Old Ebbitt Grill** at 675 15th St. NW (202-347-4800) attracts the National Theatre crowd and White House staffers. On the Hill, staffers frequent the **Hawk and Dove** at 329 Pennsylvania Ave. SE (202-543-3300). **Bullfeathers** at 410 1st St. SE (202-543-5005), a few steps from the Republican National Club, has half-price burgers on Tuesday nights and scads of staffers every night. A second location is in Old Town Alexandria at 112 King St. (703-836-8088). The **Union Street Public House** at 121 S. Union St. in Alexandria (703-548-1785), with its microbrewery and excellent steak sandwiches, is always on the Washingtonian's Best 100 Bargains. In Bethesda, **Black's Bar & Kitchen** at 7750 Woodmont Ave. (301-652-6278) features Gulf Coast cuisine with an emphasis on seafood and steaks.

The well-known national chain **Planet Hollywood** at 1101 Pennsylvania Ave. NW (202-783-7827) is positioned near several hotels and across the street from the Post Office Pavilion. Inside, movie memorabilia adorns the walls, including costumes from "Planet of the Apes" and the model of the "Death Star" used in "Return of the Jedi."

Barbecue

The Memphis barbecue at **Red Hot & Blue** at 1600 Wilson Blvd. in Arlington (703-276-7427) remains consistently popular. If you do not want to wait in line, you can order from the carry-out store about a mile up Wilson Blvd. Red Hot & Blue has several locations in the area, including Laurel at 677 Main St. (301-953-1943) and Manassas at 8637 Sudley Rd. (703-330-4847). Consult your phone directory for one in your neighborhood.

Three Pigs of McLean at 1394 Chain Bridge Rd. (703-356-1700) serves good hickory-smoked barbecue in very informal surroundings. At **Old Glory**, 3139 M St. NW (202-337-3406), you can choose among seven sauces to season your ribs. Portions for both appetizers and entrees are large and the frosty-mugged root beer helps wash it down. **Rocklands** at 4000 Fairfax Dr. in Ballston (703-528-9663), and its tiny carryout location at 2418 Wisconsin Ave. NW (202-333-2558) in Glover Park, offers an array of delicious smoked meats and side dishes made with the freshest ingredients.

Just Burgers

George Washington University students would be lost without **Lindy's Bon Apetit** at the corner of 21st and Eye Sts. NW (202-452-0055), affectionately called "The Bone." In good weather you can sit at one of the couple of outdoor tables, but it is mostly carry-out. You can order from the same extensive burger menu upstairs at the **Red Lion Pub**. Capitol Hill's **Li'l Pub** at 655 Pennsylvania Ave. SE (202-543-5526) serves huge burgers (about 11 ounces pre-cooked). Departing from traditional sit-down burger places, **Five Guys** at 4626 King St. (703-671-1606) in Alexandria sells its bargain burgers and fries for carry out only. These "guys" have other locations at 6541 Backlick Rd., Springfield (703-913-1337) and 107 N. Fayette St., Alexandria (703-549-7991).

All-Night Diners

If you are prone to the midnight munchies, you have some good options. Georgetown's French café, **Au Pied de Cochon** at 1335 Wisconsin Ave. NW (202-337-6400), is open around the clock. **Bob & Edith's Diner** in Arlington at 2310 Columbia Pike (703-920-6103) offers night owls the regular diner fare—eggs, coffee, waffles, pies, not to mention interesting patrons. You will find a fairly large menu and wonderful desserts at the **Amphora** at 377 Maple Ave. West in Vienna (703-938-7877). Each booth comes with an individual juke box. **Amphora's Diner Deluxe** is located at 1151 Elden St., Herndon (703-925-0900). The old suburban stand-by, **Tastee Diner**, is also open 24 hours a day, seven days a week, with locations in Fairfax at 10536 Lee Hwy. (703-591-6720), in Silver Spring at 8516 Georgia Ave. (301-589-8171), in Laurel at 118 Washington Blvd. (301-953-7567) and in Bethesda at 7731 Woodmont Ave. (301-652-3970).

The **Afterwords Cafe** at 1517 Connecticut Ave. NW (202-387-1462) in Dupont Circle can be a perfect place to go for dessert and coffee any night. On weekends, the restaurant, attached to Kramerbooks, stays open all night. Besides the excellent desserts, the Afterwords Cafe offers a selection of vegetarian and southwestern dishes. The **American City Diner** at 5532 Connecticut Ave. NW (202-244-1949) is also open around the clock on Friday and Saturday.

While not quite 24-hour diners, Diner-X-Press and the Silver Diner chain stay open until the early morning hours. **Diner-X-Press**, at 1101 Clopper Rd. in Gaithersburg (301-330-8700), is part of Bowl America Gaithersburg and is open until 1:00 a.m. weekdays, and 2:00 a.m. weekends. The **Silver Diner** is open until 2:00 a.m. weekdays and 3:00 a.m. weekends. The Silver Diner chain has numerous restaurants in the area so check the phone directory for a site near you.

One-of-a-Kind American

Stop for a meal at the local landmark, **Sholl's Colonial Cafeteria**, at 1990 K St. NW (202-296-3065). It's best known for down-home basic cooking and low prices. Just remember to bring your wallet—it's cash only here as well as at another enduring favorite, **CF Folks Restaurant**. Located at 1225 19th St. NW (202-293-0162), CF Folks offers a lunch special that changes ethnicity daily. This tiny spot is only open on weekdays from 11:45 a.m. to 2:30 p.m. Its menu is limited, but the food will keep you coming back.

Asian

What started as a hybrid cuisine, today's Pan-Asian dishes are fun and flavorful, and usually feature dumplings, skewers, or noodles—especially noodles. This cooking "genre" is on display at several local establishments, which are standing-room-only popular. Some of the best are listed here.

Asia-Nora at 2213 M St. NW (202-797-4860) features New Asian cooking with all organic ingredients, and offers 20 types of infusion teas. Every detail of the food and decor has been attended to, including the handmade dinner plates.

Pan Asian Noodles and Grill at 2020 P St. NW (202-872-8889) and 1018 Vermont Ave. NW (202-783-8899) is a cross between a Japanese noodle shop and a Thai restaurant, serving both spicy and mild noodle dishes.

Teaism, an Asian teahouse at 2009 R St. NW (202-667-3827), is open for breakfast, lunch and dinner. Carefully chosen food to accompany their teas is prepared in their kitchen featuring tandoori dishes and flatbreads. The menu also features sandwiches, salads, soups and rice, with condiments such as chutneys and raita.

The Pan-Asian noodle house, **Oodles Noodles**, has two sites in the area, one at 1120 19th St. NW (202-293-3138) and the other at 4907 Cordell Ave. in Bethesda (301-986-8833). The emphasis here is on Malaysian and Indonesian cooking.

Additional Pan-Asian offerings include **Zuki Moon**, an Asian noodle and grille cafe, located in the George Washington Inn at 824 New Hampshire Ave. NW (202-333-3312). **Raku—An Asian Diner** is located at 1900 Q St. NW (202-265-7258), and in Bethesda at 7240 Woodmont Ave. (301-718-8681).

Chinese

Washington's Chinatown sits between the DC Convention Center and Capitol Hill. The entrance to Chinatown at 7th and H Sts. NW features the impressive Friendship Archway, the largest single-span Chinese arch in the world. The neighborhood highlight is the annual Chinese New Year celebration and parade. Reminiscent of the larger Chinatown neighborhoods in San Francisco and New York, this area has a number of its own special treasures. From the Gallery Place Metro station at Chinatown's entrance, you can walk to **Mr. Yung's** at 740 6th St. NW (202-628-1098), which presents customers nearly 30 different dim sum choices. **Hunan Chinatown** at 624 H St. NW (202-783-5858) has won the *Washingtonian's* 50 Best Restaurants Award for over 10 consecutive years. It offers delicious food, an unpretentious atmosphere despite its white tablecloths, and a friendly staff.

Tony Cheng's Mongolian Restaurant at 619 H St. NW (202-842-8669) allows you to concoct your own all-you-can-eat entrees. You choose from a buffet of fresh meats and vegetables and Tony's chefs grill your dishes right in front of you. On Sunday mornings, Tony Cheng's offers an extensive dim sum brunch. **Tony Cheng's Seafood Restaurant** (202-371-8669) is upstairs. You can guess its specialty.

City Lights of China at 1731 Connecticut Ave. NW (202-265-6688) prepares Dupont Circle's best Chinese food. It is so good that its patrons quickly become regulars, although passersby can easily miss it as it is located in the basement of a townhouse.

Charlie Chiang's has maintained high quality and prompt service at each of its location as it has continued to branch out into the suburbs. The location at 4250 Connecticut Ave. NW (202-966-1916) has an express lunch counter on the ground floor. Other locations are in the District at 1912 Eye St. NW (202-293-6000) and at 629 H St. NW (202-219-9696). The Virginia suburbs locations are in Alexandria at 660 S. Pickett St. (703-751-8888), in the Shirlington area of Arlington at 4060 S. 28th St. (703-671-4900), in Reston at 11832 Sunrise Valley Dr. (703-620-9700) and in Herndon at 13059 Worldgate Drive (703-469-9118).

Top-of-the-line **Mr. K's**, at 2121 K St. NW (202-331-8868), serves Cantonese Chinese food in elegant surroundings. When the Republicans were in the White House, many Washingtonians went to **Peking Gourmet** at 6029 Leesburg Pike (703-671-8088) because it was one of President Bush's favorites. The restaurant looks modest from the outside; inside, the walls of this brightly lit restaurant are covered with pictures of Washington's notables. Peking Gourmet's primary specialty is Peking duck.

The best strategy when going to **Good Fortune** at 2646 University Blvd. in Wheaton (301-929-8818) is to bring along a group of friends. Its Cantonese menu lists more than 200 dishes begging to be tried. If you make it there for lunch, you will find dim sum being served.

In Virginia, **P.F. Chang's China Bistro** in Tysons Galleria at 1716-M International Drive, McLean (703-734-8996), is a popular restaurant serving tasty and eye-appealing dishes ranging from tame to firey hot. Not far away in Vienna, **Wu's Garden** at 418 Maple Ave. East (703-281-4410) serves authentic dishes made with their own farm-grown produce.

For Chinese food in less than five minutes and under five dollars, served in carry-out containers, try any one of the several **China Cafes**. Three popular locations in the District draw big lunch crowds—1411 K St. NW (202-393-6277), Dupont Circle at 1723 Connecticut Ave. NW (202-234-4053), 1990 M St. NW(202-457-0466) and McPherson Sq., 1018 Vermont Ave. NW (202-628-1350). The daily specials are always punctual and delicious.

For dim sum in Northern Virginia, you have several options. Clarendon's **Hunan Number One** at 3033 Wilson Blvd. (703-528-1177) serves its dim sum daily between 11:00 a.m. and 3:00 p.m. Weekends offer the best selection. **Fortune Chinese Seafood Restaurant** in Baileys Crossroads at 5900 Leesburg Pike (703-998-8888) has a more extensive daily selection. Despite Fortune's large size, lunch hours can be crowded and you may have to wait. **Fortune of Reston** is located at 1428 North Point Village (703-318-8898) and **Fortune of Seven Corners** is at 6249 Seven Corners Center, Falls Church (703-538-3333). In Rosslyn, you'll find **China Garden**, downstairs in the USA Today building in Rosslyn at 1100 Wilson Blvd (703-525-5317).

Ethiopian and Afghan

The first Ethiopian and Afghan restaurants in the nation were established in the District and remain some of the best in the country. You will quickly discover the best choices are in Adams Morgan. **Red Sea** at 2463 18th St. NW (202-483-5000) and **Meskerem** at 2434 18th St. NW (202-462-4100) are right across the street from each other and are rightfully the most popular Ethiopian restaurants in town. For those who have never eaten Ethiopian food, diners eat the spicy stews with their fingers and injera (something like a moist, doughy tortilla). While you might be tempted to ask for a fork, don't do it. It might be considered impolite and it definitely spoils the experience. In Georgetown, you can enjoy Ethiopian cuisine at **Zed's** at 1201 28th. St. NW (202-333-4710). **Addis Ababa** at 2106 18th St. NW (202-232-6092) is known as the Ethiopians' Ethiopian restaurant.

Bethesda's Afghan restaurant, **Faryab**, is located at 4917 Cordell Ave. (301-951-3484). Aushak, the mainstay of any Aghan menu, is especially good here. **Panjshir II** at 224 Maple Ave. West in Vienna (703-281-4183) is a family-owned-and-operated Afghan restaurant. The menu includes a range of beef, lamb, poultry and vegetarian dishes. On first glance, the decor appears to be formal, but the ambiance is actually comfortable and relaxed. The owners wait on customers and are very entertaining. Panjshir's other location is at 924 W Broad St. in Falls Church (703-536-4566).

Also in Virginia is **Afghan**, with locations at 2700 Jefferson Davis Hwy., Alexandria (703-548-0022) and 6271 Old Dominion Drive, McLean (703-734-0909). The menu is small, primarily meat or vegetable kebabs, the bread is baked in a clay oven, and the restaurant is frequented by Afghan families.

French

Washington has numerous French restaurants, ranging from casual to expensive. For casual French fare 24 hours a day, you can eat at **Au Pied de Cochon** at 1335 Wisconsin Ave. NW (202-333-5440). Just off M St. toward the Potomac is another Georgetown favorite, **Café La Ruche**, at 1039 31st St. NW (202-965-2684). This small café right near the C&O Canal serves lighter fare such as soups, salads and sandwiches as well as fruit tortes for dessert. When the weather permits, the tables in the garden can provide a peaceful lunch-time interlude. A favorite spot for many Georgetowners is **Bistrot Lepic**, a small French bistro at 1736 Wisconsin Ave. NW (202-333-0111).

Le Bistro Français at 3128 M St. NW (202-338-3830) boasts fresh seafood every day and specializes in southern French cuisine. Be sure to ask for a sample of their homemade pâtés when ordering. The chef at Cleveland Park's **Lavandou Restaurant** at 3321 Connecticut Ave. NW (202-966-3002) also serves dishes from the popular Provence region in the south of France. Lavandou continues serving to a packed house, despite recently doubling its size.

For French fare with a view of the Potomac, dine at **Le Rivage**, 1000 Water St. SW (202-488-8111). This waterfront restaurant specializes in seafood, but there are many other choices. Outdoor seating is available during warm weather.

For French wining and dining on the Hill, staffers take to **La Colline** at 400 North Capitol St. NW (202-737-0400) or **La Brasserie** at 239 Massachusetts Ave. NW (202-546-9154).

Indian

Just across Rock Creek Park from Adams Morgan and Dupont Circle, two Indian restaurants neighbor each other on Connecticut Ave.—**Rajaji** at 2603

Connecticut Ave. NW (202-265-7344) and **Taste of India** at 2623 Connecticut Ave. NW (202-483-1115). Rajaji will satisfy those who enjoy spicy curries, while Taste of India caters to those who prefer milder Indian food. Also on Connecticut Ave. is the **Bombay Club** at 815 Connecticut Ave. NW (202-659-3727), offering refined dining featuring traditional Indian cuisine with the addition of seafood in a quietly elegant dining room. The **Bombay Palace** (202-331-4200) at 2020 K St. NW features some wonderful vegetarian cuisine and is a good choice if you are considering dining with a large crowd. Near K St., you will find **Aroma Indian Restaurant** at 1919 Eye St. (202-833-4700). In Georgetown, **Aditi** at 3299 M St. NW (202-625-6825) receives high praise for its Indian food. North on Wisconsin Ave., you'll find the upscale **Heritage India** at 2400 Wisconsin Ave. NW (202-333-3120). The elegant dining room is an enchanting background for the feast you will be offered here, from mouth-watering Tandoori meats and curries of all varieties, to vegetarian entrees that are not to be missed.

LOCAL DINING WEBSITES

Dining Web
http://diningweb.com
Free on-line database, searchable by name, address, price range, neighborhood or cuisine.

Washingtonian Online
www.washingtonian.com
Online version of the monthly magazine; includes lists of best restaurants, reader surveys, a calendar of wine and food events, and a place to leave questions and comments for the magazine's restaurant critic.

Digital City Washington
www.digitalcity.com
Electronic database of information about Washington; includes information about restaurants and a link to the National Restaurant Register's Menu-Online, an interactive information service providing actual menus and other restaurant information.

Indian restaurants are no longer only located downtown. More of these restaurants are opening in the suburbs to the delight of those who simply want good neighborhood restaurants. For example, in Maryland, **Tiffin Restaurant** at 1341 University Blvd. East, Langley Park (301-434-9200), is an especially popular place for lunch. Patrons begin lining up before noon to partake of the buffet which includes selections of traditional Indian dishes and condiments. **Bombay Gaylord**, 8401 Georgia Ave., Silver Spring (301-565-2528), is a casual and inexpensive neighborhood restaurant frequented by regulars. Among the choices available to Virginia residents is the **Bombay Curry Company**, 3110 Mount Vernon Ave., Alexandria (703-836-6363), which offers a modestly priced menu, some complex curries and a good Sunday brunch.

Italian

Arguably the best-valued Italian restaurant in the District, **I Matti** in Adams Morgan at 2436 18th St. NW (202-462-8844) prepares fresh bread, gourmet pizza, innovative pasta, roast meat (including rabbit) and seafood in an up-scale, trendy atmosphere. I Matti is a more affordable and casual version of the Downtown restaurant **I Ricchi**, at 1220 19th St. NW (202-835-0459), serving excellent authentic Tuscan cuisine. **Galileo** at 1110 21st St. NW (202-293-7197) caters to those who enjoy making deals over some of the finest Italian cuisine anywhere. Their new Laboratorio Galileo is a glass-walled kitchen and dining area where, for $95 per person and advance reservations, you can watch the chef prepare your meal.

RESTAURANT DELIVERIES

The hectic lifestyle of people living in the metropolitan DC area has been a major influence on the fast-rising industry of "delivering restaurants" directly to your door. The next time you are up against a deadline, or too tired at the end of the day, call one of the delivery services listed below to find out exactly where they deliver, their rates and the restaurants they serve.

A La Carte Express
202-232-8646

Waiter on the Way
301-869-0300

Restaurants on the Run
703-820-1000

Takeout Taxi:

District
202-986-0111

Bethesda and Rockville
301-571-0111

Northern Virginia
703-578-3663
703-435-3663

A.V. Ristorante Italiano at 607 New York Ave. NW (202-737-0550) is legendary in Washington. This restaurant has the quintessential neighborhood ambiance Italian restaurants are known for—Chianti bottles for candle holders, dark red walls and red-checked tablecloths. Its pizza and pasta dishes are terrific and you will definitely get your money's worth, especially on the meat platters.

Downtown dining received a shot in the arm with the spate of building in the area across from the National Archives. One dining addition is **Bertollini's** at 801 Pennsylvania Ave. NW (202-638-2140). Bertollini's also can be found at White Flint Mall on Rockville Pike (301-984-0004).

The three locations for **Il Radicchio**—at 1509 17th St. NW (202-986-2627), 1211 Wisconsin Ave. NW (202-337-2627) and at 1801 Clarendon Blvd., Arlington (703-276-2627)—each has excellent pizza and a unique way of serving spaghetti. After you buy the first bowl, you can refill for free and buy just the sauces. Not far from Il Radicchio is the more refined **Filomena Ristorante of Georgetown** at 1063 Wisconsin Ave. NW (202-338-8800), known for its pastas and seafood.

Paolo's at 1303 Wisconsin Ave. NW (202-333-7353), a trendy, up-scale Italian café, serves delicious pastas, pizzas and salads. If you would like to avoid the crowds, try late lunches or weekend brunches. Paolo's has another location in the Reston Town Center (703-318-8920).

The budget-minded will enjoy Adams Morgan's **Spaghetti Garden** at 2317 18th St. NW (202-265-6665), especially when you can sit out on its rooftop on a warm summer evening. At **Pasta Mia**, 1790 Columbia Rd. NW (202-328-9114) in Adams-Morgan, enjoy the all-pasta entrees while sitting at small tables with red checked cloths adorned with bottles of olive oil.

Farther out, **Da Domenico Ristorante** at 1992 Chain Bridge Rd. in McLean (703-790-9000) receives rave reviews. It is known for its pork chops and clams, and rumor has it that it has the best martinis around.

Family-style Italian dining has gained popularity in the area and is available at two popular, primarily suburban, restaurants. If you are looking for an abundance of food at moderate prices, try **Maggianno's Little Italy** in Tysons Galleria at 1790-M International Dr., McLean (703-356-9000) or at 5333 Wisconsin Ave. in Chevy Chase (301-966-5500). Another very popular family-style Italian restaurant is **That's Amore** with sites at 5225 Wisconsin Ave. NW (202-237-7800); in Maryland at 15201 Shady Grove Rd., Rockville (301-670-9666); and in Virginia at 150 Branch Rd. SE, Vienna (703-281-7777). Both of these chains are expanding, so watch for locations opening near you.

For good pasta and pizza, treat yourself to a meal at the **Red Tomato**, 2030 M Street NW (202-463-9030) and St. Elmo Ave. Bethesda (301-652-4499). The business lunch crowd meets here and it's a good place for the singles social scene.

Japanese

A popular spot for Japanese cuisine is **Perry's** at 1811 Columbia Rd. NW (202-234-6218). Typical of restaurants in Adams Morgan, Perry's offers its diners lots of atmosphere. During the spring and summer months, you can eat your dinner on their rooftop deck overlooking the city.

At the **Japan Inn** at 1715 Wisconsin Ave. NW (202-337-3400), you can sit at a communal table and

SUSHI

Asian Flavor
128 W. Maple Ave., Vienna
703-938-9800

Japan Inn
1715 Wisconsin Ave. NW
202-337-3400

Kaz Sushi Bistro
1915 I St. NW
202-530-5500

Matuba
2915 Columbia Pike
703-521-2811
4918 Cordell Ave., Bethesda
301-652-7449

Spices Asian Restaurant & Sushi Bar
3333-A Connecticut Ave. NW
202-686-3833

Sushi Chalet
4910 Fairmont Ave., Bethesda
301-652-773
323 Muddy Branch Rd., Gaithersburg
301-948-7373

Sushi-Ko
2309 Wisconsin Ave. NW
202-333-4187

Tako Grill
7756 Wisconsin Ave., Bethesda
301-652-7030

Yosaku
4712 Wisconsin Ave. NW
202-363-4453

watch your order being cooked on a grill in front of you. Or, you can reserve a private room, sit at a low table, and be served by a kimono-clad waitress.

Located at 6715 Lowell Ave., McLean, **Tachibana Japanese Restaurant** (703-847-1771) is considered by some to be the best Japanese restaurant in the entire metropolitan DC area.

Tako Grill at 7756 Wisconsin Ave. in Bethesda (301-652-7030) departs from the regular sushi and sake restaurants. Diners can feast on robatayaki (grilled fish, meat and vegetables) and other less common dishes, as well as the more typically Japanese staples (sushi, teriyaki, yosenabe and tempura).

At **Matuba**, 2915 Columbia Pike, Arlington (703-521-2811), and at 4918 Cordell Ave., Bethesda (301-652-7449), you will find a variety of traditional Japanese noodle, meat and fish dishes in addition to their acclaimed sushi.

Kosher

Most of Washington's kosher restaurants are to be found in the area's largest Jewish communities. All of the restaurants listed below are under the supervision of the Vaad of Washington.

The **H St. Hideaway** at 2300 H St. NW (202-452-1161) caters mostly to George Washington University students who are on the Kosher meal plan, but is also open to the public. It serves meat and vegetarian dishes and is open for dinner Monday through Thursday, 5:00 p.m. to 8:30 p.m.

L'Etoile at 1310 New Hampshire Ave. (202-835-3030) is the first Kosher French restaurant in Washington, DC. Reservations with a credit card are required for Friday dinner and Saturday lunch because Jewish law forbids exchanging money on the Sabbath.

Nuthouse at 11419 Georgia Ave. in Wheaton (301-942-5900) specializes in pizza, falafel and salads and is open until 1:30 a.m. on Saturday nights.

The **Royal Dragon** at 4840 Boiling Brook Pkwy. in Rockville (301-468-1922) serves Glatt kosher Chinese food.

Mediterranean and Middle Eastern

In Tenleytown, **Cafe Olé** at 4000 Wisconsin Ave. NW (202-244-1330), offers primarily mezze—small dishes like tapas—and sandwiches. There's also a wine and cheese bar, and an espresso bar.

The **Lebanese Taverna** at 2641 Connecticut Ave. NW (202-265-8681) sits among a row of ethnic restaurants across from the Woodley Park Metro station. Sit outside and watch the world go by as you enjoy excellent food with well-timed service. The original location, usually busy and quite neighborly, can be found at 5900 Washington Blvd., Arlington (703-241-8681).

Bacchus at 1827 Jefferson Pl. NW (202-785-0734) also has excellent Lebanese food. This intimate restaurant is neatly tucked away in the basement of a Dupont Circle townhouse. A second Bacchus, in Bethesda at 7945 Norfolk Ave. (301-657-1722), promises much of the same.

Mama Ayesha's (formerly the Calvert Cafe) at 1967 Calvert St. NW (202-232-5431) is just over the Calvert St. Bridge in Adams Morgan. Venture in to this recently renovated establishment for some very good traditional dishes at reasonable prices.

At **Zorba's Cafe** in Dupont Circle at 1612 20th St. NW (202-387-8555), you can enjoy eating your gyros outside while listening to Greek music played over a loudspeaker. Also in the Dupont area is **Skewers**, 1633 P St. NW (202-387-7400), an enduring restaurant featuring moderately priced kebabs and mezze.

In Bethesda, **Levante's**, at 7262 Woodmont Ave. (301-657-2441) serves authentic food and amazing bread from their wood-burning oven. **Mykonos Grill**, at 121 Congressional Lane in Rockville (301-770-5999), is a branch of downtown's longtime staple, **Mykonos**, at 1835 K St. (202-331-0370). Here you can make a delightful meal by choosing from their wide selection of starters.

ECONOMICALLY EATING

A wonderful resource for the budget-minded as well as the adventurous is the ***Entertainment Guide***. These coupon books (one for Virginia and DC and another for Maryland and DC) offer discounts at hundreds of restaurants, as well as many area theaters and concert halls. The ***Entertainment Guide*** costs $35 (plus $4 s/h if you order by mail), but practically pays for itself with just three restaurant visits. ***Entertainment Guides*** can be purchased directly from the publisher by credit card (703-207-0770). Pick up a copy or write to them at Entertainment Publications, 2812 Old Lee Hwy., Suite 200, Fairfax, VA 22031. For additional information about their services and products, visit their website at www.entertainment.com.

To enjoy a full restaurant experience on a budget, check out early-bird prices. A number of restaurants, especially those in the Downtown theater areas, offer fixed price pre-theater menus, generally available from 5:00 to 7:00 p.m. or until 7:30 p.m.

Kabul Caravan at 1725 Wilson Blvd. (703-522-8394) serves authentic fare in Arlington. Its rather unpretentious exterior disguises the cozy, romantic interior. Also in Virginia is **Aegean Taverna** at 2950 Clarendon Blvd., Arlington (703-841-9494) which offers very good food in a festive ambiance.

Topkapi Restaurant in Fairfax at 3529 Chain Bridge Rd. (703-273-4310) is a Turkish restaurant in disguise. Camouflaged among entrees such as tortellini and prime rib, the menu lists a banquet of tasty Turkish dishes. Topkapi also has restaurants in Ballston Commons (703-525-8468) and at 5801 Duke St. in

Alexandria (703-941-9433). While in Alexandria, try the lavish Sunday brunch at **Taverna Cretekou**, 818 King St., in Alexandria (703-548-8688).

Mexican and Southwestern

For Mexican food, one of Washington's best deals is **El Tamarindo** at 1785 Florida Ave. NW (202-328-3660). El Tamarindo offers cheap (and good) pitchers of margaritas and solid, no-frills Mexican and Salvadoran dishes. In addition to its primary location on Florida Ave., El Tamarindo has two other locations—3015 M St. NW (202-337-9291) and 7331 Georgia Ave. NW (202-291-0525). If you are part of a large group, you should go to the Wisconsin Ave. location.

Lauriol Plaza at 1835 18th St. NW (202-387-0035) makes for the most romantic of any Mexican meal. And prices are a bargain, considering the portion sizes. Besides excellent fajitas, Lauriol Plaza offers a number of offbeat Spanish and Latin American dishes. The same owners manage **Cactus Cantina**, near the National Cathedral, at 3300 Wisconsin Ave. NW (202-686-7222). During warm weather, the tables outside the restaurant are a perfect spot for sipping margaritas and sharing nachos and a delicious salsa. Cactus Cantina tends to attract a younger crowd than Lauriol Plaza.

Austin Grill's bar at 2404 Wisconsin Ave. NW (202-337-8080) serves excellent margaritas making it a popular after-work hangout. The restaurant space is somewhat limited at this location. You'll find a second DC spot in the Lansburgh Bldg., at 750 E St. NW (202-393-3776). In Maryland, Austin Grill is located at 7278 Woodmont Ave., Bethesda (301-656-1366). **South Austin Grill** at 801 King St. in Alexandria (703-684-8969) and Austin Grill in Springfield, located at 8430A Old Keene Mill Rd. (703-644-3111), serve more of the same excellent food and margaritas. Each month, the Austin Grill restaurants donate a portion of dinner proceeds to a local charity. The restaurant and the charity rotate each month.

Enriqueta's at 2811 M St. NW in Georgetown (202-338-7772) serves authentic Mexican food, as opposed to the "north of the border" Tex-Mex version. The brightly painted chairs in this restaurant add to the casual and colorful environment of this Georgetown landmark.

Tex-Mex has been made into big business at **Rio Grande Cafe**. Three extremely popular locations—Ballston, Bethesda and Reston—promise long lines, especially on weekends. Take advantage of their fresh chips and salsa while you wait. In Ballston, Rio Grande is at 4301 North Fairfax Dr. (703-528-3131), just down the street from the Ballston Metro station. The Bethesda location is at 4919 Fairmont Ave. (301-656-2981) and the Reston restaurant is at 1827 Library St. in the Reston Town Center (703-904-0703). **Cottonwood Cafe** at

4844 Cordell Ave, Bethesda (301-656-4844) is noted for its seafood and paella, and is considered more upscale and pricier than the Rio Grande Cafe.

On the Hill, **La Lomita Dos** at 308 Pennsylvania Ave. SE (202-544-0616) serves Mexican food in more typical surroundings. Sombreros and piñatas decorate the small white-stucco dining room. The original **La Lomita** is at 1330 Pennsylvania Ave. SE (202-546-3109).

The tastes of southwestern cuisine are to be found in grand style at the **Red Sage** at 605 14th St. NW (202-638-4444). With its $5 million decor, the Red Sage is a spectacularly fanciful vision of the West. It is under the same ownership as the famous Coyote Cafe in Santa Fe.

Pizza

Over the years, **Armand's** has been recognized as the place to go for pizza. Armand's original pizzeria at 4231 Wisconsin Ave. NW (202-686-9450) serves "Chicago-style" pizza in a casual, family atmosphere. Armand's has now spread throughout the District and the suburbs.

Thin-crust pizza connoisseurs will enjoy **Faccia Luna** at 2400 Wisconsin Ave. NW (202-337-3132), and **Il Forno Pizzeria** at 4926 Cordell Ave. in Bethesda (301-652-7757) and 8941 N. Westland St. in Gaithersburg (301-977-5900). Faccia Luna tops its pies with interesting items such as tuna, eggplant, spinach and pesto. Faccia Luna has two Virginia locations, in Arlington at 2909 Wilson Blvd. (703-276-3099) and in Alexandria at 823 S. Washington St. (703-838-5998). Il Forno bakes its pizza in a wood-burning oven, producing amazing results.

Some locals find that the best pizza in Washington comes out of the wood-burning stove at **Pizzeria Paradiso**, 2029 P St. NW (202-223-1245). The thick, flavorful, chewy crust is truly paradise, particularly when accented by any of the dozen or so fresh, high-quality toppings available. The small dining room fills up quickly, so be prepared to wait for dinner.

Other locals will swear that **Luigi's** makes the best pizza. Luigi's, at 1132 19th St. NW (202-331-7574), is one of the few pizza places in the area that offer a wide range of toppings, including calamari, clam, pineapple and more. Diners can choose to sit inside or in a glassed-in patio out front. Beware of the blue margarita—one is plenty.

Imported from Beverly Hills, the **California Pizza Kitchen** (CPK) not only serves delicious individual gourmet pizzas, but also offers terrific salads to start and desserts to finish. You will find this restaurant located all over town, including 5345 Wisconsin Ave. NW (202-363-6650) and 1220 Connecticut Ave. NW (202-331-4020); in Montgomery Mall at 7101 Democracy Blvd.

STEAK AND BEEF HOUSES

Capital Grille
601 Pennsylvania Ave. NW
202-737-6200

JW's View Steakhouse
1401 Lee Highway, Arlington
703-524-6400

Les Halles de Paris
1201 Pennsylvania Ave. NW
202-347-6848

Max's of Washington
1725 F St. NW
202-842-0070

Morton's of Chicago*
3251 Prospect St. NW
202-342-6258
1050 Connecticut Ave. NW
202-955-5997

Palm*
1225 19th St. NW
202-293-9091

Prime Rib
2020 K St. NW
202-466-8811

Ruth's Chris Steakhouse*
1801 Connecticut Ave. NW
202-797-0033

Sam & Harry's*
1200 19th St. NW
202-296-4333

Smith & Wollensky
1112 19th St.
202-466-1100

*and other locations

(301-469-5090); and in Pentagon Center at 1201 S. Hayes St. (703-412-4900) and in Tysons Corner Center, Lower Level (703-761-1473). Their other locations are too numerous to mention, but can be found in any local phone book.

If you are really hungry, try **Generous George's Positive Pizza and Pasta Place** at 3006 Duke St. in Alexandria (703-370-4303), 7031 Little River Turnpike in Annandale (703-941-9600) and 6131 Backlick Rd. in Springfield (703-451-7111). As its name suggests, Generous George's fare is king-sized—enormous pizzas, huge salads and gigantic pasta dishes. Quality does not suffer from the emphasis on quantity. In the Torpedo Factory Food Pavilion in Old Town Alexandria, you will find **Radio Free Italy** (703-683-0361). "Pizza and pasta with frequency" is their motto and Marconi is the house beer.

While pizza is what put **Julio's**, at 1604 U St. NW (202-483-8500), on the map, this restaurant is best known for its Sunday brunches and happy hours. Brunches are all-you-can-eat and there is plenty to choose from, including, of course, pizza.

Seafood

Seafood lovers in your crowd will want to take advantage of Maryland's specialty—soft-shell crabs. It may be a little disconcerting at first to eat the whole thing—shells, claws and all—but it is a treat not to be missed. For the freshest crab, make a trip to Maryland's Eastern Shore during the summer months. Just hop on Route 50 East and keep driving. You will know when to stop—when you see corner stands along the highway selling fresh crab and other seafood.

If you want to stay closer to the District, go to the waterfront in Southwest (Metro's Green Line to Waterfront). Along Water St., you will see **Phillips Flagship** at 900 Water St. (202-488-8515); and the **Gangplank** at 600 Water St. (202-554-5000); and **Zanzibar on the Waterfront**, an African restaurant with a Caribbean flare, at 700 Water St. SW (202-554-9100). **Le Rivage**, a French seafood restaurant mentioned previously, is also on this street. The **Market Inn**, a long-time DC establishment at 200 E St. SW (202-544-2100), serves fresh seafood daily and is known for its Sunday brunch.

Tony & Joe's Seafood Place at 3000 K St. NW (202-944-4545) is farther up the Potomac in Georgetown's Washington Harbour complex. Some prefer its less expensive sister restaurant, the **Dancing Crab** at 4611 Wisconsin Ave. NW (202-244-1882), at the corner of Wisconsin Ave. and Brandywine St. NW. This restaurant serves all-you-can-eat crab dinners during the summer. During the winter months, the Dancing Crab offers an all-you-can-eat raw bar.

Kinkead's at 2000 Pennsylvania Ave. NW (202-296-7700) is one of the area's more popular restaurants. It specializes in fresh seafood dishes, with inventive flavor combinations and creative presentations. Kinkead's restaurant has two floors—a formal dining room upstairs, and a bar/lounge area where you can eat and listen to a terrific jazz pianist, Hilton Felton.

The popular Massachusetts chain, **Legal Sea Foods**, has opened restaurants at 2020 K St. NW (202-496-1111) and in Tysons Galleria (703-827-8900) in Virginia. An old-time local favorite is **O'Donnell's Restaurant** at 8301 Wisconsin Ave. (301-656-6200), serving seafood for over 70 years, along with tasty, traditional rum buns. O'Donnell's also has a restaurant at 311 Kentlands Blvd. in Gaithersburg (301-519-1650).

The Pacific Northwest favorite, **McCormick & Schmick's**, has arrived on the scene with a restaurant in DC at 1652 K St. NW (202-861-2233), in Bethesda at 7401 Woodmont Ave., Bethesda—North Lane (301-961-2626), in Reston Town Center (703-481-6600) and in Virginia at 8484 Westpark Drive, McLean (703-848-8000). Oregonians and Washingtonians are delighted to have their Dungeness crab, Petra sole, and Pacific coast salmon and prawns so readily available. Their **M&S Grill** is located at 600 13th St. NW (202-347-1500).

Pesce Trattoria at 2016 P St. NW (202-466-3474), a combination fish market and restaurant, is reported to serve the freshest fish in Washington. It was opened by chefs of two four-star restaurants as another outlet for their source of supremely fresh fish. You can either take the fish home and cook it yourself or have it prepared for you and dine on the premises.

VEGETARIAN EATING

There are a number of specifically vegetarian restaurants in the area for the meatless devotee. Some of the most popular are listed here. Check with local health food stores for other suggestions.

Berwyn Cafe
5010 Berwyn Rd., College Park
301-345-6655

Delights of the Garden
2606 Georgia Ave. NW
202-328-7685

Swagat
2063 University Blvd. East, Adelphi
301-434-2247

Sunflower
2531 Chain Bridge Rd., Vienna
703-319-3888

Thyme Square
4735 Bethesda Ave., Bethesda
301-657-9077

Udupi Palace
1329 University Blvd. East,
Langley Park
301-434-1531

DC Coast at 1401 K St. NW (202-216-5988) is one of the hottest spots in town for business lunches and dinner. Don't miss the crab cakes or the soft-shell crab here.

Arlington is home to the **Chesapeake Seafood and Crab House and An-Loc Landing Vietnamese Restaurant and Pho** at 3607 Wilson Blvd. (703-528-8896). If the name seems like a mouthful, you should see the menu—a full 15 pages of items ranging from basic seafood to exotic Vietnamese dishes. Despite the incongruity of it all—the menu covers "authentic Vietnamese and Chinese, along with a variety of typically French and American seafood cuisines"—this restaurant pulls it off. The crab and Vietnamese dishes are excellent and plenty of outdoor seating makes the Crab House a must on a summer evening.

Crisfield's (301-589-1306) original location at 8012 Georgia Ave. in Silver Spring is known for its long lines, coffee-shop decor and amazing seafood. To ease the wait, a second Silver Spring location has opened at 8606 Colesville Rd. (301-588-1572).

Andalucia at 4931 Elm St., Bethesda (301-907-0052) and 12300 Wilkins Ave., Rockville (301-770-1880) features Southern Spanish seafood dishes.

The **Bethesda Crab House** at 4958 Bethesda Ave. (301-652-3382) serves up crab on long picnic tables under a sprawling awning; the outdoor seating is nice on a warm evening. If you are with a small group, be prepared—the waiters move parties from table to table to make way for the larger groups constantly arriving.

Fish Market at 105 King St. in Old Town Alexandria (703-836-5676) has a double personality—upstairs a lively crowd sings along in a pub-like atmosphere, while downstairs a more sedate group concentrates on eating and drinking. The Fish Market's huge 32-ounce "schooners" of beer make it a popular spot on the weekends, particularly for the 20-something crowd. The **Warehouse Bar & Grill** at 214 King St. (703-683-6868) serves seafood with a New Orleans twist. The soups and seafood chowders should not be overlooked. **Blue Point Grill** at 600 Franklin St. (703-739-0404) in Alexandria is affiliated with Sutton Place Gourmet. The menu starts with more than a dozen varieties of the day's fresh fish.

Southern/Soul/Caribbean

This category covers a wide range of cooking styles and regions. Meals may be accompanied by live music or other entertainment, often with a late-night dining option. Come prepared to eat your heart out and then some, where multi-course dining usually rules.

B Smith's, 50 Massachusetts Ave. NE, Union Station (202-289-6188) offers a full range of Southern foods from red beans and rice to ribs to coconut cake for dessert. **Georgia Brown's** at 950 15th St. NW (202-393-4499) is an upscale restaurant offering a gourmet Southern menu that is very popular with the downtown business crowd.

You can dine on soul food at **Florida Avenue Grill** at 1100 Florida Ave. NW (202-265-1586), one of DC's landmark restaurants.

If Caribbean dishes are your desire, try either **Zanzibar on the Waterfront**, 700 Water St. SW (202-554-9100) which is "African with a Caribbean flare," or **BET on Jazz** at 730 11th St. NW (202-393-0975) offering "New World Caribbean Cuisine," which is a full-dress supper club with live music on the weekends. **Cafe Atlántico**, 405 8th St. NW (202-393-0812), offers Latin and Caribbean cuisine that is a feast for the eyes as well as the palette.

Thai

One of the more interesting trends in Asian dining is the explosion of restaurants specializing in Thai cuisine. Until recently, most Thai restaurants were located in the suburbs. Fortunately, downtown DC now has a few choices, including **Sala Thai** in Dupont Circle at 2016 P St. NW (202-872-1144); **Haad Thai** near the Convention Center at 1100 New York Ave. (entrance on 11th St.); and in the West End, **Thai Kitchen** at 2311 M St. NW (202-452-6090). At **Duangrat's**, 5878 Leesburg Pike (703-820-5775), waitresses in beautiful silk gowns serve some of the area's best Thai food. **Tara Thai** in Vienna at 226 Maple Ave. West (703-255-2467), in Falls Church at 7501 Leesburg Pike (703-506-9788), and in Bethesda at 4828 Bethesda Ave. (301-657-0488), is an award-winning restaurant specializing in seafood. This restaurant is expanding throughout the area; consult the phone book for the location nearest you.

Perhaps the best endorsement for Bethesda's **Bangkok Garden** at 4906 St. Elmo Ave. (301-951-0670) is that it has two menus—one in English for Americans and one in Thai for its many Thai customers. The cook often goes easy on the spices for American customers. If you want the hot stuff, be sure to ask for it.

Vietnamese

If you have never had Vietnamese food, you have been missing something special. Vietnamese food is similar to Chinese food, but tends to be sweeter and more delicate. The Clarendon section of Arlington is absolutely the best place to go—locally—for the exotic flavors of this Asian cuisine. A host of Vietnamese restaurants compete within a several-block radius of the Metro station: **Cafe Saigon** at 1135 North Highland St. (703-243-6522), **Nam-Viet** at 1127 North Hudson St. (703-522-7110) and **Queen Bee** at 3181 Wilson Blvd. (703-527-3444). These restaurants all offer fine cuisine at relatively inexpensive prices.

Any of the area's Pho restaurants are sure to please when you are in the mood for noodle soup or other Vietnamese dishes. **Pho 75** at 1711 Wilson Blvd. in Arlington (703-525-7355) has been around for years, and has expanded to three other locations including 3103 Graham Rd., Unit B, Falls Church (703-204-1490); 711 Hungerford Dr., Rockville (301-309-8873); and 1510 University Blvd. East, Langley Park (301-434-7844). **Pho 95** can be found at 785-H Rockville Pike (301-294-9391). Check your phone book for other Pho sites near you.

In Georgetown, **Vietnam Georgetown Restaurant** at 2934 M St. NW (202-337-4536) and **Saigon Inn** at 2928 M St. NW (202-337-5588) sit side by side.

Etc...

Cities at 2424 18th St. NW in Adams Morgan (202-328-7194) offers a unique approach to the dining experience. Every few months, Cities changes its entire decor and revamps its menu to celebrate the cuisine of a different city. Regional wines are also selected to round out the cultural experience.

Jaleo at 480 7th St. NW (202-628-7949) recreates the taste, feel and atmosphere of a Spanish tapas restaurant. At Jaleo, customers casually linger over the small appetizers with a glass of one of the fine sherries in the restaurant's extensive selection. With a constant crowd in the bar area, Jaleo makes for an appealing night out. Just up the street is **Coco Loco** at 810 7th St. NW (202-289-2626), another popular tapas restaurant. In addition, they offer a fixed-price, all-you-can-eat, traditional Brazilian mixed grill.

If you are a hungry art lover, **Utopia** at 1418 U St. NW (202-483-7669) will leave you doubly satisfied. The owner of this restaurant and bar is a painter and the space doubles as an art gallery for his work and the work of other local artists. Utopia's high ceiling (the building used to be a garage) leaves ample wall space for paintings and prints. There is also a full bar with weekday happy hour.

The **State of the Union**—the former Soviet Union that is—at 1357 U St. NW (202-588-8810) offers Russian-American cuisine. The menu even lists a shot of Vodka as an appetizer. Like many of the other restaurants and bars on U St., the owners had local artists decorate the interior. In this case, even the bathrooms are works of art.

Authentic Malaysian food is available at the **Straits of Malaya** at 1836 18th St. NW (202-483-1483) in Adams Morgan. Enjoy your summer meal on their rooftop restaurant.

Shamshiry, a Persian kebab restaurant at 8607 Westwood Center Dr., Vienna (703-448-8883), offers a limited menu of beef, chicken and salmon kebabs, each served with mounds of fluffy rice. As you enter Shamshiry, you are greeted with the memorable sight of a large window overlooking the skewers on the grill, and the enormous pots of rice in the background.

For authentic Moroccan cuisine and atmosphere, plan a dinner at **Marrakesh** at 617 New York Ave. NW (202-393-9393). The evening features a fixed-price seven-course meal eaten with the hands using broken bread. Belly dancing is the featured entertainment. This restaurant accepts no credit cards, so be sure to take along cash or your checkbook.

Authentic Jamaican cuisine is available at Adams Morgan's **Montego Cafe** at 2437 18th St. NW (202-745-1002) where reggae music and jerk chicken are only part of the colorful tropical atmosphere.

For That Special Evening

To begin a special evening, start with drinks at the **Terrace at the Hotel Washington** at 515 15th St. NW (202-638-5900), overlooking the Mall and the White House. When you enter the hotel, take the elevator to the top floor. If you are looking for something with a dash of Victorian romance for dinner afterwards, try the nearby **Morrison Clark Inn** at 1015 L St. NW (202-898-1200).

The chic atmosphere at **I Matti** at 2436 18th St. NW (202-462-8844) makes it a great place to begin an evening in Adams Morgan. In Georgetown, **Ristorante Piccolo** at 1068 31st St. NW (202-342-7414) offers intimate candle-lit tables and good Italian cuisine, making it a great spot for dinner before wandering around the neighborhood.

If you are in the mood for French cuisine, try **Le Gaulois Cafe Restaurant** at 1106 King St. in Alexandria (703-739-9494), which has received rave reviews for both food and atmosphere. The fireplace definitely adds to the experience. Be sure to call ahead and make reservations.

Another favorite is Potomac's **Old Angler's Inn** at 10801 MacArthur Blvd. (301-365-2425). This country inn, within walking distance of the C&O Canal Towpath, features regional cuisine with a French accent. In the winter, try to get a spot next to the fireplace. In the summer and spring, take advantage of the outside terrace.

America's first restaurant to be "certified organic," **Restaurant Nora** at 2132 Florida Ave. NW (202-462-5143) is Washington's answer to Chez Panisse, the Berkeley restaurant that started the nouvelle cuisine trend. From appetizers to desserts, everything is freshly made from organic ingredients. They always have one selection from every course of a meal for vegetarians.

The **Iron Gate Inn** at 1734 N St. NW (202-737-1370), a Middle Eastern restaurant in an old carriage house just off Dupont Circle, is another popular favorite. In the summer, take advantage of its wonderful courtyard. Meals are just as romantic in the winter when you can sit indoors in a cozy room with a fireplace.

For refined French dining in elegant surroundings, you'll definitely want to spend an evening at **Lespinasse**, in the Sheraton-Carlton Hotel, 923 16th St. NW (202-879-6900).

In Georgetown, you'll find **Michel Richard Citronelle** in the Latham Hotel at 3000 M St. NW (202-625-2150). This is among the most expensive restaurants in town, and deservedly so.

LaFerme at 7101 Brookville Rd. in Chevy Chase, MD (301-986-5255) offers a close-in French country dining experience.

To cap off an evening out with a drink and a bit of jazz, stop by **Café Lautrec** (202-265-6436) at 2431 18th St. NW in Adams Morgan. You cannot miss the restaurant, thanks to the mural of Lautrec painted on the building. This café has nightly live entertainment and on the weekends, tap dancing on the bar.

If you are in the mood for something a little quieter to finish off the evening, try **Dolce Finale** (202-667-5350). You will have to look closely to find this spot—tucked away under **Petitto's Restaurante d'Italia** at 2653 Connecticut Ave. NW in Woodley Park. The tiny basement café, with seating for just over a dozen people, has excellent desserts and is open until 1:30 a.m. on weekends.

For the ultimate special evening, slip away to the quiet atmosphere of a warm and inviting French country inn. **L'Auberge Chez François** (703-759-3800) is located at 332 Springvale Rd. in Great Falls and has been rated by the *Washingtonian* reader survey for over 10 years in a row as the area's best place to eat.

Reservations at this gem are difficult to get due to its well-deserved popularity.

Bars and Pubs

When you are out for the evening and want more than just a good meal, you don't have to go far. The metropolitan area is full of evening spots, including traditional bars and Irish pubs, casual and classy coffee bars, and a wide variety of night clubs.

Traditional Bars

When Washingtonians want to engage in a friendly game of bar golf or go on a more casual pub crawl, they head for the busy streets of Georgetown. Prices reflect the neighborhood's trendy status. Old Town's King St. draws much the same crowd. In Dupont Circle, the bars around 19th and M Sts. are the place to go. Below are highlights of some of Washington's many notable bars.

The **Brickskeller** at 1523 22nd St. NW (202-628-0202) boasts over 500 different types of beer from all over the world. The Brickskeller is a better place to go to catch up with a long-lost pal than to meet a new friend. Unlike most bars, no one mills about or dances; instead the host will ask you to choose a table.

On weekdays, the **Bottom Line** at 1716 Eye St. NW (202-298-8488) features free munchies including tacos, buffalo wings and egg rolls, making this a popular watering hole for nearby workers. On the weekends, college students pack this bar to drink and dance. Do not mistake the **Third Edition** at 1218 Wisconsin Ave. NW (202-333-3700) in Georgetown for a bookstore. It is a hot spot for the college crowd, especially on weekends.

The area around 19th and M Sts. includes a number of happy hour spots. Washingtonians and suburbanites flock to **Madhatter** at 1831 M St. NW

BREW PUBS AND MICROBREWERIES

DC

Capitol City Brewing Company
11th and H Sts. NW
202-628-2222
2 Massachusetts Ave. NE
202-842-2337
7735 Old Georgetown Rd., Bethesda
301-652-2282
4001 S. 28th St., Arlington
703-578-3888

John Harvard's Brew House
1299 Pennsylvania Ave. NE
202-783-2739

Maryland

Olde Towne Tavern & Brewing Company
227 E. Diamond Ave., Gaithersburg
301-948-4200

Rock Bottom Restaurant and Brewery
7900 Norfolk Ave., Bethesda
301-652-1311
Rock Bottom Brewery additional site:
4238 Wilson Blvd., Arlington
703- 516-7688
and their
District Chophouse & Brewery
509 7th St. NW
202-347-3434

Virginia

Virginia Beverage Company
607 King St., Alexandria
703-684-5397

IRISH PUBS

Biddy Mulligan's
1500 New Hampshire Ave. NW
202-483-6000

Dubliner
4 F St. NW
202-737-3773

Fadó
808 7th St. NW
202-789-0066

Ireland's Four Courts
2051 Wilson Blvd., Arlington
703-525-3600

Ireland's Four Provinces
(referred to as the Four Ps)
3412 Connecticut Ave. NW
202-244-0860
and
105 W. Broad St.
703-534-8999

Kelly's Ellis Island
3908 12th St. NE
202-832-6117

Kelly's Irish Times
14 F. St. NW
202-543-5433

Murphy's Grand Irish Pub
713 King St., Alexandria
703-548-1717

Murphy's of DC
2609 24th St.
202-462-7171

Pat Troy's Restaurant and Pub
111 N. Pitt St. Alexandria
703-549-4535

(202-833-1495), **Sign of the Whale** at 1825 M St. NW (202-785-1110) and particularly **Rumors** at 1900 M St. NW (202-466-7378). Another popular place is **Mister Days Sports Rock Cafe** at 1111 19th St. NW (202-296-7625), just off 19th St. in the back alley. A second Mister Days location is at 3100 Clarendon Blvd., Arlington (703-527-1600). **Club Odds** at 1160 20th St. NW in Dupont (202-296-8644) is a popular college crowd hangout that offers dancing in the evening. **Deja Vu** at 2119 M St. NW (202-452-1966) attracts a slightly older and more international crowd. Just a few blocks away is the **Front Page** at 1333 New Hampshire Ave. NW (202-296-6500). It lacks the reputation of the M St. bars, yet draws large crowds. Another good spot is **Ha'penny Lion** at 1101 17th St. NW (202-296-8075).

The **Capitol City Brewing Company** (202-628-2222) serves all kinds of beer, most brewed on the premises. A rotating production schedule assures that there are lots of new ales, Pilseners and porters to try on a regular basis. The menu ranges from steaks, sausages and burgers to salmon, shrimp and other seafood. The brewery attracts a mostly young, professional crowd and has a popular happy hour. Other locations are at 2 Massachusetts Ave. NE (202-842-2337), 7735 Old Georgetown Rd., Bethesda (301-652-2282) and 4001 S. 28th St., Arlington (703-578-3888).

A wide variety of local talent can be seen at the **Grog & Tankard** at 2408 Wisconsin Ave. NW (202-333-3114), and live blues & jazz can be heard at **Capital Blues** at 2651 Connecticut Ave. NW (202-232-2300).

In the New U and Adams Morgan areas, the best places to go for a beer without giving up your entire wallet are **Stetson's** at 1610 U St. NW (202-667-6295) and **Millie & Al's** at 2440 18th St. NW (202-387-8131).

Several bars line Pennsylvania Ave. between 2nd and 7th Sts. SE on Capitol Hill. Among them you will find the **Tune Inn** (202-543-2725) and **Hawk and Dove** (202-543-3300). Both cater to the budgets of congressional staff and interns, who make up the majority of the crowd. Several congressmen are occasionally known to join their staffers at these spots, especially the Tune Inn. Other staffers trek over to **My Brother's Place** at 237 2nd St. NW (202-347-1350).

Whitey's at 2761 North Washington Blvd. (703-525-9825) is the place where a young crowd comes to enjoy beer, live music and a large back room with a pool table, pinball machines, dart boards and fooz ball table. Whitey's is easy to spot—just look for its neon "EAT" sign out front.

IOTA at 2832 Wilson Blvd. (703-522-8340) attracts the twenty- and thirty-somethings who congregate here to drink beer and listen to local alternative country and other entertainment. Across the street is the **Galaxy Hut** at 2711 Wilson Blvd. (703-525-8646).

Gay Bars and Restaurants

The Dupont Circle area is very much the center of Washington's gay community and is home to several of the city's gay restaurants and bars. **JR's Bar & Grill** at 1519 17th St. NW (202-328-0090) attracts the young, preppie crowd. Its popular happy hours draw a regular following. Also on 17th St. you will find several gay-oriented restaurants including **Annie's Paramount Steak House** at #1609 (202-232-0395) and the **Trio Restaurant** at #1537 (202-232-6305). Around the corner is the popular **Cafe Luna** at 1633 P St. NW (202-387-4005). Capitol Hill has **Two Quail** at 320 Massachusetts Ave. NE (202-543-8030), an excellent restaurant. **Mr. Henry's Capitol Hill Restaurant** at 601 Pennsylvania Ave. SE (202-546-8412), and its counterpart **Mr. Henry's Upstairs** also at 601 Pennsylvania Ave. SE (202-546-6886), both serve burgers and beer in a relaxed atmosphere. Of all these, Annie's is the place to go to see and be seen.

The Levi/Leather crowd hangs out at **DC Eagle** at 639 New York Ave. NW (202-347-6025) and the **Fireplace** at 2161 P St. NW (202-293-1293). Those looking for country and western bars can go to **Remingtons**, on the Hill at 639 Pennsylvania Ave. SE (202-543-3113), one of the friendliest bars in the city. As is true in a number of big cities, gay bashing is no stranger to Washington, so be careful and pay attention to where you walk.

Coffee and Tea

The coffee bar invasion landed a few years back, conquered this metropolitan area and has never turned back. Heard on every city street, the buzz of the espresso machine seems here to stay.

Since its arrival in the early '90s, **Starbucks** has opened over 50 sites in the area including those at 3430 Wisconsin Ave. NW (202-537-6879), 1501 and 5500 Connecticut Ave. NW (202-588-1280 and 202-244-9705), 5438 Westbard Ave. in Bethesda (301-718-6339), 10116 River Rd. in Potomac (301-299-9226), at 532 King St. in Old Town Alexandria (703-836-2236), and in the Lyon Village Shopping Center at Lee Hwy. and Spout Run in Arlington (703-527-6506). Website: www.starbucks.com.

Quartermaine Coffee Roasters at 3323 Connecticut Ave. NW (202-244-2676) and at 441 4th St. NW (202-347-1760) plans similar growth. Quartermaine roasts its coffee at their plant in Rockville at 4972 Wyaconda Rd. Its Bethesda store is located at 4817 Bethesda Ave. (301-718-2853) and its Chevy Chase site is at 36 Wisconsin Circle, Chevy Chase (301-951-0132). If you are interested in taking a tour of the roasting plant, just call 301-230-4600. Their website is at www.quartermaine.com.

In addition to the larger chains of coffee bars, there are a number of local ones. The **Café des Amis du Café** at 1020 19th St. NW (202-466-7860) is a great choice in the Downtown area.

Dupont Circle hosts **Kramerbooks & Afterwords Cafe** at 1517 Connecticut Ave. NW (202-387-1462), which aims to please the hungry bookworm. Kramer's is two places in one—a bookstore and a café. Aside from cakes and pastries, Kramer's offers an eclectic, somewhat pricy dinner menu and is best known as a late-night hangout after everything else closes—the café and bookstore are open all night on Friday and Saturday.

The **Java House** at 1645 Q St. NW (202-387-6622) stocks over 70 kinds of beans from all over the world. The beans are roasted and flavored on the premises. Indoor and outdoor seating is available for those who want to take advantage of the light sandwich and coffee menu.

Jolt 'n Bolt Coffee and Tea House, at 1918 18th St. NW (202-232-0077), is a quiet neighborhood place. **Soho Tea & Coffee** at 2150 P St. NW (202-463-7646) is very popular with Generation Xers as well as smokers, with eclectic concerts on Friday nights.

At **Xando** (pronounced "Zando"), you will find coffee by day and cocktails by night. Light sandwich fare and baked goods are offered, and you can make S'mores right at your table. Located at 1350 Connecticut Ave. (202-296-9341), it is conveniently located next to the Cineplex Odeon theater and the Dupont Circle Metro station. Other locations are at 1647 20th St. NW (202-332-6364) and at 301 Pennsylvania Ave. SE (202-546-5224).

If tea is your preference, there are plenty of opportunities to indulge in the delight of afternoon tea while nibbling on finger sandwiches and scones. Most of the major hotels serve daily tea somewhere between the hours of 3:00 and 5:00 p.m., with some offering as late as 6:00 p.m. There is a renewed interest in this English and Asian custom, and here are a few places beyond the hotels that may be of interest.

Teaism, an Asian teahouse at 2009 R St. NW (202-667-3827) with a second at 800 Connecticut Ave. NW (202-835-2233), offers choices from a list of dozens of teas in brewed and leaf form. Teaism is open for breakfast, lunch and dinner, and a quiet afternoon tea is best enjoyed between 3:00 and 6:00 p.m.

The **Washington National Cathedral Tour and Tea** is offered every Tuesday and Wednesday at 1:30 p.m. These docent-guided talks last about an hour and can be customized to match group interest, such as the intricate stained-glass windows, façade gargoyles and surrounding gardens. By 3 p.m., when the tour concludes, an elegant high tea is served in the Saint Paul Tower with breathtaking views of downtown Washington. At $18 per guest, these reservations go fast. Call 202-537-8993 for information and reservations.

In Georgetown try the Chinese tearoom, **Ching Ching Cha**, at 1063 Wisconsin Ave. NW (202-333-8288). You can sit at low tables with pillows or on chairs, and receive a lesson in brewing tea. Light fare is also served.

The **Alexandria Pastry Shop** at 3690-H King St. in Alexandria (703-578-4144) offers tea every Tuesday from 2:00 to 4:00 p.m. Sandwiches, sweets and scones are served on china with classical music playing softly in the background.

MASTERING DC: LOCAL FOOD & DRINK

Sandwiched between Boston Baked Beans and Key Lime Pie, the Mid-Atlantic Region is a smorgasbord of regional specialties, thanks to the mild climate, agricultural traditions, and local bounty of land and sea. Some dishes come down to us through generations of immigrants who help make this part of the country so diverse—and so tasty!

☐ **Eat the Apples:** Winchester, is the **apple capital** of Virginia, specializes in Red and Golden Delicious and Stayman varieties. Try apple pie, apple cider, apple butter, apple strudel, apple juice, apple cider…you get the apple idea.

☐ **Drink the Wine:** Tour the countryside and taste the wine at any of the close to 60 **wineries** in Virginia, concentrated in the Shenandoah Valley, throughout Central Virginia, in Northern Virginia, and on the Eastern Shore.

☐ **Taste the Ham:** Peanut-fed hogs are the secret behind the unique rich and salty taste of **Smithfield ham**. You'll find other dry-cured country hams in the area, but none have the authentic taste and international renown of the ones processed in Smithfield, VA.

☐ **Shuck the Oysters, Crack the Crabs:** The waters off the Atlantic Coast, the Chesapeake Bay, and the area's tidal rivers produce a feast of **oysters, crab, bass, shad, flounder and bluefish**. A local specialty is fried oysters and chicken salad. The famous **Chesapeake Blue Crab** is delicious any way you like it: hard shell or soft shell, as Maryland Crab Cakes, in crab bisque, or steamed and ready for cracking.

☐ **Go Dutch:** The Pennsylvania Dutch Country—in and around Lancaster, PA—is home to unique foods bought from the Old County by the Amish, Mennonite, and Brethren communities. Special dishes include **pretzels, shoofly pie, schnitz, cup cheese and sausage**.

☐ **Don't Be Chicken:** One of the most important agricultural products of Maryland and Delaware—particularly on the Eastern Shore of each state—is poultry. A local favorite is **chicken and slippery dumplings**.

☐ **Dump the Diet:** Just once, sample the ultimate southern specialty—**sausage gravy**. It's a real cholesterol feast, ground sausage cooked in a thick brown gravy and served over buttermilk biscuits. Sounds odd, tastes great, and once just might be enough.

☐ **Get Your Peanuts...Here!** No matter where you are coming from, you've probably already had **Virginia peanuts**, "the peanut of gourmets." One of the four most popular types in the country, this large-kerneled peanut is grown in Virginia, North Carolina, Tennessee, and parts of Georgia, and shipped all over the country to be enjoyed salted, butter toasted, roasted in the shell, chocolate coated, or in peanut brittle.

☐ **Go Underground:** Nearby Pennsylvania leads the nation in mushroom production, accounting for nearly half of the country's total. You'll find these delicacies particularly in the Brandywine Valley and Kennett Square area, where commercial cultivation of **mushrooms** got its US start more than a century ago.

☐ **Dine Around the World:** While you are sampling some of the many international restaurants in and around the city, don't miss the unique combinations of food and community in **DC's Chinatown and Baltimore's Little Italy** neighborhoods.

CHAPTER EIGHT

Beyond the Job

When your last e-mail is sent and you've logged off the computer, it's time to take advantage of the plentiful resources available in this rich and complex metropolitan area. You will find a surprisingly large number of social, cultural, educational, recreational and entertainment resources. You can join any of a multitude of organizations—everything from biking and hiking clubs to volunteer groups to affiliations with the Smithsonian and Kennedy Center. Organizations provide a great way to meet new friends while taking part in your favorite activities.

Activities and Social Clubs

If meeting new people in enjoyable social settings is your free-time preference, you will be glad to know about the many activity and social clubs in the area. Some focus on specific areas of interest, others are more broad-based. Some specialize in creating activities for individuals of a certain age groups, others know no limit.

Cultural Organizations

Washington, DC is home to more than 170 embassies, chancelleries and diplomatic residences representing cultures from every continent. Consequently, a number of international organizations and sponsored activities are available throughout the area. A list of several cultural organizations can be found in the Resources section to assist you in locating activities in which to participate.

Maryland Outdoors Club, Inc.

The Maryland Outdoors Club, Inc. (301-601-5007) is a nonprofit outdoors and social club focusing on a variety of activities for active individuals with common interests such as biking, camping, hiking, skiing and whitewater rafting. Although this organization is based in Maryland, it serves the entire Baltimore/Washington area. Membership rates are $35 for singles and $50 for two individuals from the same address. Learn more about this organization at www.maryland-outdoors-club.org

State Societies

Lonely for home and longing to be with people who pronounce the letter "r" just the way you do? Then join your home state society. Nominal membership fees (around $15 a year) guarantee you an invitation to every one of their social

POLITICAL ORGANIZATIONS

If you are interested in getting involved with either the Democratic or Republican parties, Washington is certainly the place to be. Call the Democratic National Committee (202-863-8000) or the Republican National Committee (202-863-8500) for specific information. These organizations can also put you in touch with other political groups from their "side of the aisle."

events. For more information on your state society, contact your state congressional delegation office.

Washington Party Group

The Washington Party Group (703-391-2708; www.partydc.com) is a social group for individuals in the 24-45 year age range. They offer a variety of events announced by monthly newsletters and mailed invitations as well as on their website. There is no membership fee; however, there is a charge for the events.

Wine Tasting Association

This non-profit organization offers such activities as wine tastings and cooking classes, including embassy events to sample the wines of a particular country. Event calendars are distributed to members to announce upcoming events, including information on dates, times and costs. Members receive discounts at area wine shops and on WTA events. Annual membership fees are $70 for an individual and $135 for two people at the same address. For additional information, call 703-765-8229 or see their website at www.winetasting.org.

EDUCATION

Washington is a city full of educational resources. With approximately 25 colleges and universities spread among the three jurisdictions, this area is rich in opportunities and deserves the reputation it has earned as a center of education and learning.

Universities

Twelve of the area's leading institutions of higher learning are members of a cooperative venture, the **Consortium of Universities of the Metropolitan Washington Area**, with offices at One Dupont Circle NW (202-331-8080; www.consortium.org). The Consortium members are the **American University**, the **Catholic University of America, Gallaudet University**, **George Mason University**, **George Washington University**, **Georgetown University**, **Howard University**, **Marymount University**, **Mount Vernon College**, **Trinity College**, the **University of the District of Columbia** and the **University of Maryland**. Through the Consortium, students enrolled in a member institution have access to the courses, faculty and libraries of all member universities.

Non-Degree Classes

Washingtonians can take advantage of having the **Smithsonian Institution** in their backyard. The Smithsonian Associates Program offers individual lectures, seminars and concerts, most of which are held in the Baird Auditorium at the American History Museum. Their continuing education arm, Campus on the Mall (202-357-3030; www.si.edu/tsa), offer courses in the arts, humanities, sciences and studio arts, together with a vast offering of lecture series. Many courses include guided tours of local museums and art galleries. Some courses even conclude with receptions at a related embassy. Classes usually meet weekly for six to eight weeks at one of the Smithsonian museums on the Mall. Virtually all locations are easily accessible by Metro.

Georgetown University's Summer and Continuing Education Program (202-687-5942; www.georgetown.edu) offers some of the best non-credit classes for adults, from Women in Western Political Thought to Screen Writing for Film and Television Movies to Chinese. There are evening and weekend courses in art history, studio arts, theater, music, literature, writing, communication, classics, religion, psychology, philosophy, history, international affairs, languages, economics, personal finance, science, computers and professional development. On-campus parking is available at a discounted rate for registered students.

Another great bargain is the **US Department of Agriculture** (202-720-5885; www.grad.usda.gov). The USDA offers over a thousand courses per year in 50 subject areas intended to help government and other organizations to increase efficiency and effectiveness. The courses are open to all and most are held week nights at various federal office buildings downtown, accessible by Metro.

Through its Center for Career Education and Workshops (CCEW), **George Washington University** (202-973-1175; www.gwu.edu/~cce) also offers non-credit professional training courses. In addition to courses in fields such as desktop publishing and financial planning, CCEW sponsors FSE, GRE, GMAT and LSAT test-prep courses at rates much lower than their commercial competitors. Courses usually last eight weeks and are held in convenient downtown buildings. You can also enroll in regular undergraduate and graduate courses at GWU as a non-matriculating student. The information desk in the lobby of Rice Hall at 2121 Eye St. NW has course catalogs and schedules.

American University (202-885-2500; www.continuinged.american.edu) offers all of its regular undergraduate and graduate courses to qualified non-degree students. All classes are given at the main campus at 4400 Massachusetts Ave. NW. Non-degree students have access to the AU libraries and to the shuttle bus from the AU-Tenleytown Metro station on the Red Line. Once registered, you can purchase a pass to use the sports center's swimming pool, racquetball courts and weight room.

The District's only public university, **University of the District of Columbia** (202-274-5000; www.udc.edu), offers both academic and non-academic classes at its main campus at 4340 Connecticut Ave. NW. District residents pay at rates substantially below those for non-residents. For professional development and leisure courses, call (202-274-5179).

Residents of Maryland and Virginia get the same advantages at their community colleges. **Montgomery College** has locations at Rockville (301-279-5000), Takoma Park (301-650-1300) and Germantown (301-353-7700), each offering a wide variety of credit and non-credit courses and seminars; see their website at www.mc.cc.md.us. You can pick up catalogs and applications at any of the campuses. **Northern Virginia Community College** has campuses in Alexandria (703-845-6200), Annandale (703-323-3000) and Woodbridge (703-878-5700). Virginia residents can expect to find course catalogs stuffed in their mailboxes on a regular basis. Visit their website at www.nv.cc.va.us.

First Class (202-797-5102; www.takeaclass.org) offers numerous, inexpensive classes that meet anywhere from one to four times. Most of the courses meet at the organization's Dupont Circle office, 1726 20th St. NW. Classes regularly feature celebrities and authors speaking on a variety of topics in an informal setting.

ENTERTAINMENT

Both the *Washingtonian Magazine* and the Friday Weekend section of the *Washington Post* contain a comprehensive listing of current exhibits, lectures, concerts, plays, performances and movies, and are a valuable resource for beyond the job activities. In addition to watching for listings of events, you can join organizations such as the **Washington Performing Arts Society** (202-833-9800; www.wpas.org), which will keep you apprised of cultural events and through which you can order subscription series. And don't forget your local arts councils as great sources of information for local events and community theater productions. The opportunities are many for both patrons and performers.

Concerts

To find out about upcoming concerts, listen to your favorite radio station or check the newspapers, especially the City Paper. Popular performers, particularly rock groups, play at **RFK Stadium** (202-547-9077), **George Mason's Patriot Center** (703-993-1000), **Warner Theatre** (202-783-4000), **Constitution Hall**

(202-638-2661), and **Nissan Pavilion at Stone Ridge** (703-754-1288).

Smaller concerts play **Lisner Auditorium** at George Washington University (202-994-1500; www.lisner.org). The **In Series**, sponsored by The George Washington University, offers cabaret, concerts, dance, readings and opera at Mount Vernon College at 2100 Foxhall Road, NW in DC. Call 202-625-4655 for information and tickets. The reputation of Alexandria's **Birchmere** at 3701 Mount Vernon Ave. (703-549-7500) continues to grow even though the space remains small. If you can get in, you will certainly enjoy the live music, ranging from folk to country and bluegrass to blues. Call Ticketmaster at 202-432-SEAT for ticket information.

During the summer, outdoor concerts and performances are held at **Wolf Trap's Filene Center**, universally known as Wolf Trap (703-255-1860; www.wolftrap.org). Part of the National Park Service, Wolf Trap generally books classical, folk and country performers, as well as storytellers and comedians. If the weather is good you can buy lawn tickets, bring a blanket and some food, and have a picnic while you enjoy the performance. For Filene Center performances only, shuttle bus service is available from the West Falls Church Metrorail station. Call 202-637-7000 for information. The **Barns of Wolf Trap** (703-938-2404), which sponsors indoor concerts and shows, is their winter site. The **Carter-Barron Amphitheater** (202-426-6837) also holds outdoor concerts. The **Merriweather Post Pavilion** (301-982-1800) in Columbia, MD is similar to Wolf Trap, but offers a wider variety of performance as it does not have to get Park Service approval for shows.

Classical music lovers will find plenty of opportunities to hear their favorite musicians and orchestras. The **John F. Kennedy Center for the Performing Arts** (202-467-4600; http://kennedy-center.org) hosts the National Symphony Orchestra as well as performances ranging from international orchestras to individuals in recital. The **French Embassy** (202-944-6000) and the **Smithsonian Associates Program** (202-357-3030; www.si.edu/tsa) both offer subscription series concerts, as do several of the universities in the area. The **Phillips Collection** offers a Sunday afternoon concert series from September through May (202-387-2151; www.phillipscollection.org).

During the summer, area monuments, various art galleries and churches host free concerts. The Smithsonian (202-357-2700; www.si.edu/activity) frequently sponsors classical concerts. Big band aficionados attend performances on the grounds of the **Washington Monument**. If you have time during the day, the

Corcoran Gallery of Art (202-639-1700) sponsors free summertime jazz. The **Washington National Cathedral** (202-537-6200) hosts free choral and chamber music concerts. From time to time, they also offer lunch-time concerts. Free Sunday night concerts are also available in the **National Gallery of Art, West Wing.**

The US Marines hold evening parades at the **Marine Corps Barracks** (202-433-6060), 8th and I Sts. SE, on Friday evenings at 8:45 p.m. from mid-May through early September. Reservations are required three weeks in advance for this spectacular show of drum and bugle corps, precision marching and silent rifle drills. Shuttle bus service is available from the free parking facilities at the Navy Yard, 11th and N Sts. SE, or take Metro's Blue or Orange Lines to Eastern Market.

Opera

The **Washington Opera** (202-295-2400; www.dc-opera.org) performs at the Kennedy Center. The **Washington Concert Opera** (202-333-1768) performs at Lisner Auditorium at 21st and H Sts. NW. This is a first rate opera without sets or costumes, with subtitles in English. **Wolf Trap Opera Company** (703-255-1935) performs in the Barns of Wolf Trap from October to May. The **Vocal Arts Society** (202-265-8177) is a series of concerts by young or overlooked singers. Performances are usually held at the French Embassy.

Theater

Washington, once considered a weak theater town, is now a prime pre-Broadway proving ground as well as a regional theater scene in its own right. Major stars make regular appearances at the Shakespeare Theatre at the Lansburgh and the Helen Hayes Awards have become an institution honoring local theater.

The **Kennedy Center** (202-467-4600; http://kennedy-center.org), perched along the banks of the Potomac River not far from the Lincoln Memorial, houses many cultural events and programs in its six theaters. Plays and comedies are usually performed in the Eisenhower Theater. The National Symphony Orchestra performs in the Concert Hall, the Washington Opera in the Opera House. The Terrace Theater is reserved for concerts and plays. Theater groups and dance troupes perform experimental works in the Theater Lab. All kinds of movies, from advanced screenings to retrospectives, can be seen at the American Film Institute theater (202-785-4600). Since 1987, the Kennedy Center's Cabaret Theater has performed a comedy whodunit called "Shear Madness." This interactive play, set in DC, lets the audience play armchair detective. The humor is based on local events and people. The Millennium Stage, located in the Grand Foyer, offers free, hour-long performances on a daily basis at 6:00 p.m.

The performances are diverse and include such events as classical music, jazz, dance troupes and storytellers. Millennium stage performances are broadcast every evening at www.kennedy-center.org/millennium.

The **National Theatre** at 1321 Pennsylvania Ave. NW (202-628-6161; www.nationaltheatre.org), a few blocks from the White House, attracts Broadway previews as well as Broadway hits on tour. The newly renovated **Warner Theatre** at 13th and E Sts. NW (202-783-4000) hosts many musicals and concerts.

Although shows at the National Theatre and Kennedy Center may command the headlines, the irreplaceable gems for Washington theater goers are the Arena and Shakespeare Theaters. Theater-in-the-round is the best-known facet of **Arena Stage** at 6th and Maine Sts. SW (202-488-3300; www.arenastage.org). Arena's own acting company produces a variety of plays, including classics, modern plays and the occasional musical. The Arena complex houses a standard stage, the Kreeger Theatre, and a performance space, the Old Vat Room.

Shakespeare is alive and well at the **Shakespeare Theatre** at the Lansburgh, 450 7th St. NW (202-393-2700; http://shakespearedc.org). Each season the company presents five productions, three of which are Shakespearean plays. Four of the performances are on the Shakespeare Theatre's home stage. The fifth performance is held at the Shakespeare Theatre Free For All at the Carter Barron Amphitheater. If you were to pick only one theater to subscribe to, the Shakespeare would be an excellent choice. The quality is superb and the price not astronomical. If the performance is sold out, standing-room-only tickets are usually available and go on sale one hour before the performance.

Each year, the **Ford's Theatre** (202-347-4833; www.fordstheatre.org), best known as the site of the assassination of President Lincoln, performs big-name, family-oriented shows and musicals. The theatre, located at 511 10th St. NW, is a national monument and the small Lincoln museum in the basement is worth the trip on its own.

The historic **Lincoln Theatre** at 1215 U St. NW (202-328-6000) was among a number of theaters, cabarets, dance halls and restaurants in what was referred to as "Black Broadway" during the first half of this century. In its heyday, it attracted some of the country's best entertainers. It was restored by the city in 1994 and today hosts musical and comedy acts. Tickets are available through Ticketmaster (202-432-SEAT). The theater is located across from the U St.-Cardoza Metro station.

Studio Theatre at 1333 P St. NW (202-332-3300; www.studiotheatre.org) offers off-beat comedy and drama on its two small stages. Studio is one of several small theaters in the 14th St. Theater District, an "unofficial" district famous for its daring and experimental theater companies. Along with the Studio Theatre, you will find the **Woolly Mammoth** at 1401 Church St. NW (202-393-3939; www.woollymammoth.net) and the **Source Theatre Company** at 1835 14th St. NW (202-462-1073; www.dcmdva-arts.org). These theaters attract local thespian groups and occasionally produce the works of local playwrights. In Northern Virginia, **Signature Theatre** at 3806 South Four Mile Run Dr. (703-820-9771; www.sig-online.org) has acquired a terrific reputation for its productions, especially of Stephen Sondheim musicals. This comparatively small company has received 19 Helen Hayes Awards. Ticket prices at all of these theaters are generally low. Also in Virginia is Fairfax's **Theatre of the First Amendment** which performs at George Mason University's Center for the Arts (703-993-8888; www.gmu.edu/cfa).

The award-winning Grupo de Actores Latino Americanos performs at the **GALA Hispanic Theatre** at 1625 Park Rd. NW (202-234-7174). They present three plays a season by Latin American or Spanish authors. One of these productions is performed in both Spanish and English, and the others are done in Spanish with simultaneous English translation. There is also a French-American theater group, **Le Néon**, at 3616 Lee Hwy. in Arlington, VA (703-243-NEON; www.leneon.org).

Each summer, Rock Creek Park and the Shakespeare Theatre sponsor a free play at the **Carter-Barron Amphitheater** at 16th St. and Colorado Ave. NW (202-426-6837; www.nps.gov/rocr/cbarron.htm). The production is usually a restaging of one of the Shakespeare Theatre's recently produced works. During the rest of the summer, the Carter-Barron is home to a series of free concerts and musical recitals from classical to jazz to pop.

If you are looking for discount theater tickets, half-price tickets can be purchased (cash only) the day of the show at **Ticketplace** located on the ground floor of the Old Post Office Pavilion at 1100 Pennsylvania Ave. NW (202-842-5387), across from the Federal Triangle Metro (Orange and Blue lines). Given the high demand, Ticketplace can afford to have limited hours; it is only open Tuesday through Saturday from 11:00 a.m. to 6:00 p.m. Tickets for shows on Sunday and Monday are sold on Saturday. You can also look into standing-room-only tickets or being an usher by checking with the box offices of the individual theaters.

Regular-price tickets can be purchased either at the theater box offices or over the phone through **Ticketmaster** (202-432-7328; www.ticketmaster.com) or

Telecharge (800-233-3123; www.telecharge.com) or **Protix** (703-218-6500; www.protix.com).

Movies

Washington is a terrific movie town. There are many first-run houses; a sizable collection of theaters specializing in classic, foreign and art films; and an annual local film festival, Filmfest DC. An influx of "future trend' theaters offers local moviegoers the choice of stadium seating, bigger screens and digital stereo with their popcorn.

Each year, hundreds of movies, new and old, from Hollywood and elsewhere are shown at the **American Film Institute (AFI) National Film Theatre** in the Kennedy Center (202-785-4600; www.afionline.org/nft/nft.frame.html). A second facility, **AFI Silver Theatre**, is scheduled to open in Silver Spring the latter part of 2000. It will be a state-of-the-art, internationally recognized film and video exhibition center offering American and international cinema, both classic and contemporary. Watch the website for details about its opening date, address and phone number.

The **Uptown Theatre**, located one block south of Cleveland Park Metro station on the Red Line at 3426 Connecticut Ave. NW (202-966-5400), generally gets the most votes as Washington's best movie theater. It has preserved the old-style seating and balcony. A remnant of the art deco period, the Uptown maintains its original huge screen. The theater shows both first-run movies and occasional classics. The **Avalon**, about a 15-minute walk from Friendship Heights Metro Station on the Red Line, is up the street from the Uptown at 5612 Connecticut Ave. NW (202-966-2600).

The **Cineplex Odeon Cinemas** (202-244-0880) is a popular modern multiplex with six screens. Located across from Friendship Heights Post Office, and 6 blocks south of the Tenleytown Metro Station on the Red Line at 4000 Wisconsin Ave. NW, they show mostly first run commercial movies with an occasional art film that appeals to other tastes. The seats are comfortable and the free parking in the underground garage is convenient. You can find a guide to Cineplex Odeon movies, by major city, on the Internet at www.cineplexodeon.com.

The **AMC Union Station** at 50 Massachusetts Ave. NE (703-998-4AMC) is the only movie house in the Northeast quadrant of the city. When the idea was first introduced to have a movie theater in the basement of the renovated train station, it was met with some skepticism. Today, nine spacious and popular theaters cater to an otherwise under-served part of the city. Each theater in the complex is named for a famous movie house from Washington's cinema history.

Both the **Arlington Cinema 'n Drafthouse** at 2903 Columbia Pike (703-486-2345) and the **Bethesda Theatre Café** at 7719 Wisconsin Ave. (301-656-3337; www.jwdc.com/movies) serve beer, wine and snacks during movies. Both show second-run movies; admission is around $5.00 on the weekends and $3.50 during the week, and $1.50 on Mondays and all shows before 5:00 p.m. On Sundays during the fall, Redskins games take over the screen and admission is free. As you enter or leave the Theatre Café, be sure to notice its marquee, which is a historic landmark.

Independent and foreign film aficionados will be pleased to know that the **Biograph** theatre, once a landmark in Georgetown, is being resurrected at a new location. Scheduled to open in 2001 as part of the Lincoln Square office building at 555 11th Street NW, it will show independent films, foreign language cinema and restored classics. Those who really love serious cinema should look into the **Key's Sunday Cinema Club** (202-965-4401) which is held at the AMC Courthouse in Virginia. Members see new, unreleased (mostly foreign) movies on Sunday mornings with free coffee during the showing and a discussion session following.

The **Cineplex Odeon** at 2772 S. Randolph in Shirlington (703-671-0910) specializes in foreign art films. Its location in Shirlington's "restaurant row" makes it convenient to grab a bite to eat either before or after the movie. For film buffs who enjoy food and drink with their cinema, **Visions** at 1927 Florida Ave. NW (202-607-4321; www.VisionsDC.com), is scheduled to open during the summer of 2000. With two screens, special programming, a bistro and a lounge, Visions is a destination for the entire evening rather than just a portion of one.

Free movies are offered at a number of places including the **National Gallery's East Wing** and the Smithsonian's **Freer Gallery**, and **Hirschhorn** and **National Air and Space Museums**.

Jazz

While not all that it once was, back in the days of Duke Ellington, Washington's jazz scene is still alive. One of the most popular clubs attracting top musicians is **Blues Alley** at 1073 Wisconsin Ave. NW (202-337-4141). An evening at Blues Alley can be quite expensive; cover charges range from $13 to $31.50, depending on the show, and there is a $7 food and beverage minimum per person. **Takoma Station Tavern** at 6914 4th St. NW (202-829-1999) features live jazz nightly, charges no cover and has just a two-drink minimum. Other local jazz spots include the **219 Club** at 219 King St. in Old Town (703-549-1141), and **Bailey's Cafe and Grill** at 1100 Wayne Ave., Silver Spring (301-495-3063). For information on the annual contemporary **Capital Jazz Fest**, jazz afficionados can call 301-218-0404 or check the Web at www.capitaljazz.com.

Comedy

Washington—particularly the government—is food for thought for many local and national comedians. Who can blame them? Many of the things that go on here can seem pretty outrageous, especially when the story is told just right. A few local comedy clubs and troupes keep Washingtonians in good spirits, even when we are laughing at ourselves.

The **Improv** is located between L and M Sts., one block from the Farragut North Metro on the Red Line, at 1140 Connecticut Ave. NW (202-296-7008); it is the local version of the nationally known club. Admission is charged.

Drawing from local talent, both **Gross National Product** and the **Capitol Steps** satirize Washington politics. Gross National Product (202-783-7212; http://home.earthlink.net/~gnpinc) is on tour for the remainder of the campaign year. Watch their website for the venue and schedule once their local performances are reconvened. On most weekends, the Capitol Steps, a nationally known musical parody group made up of current and former Congressional staffers, can be seen at **Chelsea's** at 1055 Thomas Jefferson St. NW (703-683-8330; www.capsteps.com—the final "s" is essential!). Tickets are available for the show and dinner, or you can opt to see the show only. Although an evening with the Steps is a bit pricey, they are terrific and well worth it. For a less expensive dose of the Capitol Steps, watch for one of their frequent specials on PBS, wait for one of their shows on NPR, or buy one of their compact discs.

Recreation

From park land and trails perfect for hiking and biking to sports and health clubs, from boating and sailing to golf and horseback riding, there are options in the District and the Maryland and Virginia suburbs to suit every preference.

Bicycling

Bicyclists will be glad to know that hundreds of miles of bike trails criss-cross the metropolitan area. Many cyclists favor a picturesque 15-mile stretch between Georgetown and Great Falls on the C&O Towpath. An equally beautiful trail is available on the other side of the Potomac. The paved Mount Vernon Bike Trail rambles 18 miles from Roosevelt Island to George Washington's plantation. The Washington & Old Dominion (W&OD) trail extends over 60 miles from Alexandria to Purcellville. Rock Creek Park provides another prime location, especially on weekends, when cyclists can enjoy car-free sections of Beach Drive.

Another favorite for bikers, as well as hikers, joggers, and rollerbladers is the **Capital Crescent Trail**. Originally the B&O railroad tracks, the Capital

Crescent Trail connects Georgetown to Bethesda and Rock Creek Park, and to Silver Spring. Their website at www.cctrail.org offers a map of the trail's completed and unfinished sections, a brief history of the Baltimore and Ohio Railroad tracks that preceded the trail, parking locations, news updates and a calendar of events.

One of the largest recreation areas in Maryland is the Beltsville Agricultural Park, just north of Greenbelt. This is a huge tract of government land, criss-crossed by miles of two-lane country roads. It is perfect for bicycling and on weekends you will usually see more bicycle traffic than automobiles. To get there, take the Beltway to the exit for Kenilworth Ave. and go north.

Mountain bikers may not be satisfied with local riverside or park routes. Instead, they can tackle the unrestricted system of challenging trails around Sugarloaf Mountain just outside the northwest corner of Montgomery County. To get to Sugarloaf, take I-270 North to Route 109. Follow Route 109 three miles to Comus Rd., make a right and drive (or ride) another three miles.

Lots of resources are available for people who like to bike. You can rent bikes at **Fletcher's Boathouse** at 4940 Canal Rd. NW (202-244-0461), **Thompson Boat Center** at 2900 Virginia Ave. NW (202-333-4861) or **Swain's Lock** (301-299-9006). The District's **Department of Documents** (202-727-5090) publishes bike trail maps for $3. You can pick them up or order them by mail at Suite 520, 441 4th St. NW. You can also get information from the **Potomac Pedalers Touring Club** (202-363-8687) and the **National Capital Velo Club** (301-588-2087). Enthusiasts may want to consider joining the **Washington Area Bicyclist Association** (202-628-2500; www.waba.org). This organization works to create new and better places to bicycle in the Washington area, and to ensure the safety of bicyclists.

Boating and Sailing

The waters of the C&O Canal and the Potomac River (downstream from Chain Bridge) cater to the romantic soul with canoeing and boating from May to October. You can rent both canoes and rowboats at **Fletcher's Boathouse**, 4940 Canal Rd. NW (202-244-0461). A bit farther downstream near Washington Harbour, **Thompson Boat Center** at 2900 Virginia Ave. NW (202-333-4861) rents canoes and kayaks. Recreational sculls are available to individuals providing some type of rowing certification. Thompson's proximity to the Georgetown waterfront and the Mall makes it the best starting point for watercraft tours of the city. If you would like to paddle around the Tidal Basin, you can rent a two-person paddle-boat at the **Tidal Basin Boathouse** at 1501 Maine Ave. SW (202-484-0206). The **Washington Sailing Marina** (703-548-9027), a mile south of Reagan National Airport, gives lessons and rents sailboats. Farther down the George Washington Parkway, the Mariner Sailing School at the **Belle Haven Marina** (703-768-0018) offers sailing lessons and rents canoes, kayaks and sailboats.

To meet others with similar interests, you might join the **Washington Canoe Club** (202-333-9749) or **Canoe Cruisers Association of Greater Washington** (301-656-2586; www.ccadc.org). When planning a trip, remember that flooding or severe weather can curtail these water activities. Before you venture out, call 703-260-0505 for the marine forecast.

Golf

Golfers can tee off at a number of area public golf courses. The **East Potomac Park Golf Course** (202-863-9007), located at Hains Point, has two nine-hole courses and one 18-hole course. Rolling hills and tree-lined fairways characterize the 18-hole golf course in **Rock Creek Park** (202-882-7332), located at Rittenhouse and 16th Sts. NW. Suburbanites can stroll the links closer to home at public courses in Alexandria at 6700 Telegraph Rd. (703-971-3788), in Reston at 11875 Sunrise Valley Dr. (703-620-9333), and in Wheaton at 15701 Layhill Rd. (301-598-6100). Golfers interested in joining country clubs will find a number of superb choices throughout the metropolitan Washington, DC area.

HEALTH CLUBS

Aspen Hill Club
301-598-5200

City Fitness
202-537-0539

Fitness First
301-963-1500

Muscle Beach
202-328-5200

Olympus Fitness Center
703-241-2255

Sport & Health Co.
703-556-6550

Washington Sports Club
202-332-0100

YMCA of Metropolitan Washington
202-862-9622

Health Clubs

Most of the national health club chains have facilities in the area and several local entrepreneurs have started their own health clubs. Facilities vary widely in features, but most offer at least exercise rooms and aerobics classes. Hotels, too, have gotten into the act, with most of the larger ones offering exercise rooms and pools to both their guests and local residents. With more HMOs encouraging regular exercise, check to see if your health insurance plan offers a discount at any area health clubs or rebates on premiums for health clubs members.

Hiking

For some of the area's best hiking, trails paralleling the Potomac River in Great Falls Park provide great terrain and striking vistas, such as Potomac Overlook Park in Arlington, and Huntley Meadows in Alexandria. Those looking for something closer in should head to Rock Creek Park in the District. Trails also meander through Theodore Roosevelt Island, the wildlife sanctuary just across the Potomac from the Kennedy Center. Popular hiking clubs include **Sierra Club** (202-547-5551 for their weekly activity schedule, or 703-242-0693 to speak to a staff member), **Potomac Appalachian Trail Club** (703-242-0965) and **Potomac Backpackers Association** (703-524-1185). Visit the clubs virtually at www.sierraclub.org and www.patc.net.

Information about the **Metropolitan Washington Regional Outings Program** (MWROP) of the Sierra Club can be found by calling 202-547-2326, or at their website at http://webmentor.com/mwrop/index.html. You can subscribe to a quarterly newsletter from MWROP listing hikes and backpacking trips. If you like to hike, especially if you are not familiar with the area and want to hike with people who are, this is the hardcopy source to get.

Horseback Riding

City dwellers can enjoy 17 miles of bridle paths in **Rock Creek Park** (202-362-0117), winding through some of Washington's best scenery. Escorted trail rides and lessons are available at all levels. **Wheaton Regional Park** (301-622-3311) offers horseback riding and guided hour-long trail rides on Sunday afternoon. If you are experimenting with horseback riding, don't forget to wear long pants. For all activities, call ahead for reservations.

Equestrian Enterprises in Great Falls, VA (703-759-2474) offers guided trail rides for adults through Great Falls Park. You have to call ahead to book one of the two-hour trail rides. You can also join the **Capitol Hill Equestrian Society**; call 202-828-3035 for more information.

If Polo is your game, the **Georgetown Polo Club** organizes games on the Mall near the Lincoln Memorial in West Potomac Park. Call 301-983-5229 for information.

Ice Skating

With the elegant Willard Hotel as a backdrop, ice skaters glide across the ice at the outdoor **Pershing Park Ice Rink** (202-737-6938) at Pennsylvania Ave. and 14th St. NW, just a short stroll from the White House. A few blocks away, winter enthusiasts enjoy skating at the **National Sculpture Garden Ice Rink** at Constitution Ave. and 9th St. NW (202-371-5340). Fees are assessed for skating at Pershing Park and the National Sculpture Garden. Montgomery County has several outdoor rinks including the **Wheaton Regional Park Ice Rink** (301-649-3640), the **Bethesda Metro Ice Center** (301-656-0588) and Rockville's **Cabin John Ice Rink** (301-365-2246). Cabin John is open year-round. Virginians can skate year round at the **Fairfax Ice Arena** (703-323-1131) and at **Reston Skating Pavilion** (703-318-7541). If skating means hockey playing, contact **Arc Ice Sports Rockville** (301-294-8101) or one of the **Skate Nation** facilities located in Reston (703-709-1010), Dale City (703-730-8423) or Odenton, MD (410-672-7013), which is the official training facility for the NHL's Washington Capitals.

Running

Thousands of Washingtonians fit a run into their lunch hour along the Mall, East Potomac Park, the Mount Vernon Trail or Rock Creek Park. A few runners even opt for a diabolical sprint up the imposing flight of stone steps featured in "The Exorcist" on M St. in Georgetown near the Key Bridge.

Triathlons take place in Reston, VA and Columbia, MD. The **Tri-Maryland Triathlon Club** (410-882-6103; www.triad.com) plans the "No Frills" Biathlon Series (running/biking and swimming/running) at sites throughout Maryland. *The Running Report*, available at most sports equipment stores, lists upcoming races. You can also find the Report on the Web at http://runwashington.com. Popular clubs are **DC Road Runners** (703-241-0395); **Montgomery County Road Runners Club** (301-353-0200); and **DC Front Runners** (202-628-3223), a running club for gays, lesbians and their friends.

Skiing

During the winter, cross-country skiers pick up where walkers and joggers leave off in Rock Creek Park or on the Mall. Downhill skiing—on the other hand—requires some serious driving to reach the slopes. While Virginia and Maryland have their own ski locations, Eastern Pennsylvania, about 200 miles away, is one of your best bets. Many ski fans—and fans of other kinds of fun activities—join the **Maryland Outdoors Club, Inc.** (301-601-5007). Another number you should know is the *Washington Post's* **Post-Haste Ski Report** hotline. Call 202-334-9000, ext. 4300 for the latest area ski conditions, or visit the Travel page of www.washingtonpost.com. Some of the ski areas you will find on these sites include:

Maryland

Wisp, Deep Creek Lake — 301-387-4911
www.gcnet.net/wisp

Virginia

Bryce Mountain, Basye — 540-856-2121
www.bryceresort.com

Massanutten, Harrisonburg — 540-289-9441
www.massresort.com

Wintergreen, Wintergreen — 800-325-2200
www.wintergreenresort.com

Pennsylvania

Blue Knob, Claysburg	814-239-5111 www.blueknob.com
Bear Mountain, Macungie	610-682-7100 www.skibearcreek.com
Hidden Valley, Somerset	800-458-0175 www.hiddenvalleyresort.com
Seven Springs, Champion	800-452-2223 www.7springs.com
Ski Liberty, Fairfield	717-642-8282 www.skiliberty.com
Whitetail, Mercersburg	717-328-9400 www.skiwhitetail.com

Soccer

Soccer's popularity continues to increase, as do opportunities for leagues, clubs and pickup games. Parks and Recreation Departments and many schools offer playing fields, and new facilities are being established. In Montgomery County, the area's largest soccer complex is being developed at the South Germantown Recreation Park. When completed in late 2000, **SoccerPlex** will be the largest soccer complex in the Washington area with 26 indoor and outdoor fields.

You can obtain information regarding clubs and leagues from the **Maryland State Soccer Association** (410-744-5864), the **National Capital Soccer League** (703-791-2656) or the **Virginia Soccer Association** (703-753-2432). Information is also available online where you can link directly to sites for local soccer clubs and leagues. Two websites to get you started are www.delmarweb.com/maryland and www.soccervirginia.com.

Sports on the Mall

The vast expanse of the Mall, especially around the Washington Monument, is the staging ground for many sports activities. Recreational team sports, particularly softball, have become as vital to politicking and deal-making as power lunches. Interns, legislative aides, partners and associates can be seen battling it out on the Mall grounds, both in and out of uniform. Most teams are co-ed and low-key. You should ask around your office to see about joining a team or contact the **Congressional Athletic Association** at 202-544-3333. On the Web, they are at www.congsoftball.com.

Swimming

If you do not have access to a pool, relief from Washington's hot, muggy summers can be found in any one of the area's public swimming pools. One of the city's finest pools is just off Wisconsin Ave. in Georgetown, at 34th St. and Volta Pl. NW (202-282-2366). Other public pools are the indoor pool in the **Marie Reed Recreation Center** at 2200 Champlain St. NW (202-673-7768) or the indoor **Capitol East Natatorium** at 635 North Carolina Ave. SE (202-724-4495).

Arlington's high schools have indoor pools open to the public for lap swimming on a pay-as-you-swim basis. You can try **Washington-Lee** at 1300 North Quincy St. (703-228-6262), **Wakefield** at 4901 South Chesterfield Rd. (703-578-3063) or **Yorktown** at 5201 North 28th St. (703-536-9739). Non-residents are welcome but must pay a slightly higher fee than residents pay.

RECREATION DEPARTMENTS

District of Columbia
202-673-7660

Maryland
Montgomery County
240-777-6804

Prince George's County
301-699-2407

Virginia
Alexandria
703-838-4343

Arlington County
703-228-3322

Fairfax County
703-324-4386

The **Montgomery Aquatic Center** at 5900 Executive Blvd. in North Bethesda (301-468-4211) has a 200-foot-long water slide. Water lovers can also enjoy swimming in the Center's 50-meter pool and relaxing in one of its two hot tubs. Call for current admission fees.

In Silver Spring, the **Martin Luther King Swim Center** at 1201 Jackson Rd. (301-989-1206) has a 42-yard pool, eight 25-yard lanes and a teaching pool. After your swim, you can relax in the hot tub. The **Fairland Aquatic Center** at 13820 Old Gunpowder Rd. in Laurel (301-206-2359) boasts a 50-meter Olympic-sized pool and a 20-person jacuzzi. Swims are reasonably priced both here and at the Martin Luther King Center.

Nearly every public pool has a Masters Swimming group for adults. You can receive coaching, a private swimming lesson several times a week and, periodically, the chance to compete.

Tennis

Tennis buffs can play on the same courts that have hosted major players, at the **Rock Creek Tennis Center**, 16th and Kennedy Sts. NW (202-722-5949). A large plastic bubble roof permits winter play on five of the hard courts. Hourly fees are modest for outdoor courts while indoor court fees climb sharply. Reservations must be made one week in advance.

Public tennis courts are widely available, both in the District and beyond. **Hains Point's East Potomac Tennis Center** (202-554-5962) has 19 outdoor and five indoor courts. You can also play at the outdoor courts at **Pierce Mill** in Rock Creek Park (202-426-6908). Several courts, on the 3000 block of R St. in Georgetown, are open on a first-come, first-served basis. On the Hill, you can play at Garfield Park, 3rd and Eye Sts. SE. The least well-known public courts in town are on D St. NW, right across from the State Department. Time slots are distributed to employees and the public through a lottery system. You must sign up in person at the **Federal Reserve Bank**, Constitution Ave. and 20th St. NW (202-452-3357). For a list of public tennis courts in your area, call your local recreation department. For the serious tennis player, there is the **Mid-Atlantic Tennis Association** (703-560-9480).

Spectator Sports

The Washington area has lots of spectator sports activities, both professional and college. Football, basketball, hockey, baseball, soccer, even golf and tennis stars bring together avid fans from all around the area.

Professional Sports

Liberal or conservative, Democrat or Republican, the nation's capital has one unifying force—the **Washington Redskins** (301-276-6000; www.redskins.com). Few teams have followers as devoted as Redskin fans. When the local National Football League team plays Dallas, you will hear of little else all week. Chances of seeing a Redskins game at FedEx Field are slim at best, unless you go as a guest of a season ticket holder or pay scalpers' exorbitant prices. Tickets are so hot that people fight over them in divorce settlements and pass them along in wills. You may want to get on the waiting list for season tickets. The perennial sell-outs guarantee that all games are televised. But if you still want to be there, tickets can be found. The classified section of the *Washington Post* and *Washington Times* regularly list single game and season ticket packages. If you plan to drive to a game at the FedEx Field on Rte. 202 in Landover, MD (301-276-6000), expect delays getting in and out of the parking areas. To get to the stadium from the Beltway, take Exit 17A (17B is the most congested and should be avoided), Exit 16B, or Exit 15B or 15A. Metro expands its rail service on game days, and shuttle buses are available both before and after the game at the Cheverly and Landover stations on the Orange Line, and at the Addison Road station on the Blue Line.

One side benefit to Washington's Redskin-mania is that the stores and shopping malls are fairly quiet during games. For non-football fans, Sunday afternoons can be an excellent time to shop, check out the latest show at the National Gallery of

Art, go to the movies or do just about anything unimpeded by the usual crowds. Washington also hosts professional basketball and hockey teams—the National Basketball Association's **Wizards** (www.nba.com) and the National Hockey League's **Capitals** (www.nhl.com). Both teams play at the MCI Center at Seventh and F Sts. NW (202-628-3200; www.mcicenter.com). Metro is by far the best way to travel to events at this site. The Gallery Place station (Red, Yellow and Green Lines) connects directly with the Center, and three more stations are all within easy walking distance: Metro Center (Red, Blue and Orange Lines), Archives (Yellow and Green Lines) and Judiciary Square (Red Line). Limited parking is available in neighborhood lots and garages for those who plan to drive.

The **Washington Mystics** (202-628-3200, www.wnba.com/mystics), Washington's WNBA franchise, play their home games during the summer at MCI Center. Tickets are available at 202-661-5050 (season tickets), and 202-432-SEAT (individual game tickets).

Since the Senators left in 1971, Washingtonians have longed for a baseball team they could call their own. For now, it is still the American League **Baltimore Orioles** (410-685-9800; www.theorioles.com) who play in the wonderful downtown ballpark, Oriole Park at Camden Yards (or simply Camden Yards).

To get to Camden Yards by car, take I-95 North to Baltimore. From I-95 take the I-395 Exit and follow the signs; the stadium is just off the highway. Since the Stadium is only a short stroll away from Inner Harbor, it is fun to make a day of it. Parking is cheap and you can hang out in Inner Harbor or nearby Little Italy before heading over to the game.

The Orioles regularly sell out, therefore you should plan ahead. Washingtonians (who make up nearly a third of the fans) can go to the convenient **Orioles Baseball Store** at 914 17th St. NW (202-296-2473) for tickets and memorabilia. Players make personal appearances at the store so call and check out when you can do a little "Bird-watching." You can also purchase tickets over the phone through Ticketmaster (202-432-SEAT). If you are unfamiliar with the stadium floor plans and seating, consult the front of the Bell Atlantic Yellow Pages, which contains diagrams of the major area stadiums.

The NFL's **Baltimore Ravens** (410-261-7283; www.baltimoreravens.com) play at PSINet Stadium, also at Camden Yards.

The **DC United**, a championship Major League Soccer team, meets its opponents at Robert F. Kennedy (RFK) Stadium (Metro stop: Stadium-Armory). Tickets are available through Ticketmaster. Team information and schedules are available at www.dcunited.com.

The **Professional Golfer's Association** (PGA) tour swings through Washington for the **Kemper Open**, traditionally held in late May. The **Tournament Player's Club** at Avenel in Potomac, MD (301-469-3737) hosts the event, which has attracted many top pros.

Many of the world's top male tennis players travel here in July for the **Newsweek Classic**. The top women players show up in September for the **Champions' Challenge**. Both events are held at the Washington Tennis Center at the corner of 16th and Kennedy Sts. NW. Tickets can be purchased through Pro Serv (202-721-7200).

Each February, past and future Olympic medalists assemble at George Mason University for the **Mobil 1 Invitational Track and Field Meet**. It is one of the major events of the competitive circuit. Seating is limited and tickets go quickly. For ticket information, call 703-993-3270.

Serious runners may want to begin training for Washington's biggest marathon. In late October, the **Marine Corps Marathon** tests the mettle of more than a few good men and women. The race begins at the Iwo Jima Memorial in Rosslyn and finishes 26 miles later at the same spot. It attracts thousands of runners each year. For information on advance registration, which is required, and the current entrance fee rate, call 703-690-3431. The Marine Corps Marathon's website is http://issb-www1-mqg.usmc.mil/marathon/.

College Athletics

There are many schools in and around Washington with excellent, nationally competitive athletic programs, both men's and women's. The Fall 1999 *Sports Illustrated for Women* ranked Maryland eighth and Virginia thirteenth in country for women's athletics. The **University of Maryland's** basketball teams play their home games at Cole Field House and football at Byrd Stadium on the Maryland campus. The **Terrapins** (www.umterps.com) compete in the Atlantic Coast Conference against schools like Duke, North Carolina and Virginia. Tickets for either sport can be ordered in advance by phone (301-314-7070) or mail (PO Box 295, College Park, MD 20741). The University's website is www.umcp.umd.edu.

The MCI Center hosts the **Georgetown Hoyas** men's basketball team (202-687-HOYA; www.guhoyas.com) and the Hoyas play football at Kehoe Field. Contests against Big East Conference rivals sell out quickly. Tickets can be purchased at Georgetown or through Ticketmaster (202-432-SEAT).

VOLUNTEERING AU NATURAL

Protecting and restoring local resources naturally go hand-in-hand with volunteering. For the environmentally inclined, here are a few ideas to get you going:

DC

The EnvironMentors Project
202-347-7766;
www.scarlson@environmentors.org
Matches environmental professionals with DC high school students to focus on science and community service projects.

National Zoo
202-673-4961; www.fonz.org/getinv.htm
Choose from caring and feeding the animals to conducting tours to working at special events.

MD

The Anacostia Watershed Society
301-699-6204; www.anacostiaws.org
Works to protect and restore the river and watershed; river day trips and focused clean-up projects are making a difference.

Maryland/DC Chapter of The Nature Conservancy
301-656-8673; www.tnc.org
Focuses on preserving plants, animals and natural communities that represent the diversity of life by protecting the lands and water they need to survive.

The Oyster Recovery Partnership
410-269-5570
Works to restore oysters to Chesapeake Bay. Join this group to learn about the Bay while contributing to an important mission.

VA

The Potomac Appalachian Trail Club
703-242-0693; www.patc.net
Maintains and improves 970 miles of hiking trails, 30 shelters, and 28 cabins in Washington, DC, Maryland, Virginia, West Virginia and Pennsylvania, including 240 miles of the Appalachian Trail.

The **Howard University** men's basketball team, the **Bison**, play at Burr and play football at Greene Stadium on the University campus. Tickets are available at Cramton Auditorium box office (202-806-7199) or from Ticketmaster (202-432-SEAT). Howard University's website is www.howard.edu/.

George Washington University (202-994-6650; www.gwu.edu) has no football team. The basketball and volleyball teams, known as the **Colonials**, play at Charles E. Smith Center located at 600 22nd St. NW. GWU baseball is played at Barcroft Park and soccer is at South Riding Field. Tickets to their games are available from Ticketmaster (202-432-SEAT).

VOLUNTEER ACTIVITIES

Volunteering for a cause has always made a difference...in the cause itself, and in the life of the volunteer. And choosing among the countless organizations and groups to work with has never been easier, with the aid of local clearinghouses, or just by getting on-line. Whether you are new to the Washington, DC area or have lived here for years, it's a great time to care.

10 TIPS FOR VOLUNTEER SAVVY

(1) Do your research. Choose issues and programs important to you.

(2) Understand your natural and special skills and abilities.

(3) Consider a fresh idea, far away from your daily routine.

(4) Combine goals: plant trees and...lose weight!

(5) Don't over-commit! Nobody wins.

(6) Be prepared for a possible interview.

(7) Think about volunteering as a family.

(8) Volunteer—virtually.

(9) Expect a surprise, there are volunteer experiences you've never even dreamed of.

(10) Bring your heart and sense of humor.

Now more than ever, local schools need your volunteering expertise. This is particularly true as expectations and standards have become more rigorous. A child can benefit exponentially from a little one-on-one from the heart. To volunteer, contact a school district in your area (see Chapter 10's feature page listing of area schools).

Today, due in part to a spirited commitment by local corporations, the volunteer experience has become downright mainstream and more than just an activist's pursuit. America Online in Dulles recently introduced its new online database of over 600,00 charities and 20,000 volunteer opportunities. The website, www.helping.org, allows the user to search by location and topic, bringing you detailed information about volunteering opportunities as close as your zip code. Another online resource for both organizations and volunteers is www.volunteermatch.org. Match your skills, time and/or resources with nonprofit community-based organizations and causes in your area.

One of the easiest ways to get involved is to contact your community's volunteer clearinghouse, which serves as an information bank, providing details on hundreds of community service opportunities. **Greater DC Cares** (202-289-7378; www.dc-cares.org), a 10-year-old nonprofit organization, annually facilitates 100,000 volunteer hours for 100 local nonprofits. Four years ago, they began **Business Shares**, a program that works within a company to help create its own volunteer programs. Greater DC Cares coordinates and manages projects in seven critical areas: children and families, elderly, hunger and homelessness, affordable housing, environment, people living with disabilities, and people affected by HIV/AIDs.

Another major DC clearinghouse is called **DoingSomething** (202-393-5051; www.doingsomething.org). Its all-electronic newsletter provides a weekly listing of opportunities to both help and connect with others. On the social side, DoingSomething volunteers get together monthly to meet and relax with fellow members.

Along those same lines, if you're single and interested in group volunteering activities, the **Single Volunteers of DC** (www.singlevolunteers.org) may be just right for you. Project leaders work with interested non-profit organizations to find projects where SVDC volunteers can help. Available singles are brought together in a productive, positive environment. Regular opportunities to meet on a strictly social level are built into the program, resulting in a great way to meet people.

For Maryland and Virginia neighbors willing to roll up your shirtsleeves and get involved, contact the appropriate volunteer office below to learn about the ways in which you can make a difference in your community.

Maryland

Montgomery County Volunteer and Community Service Center
401 Hungerford Dr., First Floor, Rockville, MD
240-777-2600
www.co.mo.md.us/services/volunteer

Prince George's Voluntary Action Center
5012 Rhode Island Ave., Hyattsville, MD
301-699-2797

Virginia

Alexandria Volunteer Bureau
2210 Mount Vernon Ave., Alexandria, VA
703-836-2176
www.needsyou.org/avb.htm

Arlington County Volunteer Office
800 S. Walter Reed Dr., Arlington, VA
703-228-5811
www.co.arlington.va.us/volunteer

Volunteer Fairfax
10530 Page Ave. Fairfax, VA
703-246-3460
www.btg.com/volsrus

Prince William County
9248 Center St. Manassas, VA
703-369-5292
www.pwcweb.com/vac

Loudoun County Volunteer Center
One Harrison St. SE Leesburg, VA
703-777-0113

EVENTS & FESTIVALS

January/February

Martin Luther King Jr.'s Birthday
The National Park Service sponsors a ceremony at the Lincoln Memorial, the site of the famous 1963 "I Have a Dream" speech.

Chinese New Year Parade
Chinatown celebrates with fireworks and elaborately costumed parade participants.

George Washington's Birthday Parade
Old Town Alexandria hosts a parade; Mount Vernon, George Washington's home, holds special activities.

Baltimore Craft Show
The ACC Craft Fair is held at the Baltimore Convention Center at Pratt and Sharp Sts. It's the largest juried craft show in the United States featuring crafts in fine art form and museum quality.

March/April

St. Patrick's Day Parade
Bagpipers, bands and floats parade through Old Town Alexandria and along Constitution Ave.

Smithsonian Kite Festival
Fly your kite with hundreds of others on the Washington Monument grounds.

Cherry Blossom Festival
The local week-long rite of spring celebrates one of the area's most beautiful sights. Short-lived blossoms, concentrated along the Tidal Basin, peak between mid-March and mid-April.

Duke Ellington Birthday Celebration
Celebrate the music of this DC-born jazz star with a concert at Freedom Plaza, 13th St. and Pennsylvania Ave. NW.

Washington Flower and Garden Show
Washington area landscape designers display gardens filled with thousands of flowers and trees, and offer lectures and demonstrations at the Washington Convention Center.

Smithsonian Craft Show
This event features the creations of more than 100 international artists at the National Building Museum.

White House Easter Egg Roll
Children eight and under, accompanied by adults, gather on the White House South Lawn.

May/June

Filmfest DC
Over 50 international and American independent films are shown all over town.

Malcolm X Day
A day to honor Malcolm X is held in Anacostia Park in Southeast DC, featuring speeches, exhibits, music and food.

Gay Pride Day
This march to promote gay rights begins at 16th and W Sts. and ends at 24th and N Sts.

Festival of American Folklife
In late June to early July, the Smithsonian presents a slice of American Folklife on the Mall.

Memorial Day Weekend Concert
The National Symphony Orchestra performs an outdoor concert on the West Lawn of the US Capitol.

Annual Goodwill Embassy Tour
Selected embassies open their doors to the public to benefit Davis Memorial Goodwill Industries.

Marine Band's Summer Concert Series
Starting in June, evening performances are Wednesdays at the US Capitol and Sundays at the Ellipse across from the White House.

Caribbean Festival This annual festival on Georgia Ave. NW features an elaborate parade and programs about Caribbean cultures.

National Capital Barbecue Battle
The annual event includes entertainment, children's activities, cooking demonstrations and a cooking contest to determine the National Barbecue Championship winners. Staged between 9th and 13th Sts. on Pennsylvania Ave.

Virginia Renaissance Faire
This festival, with medieval entertainment, sports, music and storytellers, features costumed actors and runs through six weekends in Fredericksburg, VA.

JULY/AUGUST

Fourth of July
This holiday is a day of free celebrations—a dramatic reading of the Declaration of Independence, a parade down Constitution Ave., an evening performance of the National Symphony Orchestra, and a tremendous fireworks display on the Mall.

Latin American Festival
For two days at the end of July, the mall comes alive with Latin American music, food, dance and crafts.

SEPTEMBER/OCTOBER

Black Family Reunion
In early September, the National Council of Negro Women sponsors an event with storytellers, music, art, food and other activities, on the Washington Monument grounds.

Adams Morgan Day
A street festival along 18th St. NW, on the second Sunday in September, celebrates the multicultural flavor of this neighborhood.

Taste of DC
Each October, the DC Committee to Promote Washington offers Taste of DC, featuring food from local restaurants, to promote area tourism and benefit local charities.

Marine Corps Marathon
In late October, thousands of runners race from the Iwo Jima Memorial in Arlington through downtown DC.

Halloween
Wisconsin Ave. and M St. in Georgetown are closed to traffic as thousands of costumed pedestrians descend upon an eight-block area.

NSO Labor Day Concert
The National Symphony Orchestra ends its season with a concert on the West Lawn of the Capitol.

Maryland Renaissance Festival
Medieval games, music, food and entertainment are featured along with the opportunity to actively participate in an historical reenactment. Runs over nine weekends in Crownsville, MD (near Annapolis).

NOVEMBER/DECEMBER

National Christmas Tree Lighting
Join the President—and a few thousand locals and tourists—for this annual ritual on the Ellipse, south of the White House.

Washington Craft Show
In November, a juried show of fine contemporary American crafts featuring 175 artisans from across the country is held at the Washington Convention Center.

People's Christmas Tree Lighting
The event occurs on the west side of the US Capitol, accompanied by a military band concert.

White House Christmas Candlelight Tours
Evening tours are given of the White House Christmas decorations.

MASTERING DC: BEST VIEWS OF THE CITY

Known for its monuments, cherry trees, and green spaces, Washington, DC is a beautiful city by day or by night. You won't find many natural high points from which to view the city but there are several buildings and monuments throughout the area that provide good vantage points.

☐ **Check the Time:** Tour the **Old Post Office Clock Tower,** the city's first clock tower and modern "skyscraper." View the city from the Observation Deck high above Pennsylvania Ave. and walk through the tower to see the Congress Bells...and on Thursdays to hear them too.

☐ **Go to the Top:** Ride the elevator or walk to the top of the **Washington Monument** for unobstructed views of the city and major landmarks in all directions.

☐ **Get a Monumental View:** Look across the Mall from the Capitol to Lincoln Memorial, standing on the **West Capitol steps**.

☐ **Appreciate L'Enfant's Vision:** View the Capital City from the **Custis-Lee Mansion** and from L'Enfant's grave site at **Arlington National Cemetery.** It's one of the loveliest views around.

☐ **Ring in the Evening:** Picnic at the **Netherlands Carillon** on a Saturday afternoon (spring) and early evening (summer) and listen to the free carillon concerts. Climb the staircase during the concert to watch the carilloneur at work and enjoy panoramic views of the city.

☐ **Look Down From on High:** View the cathedral grounds, the city, and beyond from the Pilgrim Observation Gallery at **Washington National Cathedral**.

☐ **See the City at Night:** Stand on the steps of the **Lincoln Memorial** for a panorama across the Reflecting Pool to the lighted Capitol dome, or view the city from the **Jefferson Memorial** across the Tidal Basin.

☐ **Wine and Dine:** For a unique view of the city overlooking rooftops of the Treasury building and others near the White House, have drinks and/or dinner at the **Hotel Washington Sky Terrace Lounge** (515 15th St. NW; 202-638-5900) from May to October.

☐ **Dine High:** Above the Potomac River that is, at **J.W.'s Steakhouse** atop the Key Bridge Marriott Hotel (1401 Lee Hwy., Arlington; 703-413-5500). Situated directly opposite the Georgetown University campus, you may even see crewing practice from the University toward downtown.

☐ **Dine Down by the River Side:** Try **Sequoia** (202-944-4200) at Washington Harbour in Georgetown, **Aquarelle** (202-298-4455) in the Watergate Hotel, or **Le Rivage** (202-488-8111) or **Zanzibar on the Waterfront** (202-554-9100) at the wharf area in Southwest DC.

☐ **Cross the River:** The Doubletree Hotel (300 Army-Navy Dr., Crystal City) offers two views, from the restaurant **Windows Over Washington** (703-416-3894) and from the revolving **Skydome** nightclub above the restaurant (703-416-3873).

☐ **Check Out the Roof Tops:** View the Capitol dome and the Library of Congress copper roof from the **Capitol View Club** atop the Hyatt Washington (400 New Jersey Ave. NW; 202-737-1234). Note that this membership club is open to the public in the evening.

Washington Weekends

As a major world capital set in the midst of an area rich in history, culture and natural beauty, Washington offers an unlimited choice of activities for those seemingly all too rare free weekends. You will find, however, that the tremendous number of attractions—both within the Beltway and throughout the general mid-Atlantic region—just might tempt you to shift your priorities.

Besides word of mouth, one of the best ways to learn about what's going on is to check the Weekend section of the *Washington Post* each Friday. Here you will find details on special events, local exhibits, movie and theater listings, and sports events. Washington's free *City Paper* is also an excellent resource. In addition to its regular column, "City Lights," highlighting the week's best events, the *City Paper* contains numerous ads for some of the area's best night life. Also, remember to peruse the local interest section of your favorite bookstore (see Chapter 6 for ideas) for guide books on various aspects of the metropolitan DC area. Or go online to locate the many DC-related websites (see Chapter 5 for listing). This chapter directs you to many of the more prominent sites in the area to get you on your way to some great Washington weekends.

The Weekend Tourist

It used to be that some area residents felt that going to the top of the Washington Monument or taking a cruise on the Potomac was just for tourists. Increasingly, however, suburban Maryland and Virginia residents are being drawn to the city to take advantage of the rich cultural and social life unavailable in the suburbs. They become weekend city dwellers—social commuters—who spend Friday and Saturday nights savoring the city without the hassle of commuting. Whether you choose to live in the city or the suburbs, take a break from your routine to see some of the sights the area has to offer. If you live outside city limits, become a social commuter—book a room at a local hotel, a B&B or stay with a friend. You will end up with a whole new perspective on the city.

Sightseeing Tours

If you aren't sure where to start or you would like to get a good initial overview of the sights, try one of the area's many sightseeing tours, such as the quick, motorized preview provided by **Tourmobile** (202-554-5100; www.tourmobile.com). The red, white and blue Tourmobile cruises through Washington stopping at 25 of its most popular sights. With unlimited boarding and reboarding, you can easily customize the tour. Tickets are available from the drivers at any of the nine ticket locations, or in advance through Ticketmaster.

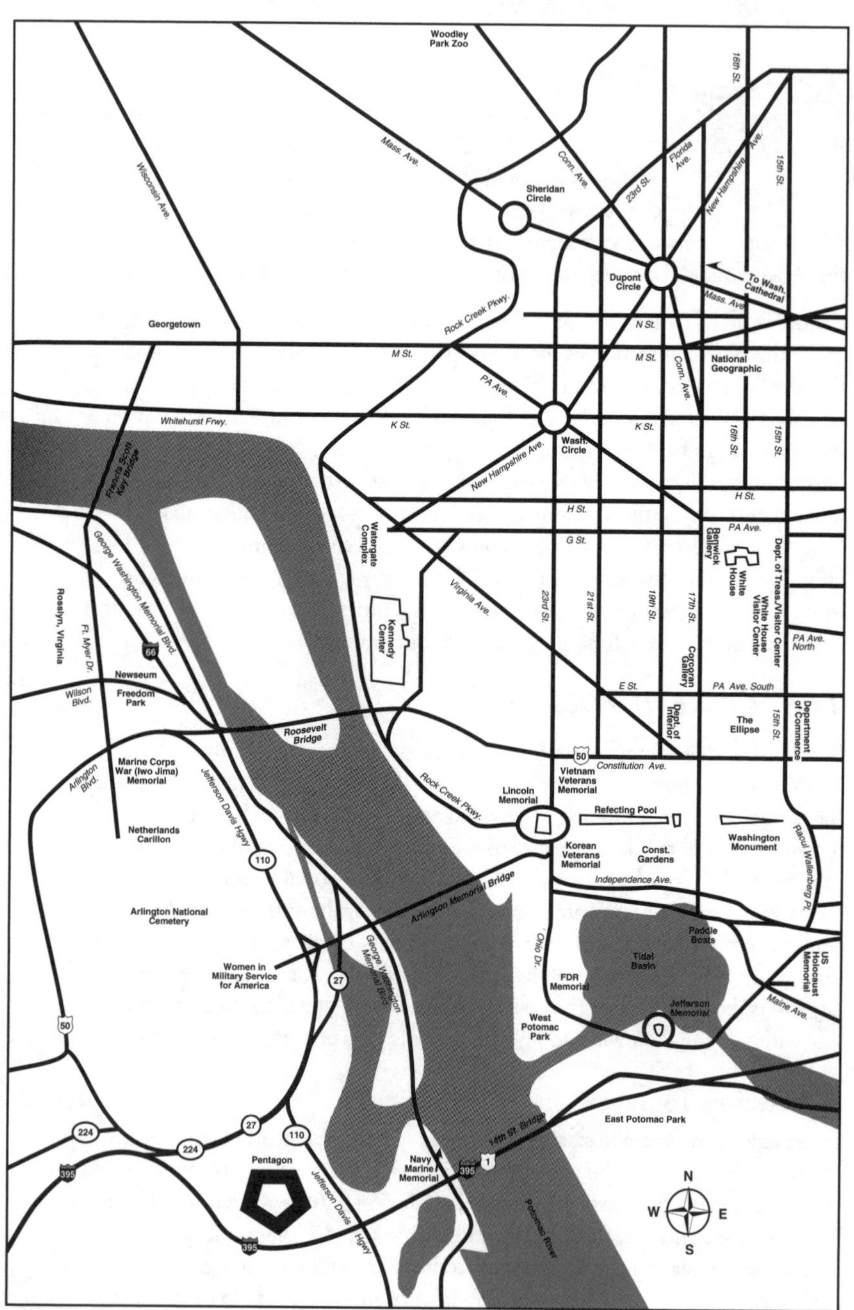

POINTS OF INTEREST

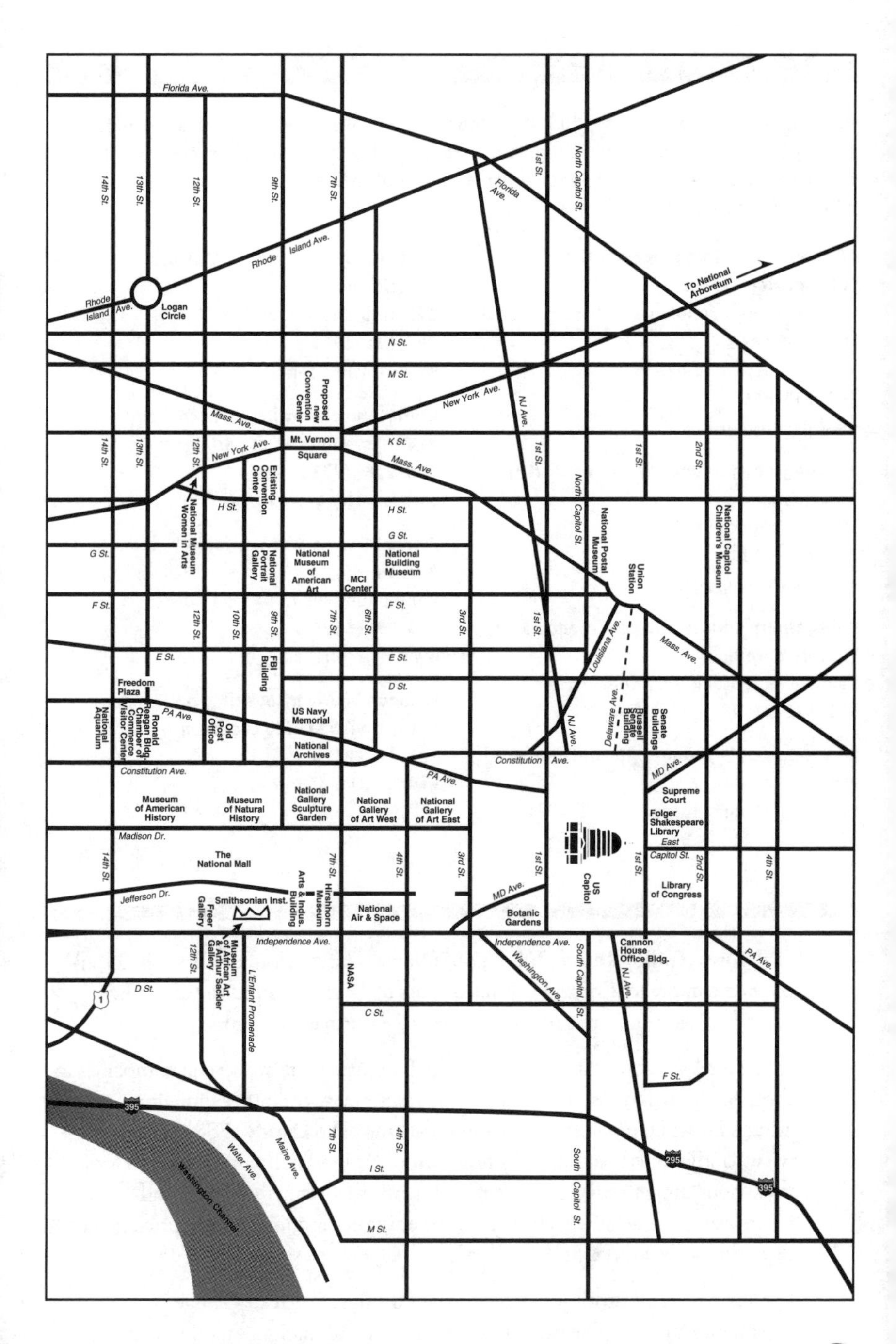
Florida Ave.
14th St.
13th St.
12th St.
9th St.
7th St.
1st St.
North Capitol St.
Florida Ave.
Rhode Island Ave.
Rhode Island Ave.
Logan Circle
To National Arboretum
N St.
M St.
Proposed new Convention Center
New York Ave.
NJ Ave.
Mass. Ave.
Mt. Vernon Square
K St.
New York Ave.
Existing Convention Center
Mass. Ave.
2nd St.
H St.
National Museum Women in Arts
National Postal Museum
National Capitol Children's Museum
G St.
National Portrait Gallery
National Museum of American Art
MCI Center
National Building Museum
Union Station
F St.
10th St.
6th St.
3rd St.
Louisiana Ave.
Mass. Ave.
E St.
FBI Building
Freedom Plaza
D St.
National Aquarium
Ronald Reagan Bldg. Chamber of Commerce Visitor Center
PA Ave.
Old Post Office
US Navy Memorial
National Archives
Delaware Ave.
Russell Senate Building
Senate Buildings
NJ Ave.
Constitution Ave.
Constitution Ave.
PA Ave.
MD Ave.
Museum of American History
Museum of Natural History
National Gallery Sculpture Garden
National Gallery of Art West
National Gallery of Art East
Supreme Court
Folger Shakespeare Library
Madison Dr.
East Capitol St.
The National Mall
Hirshhorn Museum
Arts & Indus. Building
4th St.
US Capitol
Library of Congress
Jefferson Dr.
Smithsonian Inst.
Freer Gallery
National Air & Space
MD Ave.
Botanic Gardens
Independence Ave.
Independence Ave.
Washington Ave.
South Capitol St.
Cannon House Office Bldg.
PA Ave.
Museum of African Art & Arthur Sackler Gallery
L'Enfant Promenade
NASA
D St.
1
C St.
F St.
395
Water Ave.
Maine Ave.
Washington Channel
I St.
295
395
M St.

WASHINGTON DC—THE AMERICAN EXPERIENCE

Washington has approximately 20 million domestic and international visitors annually, making tourism the second most important industry after the federal government. The following visitor centers stand ready with a wealth of information for everyone—newcomer, tourist and local alike.

DC Chamber of Commerce Visitor Information Center
Ronald Reagan Building and International Trade Center
1300 Pennsylvania Ave. NW
202-638-DCCC
www.dcchamber.org

Washington, DC Convention and Visitors Association
1212 New York Ave. NW
202-780-7000
www.washington.org

Montgomery County, MD Conference & Visitors Bureau
12900 Middlebrook Rd., Germantown
301-428-9702

Prince George's County, MD Conference & Visitors Bureau
9200 Basil Court, Largo
301-972-8300

Alexandria Convention & Visitors Association
221 King St., Alexandria
703-838-4200
www.funside.com

Arlington Convention & Visitors Service
2100 Clarendon Blvd., Arlington
703-228-3988
www.co.arlington.va.us

Fairfax County Convention & Visitors Bureau
8300 Boone Blvd., Tysons Corner
703-790-3329
www.visitfairfax.org

Loudoun Tourism Council
108-D South St. SE, Leesburg
703-772-2170
www.visitloudoun.org

Old Town Trolley Tours (202-832-9800; www.historictours.com/washington) provide comprehensive and fun-filled tours of 19 sites around the city. There is free reboarding at every site on these daily 2-hour narrated tours.

If you are looking to take a cruise on the Potomac, there are several companies in the area that will transport you past the monuments and other shoreline attractions while providing dinner and dancing. The **Dandy** (703-683-6076; www.dandydinnerboat.org) sails from Prince St. in Old Town Alexandria for a three-hour dinner cruise past the monuments, the Kennedy Center and Georgetown. Check the website for further information, including pricing and departure/arrival times.

For a trip with a historical twist, take the **Potomac Spirit** to George Washington's estate. The captain will point out landmarks along the way and you will have two hours to explore the mansion and gardens at Mount Vernon before the return trip to Washington. The sister ship, **Spirit of Washington**, sails down the Potomac to Alexandria past the monuments and Old Town with either live music from the 1940s through the 1990s or a Cabaret-style show. Both ships are part of the Potomac Spirit fleet (202-554-8000) and depart from Pier 4 at 6th and Water Sts. SW. Moonlight party cruises are also available.

The most unique Potomac dinner cruise option is offered by Odyssey Cruise Line (202-488-6000; www/odyssey-cruises.com), which also has ships in Chicago and Boston. The **Odyssey III**, a $6 million craft constructed specifically to navigate under all the Potomac bridges, is the only ship of its kind in US waters. Its outside decks and glass ceilings offer breathtaking views of the Capitol, monuments, Georgetown and the Kennedy Center. The Odyssey departs from the Gangplank Marina at 6th and Water Sts. SW, a short walk from the Green Line Waterfront Metro station. If you drive, complimentary parking is available in the lot across from the Gangplank restaurant at 7th and Water Sts. SW. Your cruise options include Sunday Jazz Brunch, lunch Monday through Saturday, dinner each night and moonlight cruises.

The Potomac Riverboat Company (703-684-0580) offers several cruises that set sail from behind the Torpedo Factory Arts Center in Old Town Alexandria. Reservations are recommended for these short trips, which usually depart every hour on the hour. For example you can enjoy a leisurely 90-minute cruise aboard the **Matthew Hayes** as you sail past the Lincoln Memorial, Jefferson Memorial, Washington Monument and the Kennedy Center. See Alexandria by water and enjoy a

GUEST ACCOMMODATIONS

Are you a social commuter looking for a weekend room in the city? Do you have family, friends or business colleagues coming to visit and no extra room? One stop reservation services, with up to 30-50% off normal rates, are offered on hotels in DC and nearby Maryland and Virginia suburbs. They provide professional meeting placement services for groups of all sizes. These services are available through their offices during working hours, or on-line at any time.

Capitol Reservations
202-452-1270
800-847-4832
www.visitdc.com

Capitol Reservations specializes in booking hotel rooms for business and leisure travelers, and arranging complete tour packages in Washington, DC and the Mid-Atlantic region.

Washington DC Accommodations
202-289-2220
800-554-2220
www.dcaccommodations.com

Washington DC Accommodations is a hotel reservation and meeting planning service with complete and personal knowledge of the hotels, conference centers and specialty inns of DC. They pride themselves on personal service in matching you with a hotel that perfectly suits your needs. In 1999, they were awarded the Small Business of the Year Award by the DC Chamber of Commerce.

40-minute narrated sightseeing cruise on the Potomac River aboard the **Admiral Tilp**. Or cruise the Potomac on the **Miss Christin** from Old Town to George Washington's home at Mount Vernon.

Cruise times for all of these ships vary depending upon the time of year and the day of the week. You should call ahead to check specific departures for the cruise you want to take.

In addition to tours by bus and by boat, Washington and several of the suburban towns offer pleasant and informative walking tours. **DC Walking Tours**, Inc. (202-237-7534; www.dcwalkingtours.com) will provide you with an insightful look at the city behind-the-scenes. For international participants, they offer foreign language interpreters free of charge. **Georgetown Walking Tours** (301-588-8999; www.tourdc.com) specializes in the history and glamour of this famous neighborhood. For other suggestions and schedules, be sure to check area parks and recreation departments, the *Washington Post* and the *Smithsonian Associates*.

For a unique touring experience, try one of Washington's many and varied specialty tours. For the athletically inclined, **Bike the Sites, Inc.** (202-966-8662; www.bikethesites.com) will take you on a three-hour guided tour to 55 landmarks along scenic paths and trails. Bicycles, helmets, water and snacks are provided. Contact them for specific information on company policies, age restrictions and pricing.

With **DC Ducks: The Boats on Wheels** (202-832-9800) you will tour the Mall by land, then splash into the Potomac River on the boats with wheels. Fully narrated 90-minute tours using rebuilt WWII amphibious vessels depart from Union Station.

Hosted by Gross National Product, a local improvisational comedy group, **Scandal Tours** provides an irreverent and hilarious look at Washington's infamous scandal sites. Tours run Saturdays from the Old Post Office Pavilion from April Fools Day through Labor Day weekend. For reservations and current rates contact them at 202-783-7212, or at http://home.earthlink.net/~gnpinc.

Several groups offer cultural and heritage tours. The **DC Chamber of Commerce** offers narrated sightseeing tours of DC's diverse neighborhoods with packages that include entertainment and a meal. Call 202-638-3222 for information on these specific tours, or visit them at www.dcchamber.org. **Capital Entertainment Service** in Washington, DC (202-636-9203) and **Site Seeing Tours, Inc.** of Silver Spring, MD (301-445-2098) specialize in African-American heritage and historical sites.

Museums, Monuments and Memorials

For a quick overview of Washington, start at the Mall, the expansive public space between Constitution and Independence Aves. This sweeping promenade of gardens, museums and famous monuments extends from the **US Capitol** at the east end all the way to the **Lincoln Memorial** at the west end. Along the way, you will find famous sights including the memorials to the **Vietnam** and **Korean War Veterans** as well as the **Washington Monument** and its **Reflecting Pool**. Nearby you will find the **Tidal Basin,** the **Thomas Jefferson Memorial,** and the **Franklin Delano Roosevelt Memorial** as well as two beautiful public spaces, East and West Potomac Parks. On the Mall, between 3rd and 14th Sts., sit some of the city's best museums.

The Smithsonian Institution

You could visit a different museum every day for two weeks and still not have covered all of the **Smithsonian Institution**. With 15 sites today in DC alone, the Smithsonian was founded back in 1846 on a bequest from James Smithson, a distinguished English scientist. Today, the Smithsonian is one of the world's great museum complexes as well as a preeminent research institution. All museums are open daily, except Christmas Day. Extended spring and summer hours are established each year. Admission to all museums is free. Many of these facilities have museum shops and cafeterias, so you can make your visit a multi-purpose one. Visitor information is available from 9:00 a.m. to 5:00 p.m. daily, at 202-357-2700 (TDD 202-357-1729, recorded information 202-357-2020, Spanish 202-633-9126). You can also visit the Smithsonian at www.si.edu.

Along the Mall, you can visit several of the Smithsonian facilities, including the main building at 1000 Jefferson Dr. SW. The original Smithsonian Institution Building, known as "The Castle," stands as an icon for the Smithsonian and is recognized across the country and around the world. It houses the Smithsonian Information Center and administrative offices. The Smithsonian facilities on the Mall are easily reached by any of three Metro stations—Smithsonian, Federal Triangle and L'Enfant Plaza. Check the address of the museum, or ask the attendant at the Metro kiosk before boarding the train, to see which one is most convenient.

Arthur M. Sackler Gallery, 1050 Independence Ave. SW. This gallery, opened in 1987, has a permanent collection of Asian art from ancient times to the present as well as exhibitions of related works of art on loan. Website: www.si.edu/asia.

Arts and Industries Building, 900 Jefferson Dr. SW. Opened in 1881, this landmark castle-like structure of red brick and Ohio sandstone served as the first home of what was then called the National Museum. The Smithsonian complex

The Library of Congress allows you to make prints from their photography collection (the largest in the world). You will find photographs of Washington, DC among those included in the archives of the Prints and Photographs Reading Room (http://lcweb.loc.gov/rr/print) in the James Madison Building. Take your order to the Photo Duplication Office in the Adams Building. The charge is $15 for B&W 8 x 10 reprints; color prints are $25. Allow four to six weeks for prints to be ready.

grew and flourished from this original structure. Today the Arts and Industries features changing exhibitions and the Discovery Theater for children. Website: www.si.edu/ai.

Freer Gallery of Art, 12th St. and Jefferson Dr. SW. The Freer Gallery was opened to the public in 1923 and was the first Smithsonian museum of fine arts. Today it offers a world-renowned collection of Asian and 19th- and early 20th-century American Art. Website: www.si.edu/asia.

Hirshhorn Museum and Sculpture Garden, 7th St. and Independence Ave. SW. The focus of the Hirshhorn collection is 19th-and 20th-century painting and sculpture. Changing exhibitions explore the newest trends in modern art. A sunken sculpture garden is located on the Mall side of this distinctive circular museum. Website: www.si.edu/hirshhorn.

National Air and Space Museum, 6th St. and Independence Ave. SW. This museum—the most visited in the world—contains exhibits on the history of aviation, space science and space technology. Highlights include shows at the Einstein Planetarium and the Langley IMAX® theater. Website: www.nasm.si.edu.

National Museum of African Art, 950 Independence Ave. SW. The focus of this museum is the art and culture of Africa, displayed in both permanent and rotating exhibits. Originally established in the Frederick Douglass House on Capitol Hill in 1964, it was officially merged with the Smithsonian in 1979 and moved to the Mall. Website: www.si.edu.nmafa.

National Museum of American History, 14th St. and Constitution Ave. NW. Here you will see exhibits on the history of science, technology and culture in America. Young people can enjoy—and learn from—hands-on experiences in the Science Center and the History Room. Tickets are required on weekends, however they are free. Children ages 5-12 must be accompanied by an adult. Website: www.americanhistory.si.edu.

National Museum of Natural History, 10th St. and Constitution Ave. NW. In addition to the Hope Diamond and "Henry," the museum's 13-foot-tall African bull elephant, this museum includes a 487-seat IMAX® theater with a 3-D screen (tickets are required), a spacious Atrium Café, and gift shops. Visitors can plan their visit to this sprawling museum via an electronic bulletin board near

SITES ON THE HORIZON

The **National Museum of the American Indian**, under construction at Third Street and Independence Ave. SW, fills the last open space on the Mall. The design, a collaborative process among North American tribes, is dedicated to the preservation, study and exhibition of historic and contemporary culture of Native Americans. This latest museum created by the Smithsonian Institution is scheduled to open in 2002. You can check on the museum's progress at www.si.edu./cgr-brn/nav.cgi.

A site on the Tidal Basin has been selected for the **Martin Luther King Jr. Memorial**. Once the design has been approved, the memorial to the slain civil rights leader will be built between the Lincoln and Jefferson memorials and near the tribute to Franklin D. Roosevelt.

Groundbreaking for the **World War II Memorial** is scheduled by Veterans Day 2000. The Rainbow Pool, located at the eastern end of the Reflecting Pool on the Mall, is at the center of the memorial plan. Website: www.wwiimemorial.com.

The **National Japanese American Memorial**, commemorating the internment of 120,000 Japanese Americans and Japanese aliens during World War II, is expected to be completed the autumn of 2000. The memorial faces the Capitol from the triangular park bounded by Louisiana and New Jersey Aves. and D St. NW. Website: www.njamf.org.

The city of Washington will have a museum that celebrates its past and present. The former Carnegie Central Library building at Mount Vernon Square between 7th and 9th Sts. will be converted to the **City Museum** beginning in 2001 with an anticipated opening in 2003. Operated by the Historical Society of Washington, it will house District archives and artifacts, a multimedia theater, and will serve as a visitor center to introduce people to the nonfederal part of the city.

The **Air Force Memorial** will be located in Arlington near the Netherlands Carillon and the Marine Corps' Iwo Jima Memorial. Dedication of the star-shaped monument is expected in 2002. Website: www.airforcememorial.org.

the main gift shop that lists screening times at the IMAX®, the day's special events and ongoing exhibitions. Renovation of this museum continues with completion expected in 2002 at which time the new Discovery Room will open on the top level. Website: www.mnh.si.edu.

In addition to the locations along the Mall, there are several Smithsonian buildings in other parts of town. These include:

National Portrait Gallery, 8th and F Sts. NW. The Gallery is best known for its portraits of distinguished Americans. It also includes sculptures, paintings, photographs and the *Time* magazine cover collection. The Gallery is housed in the historic Old Patent Office Building along with the National Museum of

American Art. The building was closed to the public for a three-year renovation project beginning in January 2000. Metro: Gallery Place. Website: www.npg.si.edu.

National Postal Museum, 2 Massachusetts Ave. and N. Capitol St. NE. As you might expect, this museum offers a history of postal communication and philately. It features interactive displays and the largest stamp collection in the world. Metro: Union Station. Website: www.si.edu/postal.

National Zoological Park, 3000 Connecticut Ave. NW. Washington's zoo is home to some 5,000 animals in a beautiful 163-acre park, right in the midst of town. Exhibits include Amazonia, a re-created microcosm of the world's largest rain forest. Metro: Cleveland Park or Woodley Park-Zoo/Adams Morgan. Website: www.si.edu/natzoo.

Renwick Gallery, 17th St. at Pennsylvania Ave. NW. The Renwick has a permanent collection and exhibitions of American crafts, design and contemporary arts. Metro: Farragut West. Website: http://nmaa-ryder.si.edu.

Anacostia Museum, 1901 Fort Place SE. In this community-based museum, you will find a national resource for identifying, documenting, protecting, and interpreting African-American history and culture. The museum's primary focus is on Washington, DC and the rural South. The museum closed for renovation in January 2000 and reopening is planned for Spring 2001. Website: www.si.edu/anacostia.

National Museum of American Art, 8th and G Sts. NW. Painting, sculpture, graphics, folk art and photography from the 18th-century to the present are available here, as well as special exhibitions of American art. Along with the Portrait Gallery, the National Museum of American Art occupies the historic Old Patent Office Building. The museum closed its doors in January 2000 for a three-year

VIP TOURS

US Congressional offices can assist in arranging VIP tours at a number of federal buildings such as the White House, the Capitol, the Kennedy Center and the Federal Bureau of Investigation (FBI), as well as some non-federal buildings such as Washington National Cathedral. While these VIP tours typically do not provide different views from those available on a public tour, a reservation can minimize the time you have to wait in line.

There are limited numbers of these free tickets and they go quickly, so try to make your request at least several months in advance. You can obtain maps and information on DC sightseeing as well as VIP tour ticket availability by writing the Congressional Representative for your district in care of the US House of Representatives, Washington, DC 20515. Or contact your Representative's office by calling the Capitol switchboard at 202-224-3121.

You will need to provide a contact name, home address, and both day and evening phone numbers; the size of your party; the tour sites you wish to visit; and your preferred dates. If available, tickets will be mailed a week or two before your scheduled tour.

renovation. Much of its art will be on traveling shows across the country during this period under the name Smithsonian's American Art Museum. Several works too large to tour will go on extended loan to various institutions in the local area. Consideration is being given to changing the name of the museum to avoid confusion with the National Gallery of Art, however such a move will require the approval of Congress. Website: www.nmaa.si.edu.

Other Museums

In addition to the Smithsonian museums, the Washington area boasts about 66 museums off the Mall. Of these, one of the best known and most often visited is the **National Gallery of Art**. The museum was founded in 1937, the result of the dream of Andrew Mellon who wanted to create a gallery of art for the people of the United States. The combination of public and private support is built into the foundation of this great gallery. Donations from the Mellon family funded the construction of both the West and East Buildings. Paintings and sculpture first given by Mellon formed the nucleus of high quality of work around which the collection has grown. Private donations from generous individuals, foundations and corporations have paid for every work of art in the collection. Federal funds ensure the operation, maintenance, protection and care of the nation's art collection and enable the Gallery to be experienced free of charge.

The East and West Buildings of the National Gallery of Art (202-737-4215; www.nga.gov) face each other at the corner of Constitution Ave. and 4th St. NW. The West Building houses works from the 13th to the early 20th century, including paintings by Raphael, Rembrandt and Monet. Across the street, I.M. Pei's East Building displays modern art and the museum's special exhibits. The gift shop will thrill with its wide variety of artistic treasures for sale. An underground tunnel allows you to move easily between the East and West Buildings. Metro: Archives-Navy Memorial or Judiciary Square.

The **National Gallery of Art's Sculpture Garden** is located at Seventh St. and Constitution Ave. NW. Built with Tennessee Pink marble in keeping with the construction of both the Gallery's East and West Buildings, the new tree- and art-filled park contains predominantly abstract sculptures by some of the century's most luminous artists. The Sculpture Garden, along with its neighbor to the south, the Hirshhorn Museum and Sculpture Garden, now provide two destinations for sculpture seekers to enjoy.

The **US Holocaust Memorial Museum** is located near the Mall at 100 Raoul Wallenberg Pl. SW, between 14th and 15th Sts. (202-488-0400). This private museum documents the horrors of the Holocaust through artifacts, exhibits, film and photography. Use the address www.ushmm.org to reach the US Holocaust Museum's website. Metro: Smithsonian.

The impressively spacious **National Building Museum** in the Pension Building (202-272-2448) fills the block formed by F and G Sts. and 4th and 5th Sts. NW. The collection focuses on major building projects throughout the country. One of its permanent exhibits is on the history of Washington, DC. It includes interactive displays as well as scale models of the major monuments created for the visually impaired to experience through touch. Braille identification signs are attached to each model. Metro: Judiciary Square. Website: www.nbm.org.

The **National Museum of Women in the Arts** at 1250 New York Ave. NW (202-783-5000; www.nmwa.org) is the first museum in the world dedicated to women artists. Ironically, the building is a former Masonic Temple. Metro: McPherson Square or Metro Center.

The Kreeger Museum is located at 2401 Foxhall Rd. NW (202-338-3552; www.kreegermuseum.com). Often referred to as "The Jewel on Foxhall," it features 19th- and 20th-century paintings and sculpture plus African and other non-Western art. Tours are available and reservations are required. There is free parking on the grounds and you can reach the museum by taxi. It is not, however, convenient by public transportation. Children under the age of 12 are not allowed in this museum.

The **B'nai B'rith Klutznick National Jewish Museum,** located at 1640 Rhode Island Ave. NW (202-857-6583; www.bnaibrith.org), explores four millennia of Living Judaism and includes the work of contemporary artists. Metro: Farragut North.

The **Newseum,** opened in 1997 across the Potomac River in Rosslyn, VA at 1101 Wilson Blvd. (703-284-3544 or 888-NEWSEUM). Here you can explore the history of news from print to broadcast to electronic media. Visitors can relive great moments in history in the large high-definition video theater and watch the news as it happens from around the world on the Video News Wall. Through interactive displays, you can investigate a story, edit a front page, or videotape yourself as a television news anchor or radio announcer. Walk outside to the adjacent **Freedom Park** for a view of Washington along the Potomac River. The structure at the center of the park is the Journalists Memorial, which pays tribute to journalists who have lost their lives while attempting to report the news from around the world. Interestingly, the park is built on a section of elevated highway that was never completed. Use www.newseum.org to find out more about the museum. Metro: Rosslyn.

Washington's Many Monuments

With over two hundred years of history, Washington has plenty of famous people and events represented by its many public monuments.

The major presidential monuments are those of Lincoln, Washington, Jefferson and Roosevelt (FDR), all of which are open on weekends. The **Lincoln Memorial** is located at the far west end of the Mall, at 23rd St. The Memorial's 36 columns represent the number of states in the Union at Lincoln's death. The names of the 48 states in the union when the memorial was dedicated on May 30, 1922, are carved around the frieze, and plaques for both Alaska and Hawaii have been added to the front steps. The closest Metro is Foggy Bottom-GWU; from there it is an eight-block walk south on 23rd St. Website: www.nps.gov/linc.

The **Washington Monument** is located on the western half of the Mall, on Constitution Ave. NW between 15th and 17th St. To get there, take the Metro to either the Smithsonian or the Federal Triangle station. It is well worth the wait in line to take the elevator to the top for a panoramic view of the city. The summer of 2000 marked the end of two years of repair and renovation to the world's tallest freestanding marble obelisk. Visitors will use new elevators for the 70-second ride to the top of the 555-foot monument and view the sights in the comfort of a new air conditioning system. You can obtain free tickets the day of your visit at the 15th St. Kiosk at the base of the monument. Advance tickets can be purchased through Ticketmaster (800-551-7328); note that while all tickets themselves are free, there is a $1.50 per-ticket charge and a $0.50 handling fee per Ticketmaster order. Website: www.nps.gov.wamo.

HISTORICAL SOCIETY OF WASHINGTON

The city of Washington boasts 37 historic districts, 557 buildings, and 100 parks and other historic sites listed on the National Register of Historic Places. The Historical Society of Washington is devoted to making the history of the Washington metropolitan area and its people accessible and understandable to the public. It offers an extensive research library, publications, exhibitions and, as part of their educational programs, a continuing series of workshops focused on various local history topics—including neighborhood history, history of buildings, and historic photographs. Also available are exhibits of picture postcards and tourist memorabilia and videos of Washington's history and neighborhoods.

The Historical Society of Washington is appropriately located in one of DC's historic mansions, the Heurich Mansion at 1307 New Hampshire Ave. NW, once home to DC beer baron Christian Heurich; tours of the mansion are also available. For further information, contact the society at 202-785-2068 or at www.hswdc.org.

Surrounded by cherry trees south of the Tidal Basin, the **Thomas Jefferson Memorial** on Ohio Dr., south of the Tidal Basin, contains a bronze-standing statue of Jefferson and carved excerpts from four of his writings. There is no direct Metro access to this monument, but in the summer, you can travel there by paddle boat, for rent at the Tidal Basin. Website: www.nps.gov/thje.

The **Franklin Delano Roosevelt (FDR) Memorial**, the area's fourth major presidential monument, opened in May 1997. The memorial is a powerful tribute to the man and his 12-year presidency. Spread over seven acres, the memorial wends its way along the famous Cherry Tree Walk on the Tidal Basin in West Potomac Park. The site has waterfalls, native trees and shrubs, and quotations carved in walls of granite. Among the figurative sculpture is a statue of Eleanor Roosevelt, the only First Lady represented in a presidential memorial. Four outdoor galleries depict the great social, economic and cultural changes that marked FDR's four terms in office, from the Great Depression to World War II. More than 6,000 tons of granite, enough to erect an 80-story building, were used in the construction of this site. The first of the memorials purposely designed as wheelchair-accessible, the memorial shows Roosevelt, but not his wheelchair. This fact caused so much controversy—both before and after the memorial's opening—that President Clinton had to introduce special legislation for the statue to be commissioned and placed at the site. Metro: Smithsonian. Website: www.nps.gov/fdrm.

War Memorials

Memorials to wars and military service dot the area. The two best-known are the **Marine Corps War Memorial (Iwo Jima Statue)** and the **Vietnam Veterans Memorial**. The Iwo Jima Statue, depicting the raising of the American Flag on Iwo Jima during World War II, is located on N. Ft. Myer Dr. and Marshall Dr. in Arlington, VA. Take the Metro to the Rosslyn station, then go six blocks south on Ft. Myer Dr.

The **Vietnam Veterans Memorial** is on the Mall, between 21st and 22nd Sts. The black granite structure, known as "The Wall," bears the names of the 58,000 soldiers lost in the Vietnam War, listed in chronological order. If you are looking for the name of someone in particular, check the alphabetical directories along the walkway leading to the wall. Subsequent to the dedication of the memorial in 1982, the Statue of the Three Servicemen was added to the site in 1984, and the Women of Vietnam War statue was added in 1993. Website: www.nps.gov/vive.

The **Korean War Veterans Memorial** is nearby, on the opposite side of the Reflecting Pool. Here, 19 statues depict soldiers on patrol in the rugged terrain and harsh weather of Korea. Granite curbs and slabs list names of countries that sent troops and/or provided medical services. Also depicted are unnamed men and women who served in the defense of South Korea. Website: www.nps.gov/kwvm.

The **US Navy Memorial** at 8th St. and Pennsylvania Ave. NW features a large map of the world, inlaid in the granite plaza. The "Lone Sailor," a Stanley Bleifeld sculpture, keeps watch. Nearby are two edifices with bronze sculpture panels and a visitors center. The Navy Memorial's website is at www.lonesailor.org.

The **African-American Civil War Memorial**, at 10th and U Sts. NW in the historic Shaw neighborhood, recognizes the heroism of the 185,000 African-American soldiers who fought for the Union.

Once you venture outside the District, more sites await nearby, in addition to the Iwo Jima Statue. **Arlington National Cemetery** (www.mdw.army.mil/cemetery), a memorial in its own right, rests silently across the Potomac River from the Lincoln Memorial. Originally the home of Robert E. Lee, it was turned into a cemetery for fallen Union soldiers and is now the last resting place for casualties of war, veterans and their spouses. You can wander the grounds and watch the changing of the guard as it keeps vigil over the **Tomb of the Unknowns** (commonly referred to as the Tomb of the Unknown Soldier). However, the crypt that once contained the remains of an American serviceman from the Vietnam War will remain empty, possibly forever, because of advances in DNA testing. The eternal flame burns in remembrance at the grave site of President John F. Kennedy and his wife, Jacqueline Kennedy Onassis. His brother Robert rests nearby beneath a simple white cross against a gently sloping, grass-covered hill.

In October 1997, the **Women in Military Service for America Memorial** was dedicated at the entrance to Arlington National Cemetery. The first memorial to honor military women from all eras and services, it incorporates the refurbished entrance to the cemetery. It features a fountain and reflecting pool, as well as etched transparent glass tablets that bring in natural light. Also included are a theater, exhibit gallery and Hall of Honor. Metro: Arlington Cemetery. Learn more about this memorial at their website www.womensmemorial.org.

Along the George Washington Memorial Parkway between Memorial Bridge and the 14th St. Bridge is the **Navy-Marine Memorial**. This popular outdoor sculpture of gulls in flight above graceful waves is a monument to American sailors and marines who died at sea during World War I.

Another type of war memorial is the **Army Museum at Fort George G. Meade** near Odenton, MD (301-677-6261). This site houses a collection of weapons, gear and memorabilia dating from as far back as the American Revolution. Recently, the museum has added an annex to house two World War I era tanks—the Mark VIII and the Renault FT-17. Interestingly, the gallery of the annex had to be built around these machines, which were too large to fit through museum doors. Fort Meade is located east of I-295, between the Patuxent Wildlife Research Center and BWI Airport, about a 30-minute drive from the Beltway.

Galleries

Art galleries can be found throughout the area. Whether your interest is American paintings and sculpture, European masterpieces, contemporary art, women's art, photography, or crafts, you are certain to find a place to view it. Here is just a sampling of what is available.

The **Corcoran Gallery of Art** at 17th St. and New York Ave. NW (202-639-1700; www.corcoran.org) is the area's oldest gallery. It features primarily American paintings and sculpture. Metro: Farragut West.

The **Phillips Collection** at 1600 21st St. NW (202-387-2151; www.phillipscollection.org.) houses European and American masterpieces. Events include workshops, lectures, benefits and opening receptions. The weekly Sunday afternoon concert series in its elegant music room is open to all visitors. Metro: Dupont Circle.

The **Kathleen Ewing Gallery**, 1609 Connecticut Ave. NW (202-328-0955; www.artline.com/plus/galleries), features a wide range of 19th- and 20th-century as well as contemporary photography. Rotating exhibits feature individual and organized groups of photographers. Metro: Dupont Circle.

Fraser Gallery, 1054 31st St. NW (202-298-6450; www.thefrasergallery.com), a recent newcomer to Washington, DC, opened its doors in 1996. This gallery shows works by artists the owner has met at outdoor art fairs all over the country. The personally selected pieces make-up an eclectic collection from lesser-known and emerging artists. Located in Georgetown, there is no immediate Metro access.

The **Galleries of Dupont Circle** offer monthly First Friday open houses from 6:00 to 8:00 p.m. Over 20 galleries are located within a historic neighborhood of embassies, fine shops and restaurants. For further information call 202-232-3610. Metro: Dupont Circle.

Or take the Dupont Circle-Kalorama Museum walk, an informal self-guided tour around the Dupont Circle area. It features the Phillips collection, the Textile Museum, the Woodrow Wilson House, the Historical Society of Washington, DC, the Anderson House and the Fondo del Sol Visual Arts Center. A brochure mapping out this tour is available at any of these museums. Several of the museums rely on private donations and request contributions at the door.

The **Indian Craft Shop**, located inside the Department of Interior, has been representing crafts from over 35 tribal areas within the United States since 1938. It is located at 1849 C St. NW (202-208-4056). Metro: Farragut West.

Located at 1300 Connecticut Ave. NW (202-628-0800; www.vsarts.org/gallery) is the **Very Special Arts Gallery**. This non-profit gallery represents professional and emerging artists with disabilities. Rotating exhibits feature originals, folk art, sculpture and crafts. Metro: Dupont Circle.

Gardens and Parks

One quarter of the District is made up of parks and open space, more than found in any other city in the nation. They range in size from circles, squares and triangles, to small community parks to the more expansive parks offering natural beauty as well as recreation. As you move throughout the city, take note of the seasonal plantings of the National Park Service in the areas it manages. They take great pride in the beauty and pleasure these plantings bring to residents and visitors alike.

US Botanic Garden at 245 First St. SW (202-225-8333 or 202-225-7099) is the oldest botanic garden in America. Its first greenhouse was constructed in 1842 and the Conservatory, completed in 1933, has been home to permanent collections of tropical, subtropical and desert plants, and a world renowned collection of orchids. The Conservatory of the US Botanic Garden is closed for renovation and will reopen in the Year 2000. In the meantime, you can enjoy a virtual visit on the Web at www.aoc.gov. Located across Independence Ave. from the Conservatory is a beautiful park featuring displays of bulbs, annuals and perennials. The park is named for Frederic Auguste Bartholdi, who designed the fountain that forms the focal point of the park. Metro: Federal Center SW.

Georgetown's **Dumbarton Oaks**, at 1703 32nd St. NW (202-338-8278; www.doaks.org), maintains spectacular public gardens. Adjacent to the gardens, the Dumbarton Oaks Museum houses, somewhat surprisingly, one of the country's best pre-Columbian and Byzantine collections. If you are visiting the gardens with someone special, you might want to stroll down nearby Lover's Lane (daylight hours only). In the Rose Gardens in Georgetown, at 31st and R Sts. NW (202-342-3200), you can see and smell hundreds of carefully tended rose bushes.

Modeled on a medieval garden, the **Bishop's Garden** is tucked away on the grounds of the majestic Washington National Cathedral at Massachusetts and Wisconsin Aves. NW (202-364-6616; www.cathedral.org/cathedral.). This secluded, contemplative garden features winding stone paths and lush boxwoods.

The **Hillwood Museum and Gardens**, at 4155 Linnean Ave. NW (202-686-8500), is the former estate of Marjorie Merriweather Post and is especially renowned for its azaleas and rhododendrons, wooden paths over Japanese bridges, a waterfall, and a lovely café. After completion of major renovations, the site is reopening in the Fall of 2000. Website: www.hillwoodmuseum.org.

AAA POTOMAC

If you are not already a member, consider joining AAA. Their services come in handy, not only when your car breaks down, but also when you need travel or local tourist information. Call AAA at 888-859-5161 for membership information, or visit their website at www.AAA.com.

The **US National Arboretum** at 3501 New York Ave. NE (202-245-2726; www.ars-grin.gov/na) is comprised of 444 acres of trees, shrubs and flowering plants from around the world, including its famous bonsai exhibit. A new attraction, the National Grove of Trees, honors the official trees of the 50 states and the District. As a work in progress, the grove will be developed over the next several years. On Saturdays and Sundays only, a guided non-stop tram tour is available during the months of April to October, visiting several of the Arboretum's outlying collections and gardens. From September to May, the Arboretum offers monthly moonlight walks covering five miles through the horticultural enclave; registration is required. Call ahead for current rates on both the tram tours and moonlight walks.

Brookside Gardens, at 1800 Glenallan Ave. in Wheaton, MD (301-949-8230; www.clark.net/pub/mncppc/montgom/parks), offers 50 acres of gardens, two conservatories, and streams flowing amid its famous azalea gardens.

Last, certainly not least, is **Rock Creek Park and Nature Center**, on Beach Dr. north of the National Zoo. Its 1,754 acres make it one of the world's largest urban parks. Rock Creek offers golf, exercise courses, jogging paths, bike trails, tennis courts and bridle paths. Enjoy nature exhibits, self-guided trails and a planetarium at the Rock Creek Nature Center, 5200 Glover Rd. NW (202-426-6829).

Sculpture

Outdoor sculpture is pervasive throughout the District of Columbia with over 370 pieces of public statuary having been documented. In addition to the well-known major monuments to past presidents, there are memorials to prominent Civil War leaders, world and national leaders, scientists, authors and artists, not to mention more equestrian statues than any city in the country.

When you are on the Hill visiting the Capitol building, you will see the statues of **James Garfield**, 20th President, at First St. and Maryland Ave., and both **Ulysses S. Grant**, 18th President, at First St. NW, and **Chief Justice John Marshall** on the west side of the Capitol. In the Mall area, the statue of **Albert Einstein**, formulator of the theory of relativity, should not be missed. It is appropriately located near the National Academy of Sciences and Engineering at 22nd St. and Constitution Ave. NW.

As you travel around the downtown area, you'll notice that traffic circles bear the names and statues of Civil War heroes. Among the other statuary in the downtown area is a tribute to the father of Protestantism, **Martin Luther**, located in front of the Luther Memorial Church at Thomas Circle at 14th St. and Massachusetts Ave.,

Along Embassy Row in the 3100 block of Massachusetts Ave. near the British Embassy and the Naval Observatory, you'll find sculptures of **Winston Churchill**, British Prime Minister, statesman and author, and **Kahlil Gibran**, philosopher, artist and author of *The Prophet* .

The Gallaudet University grounds at 800 Florida Ave. NE include statues of **Thomas Hopkins Gallaudet**, educator of the deaf, and his first student, **Alice Cogswell**, and **Edward Gallaudet**, former president of the university.

Along the 16th St. corridor, Meridian Park alone contains three statuary—**Jeanne d'Arc**, French heroine and martyr, **James Buchanan**, 15th President, and **Dante**, the Italian poet.

Other Points of Interest

Washington's two most famous sites are the Capitol and the White House. The **Capitol** building, the seat of the legislative branch of the government, is located at the east end of the Mall at 1st St. between Independence and Constitution Aves. (202-225-6827; www.aoc.gov). The **White House**, official home of the President of the United States, is almost as well known by its address—1600 Pennsylvania Ave. NW (202-456-7041). Tours of both sites are free and make for a fascinating trip through the history of the city and the nation. You can visit the White House without leaving the comfort of your own home; the other presidential address is www.whitehouse.gov on the Internet.

At the **National Archives**, Constitution Ave. at 8th St. NW (202-501-5000), you can see the original Declaration of Independence, US Constitution and Bill of Rights. These Charters of Freedom are kept on display in helium-filled cases

BED & BREAKFASTS

Bed and Breakfast establishments (B&Bs) offer a variety of weekend escapes both within the metropolitan DC area and in the myriad small towns and villages within a few hours of the District. In-town B&Bs are becoming an increasingly popular choice among Maryland and Virginia social commuters, as well as business travelers and individual tourists and their families looking for personal service in a cozy atmosphere, perhaps among significantly historic surroundings. **Bed & Breakfast Accommodations, Ltd.**, at 202-328-3510 or at www.bnbaccom.com, can show you a selection of local historic private guest homes; small, intimate hotels and inns; romantic country inns; and self-hosted furnished apartments. B&B opportunities exist in many of the more popular DC neighborhoods including Dupont Circle, Adams-Morgan, Capitol Hill and Logan Circle with which they can also assist you with reservations. If you are interested in a weekend B&B away from DC, you may want to consult a specialized guidebook in your local bookstore. Other local resources include ads in the *Washington Post's* Sunday Travel section and Sunday Magazine.

and each night they are lowered into a 50-ton vault 20 feet below the floor. If you are interested in genealogy, you can trace your family history in the Research Room. Whether you are doing general research or genealogy research, there are rules for accessing the facilities and for using historical records. To obtain specific information, call the Public Reference information number, 202-501-5400, or the Genealogy information number, 202-501-5410. Website: www.nara.gov.

The **Washington National Cathedral**, on Wisconsin Ave. about a mile north of Georgetown (202-364-6616), dominates the local skyline. It began with Pierre L'Enfant's vision for a great "church for national purposes" in his 1791 Plans for the City of Washington. The Cathedral is built in the same style as medieval churches—stone on stone with no structural steel. The foundation stone was laid in September 1907 and the final stone was set in September 1990. Officially named the Cathedral Church of Saint Peter and Saint Paul, it is the sixth largest cathedral in the world and the second largest in the United States. More than 800,000 visitors and worshipers visit every year. The Cathedral is also the burial site of Woodrow Wilson and Helen Keller. Website: www.cathedral.org/cathedral.

Another major facet of Washington is its African-American heritage. The **Frederick Douglass National Historic Site** at 1411 W St. SE (202-426-5961; www.nps.gov/frdo) on Cedar Hill was the last residence of the famous black statesman and abolitionist. Douglass was also the first black US Marshal for the District of Columbia. The **Anacostia Museum** (1901 Fort Pl. SE) focuses on African-American art, culture and history. It houses permanent and rotating exhibits and lectures, films, workshops and performances. The historic **Lincoln Theatre** at 1215 U St. NW (202-328-9177) was originally part of the area known as "Black Broadway," and attracted the country's best African-American entertainers. By the 1950s, the theater featured primarily movies, and was, in fact, the first movie theater to offer first-run pictures to black audiences. The theater had closed back in the 1970s but was completely renovated in the early 1990s, replicating its original historical integrity. It is again open for business, featuring live performances in the heart of the revitalized U St. Corridor.

In the Capitol Hill area, you can tour several historic buildings as well as a historic market. Tour the **Library of Congress** (202-707-5000) and its domed reading room, the Great Hall and several pavilions, as well as its visitor center. While in this remarkable neighborhood, also tour the **Folger Shakespeare Library** (202-544-4600), which is the repository for the largest collection of Shakespeare documents in existence as well as being home to a noteworthy knot garden. Continue on to the **Supreme Court** (202-479-3000), open only on week days. Tour these sites virtually at www.loc.gov, www.folger.edu and http://oyez.nwu.edu/tour. And for a change of pace, end the day with a trip to **Eastern Market**, Washington's oldest market, at the corner of 7th and C Sts. SE.

Eastern Market is particularly fun on weekends, with local artists plying their wares alongside the meat, cheese, fruit and vegetable vendors.

The **National Geographic Society's Explorers Hall**, located at 17th and M Sts. NW (202-857-7588), is indeed a place to go exploring. Here a variety of interactive exhibits allow children and adults alike to view the earth from space, touch a tornado, zoom in on a live tarantula, and travel to the North Pole. Metro: Farragut North. Website: www.nationalgeographic.com.

Located at Judiciary Square on E St., between 4th and 5th St. NW, the **National Law Enforcement Officers Memorial** honors all of America's federal, state and local law enforcement officers who have been killed in the line of duty, dating back to the first known death in 1794. Bordering the Memorial's beautifully landscaped park are two tree-lined "pathways of remembrance" where the names of the fallen officers are engraved. Metro: Judiciary Square, F St. Exit. The Visitors Center is located less than two blocks away at 605 E Street NW (202-737-3400; www.nleomf.org).

Finally, just 16 miles from Washington, DC and 8 miles from historic Old Town Alexandria, **Mount Vernon**—George Washington's estate and gardens—stretches over 500 acres overlooking the Potomac River. You can tour the mansion, museums, several outbuildings and gardens. You can also get some hands-on farming experience at the Pioneer Farm site. For further information call 800-429-1520, or visit www.mountvernon.org.

Exploring Beyond the Beltway

For day and weekend trips, you can head out from Washington in just about any direction and not be disappointed. The mid-Atlantic region is full of choices, with some of the most popular ones described here. For more detailed information, you may want to purchase a guidebook for a particular area or get in touch with local chambers of commerce or visitors centers.

The Beach

The Atlantic Ocean beaches are only a few hours from the city and in the summer provide a welcome respite for heat-weary DC residents. Renting beach houses along the coast is a popular summer tradition in Washington, for couples or groups of friends. You can find out about rentals from the chamber of commerce or visitors center in the beach town of your choice, or check the classified section of the *Washington Post* for leads.

If you think parking in downtown DC is a challenge, wait until you get to the beach. Costly parking meters are in effect throughout the summer in all resort towns, with varying enforcement hours and costs. Parking in non-metered areas requires a permit in Rehoboth Beach, Dewey Beach, Bethany Beach, South Bethany and Fenwick Island. Contact the individual city/town hall for local parking permit requirements.

Ocean City, MD

Ocean City's summer weekend population can swell to as high as 200,000 as Washingtonians seek relief from the humidity. Like most beach resorts, Ocean City offers plenty of recreational choices—amusement parks, fishing, sailing, miniature golf and a few movie theaters.

The boardwalk between Somerset Avenue and Fourth Street has been rebuilt. Concrete has been replaced by wood, and a separate train lane has been added so there's more room for pedestrians. Victorian-style lighting has also been installed giving this stretch a turn-of-the-century look.

The Coastal Highway (Route 1), Ocean City's main thoroughfare, houses a multitude of hotels, condos and more than 160 restaurants. If you plan to visit during the summer season (May to mid-September), make your reservations early. Many hotels require a minimum stay of two or even three nights during peak season.

Ocean City ends its summer with SunFest, an annual bash held the third weekend after Labor Day. The city sets up four large circus tents filled with food vendors, bands, entertainers, and arts and crafts booths.

Following graduation, many area high school students participate in "Beach Week" at Ocean City. Unless you are up to dealing with thousands of newly graduated high school seniors, avoid Ocean City during the first two weeks of June. Website: www.ocean-city.com.

Distance Approximately 3 hours from the Beltway
Visitors Center 800-62-OCEAN
Directions Take Route 50 East all the way into Ocean City.

Rehoboth Beach and Dewey Beach, DE

Rehoboth is not nearly the size of Ocean City, but offers many of the same activities on a smaller scale. Like Ocean City, the restaurants along Rehoboth's boardwalk and adjacent streets keep most beach-goers happy, both in terms of price and variety. The town is filled with interesting shops, ranging from typical beach souvenirs to imported clothing and hand-made arts and crafts. **The Golf Park** at Rehoboth (302-227-2500) has a par-58 18-hole course called the Creekside, a nine-hole "wee course," a pitch and putt for beginners and juniors, and a putting green. As Rehoboth is not a long drive from the District, adventurous Washingtonians sometimes pack a round trip into a one-day excursion. If you opt to do this, leave early (preferably before dawn) to avoid the summer-long traffic jams at the Bay Bridge. If you do plan to stay for just the afternoon, take plenty of quarters. Costly parking meters must be fed every two hours.

Just 10 minutes south of Rehoboth is the two-block-wide community of Dewey Beach. Many visitors choose to rent a cottage in Dewey, as it tends to be much quieter than Rehoboth. There is always the option to migrate to the Rehoboth boardwalk for a day or evening of more activity. Website: www.beach-fun.com

Distance Approximately 2 1/2 hours from the Beltway
Chamber of Commerce 800-441-1329
Directions Take Route 50 East to Route 404 through Delaware to Route 1.

Virginia Beach, VA

Virginia Beach boasts the world's longest resort beach—38 miles along the Atlantic Ocean and Chesapeake Bay. A recently revitalized oceanfront features mini-parks, benches, landscaping and sculptures. A reconditioned bicycle trail parallels the boardwalk. The **Virginia Marine Science Museum** is located here, for those who want to enjoy marine life without getting their feet wet. For information on the museum's exhibits and attractions, including dolphin-watching boat trips, call 757-425-3474. Website: www.vabeach.com.

Distance Approximately 4 hours from the Beltway
Visitors Center 800-446-8038
Directions Take I-95 South to I-64 which circles Hampton Roads and connects with the Virginia Beach-Norfolk Expressway, Route 44. The Expressway ends at the Virginia Beach Visitor Information Center and leads visitors directly to the oceanfront resort area.

MORE BEACHES

Assateague Island, MD
410-641-1441

Atlantic City, NJ
888-AC-VISIT

Bethany-Fenwick, DE
800-962-7873

Cape Henlopen/Lewes, DE
302-645-8073

Cape May, NJ
609-884-5508

Cape Lookout National Seashore, Harkers Island, NC
252-728-2250

Chincoteague, VA
757-336-6161

Outer Banks, Kill Devil Hills, NC
252-441-8144

Annapolis, MD

Even though Annapolis is the capital of Maryland, it remains a quaint, small town. Maryland's capitol building, the circular, red-brick **State House** (410-974-3400), offers free tours at designated times and is a good place to start learning about the city's past. It is the oldest state house in continuous legislative use in the country. Students of history will be amazed—and appalled—by the prominent statue on the State House grounds, honoring Chief Justice Roger Taney. Although Taney accomplished many things in his political and judicial career, many remember him best for his decision in the Dred Scot case, where he ruled that Congress did not have the right to ban slavery in the territories.

Also in Annapolis is the **US Naval Academy** (410-263-6933). The **Naval Academy Guide Service** (410-267-3363) offers walking tours of the Academy. Visit the Academy Visitors Center at Ricketts Hall, Gate 1, for tour information. Otherwise, just wander on your own past the buildings and along the waterfront.

Annapolis is home to the private liberal arts college **St. John's College** (410-263-2371). For both bachelors and masters degrees, students learn through a unique curriculum based on the in-depth study of the great books of the western tradition. A 400-year-old tulip tree, the Liberty Tree, once graced the school grounds in front of McDowell Hall. The Sons of Liberty met beneath its branches in the days leading up to the Revolutionary War. This historic tree was removed in 1999 due to damage incurred by Hurricane Floyd.

If you saw the television mini-series or read the book, *Roots*, then you should be sure to visit the Kunta Kinte Plaque located at the head of the city dock. The plaque commemorates the 1767 arrival of Alex Haley's famous ancestor.

If shopping is your passion, you can browse in some of Annapolis' upscale stores. Clothing stores compete with antique shops for your business, with several tourist shops thrown in for good measure. There are few more relaxing pastimes than spending a lazy spring or summer afternoon feasting on crab cakes and beer in one of the restaurants around the main square. Website: www.visit-annapolis.org

Distance Approximately 45 minutes from the Beltway
Annapolis & Anne Arundel County Visitors Bureau 410-280-0445
Directions Take US 50 East to Route 70 (Rowe Blvd.) and follow signs to Annapolis.

Baltimore, MD

Located only 45 miles north of the District, Baltimore offers many surprises to the visitor, combining its heritage as a seaport with the bustle of a city revitalized in the 1980s. The **Inner Harbor** is the city's visitor and shopping mecca. A brick walkway six blocks long winds along the waterfront past many of Baltimore's tourist attractions, including **Harborplace**, the **National Aquarium in Baltimore**, the frigate **Constellation**, the **Maryland Science Center**, the **Maritime Museum** and the **American Visionary Art Museum**. **ESPN Zone Baltimore**, a sports-themed entertainment complex, and **Port Discovery**, one of the largest children's museums in the country, are also located at the Inner Harbor.

Most of the food and shopping at Inner Harbor can be found at **Harborplace** (410-332-4191) at Pratt and Light Sts. and the **Gallery** (410-828-8721) at

200 East Pratt St. If you have been to Quincy Market in Boston, South St. Seaport in New York City or Pier 39 in San Francisco, the set-up will probably look familiar. All three Inner Harbor buildings are packed with food kiosks, cafés and specialty stores.

The **Maryland Science Center** at 601 Light St. (410-685-5225) is an exciting museum with hands-on or participatory exhibits. The Science Center also boasts a planetarium and five-story IMAX® theater. An admission fee is charged.

The modernist, triangular-shaped **National Aquarium in Baltimore** (410-576-3800) houses over 5,000 aquatic animals and a permanent exhibit, Amazon River Forest, a re-creation in cross-section of a black-water Amazon tributary and part of its surrounding forest. On weekends, waiting in the ticket line for this popular site can take over an hour, so unless you plan to get there early, you may want to order tickets in advance through Ticketmaster.

The **Baltimore Maritime Museum** (410-396-3854), next to the Aquarium, offers a self-guided tour of the **USS Torsk** submarine, noted for sinking the last warship in World War II, and the lightship **Chesapeake**, once a floating lighthouse. The frigate **USS Constellation**, first launched from Baltimore Harbor in 1797, is the only surviving Civil War-era naval vessel and the last all-sail warship that the US Navy ever built.

Baseball fans will be familiar with one of the game's gems, **Oriole Park at Camden Yards** (410-685-9800; www.theorioles.com). Just a short stroll from the Inner Harbor and right off I-95, this park's convenience is surpassed only by its marvelous ambiance. You do not need to be a fan of the Orioles, or even of baseball, to have a great time there.

Sports fans can take advantage of the sports bar, **Balls,** at 200 West Pratt St. (410-659-5844), right across from Camden Yards. Baseball fans might be interested in stopping by the Babe Ruth Birthplace and **Baltimore Orioles Museum** (410-727-1539) at 216 Emory St. on the way to the ball game.

Football fans cheer on the Baltimore Ravens in the new **PSINet Stadium** (410-230-8000; www.baltimoreravens.com) located at 1101 Russell St. at the Camden Yards site.

Located only five blocks from Inner Harbor, **Little Italy** has over 20 restaurants, ranging from inexpensive pizza parlors to elegant, somewhat pricey Italian restaurants.

For a change of pace from Inner Harbor, head to nearby **Fells Point**, one of Baltimore's historic districts. The influence of the area's 200 years of maritime history is visible in every tavern, antique store, restaurant and home.

NATIONAL PARK PASSES

The National Park Service offers several Golden Passports to help you save on entrance fees. If you plan to visit several of the many sites in, around, and within reasonable driving distance of the Washington area, you will be interested in this offer. The passports cover the holder and accompanying private party. Apply in person at any National Park or regional office of the US Park Service or Forest Service for one of the following:

The Golden Eagle Passport
$50/year

The Golden Age Passport
US residents, 62 and older
$10 one-time fee

The Golden Access Passport
Blind and permanently disabled
Free

The US National Park Service can be found on the Web at www.nps.gov

Regional National Park Guides can be obtained by calling 800-395-7275.

In the 19th century, while sailors and shipbuilders were roaming the streets of Fells Point, merchants and shoemakers were busily plying their trade up on **Federal Hill**. This historic neighborhood is only a five-minute walk south on Light St. from Inner Harbor. Cannons were placed on top of Federal Hill during the Civil War to protect the harbor, and an observation tower was built to herald arriving ships. Today, the park offers a good view of the harbor and a quiet place to picnic. Dozens of family-owned stalls, some handed down for generations, fill Federal Hill's **Cross St. Market**, each featuring something different—seafood, cheese, bread, barbecue, cookies and pastries.

Another notable Baltimore sight is **Fort McHenry** (410-962-4299) at East Fort Ave., where America's successful defense against the British in 1814 inspired Francis Scott Key to write the Star Spangled Banner.

Baltimore's **Art District** is located on Charles St., about three-quarters of a mile from the harbor. Among more than a dozen museums and galleries you will find Baltimore's gem, the **Walters Art Gallery** at 600 North Charles St. (410-547-9000). This museum houses one of the largest private collections in the world spanning 5,000 years of artistic endeavor. The **Baltimore Museum of Art** (410-396-7100), located just off North Charles St., features a collection of French Impressionist paintings and a sculpture garden. Most of the Art District museums and galleries are free to the public; a few charge a nominal admission fee. Website: www.ci.baltimore.md.us.

Baltimore has a number of sites and special collections focused on its rich African-American heritage. In addition to the Baltimore Museum of Art and the Walters Art Gallery mentioned above, visit the **Baltimore City Life Museum**, 800 E. Lombard St. (410-396-3523), the **Eubie Blake National Museum and Cultural Center**, 34 Market Pl. (410-625-3113), and the **Great Blacks in**

Wax Museum, 1601 E. North Ave. (410-563-3404). For historical information, contact the **Maryland Historical Society** at 201 W. Monument St. (410-685-3750).

Distance Approximately 45 minutes from the Beltway
Visitors Center 410-837-4636 or 800-282-6632
Directions Take the Beltway to I-95 North and follow the signs to Inner Harbor, a good starting point for access to other parts of town. If you are headed to a particular spot, call ahead for more specific directions. On weekdays, you can take the MARC commuter train from Union Station to either Camden or Pennsylvania Station in Baltimore. For more information, call 800-325-RAIL. Amtrak (800-USA-RAIL) will also take you from Union Station to Baltimore's Pennsylvania Station.

Charlottesville, VA

Charlottesville, known by some as Mr. Jefferson's city, is a charming central Virginia town, nestled in the beautiful countryside at the foot of the Blue Ridge Mountains. Visit nearby **Monticello** (804-984-9822; www.monticello.org), which Thomas Jefferson designed as his private home. Here you will quickly learn of Jefferson's wide-ranging interests in science, architecture, philosophy and the arts. The estate sits amidst beautiful gardens on top of a small mountain overlooking Charlottesville and the rolling countryside. Admission is charged and includes a guided tour.

From Monticello, you can see parts of "Mr. Jefferson's University," otherwise known as the **University of Virginia** (804-924-0311; www.virginia.edu). Jefferson founded the university, which was chartered in 1819. The grounds feature mostly neo-classical buildings, white porticos and carefully manicured gardens. The Lawn—a broad grassy expanse bordered by 19th century architecture—is the focal point of the university and a beautiful site. The school is proud of its strong academic reputation, its major teaching hospital, and its fine athletic teams, particularly in women's basketball and men's soccer and football.

Charlottesville was also home to another president, James Monroe. His estate, **Ash Lawn** (804-293-9539), famous for its boxwood gardens and strolling peacocks, has the atmosphere of an early 19th-century working plantation. Jefferson personally selected the site for Monroe's house and, on a clear day, you can see Monticello from the front porch of Ash Lawn. An admission fee is charged.

If you decide to visit either Ash Lawn or Monticello, you will probably pass by historic **Michie Tavern** (804-977-1234), on Route 53 about half a mile from Monticello. The tavern opened in 1784 and still offers native Virginia wine and fine southern cooking.

The highlight of Charlottesville's Historic District is the downtown mall, home to a small collection of antique stores, shops and art galleries and a few good restaurants. The **Old Historic Hardware Store** (804-977-1518) is an interesting place to dine, known for its meter-high beers. The **Court Square Tavern** (804-296-6111) offers more than 100 imported beers and a tasty Shepherd's Pie.

Central Virginia hosts dozens of festivals and annual celebrations. One of the most famous, the **Foxfield Steeplechase**, is Charlottesville's pride and joy, attracting people from all over each spring and fall. Website: www.ci.charlottesville.va.us.

Distance Approximately 2 1/2 hours from the Beltway
Chamber of Commerce 804-295-3141
Directions I-66 West to Route 29 South all the way to Charlottesville.

Williamsburg, VA

Williamsburg, originally the capital of Virginia, was also a training ground for the men who led America to independence. In this small city, George Washington, Thomas Jefferson, Patrick Henry and George Mason helped frame the structure of America's government. Here, the House of Burgesses adopted Virginia's Resolution for Independence in May 1776, which led to the adoption of the Declaration of Independence the following July in Philadelphia.

It is easy to picture these events in Colonial Williamsburg, for in a way, life goes on much as it did nearly 200 years ago. Thanks to generous donations from the late John Rockefeller, Jr., most of the original town was completely restored in the late 1920s and early 1930s. Along its streets you will find all the makings of a colonial town—houses, shops, taverns, gardens and even a church. Costumed actors lend a human dimension as they recreate details of 18th-century daily life. In the historic district, **King's Arms** comes highly recommended for either lunch or dinner. For some 18th-century fun, stop by **Chowning's Tavern** (804-229-2141), where you can drink ale, eat peanuts, indulge in their great barbecue sandwiches, and play games from the era, including the Most Wonderful Game of Goose and the Game of Life.

To get the most out of this excursion, plan on staying two or three days. A **Patriot Pass** allows access to Williamsburg for up to a year. During the summer and the Christmas season, call ahead for reservations. Website: www.ci.williamsburg.va.us.

The **College of William and Mary**, the second-oldest college in the United States, has been an integral part of Williamsburg since 1693. The Sir Christopher Wren Building houses the oldest classrooms in the country.

Distance Approximately 3 hours from the Beltway
Visitors Center 800-HISTORY
Directions Take I-95 South to I-64 East.

Frederick, MD

The City of Frederick, MD is located in Frederick County, which played a crucial role in many great battles in American history—the French and Indian War, the Revolutionary War, the Civil War—because of its strategic location as a transportation and trade crossroads. **Memorial Park,** at W. 2nd and Bentz Sts. in the historic downtown district, is the only place in Maryland where soldiers from every war (the French and Indian War to the Persian Gulf War) are honored in one location. Also located in the historic district is the **National Museum of Civil War Medicine** at 48 E. Patrick St. (301-695-1864), dedicated to increasing public understanding of an innovative era in medical history. History buffs may want to visit the **Historical Society of Frederick County** at 24 East Church St. (301-663-1188) and review its extensive genealogical and historic resources.

The City of Frederick is one of several Maryland towns where concentrations of antiques can be found. **Emporium Antiques** (301-662-7099) at 112 E. Patrick St. offers about 130 dealers under one roof.

One of the unique attractions in Frederick's historic downtown is the work of local artist William Cochran who uses a method called trompe l'oeil (deceive the eye). His images, Angels in Architecture, can be found throughout the downtown area. The most acclaimed of his works is the Community Bridge mural project overlooking the Carroll Creek Linear Park. What appears to be a cobblestone bridge is actually made of concrete which has been painted with stones, ivy and other images. It's worth a trip to Frederick just to see this amazing piece of work. Right next to the Community Bridge is the **Delaplaine Visual Arts Center** (40 South Carroll Street, 301-698-0656), an art gallery that exhibits a variety of works from local, national and international artists. Website: www.visitfrederick.org.

Distance Approximately 45 minutes from the Beltway
Visitors Center 800-999-3613
Directions Take Route I-270 off the Beltway and follow exits to Frederick. For directions directly to the historic district, contact the Visitors Center.

BACK TO NATURE: FINDING WILD PLACES IN & AROUND DC

In and around the city, you will find a world of wonderful ways to appreciate nature. In town, there are beautiful displays and informative exhibits at the **U.S. Botanic Garden**, **Kenilworth Aquatic Gardens**, or the **U.S. National Arboretum** ... in the gardens at **Dumbarton Oaks** or the **Franciscan Monastery** ... in **Rock Creek Park** or on **Roosevelt Island** ... and at the **National Zoo** and **National Aquarium**. Throughout the suburbs, you can visit local, regional and state parks; fine examples include Seneca Creek State Park and Rock Creek Regional Park in Maryland and Mason Neck State Park in Virginia. And not too far afield are unspoiled natural areas—from seashore to mountains—each offering opportunities to take in the beauty and wonder of nature.

On the Atlantic islands of **Chincoteague** and **Assateague** you can see wild horses, snow geese, swans, and peregrine falcons. A little further south, you can go whale-watching in winter and dolphin-watching in summer with the **Virginia Marine Science Museum** in Richmond. Many sites in the region—from Bombay Hook in Delaware to Back Bay off the coast near Virginia Beach—lie along the Atlantic flyway, providing spectacular displays of migrating and wintering birds.

In the 710,000 acres of the **George Washington** and **Jefferson National Forests** and along the **Blue Ridge**, **Massanutten**, **Shenandoah**, and **Appalachian Mountains**, you can see white-tailed deer, black bear, and bobcats. Touring the **Blue Ridge Parkway** or hiking the **Appalachian Trail** through the 200,000-acre Shenandoah National Park, you'll see even more.

Here is just a sampling of the opportunities for adventure, outdoor fun, and communing with nature, in the region and around the year. Load your camera, grab your backpack or picnic basket, and get back to nature. As you do, please remember to leave nature as you found her ... so she can continue to enrich the lives of local residents and visitors alike.

A Sampling of Nature Sites

- **Assateague Island National Seashore:** a 37-mile long windswept barrier island off the Maryland and Virginia coast and one of 10 national seashores; includes National Park, State Park, and Chincoteague National Wildlife Refuge; 1,800 acres of white sandy beaches, grassland, and dunes; wild horses, deer; 300 bird species. (NPS 410-641-1441)
- **Back Bay National Wildlife Refuge:** vital barrier island offering 7,700 acres of ocean, beach, sand dunes, shrublands, maritime forest, marsh, and bay habitats; peregrine falcon,Canada geese, heron, ibis, gulls, terns, pelicans; white-tailed deer, gray squirrel, marsh rabbit, turtles, river otter. (Virginia Beach, VA; USFWS 757-721-2412)

- **Blackwater National Wildlife Refuge:** 21,000 acres of wetlands and mixed evergreen and deciduous forest, mostly rich tidal marsh with freshwater ponds; second largest nesting population of bald eagles (after Florida); great blue herons, black ducks; endangered Delmarva fox squirrel; at peak of migration 35,000 geese and 15,000 ducks. (Cambridge, MD; USFWS 410-228-2677)

- **Bombay Hook National Wildlife Refuge:** 15,918 acres in the Delaware River and Delmarva Coastal Area ecosystem; more than one and a half million ducks, geese, and shore birds during annual migration; other wildlife year-round. (Smyra, DE; USFWS 302-653-9345)

- **Chincoteague National Wildlife Refuge:** 13,700 acres of wildlife watcher's paradise; 316 species of bird, 44 species of mammal, hundreds of snow geese during migration, mute and tundra swans, peregrine falcons. (Chincoteague, VA; USFWS 800-344-9453)

- **Huntley Meadows Park:** 1,425 acres of diverse habitats and one of the greatest varieties of plant and wildlife in the area; vast freshwater wetlands, wildflower-speckled meadows, and mature forest; fox, deer, beaver, otter, heron, dragonflies; 200 species of birds. (Alexandria, VA; Fairfax County Park Authority 703-768-2525)

- **Jug Bay National Wetlands Sanctuary:** 620-acre sanctuary and largest freshwater tidal wetlands on the East Coast; large stands of aquatic plants; rich assortment of invertebrates, fish, reptiles, amphibians, birds and mammals including bald eagle, osprey, muskrat, beaver, and turtle; mixed hardwood forests, non-tidal wetlands, agricultural fields, and streams and ponds; excellent birdwatching. (Patuxent River Park, Upper Marlboro, MD; Maryland-National Capital Park and Planning Commission 301-627-6074)

- **Mason Neck National Wildlife Refuge:** 2,227-acre refuge with several distinct ecosystems; 50-60 eagles in the winter; 1,200 pairs of great blue herons and more than 200 species of birds. (Woodbridge, VA; USFWS 703-491-6255)

- **Patuxent Research Refuge:** one of the largest forested areas in the mid-Atlantic region; provides critical breeding habitat and important nesting areas for neotropical migratory birds; 12,750 acres of forest, meadow, and wetland habitats; more than 200 species of bird. (Laurel, MD; USFWS 301-497-5760)

- **Prime Hook National Wildlife Refuge:** 8,818-acre marsh habitat for migratory waterfowl including black and wood duck, Canada geese, mallards, pintails; red and gray foxes, river otter, white-tailed deer, woodchucks, endangered Delmarva fox squirrel. (Milton, DE; USFWS 302-684-8419)

-Sheila Donoghue

NPS = *National Park Service*
USFWS = *US Fish & Wildlife Service*

MASTERING DC: THE SHENANDOAH VALLEY

Nestled between the Blue Ridge and Allegheny Mountains lies one of the most beautiful and historic regions in the eastern United States, the Shenandoah Valley. This valley was an important route west for the pioneers, figured prominently in Stonewall Jackson's 1862 valley campaign and other Civil War events, and today provides a virtually unlimited variety of recreational activities and natural beauty.

☐ **Go Underground:** Explore the **underground beauty** of Skyline Caverns in Front Royal (800-296-4545), Endless Caverns in New Market (540-896-CAVE), Luray Caverns in Luray (540-743-6551), Shenandoah Caverns near Mount Jackson (540-477-3115), or Caverns of Natural Bridge (800-533-1410) near Lexington.

☐ **Drive Into the Sunset:** The beautiful 105-mile **Skyline Drive** begins in Front Royal and runs through Shenandoah National Park. Near Waynesboro, it becomes the Blue Ridge Parkway and continues another 450 miles through valleys, forests and mountains, to Great Smoky Mountains National Park in North Carolina.

☐ **Live on the Edge:** On the western edge of the valley, visit the 1.7 million acres of the **George Washington and Jefferson National Forests** (540-265-5100). Off to the east, hike in the 1,100-acre Sky Meadows or climb Old Rag Mountain.

☐ **Party Down in the Valley:** Celebrate some of the valley's many **annual events:** Shenandoah Valley Music Festival, Arts and Crafts Show, Jazz Weekend, and Folk Festival (800-459-3396), all in Orkney Springs; the Shenandoah Apple Blossom Festival (800-230-2139) in Winchester; and Christmas open houses and candlelight tours throughout the area.

☐ **Make Yourself at Home:** Explore the area from a home base right in **Shenandoah National Park** (800-999-4714). Try the 100-year-old Skyland Lodge, the rustic cabins hidden in the trees at Big Meadows Lodge, or the furnished cottages at Lewis Mountain.

☐ **Rest, Relax & Recreate:** Ski, golf, fish, hike, play tennis or luxuriate at one of the area's **major resorts:** Wintergreen (800-266-2444), The Homestead (800-336-5771), Massanutten (800-207-MASS), Coolfont Resort (800-296-8768), or Bryce Resort (800-821-1444).

☐ **Go Natural:** Visit **Natural Bridge** (800-533-1410), a breathtaking 215-foot, 36,000-ton limestone structure. Or see **Natural Chimneys** (540-350-2510), where huge rocks tower to more than 120 feet. Resembling a medieval castle, the site inspired the 1820 creation of the Natural Chimneys Annual Jousting Tournament, the oldest continuously held sports event in the country.

☐ **Get a New Outfit:** Along the South Fork of the Shenandoah River, you'll find many **outfitters for canoeing, rafting and tubing**. One of the best known is Shenandoah River Outfitters (540-743-4159) in Luray.

☐ **Take a Bird's Eye View:** Get a unique perspective on the beauty of the valley from a **hot-air balloon**. Contact Island Balloons (800-891-3555), Bear Balloon Corp. (800-932-0152), or Balloons Unlimited (703-281-2300).

☐ **Volunteer for Nature's Sake:** Join the **Potomac Appalachian Trail Club** (703-242-0963), whose volunteers maintain more than 1,000 miles of trails along a 240-mile stretch reaching south from Pine Grove Furnace in Pennsylvania to Rockfish Cap in Central Virginia.

CHAPTER TEN

Young People

-contributed by Dartha Dragnich

There may never be a better time or place to be a child than right here and now in the Washington, DC area. Whether you reside in the area or are just visiting, there is a 100% guarantee that an abundance of kid-friendly opportunities is available for your own children, your nieces and nephews, or your friends' children. By far the best weekly resource for local exhibits and events can be found in the Saturday's Child column of the Friday *Washington Post*. Its Carousel listing offers current details on all kinds of performances, special events, nature offerings, places to go and library programs. Each weekly column usually highlights one special place or event, providing in-depth information that will probably have your youngster heading out the door before they finish reading. Also, look in the Local Interest section of area bookstores for books and pamphlets on local children and family activities. Finally, check out the Resources section of this chapter for more ideas. What follows is just a sampling of places and activities aimed at the youth in your crowd. Also included is a Feature Page providing resources for public, independent and charter schools in the metropolitan DC area.

Activities

The activity choices in the area are every bit as varied as children's interests. From amusement park rides to nature walks to watching pygmy monkeys at the aquarium, the challenge for area families is deciding what to do first. The suggestions here will get you started. And the material in the next section, Resources, will keep you going for a good long while.

Amusement Parks

Busch Gardens, the Old Country (800-722-8886; www.buschgardens.com). This may be the region's most impressive collection of serious roller coasters; set in faux 17th century Europe.

Hershey Park (800-HERSHEY; www.hersheypa.com). You'll enjoy the warehouse-sized gift shop devoted entirely to chocolate more than the actual tour. Also offers amusement park rides, a state fair, a wildlife preserve, the **Hersheypark Arena** and the **Hershey Museum**.

Paramount Kings Dominion This 400-acre theme park (804-876-5000; www.pkd4fun.com/Dominion/index.htm) north of Richmond, VA boasts seven theme areas similar to the setup at Disney parks.

PARENTS UNITED

The mission of **Parents United for the DC Public Schools** is to empower parents and the community with information and advocacy skills to help ensure educational success for all DC public school children. They publish a newsletter, ***UPDATE***, five times a year with an analysis of current school system issues. If you would like to find out about the group, schools in the city, or what you can do to support their efforts, call them at 202-518-3667, stop by their office at 1300 19th St. NW, Suite 330, or see their website at (http://media.georgetown.edu/parentsunited/).

Sesame Place (215-752-7070; www.sesameplace.com). Come for fun with Sesame Street characters, water activities, a family roller coaster, interactive science and education exhibits, and a whole lot more.

Six Flags America (301-249-1500; www.sixflags.com). Washington's closest theme-and-water park, covering over 135 acres.

Water Country USA (800-772-8886; www.watercountryusa.com). The mid-Atlantic's largest water-play park, located three miles east of Williamsburg, VA.

Aquariums

National Aquarium, 14th and Constitution Ave. NW (202-482-2825). Over 1,000 specimens of aquatic life are in residence at, of all places, the basement of the Department of Commerce building. Play with a starfish or horseshoe crab in the "Touch Tank." On specific days of the week, watch the sharks and piranhas get fed at this, the oldest aquarium in the United States. A modest admission is charged.

The **National Aquarium in Baltimore**, 501 E. Pratt St., Baltimore, MD (410-576-3800; www.aqua.org), is about a one-hour drive from DC. This extraordinary center is full of fascinating exhibits that transport you to another world. Experience an Atlantic Coral Reef, where you'll see fish being hand-fed by divers throughout the day; a Tropical Rainforest, where you'll find colorful birds, sloths and iguanas; and a Survival through Adaption exhibit featuring Congo tetras, upside-down catfish and African butterflies. The permanent Amazon River Forest exhibit includes an incredible variety of tropical fish, giant turtles, a green anaconda—one of the largest snakes in the world, as well as pygmy marmosets—the world's smallest species of monkey. There's never a dull moment at the aquarium where pools of sharks or stingrays or an electric eel may show up at any time during your visit, safely swimming in a pool, of course. Hands-on exhibits can be found in the Exploration Station as well as at the Children's Discovery Cove. Don't miss the MTV-like dolphin show, a multi-layered extravaganza featuring live dolphins, video and narration. Admission to the aquarium is charged based on age, day of the week and time of day.

Art Galleries

The **National Gallery of Art**, Constitution Ave. at 6th St. NW (202-737-4215; www.nga.gov), is always on the top 10 list of most popular art museums in the country. Its **East and West Buildings** are connected by an underground concourse with a moving walkway—similar to the traveler-friendly walkways found in airports. Even the smallest in your group can appreciate the view inside the soaring central court of the trapezoid-shaped East Building, where they'll delight in seeing a three-story-high Calder mobile and a dazzling Miro Tapestry. The West Building can be a bit overwhelming. Use its Micro Gallery to create a handy computer-generated printout of your family's own personally chosen tour of exhibits. Also, an excellent self-guided tour for children ages 4 - 8 and their families is available in the gallery shops.

Kids love visiting the **Phillips Collection**, 1600 21st St. NW at Q Street (202-387-0961; www.phillipscollection.org), because they get to walk through what was once the home of wealthy Duncan Phillips. Each elegant gallery is a room in the house, with a fancy fireplace and wonderful old-fashioned furniture. Call in advance for a Family Fun Pack before the trip or pick one up at the door.

The big news at the **Walters Art Gallery**, 600 N. Charles St. in Baltimore, MD (410-547-9000; www.thewalters.org), is the $18.5 million revitalization of its newer wing, known as the 1974 building, scheduled for completion in the fall of 2001. Despite the renovation, your family can still enjoy the best parts of the Greek, Roman and Egyptian exhibits, including a look at an Egyptian mummy. They have been moved to the 1904 building which remains open despite the dust. Watch for the new Family Arts Learning Center which will include state-of-the-art studio and workshop spaces, an updated auditorium space, and an education resource center.

Concerts

The **Washington Performing Arts Society** (202-833-9800) performs concerts and cultural enrichment programs at no charge for children, K-12, at schools throughout the metropolitan area and suburbs. Also, 12- to 18-year-olds and adults can explore the performing arts together at full-length concerts during the Family-Friendly Series of Performances. For information on these and other events, see their website at www.wpas.org.

The **Kennedy Center** supports performance and education programs for young people and families. Programs are available for children of all ages, starting at age four. Offerings include an introduction to orchestral instruments with the **National Symphony Orchestra**, theater performances and concerts, storytelling, puppetry and more, available on a subscription or individual ticket basis. Or take

EDUCATIONAL SERVICE

In addition to other publishing activities, the *Washington Post* and the *Washington Times* run important educational programs to help parents and teachers use the newspaper. You can call the *Post's* Educational Services Department at 202-334-4544 or 202-334-7972. The Education Department at the *Times* can be reached at 202-636-3370.

the family to a less-structured, hour-long concert performed every evening at 6:00 p.m. on the Millennium Stage. These free concerts are a wonderful way to introduce young people to a variety of musical talent. Further information on these programs is available at 202-416-8500.

Libraries, Reading…and More

Libraries aren't just for reading anymore, although there's plenty of that going on, too. According to the American Library Association, the Washington-area public libraries are some of the busiest in the nation. And why not, with card-carrying toddlers and 50-book checkout limits, it's a great place to read. But along with the poetry and prose, an explosion of library-sponsored activities awaits the elementary set at your local library, including author talks, storytelling, exhibits, workshops, film series, bilingual programs and multiple-sibling preschool sessions. For a general listing of city and suburban branch libraries, look in the Blue Pages of your specific area's Bell Atlantic telephone book. Also, look in the Carousel column of the *Post's* Child section, which provides an up-to-date listing of library activities for the very young in and around DC.

For a special library experience, take your family to see the **King Mural** by artist Don Miller at the **Martin Luther King Memorial Library**, 901 G St. NW (202-727-1111; http://dclibrary.org/mlk/). This carefully researched visual documentation of King's influential life is enormous in scope and emotion. No reading required.

Museums

It's little wonder that the **Smithsonian Institution**, the largest museum/research complex on the planet, has an amazing array of exhibits of particular interest to children. Be sure to inquire about the popular "Family Days," offered at various times of the year at most of the Smithsonian museums. The free-admission museums listed here are all on the Mall, between Constitution and Independence Aves., close to the Smithsonian, Federal Triangle and L'Enfant Metro stations. If you take the Metro, check with the attendant at your departure station to find out which stop is best for you. You can call the Dial-a-Museum line for daily, 24-hour recorded activity information. Call 202-357-2020 to hear the message in English or 202-633-9126 for Spanish.

The **Arts and Industries** building at 900 Jefferson Dr. SW is home to several exhibitions for children as well as the ever-popular **Discovery Theater** (202-357-1500; www.si.edu/organiza/museums/artsind). The **Museum of Natural History** (202-357-2700; www.mnh.si.edu) at 10th St. and Constitution Ave. NW has always been one of the most popular kid-targeted museums on the mall, what with the refurbished 8-ton, 13-foot African Bush Elephant, the Orkin Insect Zoo and the Dinosaur Hall. But the educational entertainment just got more fun with the introduction of Discovery Center, comprised of Washington's only state-of-the-art IMAX® 2D-3D theater, soaring Atrium Café and expanded Museum Shop. A new, expanded Discovery Room, to be located on the top floor of Discovery Center, is scheduled to open in 2002. And, depending on the weather, check out the museum's first outdoor exhibit, the Butterfly Garden, located on the 9th St. side of the museum.

A favorite of many children—of all ages—is the **National Air and Space Museum** (202-357-1400) at 7th St. and Independence Ave. SW. This museum features exhibits on the history of aviation, space science and space technology, as well as spectacular movies in its IMAX® Theater and Einstein Planetarium. For current museum information, including a schedule of daily movies, call the information line above. The museum is undergoing major renovation through 2001. Updates about the exhibits affected by the renovation can be found on the website at www.nasm.edu.

In the planning stages since the early 80s, construction is set to begin in January 2001 for a second air and space museum to be located at Washington Dulles International Airport. Completion of the Dulles Center is scheduled for the end of 2003 to coincide with the 100th anniversary of the Wright Brother's first flight.

In addition to the Smithsonian, there are a number of private museums of special note, including those listed here.

Fire Museum of Maryland, 1301 York Rd, Lutherville, MD (410-321-7500). First opened in 1971, children clamor to see the most comprehensive collection of vintage fire trucks in the area and one of the best in the country. Admission is charged. The museum is closed from November through April except for special events.

National Capital Children's Museum, 800 Third St. NE (202-675-4120). Where else can young people star in their own cartoon, visit Japan and then dance in a Mexican town plaza? Children and life are celebrated at this museum every day. Website: www.ccm.org. There is an admission fee.

National Capital Trolley Museum, Bonifont Rd. and New Hampshire Ave., Silver Spring, MD (301-384-6088). This museum features a collection of antique American and European trolleys and streetcars. Call ahead for hours of operations—which vary depending on the day and month—and for special event information. Admission is free and there's only a nominal fare charged for trolley rides.

Older children will love its exhibits on architecture and construction, but for younger kids, there is nothing like just roaming around the spectacular, yes, colossal **National Building Museum** (202-272-2448; www.nbm.org). Completed in the late 1800s, almost demolished then saved, this engineering wonder is dedicated to the building arts. Wander around the Great Hall with its eight 75-foot-tall Corinthian columns—among the tallest in the world—and central fountain measuring 28-feet across. If you feel like you're being watched, look up to see the more than 200 busts, representing building occupations, resting casually above the center court. Push button question-and-answer games and a hands-on building exhibit add to the enjoyment of this museum.

Newseum, 1101 Wilson Blvd, Arlington, VA (703-284-3544). Children can become on-the-air television or radio news announcers, have their picture put on the cover of a magazine, view television and radio shows being produced, and watch up-to-the-minute news from around the world on the block-long video news wall. Free of charge. Check out their website at www.newseum.org. A word of caution: museum content is probably best suited for the older rather than younger members of your group.

Washington Dolls' House and Toy Museum, 5236 44th St. NW (202-244-0024). Here you will find the world's largest collection of antique doll houses, toys and games, most of which are from the Victorian period. Closed on Mondays; admission is charged.

Nature Centers and Walks

Hiking and biking trails are often either too crowded or simply too treacherous to provide safe and quiet nature experiences for children. There are, however, several stroller-accessible nature walks in the area, a few of which are listed below. Call your state, regional and county parks department for information on fully accessible walks near you. Telephone numbers are listed under Recreation Centers in this chapter.

DC

Rock Creek Nature Center and Planetarium
5200 Glover Rd. NW
202-426-6829
www.nps.gov/rocr

Maryland
Clearwater Nature Center
Cosca Regional Park
11000 Thrift Rd., Clinton
301-297-4575
www.mdsci.org/edu_DSD/bio.htm

Locust Grove Nature Center
Cabin John Regional Park
7777 Democracy Blvd., Bethesda
301-299-1990

Virginia
Huntley Meadows Park
3701 Lockheed Blvd., Alexandria
703-768-2525
www.co.fairfax.va.us/parks/huntley.htm

Riverbend Nature Center
Riverbend Regional Park
8814 Jeffrey Rd., Great Falls
703-759-3211

Of special note is the **Mountain Laurel Trail** at the **National Wildlife Federation's Laurel Ridge Conservation Education Center** (703-790-4000). This trail, at 8925 Leesburg Pike in Vienna, three miles west of Tysons Corner, is perfect for families with strollers as well as for people with other special needs. The trail includes interpretive signs that are accessible from standing or sitting positions, a specially produced audio cassette tape for the hearing impaired focusing on the nonvisual elements of what might be experienced at each stop, and a large-print version of the brochure and Braille transcriptions of the signs for the visually impaired. Texture and color changes in the asphalt signal the visually impaired that they have reached an interpretive stop. Learn more about this wonderful place on the National Wildlife Federation's website at www.nwf.org.

Points of Interest

The **carousel on the Mall** at 1000 Jefferson Dr. SW is located in front of the Smithsonian Castle (202-357-2700). Built in the 1940s, it's an inexpensive delight—to ride or to watch your child ride. It operates daily, weather permitting. **Glen Echo Park's carousel** and accompanying Wurlitzer organ are circa 1920. The park is located at MacArthur Boulevard at Goldsboro Road, Glen Echo, MD (301-492-6282). Call for seasonal hours of operation.

Federal Bureau of Investigation, 9th St. and Pennsylvania Ave. NW (202-324-3447; www.fbi.gov). Look at photographs or drawings of the FBI's Ten Most Wanted individuals, learn how the FBI finds them, and conclude your visit with a marksmanship demonstration. Add exhibits of unusual firearms and memorabilia of well-known criminals and you've got one of the most popular stops in Washington. Admission is free of charge.

Kidwell Farm, 2709 West Ox Rd., Herndon, VA (703-437-9101). Part of Fairfax County's Frying Pan Park, Kidwell Farm is a real working farm. Children are fascinated with a close-up look at the old machinery still in use, petting the dozens of barnyard animals, and learning the connection between cows and milk. Open year-round, seven days a week, bring a bag lunch as no concession stands are available.

NASA/Goddard Space Flight Center, Visitor Center, Greenbelt and Soil Conservation Rds., Greenbelt, MD (301-286-8981). At this Visitor Center, you can see models of rockets and spacecraft that have made journeys into space, view the Earth and neighboring stars and planets as seen from space in a stand-up eight-screen theater, and pilot your own manned maneuvering unit and gyrochair. On the first and third Sunday of each month, visitors can watch a model rocket launch. View the website at www.gsfc.nasa.gov. Admission is free.

If everyone in your brood is at least 14-years old, make reservations to tour the largest radio station in the world, **Voice of America** (202-619-3919; www.voa.gov). With daily broadcasts in over 40 languages, far more foreign visitors than Americans usually take this interesting tour—and recognize the broadcaster's voices. See the control room, listen to a broadcast and watch a short informative film.

Recreation Centers

Children and families have an abundance of choices when it comes to recreational activities in the Washington area. In addition to programs run by local schools, each jurisdiction has its own city or county Department of Recreation. These government offices organize, run and publicize all kinds of recreational activities—playgrounds, picnic areas, courses and outings in the vicinity.

Area Departments of Recreation

District of Columbia	202-673-7660
Maryland	
Bethesda, Chevy Chase	301-983-4467
Upper Montgomery County	240-777-6804
Wheaton, Silver Spring, Takoma	301-565-7494
	www.co.mo.md.us
Prince George's County	301-699-2407
Virginia	
Alexandria	703-838-4343
Arlington County	703-228-3322
Fairfax County	703-324-4386
	www.co.fairfax.va.us

Theaters

Arena Stage, 6th and Maine Ave. SW (202-554-9066; TDD 202-484-0247). Arena Stage runs a four-part program called Theater as Discovery, targeting public school teachers and students in grades 9-12. For further information about programs at the Arena Stage, see www.arenastage.org.

Living Stage, 6th and Maine Ave. SW (202-554-9066, TDD 202-484-0247), is the social outreach company of Arena Stage. Living Stage effects social change through the art of improvisational theater. Working from the fundamental belief that everyone is an artist with the need to create, the company conducts performance workshops in regularly scheduled sessions with children, teens, and adults who otherwise lack access to avenues of creative personal development. The company offers summer camps for children and teens in separate two-week sessions by age group, 6-8, 9-12, 13-15, and 16-18. The Arena State website is at www.arenastage.org.

Kennedy Center Theater Lab at the John F. Kennedy Center for the Performing Arts, New Hampshire Ave. at Rock Creek Pkwy. The theater produces and presents professional performances at the Kennedy Center for youngsters, parents and teachers. It also provides theater training, drama and play-writing workshops, and professional training and performance opportunities for advanced theater students. Call for information at 202-467-4600, 800-444-1324, or TDD 202-416-8524. For further information about upcoming events, see www.kennedy-center.org.

Adventure Theatre (301-320-5331) at Glen Echo Park, 7300 MacArthur Blvd., Glen Echo, MD, is the grandmother of children's theater in this area. Call ahead for information and reservations, and join the flock of parents and young

SPOTLIGHT ON THE ARTS

The following major theaters, gallery and museum have each produced a unique program to introduce families and children to the wonderful world of the creative arts. And as a special treat, both the Kennedy Center (202-416-8341) and the National Theatre (202-783-3370) offer behind-the-scene tours of their stages. Reservations are required for this birds-eye view.

"Imagination Celebration"— is a way to introduce children to great artists and exciting performances from around the world. Kennedy Center (202-467-4600)

"Kidsplay"— lets parents take in four Saturday matinees, while their children are entertained a few steps away. Arena Stage (202-488-4377)

"Saturday Morning at the National"— presents free theater performances for children four and up accompanied by their parent. National Theatre (202-783-3372)

"Sunday Traditions" and Family Days — provides children with an excellent feeling about art and museums and being artists themselves. Corcoran Gallery of Art (202-639-1725)

"Young at Art"— introduces the museum's collection by presenting performers combined with hands-on art projects. Hirshhorn Museum (202-357-3235)

children who have been enjoying plays, storytelling and theater-related activities since the very early 1950s. Website: www.nps.gov/glec/adtheat.htm.

Puppet Co. Playhouse (301-320-6668), also located at 7300 MacArthur Blvd, Glen Echo, MD, offers a different puppet show each month in their 200-seat performance facility. Featuring hand puppets, rod puppets, marionettes and shadows, it is the only East Coast theater completely devoted to puppetry between New York and Atlanta. For more information about upcoming performances, see their website at www.nps.gov/glec.

Discovery Theater, located at the Smithsonian's Arts and Industries Building, 900 Jefferson Dr. SW (202-357-1500), features live performing arts presentations for young people and their families. The performances range from puppet theater, plays and mime, to music, storytelling and dance, and are a perfect way to introduce the youngest members of the family to the magical world of theater. For a current listing of events, check the website at www.si.edu./tsa/disctheater/start.htm.

Wolf Trap Farm Park for the Performing Arts, at Towlston Rd. and Route 7, Vienna, VA (703-255-1939), is America's only National Park for the performing arts. An informal story theater offers puppet shows, dance and other child-oriented entertainment, and during the summer season, features a Children's Theater in the Woods program. The annual International Children's Festival offers music, dance, costumes and crafts from around the world, and is a delightful way to bring the summer season to a close. For the latest Wolf Trap information, visit their website at www.wolf-trap.org.

Zoos and Animal Parks

National Zoological Park, 3001 Connecticut Ave. NW. The National Zoo is home to more than 5,000 animals including migratory birds, great cats, elephants, American bison and exotic reptiles such as the zoo's Komodo dragon pair. Admission is free. Recorded Zoo information is available at 202-673-4800. The zoo's website is at www.si.edu/natzoo/.

While at the zoo, experience **Amazonia**, the rain forest exhibit. Enter to view the underwater part of a river full of extraordinary tropical fish, then follow the steps up to the lush rain forest, teeming with a variety of tropical plant and animal life. Adjacent to the rain forest, the **Amazonia Science Gallery** is an actual science research laboratory for families and children. Check out the do-it-yourself computer stations and easy-to-use microscopes for magnifying creepy bugs to their super creepy-iest. Because the laboratory is devoted to topics such as animal behavior, molecular genetics, and biodiversity, some of the exhibits are better suited to the pre-teen in the family.

The **Reston Animal Park** is now located south of Leesburg on Rte 15 at 19270 James Monroe Highway, next to Sunshine Farms. This animal park has domestic and exotic animals for children to pet and feed. Information can be obtained at 703-759-3636.

Resources

A wide variety of resources exists to help you find out about other activities for young people. Area bookstores include many reference books and local guidebooks on activities for children. There are several newsletters and newspapers available either by subscription or for free at various sites in the area. Television and radio also get involved with children's programming. A sampling of these resources follows.

Books for Washington Area Families

Going Places With Children in Washington is available in most area bookstores. It is a valuable guidebook to museums, historical sights, parks, entertainment, restaurants and shopping and includes a calendar of events particularly suited to family outings. It is also available by mail order from Green Acres School, 11701 Danville Dr., Rockville, MD 20852 (301-881-4100).

The Parent Pages is a comprehensive guide to "family-friendly" products and services throughout the metropolitan area. The book is available in area bookstores or by contacting the Parent Pages, 8320 2nd Ave., Vienna, VA 22182 (703-698-8066).

Children's Bookstores

There are a number of fine specialized bookstores in the Washington area, dedicated to the interests of the younger reader. Listed here are a number of favorites.

DC

Politics and Prose
Children's Room
5015 Connecticut Ave. NW
202-364-1919
www.politics-prose.com

Sullivan's Toy Store
3412 Wisconsin Ave. NW
202-362-1343

Tree Top Toys & Books
3301 New Mexico Ave. NW
202-244-3500

Maryland
Bookoo Books for Kids
4923 Elm St., Bethesda
301-652-2794

Virginia
A Likely Story
1555 King St., Alexandria
703-836-2498
www.bookweb.org/bookstore/alikelystory

Aladdin's Lamp
126 W. Broad St., Falls Church
703-241-8281

Imagination Station
4525 Lee Hwy., Arlington
703-522-2047

Toy Corner Book Department
2918 Chain Bridge Rd., Oakton
703-255-3232

Why Not
200 King St., Alexandria
703-548-4420

Periodicals and Subscriptions

There are a number of local publications in the area focusing on the interests and needs of children. Some are focused more on support for parents and others are published for area children and teenagers. Included here are some of the major ones, but be sure to check your local library, schools and recreation centers for more ideas. Keep in mind, too, that you or your children might have something you would like to share with other families through these media outlets.

The Children's Post
51 Monroe St., Suite 1700
Rockville, MD 20850
Subscription: $17

Washington Families
Publication for Metro Washington Parents
3 Bethesda Metro Center, Suite 750
Bethesda, MD 20814
301-656-0901
http://family.com
and
462 Herndon Parkway, Suite 206
Herndon, VA 20170
703-318-1385 (VA/Metro)
Subscription: $25; free at 1,500 area locations

Washington Parent
The Parent Connection, Inc.
5606 Knollwood Rd.
Bethesda, MD 20816
301-320-2321, Subscription: $24
www.washingtonparent.com

Young DC
2025 Pennsylvania Ave. NW, #321
Washington, DC 20006
202-429-5292
Subscription: Free at 100 area locations

Television and Radio Programs

Several television channels and radio stations feature programs just for children and their families. In addition to the standard fare of the networks, you will find great shows on the three local Public Broadcasting channels—WMPT, WETA and WHUT. If you have cable, you can also tune into the Discovery Channel, Family Channel, Learning Channel, Nickelodeon and the USA Network. Across these options, you will find programming of all types for children and teenagers alike.

NOTEWORTHY NEWS

Young DC is an independent newspaper written exclusively by and for Washington, DC area teens, aged 14 to 19. The publication reflects the cultural, economic and racial diversity of the Washington community and seeks to reduce the isolation between the area's urban and suburban teens. *Young DC* is a great outlet for aspiring teen writers, editors, artists, photographers and cartoonists, giving them a chance to be seen and heard. It is distributed free of charge to more than 100 high schools and retail outlets in DC, Maryland and Virginia, including coffee shops and laundromats. The paper is particularly popular in that it covers subjects of interest to teens in a way that teens can truly appreciate.

Children's Express (CE), a news service produced "by children for everybody," is about kids reporting on the issues that affect their lives. The vision of Children's Express is "to see that the concerns and voices of children and teens are heard, respected, and acted upon." CE's worldwide headquarters is in Washington, DC. Full details as to how your child or teen can write an editorial or story, respond to a poll, give feedback on stories or subscribe to the CE list service, can be found by accessing their website at www.cenews.org/index.htm.

WASHINGTON AREA SCHOOLS

The Washington metropolitan area schools are among the best in the nation. In addition to the extensive public school systems in DC, Maryland and Virginia, there is a substantial number of excellent independent and private schools as well. You can find a comprehensive overview of area schools by going online at www.washdc.org/education.html. Detailed school information is provided, from public to private, primary to college-level as well as listings for other school-related sites and education-related organizations.

For information about a specific **public school** or district, the websites below contain a wealth of information, including school policies, curricula and calendars of events. You can obtain a listing of local area **independent and private schools** from the associations of independent schools also given below. Their websites allow you to search for schools by grade, state and type.

Charter schools are independent public schools, developed and run by educators, parents, community leaders, educational entrepreneurs and others. Local or state educational organizations monitor their quality and integrity, but allow them to operate away from traditional public school policy. Particularly in the District, charter schools have caught on as an innovative public school choice. For further information about charter schools, contact The Center for Education Reform, 1001 Connecticut Ave. NW, Suite 204, Washington, DC 20036 (202-822-9000).

Public and Independent School Information

District of Columbia
415 12th St. NW
Washington, DC 20004
202-724-4222
www.k12.dc.us

Maryland State Department of Education
200 W. Baltimore St.
Baltimore, MD 21202
410-767-0462
www.msde.state.md.us

Anne Arundel County
2644 Riva Road
Annapolis, MD 21401
410-222-5191
www.aacps.org

Calvert County
1305 Dares Beach Rd.
Prince Fredrick, MD 20678
410-535-1700
www/calvertnet.k12.md.us

Charles County
P.O. Box D
5980 Radio Station Rd.
La Plata, MD 20646
301-932-6610
www.ccboe.com

Frederick County
115 East Church St.
Frederick, MD 21701
301-694-1310
www.co.frederick.md.us/fcps

Howard County
10910 Route 108
Ellicott City, MD 21042
410-313-6600
www.howard.k12.md.us

Montgomery County
850 Hungerford Dr.
Rockville, MD 20850
301-279-3167
www.msde.state.md.us

Prince George's County
14201 School La.
Upper Marlboro, MD 20772
301-952-6000
www.pgcps.pg.k12.md.us

St. Mary's County
P.O. Box 641
41170 Baldridge St.
Leonardtown, MD 20650
301-475-4230
www.smcps.k12.md.us

Virginia State Department of Education
James Monroe Building
101 N. 14th St.
Richmond, VA 23219
800-292-3820
www.pen.k12.va.us

Alexandria City
2000 N. Beauregard St.
Alexandria, VA 22311
703-824-6600
www.acps.k12.va.us

Arlington County
1426 N. Quincy St.
Arlington, VA 22207
703-228-6000
www.arlington.k12.va.us

Fairfax County
10700 Page Ave.
Fairfax, VA 22030
703-246-3646
www.fcps.k12.va.us

Falls Church
803 E. Broad St.
Falls Church, VA 22046
703-208-7784

Fauquier County
320 Hospital Drive
Warrenton, VA 20186
540-351-1000
www.libertyhs.com

Loudoun County
102 N. Street, NW
Leesburg, VA 20176
703-771-6400
www.loudoun.k12.va.us

Manassas City
9000 Tudor Ln.
Manassas, VA 20110
703-257-8800
www.manassas.k12.va.us

Prince William County
P.O Box 389
Manassas, VA 20108
703-791-8712
www.pwcs.edu

Stafford County Public Schools
1739 Jefferson Davis Highway
Stafford, VA 22554
540-658-6000
www.pen.k12.va.us/Div/Stafford

For information on independent and private schools, contact one of the following:

Association of Independent Schools of Greater Washington
P.O. Box 9956
Washington DC 20016
202-537-1114
(Prefers to be contacted by mail.)
www.nais.org

Association of Independent Maryland Schools
P.O. Box 802
Severna Park, MD 21146
301-621-0787
www.aimsmd.org

Virginia Association of Independent Schools
8001 Franklin Farms Dr.
Suite 100
Richmond, VA 23229
804-282-3592
www.info@vais.org

MASTERING DC: HISTORIC TOWNS

Throughout the mid-Atlantic there are hundreds of places to visit where you can easily imagine early American life in the 1700s and 1800s. From frontier town to bay-side port...hunt country village to mountain spa town...the past awaits you.

☐ **Head for the Gap:** Located near a major gap in the Appalachian Mountains, **Cumberland, MD** is an early frontier town where the B&O Railroad, C&O Canal and National Road converged in the first half of the 19th century. The town is on the National Register of Historic Places.

☐ **Discover the Treasure:** Also on the National Register is **Brunswick, MD**, a classic 1900s railroad town. The Railroad Museum, an "undiscovered treasure," tells the history of the town. Other claims to fame: country singer Patsy Cline and the Blair Witch.

☐ **Sample the Vintage Port:** Once a thriving colonial village, **St. Michaels, MD** is a tiny yet well-preserved port popular for its quiet charm, historic streets, and Victorian homes. It also attracts for boaters, sailors, cyclists, golfers and fishing aficionados.

☐ **Live the History:** The state's colonial capital until 1695, **St. Mary's City, MD** is today home to an 800-acre living-history museum with recreated town, archeological digs, and an Indian hamlet.

☐ **Think Small, Very Small:** Then visit **Waterford, VA**, a 19th century village in the heart of Virginia hunt country. The entire town, of 200 people, is a National Historic Landmark: a hilly little village with Federal brick houses, spacious Victorian homes, and simple Quaker buildings.

☐ **Join the Hunt:** For a blend of colonial charm and horsey chic, it's **Middleburg, VA**, the "Nation's Horse and Hunt Capital." The town dates from 1728; many early stone buildings still stand. Foxhunting, steeplechase events, and little inns characterize this tiny town of 600 residents.

☐ **Visit the First Washington:** In 1749, 17-year-old George Washington surveyed a thriving frontier trading post. Named for him, **Washington, VA** is often called "Little Washington." Among the authentic colonial period structures are homes built by the first frontiersmen.

☐ **Take the (Bath) Waters:** The country's first spa was frequented by Native Americans long before the colonists came ashore. Established in 1776 as Bath, in honor of Bath, England, **Berkeley Springs, WV** is better known by the name that honors the healing mineral waters that ran down from from Warm Springs Ridge.

☐ **Go Off to College:** Chartered in 1762 as Mecklenburg, VA, **Shepherdstown, WV** may be the oldest town in the state. Situated on a bluff overlooking the Potomac River, the area was home to Native Americans generations before the Europeans arrived. At the core of the community's economy is Shepherd College, established in 1872 as a "Classical and Scientific Institute."

☐ **Visit the Town That Time Almost Forgot:** A center of trade until the 1824 fire destroyed the business district...on the New Castle Frenchtown Railroad until the tracks were re-routed...isolated, but not forgotten, **New Castle, DE** is today a carefully preserved town of Colonial and Federal architecture. Once a year, on the third Saturday in May, the town opens its doors to the public for A Day in Old Newcastle (302-323-4453).

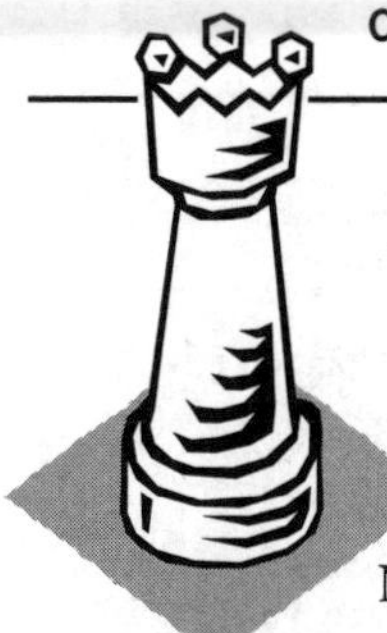

CHAPTER ELEVEN

Resources

Emergency Numbers

Ambulance, Fire, Police	**911**
National Capital Poison Center	**202-625-3333**

Useful Numbers

Automobile and Truck Rental

Alamo	800-327-9633
Avis	800-831-2847
Budget	800-527-0700
Hertz	800-654-3131
National	800-227-7368
Thrifty	800-367-2277

City and County Governments

District of Columbia	202-727-1000
Maryland	
Montgomery County	240-777-1000
Prince George's County	301-350-9700
Virginia	
Alexandria City	703-838-4000
Arlington County	703-228-3000
Fairfax County	703-324-4636
Falls Church City	703-248-5003
Loudoun County	703-777-0212
Prince William County	703-792-6000

Consumer Information

Better Business Bureau	202-393-8000
Washington Consumers' Checkbook	202-347-7283
Yellow Pages: InfoScene	
District of Columbia	202-628-0202
Maryland	301-294-6464
Virginia	703-717-1000

Cultural Organizations

Alliance Française	202-234-7911
Brazilian-American Cultural Institute, Inc.	202-362-8334
The Canadian Club of Washington, DC	703-527-7270
Global Nomads International	202-466-2244
The Goethe Institute	202-289-1200
Irish American Club of Washington, DC	301-625-6516
The Italian Cultural Society of Washington, DC	202-333-2426
The Japan-America Society of Washington, DC, Inc.	202-883-2210
Meridian International Center	202-667-6800
Mexican Cultural Institute	202-728-1628
Society for the Preservation of the Greek Heritage	202-363-4337

Embassies

Located in DC (see pages 283-292)	www.embassy.org
US Embassy & Consulate Websites Worldwide	http://travel.state.gov

Gay and Lesbian Resources

AIDS Hotline (English)	800-342-AIDS
AIDS Hotline (Spanish)	800-344-7432
HIV Testing	202-332-3926
Gay and Lesbian Switchboard	202-833-3234
Directory of *The Other Pages*	202-265-5073
Online Information	www.gay.net
Travelers' Information Site	www.outandabout.com

Hospitals

District of Columbia

Children's Hospital National Medical Center 111 Michigan Ave. NW	202-884-5000 202-884-3444 (TDD)
Columbia Hospital for Women Medical Center 2425 L St. NW	202-293-6500
DC General Massachusetts Ave. and 19th St. SE	202-675-5000 202-675-5154 (TDD)
George Washington University Hospital 901 23rd St. NW	202-994-1000 202-994-5610 (TDD)

Georgetown University Medical Center 3800 Reservoir Rd. NW	202-687-2000 202-687-4639 (TDD)
Greater Southeast Community Hospital 1310 Southern Ave. SE	202-574-6000
Howard University Hospital 2041 Georgia Ave. NW	202-865-6100
Medlink Hospital at Capitol Hill 700 Constitution Ave. NE	202-546-5700
National Rehabilitation Hospital 102 Irving St. NW	202-865-6100
Providence Hospital 1150 Varnum St. NE	202-269-7000
Psychiatric Institute of Washington 4228 Wisconsin Ave. NW	202-965-8200
Sibley Memorial Hospital 5255 Loughboro Rd. NW	202-537-4000
Washington Hospital Center 110 Irving St. NW	202-877-7000
Maryland	
Doctor's Community Hospital 8118 Good Luck Rd., Lanham	301-552-8118 301-552-8078 (TDD)
Holy Cross Hospital 1500 Forest Glen Rd., Silver Spring	301-754-7000 301-754-7406 (TDD)
NIH - Clinical Center 9000 Rockville Pike, Bethesda	301-496-2563
Prince George's Hospital Center 3001 Hospital Dr., Cheverly	301-618-2000
Suburban Hospital 8600 Old Georgetown Rd., Bethesda	301-896-3100 301-896-2010 (TDD)
Washington Adventist Hospital 7600 Carroll Ave., Takoma Park	301-891-7600 301-891-5444 (TDD)
Virginia	
The Arlington Hospital 1701 N. George Mason Dr., Arlington	703-558-5000

Inova Alexandria Hospital
4320 Seminary Rd., Alexandria 703-504-3000

Inova Fair Oaks Hospital
3600 Joseph Siewick Dr., Fairfax 703-391-3600

Inova Fairfax Hospital
3300 Gallows Rd., Falls Church 703-698-1110

Loudoun Hospital Center
224 Cornwall St., Leesburg 703-777-3300

Prince William Hospital
8700 Sudley Rd., Manassas 703-631-0096

Humane Society

District of Columbia
7319 Georgia Avenue NW 202-723-5730

Maryland
Montgomery County
14645 Rothgeb Dr., Rockville 301-279-1823

Prince George's County
8311 D'Arcy Rd., Forestville 410-499-8300

Virginia
Alexandria
910 S. Payne St., Alexandria 703-838-4774

Arlington County
2650 S. Arlington Mill Dr., Arlington 703-931-9241

Fairfax County
4057 Chain Bridge Rd., Fairfax 703-385-7387

Loudoun County
PO Box 601, Leesburg 703-777-2912

Prince William County
14807 Dumfries Rd., Manassas 703-792-6465

Lawyer Referral Service

District of Columbia 202-337-4686
Montgomery County 301-279-9100
Prince George's County 301-952-1440
Northern Virginia 800-552-7977

Medical and Health Services

AIDS Hotline (English)	800-342-AIDS
AIDS Hotline (Spanish)	800-344-7432
HIV Testing	202-332-3926
National Domestic Violence Hotline	800-799-SAFE
Planned Parenthood Clinic	
District of Columbia	202-347-8512
Silver Spring, Maryland	301-608-3448
Northern Virginia	703-533-5651
Rape Crisis Hotline	
District of Columbia	202-333-7273
Montgomery County	301-315-4357
Prince George's County	301-618-3154
Northern Virginia	703-527-4077
Suicide Hotline	
District of Columbia	202-561-7000
Montgomery County	301-738-2255
Prince George's County	301-577-4866
Northern Virginia	703-527-4077
Youth Crisis Hotline	800-HIT-HOME
Whitman-Walker Clinic	202-797-3500

Medical Referral Services

Dentist Referrals	
District of Columbia	202-547-7615
Montgomery County	800-422-8338
Prince George's County	301-345-4196
Northern Virginia	703-691-2424
Doctor Referrals (Metro area)	202-877-3627

Pet Movers

Air Animal (Nationwide)	800-635-3448
Cosmopolitan Canine Carriers, Inc. (Domestic and International)	800-738-7356

Pharmacies, 24-Hour CVS/Pharmacies

DC

Dupont Circle, 6-7 Dupont Circle NW	202-785-1466
14th St. Area, 1121 Vermont Ave. NW	202-628-0720
Tenleytown, 4555 Wisconsin Ave, NW	202-537-1587

Maryland

Bethesda-Chevy Chase, 6917 Arlington Rd.	301-656-2522
District Heights, Silver Illil Plaza	301-736-3994
Gaithersburg Square, Gaithersburg	301-948-3250
Greenbelt, 5910 Greenbelt Rd.	301-441-8810
Langley Park Shopping Center	301-434-3121

Virginia

Alexandria, 5101 Duke St.	703-823-7430
Arlington, 3133 Lee Highway	703-522-0260
Fairfax, Greenbriar Shopping Center	703-378-7550
Falls Church, 8124 Arlington Blvd.	703-560-7280
Springfield, 6436 Springfield Plaza	703-451-1400

Police Non-Emergency Calls

Alexandria	703-838-4444
Arlington	703-558-2222
Bethesda-Chevy Chase	301-652-9200
District of Columbia	202-727-1010
Falls Church	703-248-5054
Montgomery County	240-773-5390
Prince George's County	301-336-8800

Postal Service Answer Line (24 hour) 800-725-2161

Religious Organizations

Buddhist	202-723-0773
Catholic Information Center	202-783-2062
Episcopal Diocese of Washington	202-537-6555
Friends Meeting of Washington	202-483-3310
Interfaith Conference of Metropolitan Washington	202-234-6300
Islamic Center	202-332-8343
Jewish Information and Referral Service	301-770-4848
Presbyterian	202-543-1126
Unitarian Universalist Church of Arlington	703-892-2565

Schools

(see page 272)

Time (local area code required in MD and VA) 844-1212

Naval Observatory Clock	202-762-1401

Travel Resources (International)

Passport Applications or Renewals

Washington Passport Agency	202-647-0518
1111 19th St. NW (by appointment only)	http://travel.state.gov

Immunizations/Testing

Travelers Medical Service of Washington

2141 K St. NW	202-466-8109

Foreign Currency

The American Express Travel Service Offices

1150 Connecticut Ave. NW	202-457-1300
5300 Wisconsin Ave. NW (Mazza Gallerie)	202-362-4000
10480 Little Patuxent Pkwy., Columbia	410-997-1100
1100 S. Hayes, Arlington	703-415-5400
Springfield Mall, Springfield	703-971-5600
Tysons Galleria, McLean	703-893-3550
American Express 24-Hour Refund/Purchase	800-221-7282

Ruesch International

700 11th St. NW	202-408-1200

Thomas Cook Currency Services 800-287-7362

Travel Advisories

US State Department
Office of Overseas Citizens Services

Telephone	202-647-5225
Automated Fax Service	202-647-3000
Internet	http://travel.state.gov

US Capitol Switchboard 202-224-3121

Veterinarians/Animal Hospitals (24 Hour)

DC

Friendship Hospital for Animals

4105 Brandywine St. NW	202-363-7300

Maryland
Four Corners Animal Hospital
105 University Blvd. W, Silver Spring 301-593-6330

Virginia
Alexandria Veterinary Emergency Service
2660 Duke St., Alexandria 703-823-3601

Washington Animal Rescue League 202-726-2556

Washington, DC Convention and Visitors Association 202-789-7000

Weather (local area code required in MD and VA) 936-1212
National Weather Service Forecast Line:
Local and Extended 703-260-0307

Weather-related Websites

Weather www.nws.noaa.gov
www.weather.com

Earthquakes http://quake.wr.usgs.gov

Hurricanes www.nhc.noaa.gov

Zip Codes 202-635-5300
www.usps.gov/ncsc

EMBASSIES

ALBANIA
Embassy of the Republic of Albania
1511 K St. NW, 20005
202-223-4942

ALGERIA
Embassy of the Democratic
and Popular Republic of Algeria
2118 Kalorama Rd NW, 20008
202-265-2800

ANGOLA
Embassy of the Republic of Angola
1615 M St. NW, 20036
202-785-1156

ANTIGUA AND BARBUDA
Embassy of Antigua and Barbuda
3216 New Mexico Ave. NW, 20016
202-362-5211

ARGENTINA
Embassy of the Argentine Republic
1600 New Hampshire Ave. NW, 20009
202-238-6400

ARMENIA
Embassy of the Republic of Armenia
2225 R St. NW, 20008
202-319-1976

AUSTRALIA
Embassy of Australia
1601 Massachusetts Ave. NW, 20036
202-797-3000

AUSTRIA
Embassy of Austria
3524 International Court NW, 20008
202-895-6700

AZERBAIJAN
Embassy of the Republic of Azerbaijan
927 15th St. NW, 20005
202-842-0001

BAHAMAS
Embassy of the Commonwealth
of the Bahamas
2220 Massachusetts Ave. NW, 20008
202-319-2660

BAHRAIN
Embassy of the State of Bahrain
3502 International Dr. NW, 20008
202-342-0741

BANGLADESH
Embassy of the People's
Republic of Bangladesh
2201 Wisconsin Ave. NW, 20007
202-342-8372

BARBADOS
Embassy of Barbados
2144 Wyoming Ave. NW, 20008
202-939-9200

BARBUDA
See Antigua and Barbuda

BELARUS
Embassy of the Republic of Belarus
1619 New Hampshire Ave. NW, 20009
202-986-1604

BELGIUM
Embassy of Belgium
3330 Garfield St. NW, 20008
202-333-6900

BELIZE
Embassy of Belize
2535 Massachusetts Ave. NW, 20008
202-332-9636

BENIN
Embassy of the Republic of Benin
2737 Cathedral Ave. NW, 20008
202-232-6656

BOLIVIA
Embassy of the Republic of Bolivia
3014 Massachusetts Ave. NW, 20008
202-483-4410

BOSNIA AND HERZEGOVINA
Embassy of the Republic of Bosnia and Herzegovina
2109 E St. NW, 20037
202-337-1500

BOTSWANA
Embassy of the Republic of Botswana
1531-1533 New Hampshire Ave. NW, 20036
202-244-4990

BRAZIL
Brazilian Embassy
3006 Massachusetts Ave. NW, 20008
202-238-2700

BRUNEI
Embassy of the State of Brunei Darussalam
2600 Virginia Ave. NW, 20037
202-342-0159

BULGARIA
Embassy of the Republic of Bulgaria
1621 22nd St. NW, 20008
202-387-7969

BURKINA FASO
Embassy of Burkina Faso
2340 Massachusetts Ave. NW, 20008
202-332-5577

BURUNDI
Embassy of the Republic of Burundi
2233 Wisconsin Ave. NW, 20007
202-342-2574

CAMBODIA
Royal Embassy of Cambodia
4500 16th St. NW, 20011
202-726-7742

CAMEROON
Embassy of the Republic of Cameroon
2349 Massachusetts Ave. NW, 20008
202-265-8790

CANADA
Embassy of Canada
501 Pennsylvania Ave. NW, 20001
202-682-1740

CAPE VERDE
Embassy of the Republic of Cape Verde
3415 Massachusetts Ave. NW, 20007
202-965-6820

CENTRAL AFRICAN REPUBLIC
Embassy of Central African Republic
1618 22nd St. NW, 20008
202-483-7800

CHAD
Embassy of the Republic of Chad
2002 R St. NW, 20009
202-462-4009

CHILE
Embassy of Chile
1732 Massachusetts Ave. NW, 20036
202-785-1746

CHINA
Embassy of the People's Republic of China
2300 Connecticut Ave. NW, 20008
202-328-2500

COLOMBIA
Embassy of Colombia
2118 Leroy Pl. NW, 20008
202-387-8338

CONGO, DEMOCRATIC REPUBLIC OF
Embassy of the Democratic Republic of Congo
1800 New Hampshire Ave. NW, 20009
202-234-7690

COSTA RICA
Embassy of Costa Rica
2114 S St. NW, 20008
202-234-2945

COTE D'IVOIRE
Embassy of the Republic of Cote d'Ivoire
2424 Massachusetts Ave. NW, 20008
202-797-0300

CROATIA
Embassy of the Republic of Croatia
2343 Massachusetts Ave. NW, 20008
202-588-5899

CYPRUS
Embassy of the Republic of Cyprus
2211 R St. NW, 20008
202-462-5772

CZECHOSLOVAKIA
Embassy of the Czech Republic
3900 Spring of Freedom St. NW, 20008
202-363-6315

DENMARK
Royal Danish Embassy
3200 Whitehaven St. NW, 20008
202-234-4300

DJIBOUTI
Embassy of the Republic of Djibouti
1156 15th St. NW, 20005
202-331-0270

DOMINICA
Embassy of the Commonwealth of Dominica
3216 New Mexico Ave. NW, 20016
202-364-6781

DOMINICAN REPUBLIC
Embassy of the Dominican Republic
1715 22nd St. NW, 20008
202-332-6280

ECUADOR
Embassy of Ecuador
2535 15th St. NW, 20009
202-234-7200

EGYPT
Embassy of the Arab Republic of Egypt
3521 International Court NW, 20008
202-895-5400

EL SALVADOR
Embassy of El Salvador
2308 California St. NW, 20008
202-265-9671

EQUATORIAL GUINEA
Embassy of the Equatorial Guinea
1712 I St. NW, 20006
202-296-4174

ERITREA
Embassy of the State of Eritrea
1708 New Hampshire Ave. NW, 20009
202-319-1991

ESTONIA
Embassy of Estonia
2131 Massachusetts Ave. NW, 20008
202-558-0101

ETHIOPIA
Embassy of Ethiopia
2134 Kalorama Rd. NW, 20008
202-234-2281

EUROPEAN UNION
Delegation of the European Commission
2300 M St. NW, 20007
202-862-9500

FIJI
Embassy of the Republic of Fiji
2233 Wisconsin Ave. NW, 20007
202-337-8320

FINLAND
Embassy of Finland
3301 Massachusetts Ave. NW, 20008
202-298-5800

FRANCE
Embassy of France
4101 Reservoir Rd. NW, 20007
202-944-6000

GABON
Embassy of the Gabonese Republic
2034 20th St. NW, 20009
202-797-1000

GAMBIA, THE
Embassy of The Gambia
1155 15th St. NW, 20005
202-785-1399

GEORGIA
Embassy of the Republic of Georgia
1615 New Hampshire Ave. NW, 20009
202-393-6060

GERMANY, FEDERAL REPUBLIC OF
Embassy of the Federal Republic of Germany
4645 Reservoir Rd. NW, 20007
202-298-8141

GHANA
Embassy of Ghana
3512 International Dr. NW, 20008
202-686-4520

GREAT BRITAIN
See United Kingdom of Great Britain and Northern Ireland

GREECE
Embassy of Greece
2221 Massachusetts Ave. NW, 20008
202-939-5800

GRENADA
Embassy of Grenada
1701 New Hampshire Ave. NW, 20009
202-265-2561

GRENADINES
See Saint Vincent and the Grenadines

GUATEMALA
Embassy of Guatemala
2220 R St. NW, 20008
202-745-4952

GUINEA
Embassy of the Republic of Guinea
2112 Leroy Pl. NW, 20008
202-483-9420

GUINEA-BISSAU
Embassy of the Republic of Guinea-Bissau
1511 K St. NW, 20005
202-347-3950

GUYANA
Embassy of Guyana
2490 Tracy Pl. NW, 20008
202-265-6900

HAITI
Embassy of the Republic of Haiti
2311 Massachusetts Ave. NW, 20008
202-332-4090

HERZEGOVINA
See Bosnia and Herzegovina

The HOLY SEE
Apostolic Nunciature
3339 Massachusetts Ave. NW, 20008
202-333-7121

HONDURAS
Embassy of Honduras
3007 Tilden St. NW, 20008
202-966-7702

HUNGARY
Embassy of the Republic of Hungary
3910 Shoemaker St. NW, 20008
202-362-6730

ICELAND
Embassy of Iceland
1156 15th St. NW, 20005
202-265-6653

INDIA
Embassy of India
2107 Massachusetts Ave. NW, 20008
202-939-7000

INDONESIA
Embassy of the Republic of Indonesia
2020 Massachusetts Ave. NW, 20036
202-775-5200

IRELAND
Embassy of Ireland
2234 Massachusetts Ave. NW, 20008
202-462-3939

IRELAND, NORTHERN
See United Kingdom of Great Britain and Northern Ireland

ISRAEL
Embassy of Israel
3514 International Dr. NW, 20008
202-364-5500

ITALY
Embassy of Italy
1601 Fuller St. NW, 20009
202-328-5500

IVORY COAST
See Cote d'Ivoire

JAMAICA
Embassy of Jamaica
1520 New Hampshire Ave. NW, 20036
202-452-0660

JAPAN
Embassy of Japan
2520 Massachusetts Ave. NW, 20008
202-238-6700

JORDAN
Embassy of the Hashemite Kingdom of Jordan
3504 International Dr. NW, 20008
202-966-2664

KAZAKHSTAN
Embassy of the Republic of Kazakhstan
3421 Massachusetts Ave. NW, 20008
202-333-4504

KENYA
Embassy of the Republic of Kenya
2249 R St. NW, 20008
202-387-6101

KOREA
Embassy of Korea
2450 Massachusetts Ave. NW, 20008
202-939-5600

KUWAIT
Embassy of the State of Kuwait
2940 Tilden St. NW, 20008
202-966-0702

KYRGYZSTAN
Embassy of the Kyrgyz Republic
1511 K St. NW, 20005
202-347-3732

LAOS
Embassy of the Lao People's Democratic Republic
2222 S St. NW, 20008
202-332-6416

LATVIA
Embassy of Latvia
4325 17th St. NW, 20011
202-726-8213

LEBANON
Embassy of Lebanon
2560 28th St. NW, 20008
202-939-6300

LESOTHO
Embassy of the Kingdom of Lesotho
2511 Massachusetts Ave. NW, 20008
202-797-5533

LIBERIA
Embassy of the Republic of Liberia
5303 Colorado Ave. NW, 20011
202-723-0437

LITHUANIA
Embassy of the Republic of Lithuania
2622 16th St. NW, 20009
202-234-5860

LUXEMBOURG
Embassy of the Grand Duchy of Luxembourg
2200 Massachusetts Ave. NW, 20008
202-265-4171

MACEDONIA
Embassy of the Republic of Macedonia
3050 K St. NW, 20007
202-337-3063

MADAGASCAR
Embassy of the Democratic Republic of Madagascar
2374 Massachusetts Ave. NW, 20008
202-265-5525

MALAWI
Embassy of Malawi
2408 Massachusetts Ave. NW, 20008
202-797-1007

MALAYSIA
Embassy of Malaysia
2401 Massachusetts Ave. NW, 20008
202-328-2700

MALI
Embassy of the Republic of Mali
2130 R St. NW, 20008
202-332-2249

MALTA
Embassy of Malta
2017 Connecticut Ave. NW, 20008
202-462-3611

MARSHALL ISLANDS
Embassy of the Republic of the Marshall Islands
2433 Massachusetts Ave. NW, 20008
202-234-5414

MAURITANIA
Embassy of the Islamic Republic of Mauritania
2129 Leroy Pl. NW, 20008
202-232-5700

MAURITIUS
Embassy of Republic of Mauritius
4301 Connecticut Ave. NW, 20008
202-244-1491

MEXICO
Embassy of Mexico
1911 Pennsylvania Ave. NW, 20006
202-728-1600

MICRONESIA
Embassy of the Federated States of Micronesia
1725 N St. NW, 20036
202-223-4383

MOLDOVA
Embassy of the Republic of Moldova
2101 S St. NW, 20008
202-667-1130

MONGOLIA
Embassy of Mongolia
2833 M St. NW, 20007
202-333-7117

MOROCCO
Embassy of the Kingdom of Morocco
1601 21st St. NW, 20009
202-462-7979

MOZAMBIQUE
Embassy of the Republic of Mozambique
1990 M St. NW, 20036
202-293-7146

NAMIBIA
Embassy of the Republic of Namibia
1605 New Hampshire Ave. NW, 20009
202-986-0540

NEPAL
Royal Nepalese Embassy
2131 Leroy Pl. NW, 20008
202-667-4550

NETHERLANDS
Royal Netherlands Embassy
4200 Linnean Ave. NW, 20008
202-244-5300

NEVIS
See Saint Kitts and Nevis

NEW ZEALAND
Embassy of New Zealand
37 Observatory Circle NW, 20008
202-328-4800

NICARAGUA
Embassy of Nicaragua
1627 New Hampshire Ave. NW, 20009
202-939-6570

NIGER
Embassy of the Republic of Niger
2204 R St. NW, 20008
202-483-4224

NIGERIA
Embassy of the Federal Republic of Nigeria
1333 16th St. NW, 20036
202-986-8400

NORWAY
Royal Norwegian Embassy
2720 34th St. NW, 20008
202-333-6000

OMAN
Embassy of the Sultanate of Oman
2535 Belmont Rd. NW, 20008
202-387-1980

PAKISTAN
Embassy of Pakistan
2315 Massachusetts Ave. NW, 20008
202-939-6200

PALAU
Embassy of the Republic of Palau
1150 18th St. NW, 20036
202-452-6814

PANAMA
Embassy of the Republic of Panama
2862 McGill Terrace NW, 20008
202-483-1407

PAPUA NEW GUINEA
Embassy of Papua New Guinea
1779 Massachusetts Ave. NW, 20036
202-745-3680

PARAGUAY
Embassy of Paraguay
2400 Massachusetts Ave. NW, 20008
202-483-6960

PERU
Embassy of Peru
1700 Massachusetts Ave. NW, 20036
202-833-9860

PHILIPPINES
Embassy of the Philippines
1600 Massachusetts Ave. NW, 20036
202-467-9300

POLAND
Embassy of the Republic of Poland
2640 16th St. NW, 20009
202-234-3800

PORTUGAL
Embassy of Portugal
2125 Kalorama Rd. NW, 20008
202-328-8610

QATAR
Embassy of the State of Qatar
4200 Wisconsin Ave. NW, 20016
202-274-1600

ROMANIA
Embassy of Romania
1607 23rd St. NW, 20008
202-332-4846

RUSSIA
Embassy of the Russian Federation
2650 Wisconsin Ave. NW, 20007
202-298-5700

RWANDA
Embassy of the Republic of Rwanda
1714 New Hampshire Ave. NW, 20009
202-232-2882

SAINT KITTS AND NEVIS
Embassy of St. Kitts and Nevis
3216 New Mexico Ave. NW, 20016
202-686-2636

SAINT LUCIA
Embassy of Saint Lucia
3216 New Mexico Ave. NW, 20016
202-364-6792

SAINT VINCENT AND THE GRENADINES
Embassy of Saint Vincent and the Grenadines
3216 New Mexico Ave. NW, 20016
202-364-6730

SAUDI ARABIA
Embassy of Saudi Arabia
601 New Hampshire Ave. NW, 20037
202-342-3800

SENEGAL
Embassy of the Republic of Senegal
2112 Wyoming Ave. NW, 20008
202-234-0540

SIERRA LEONE
Embassy of Sierra Leone
1701 19th St. NW, 20009
202-939-9261

SINGAPORE
Embassy of the Republic of Singapore
3501 International Place NW, 20008
202-537-3100

SLOVAKIA
Embassy of the Slovak Republic
2201 Wisconsin Ave., 20007
202-965-5160

SLOVENIA
Embassy of the Republic of Slovenia
1525 New Hampshire Ave. NW, 20036
202-667-5363

SOUTH AFRICA
Embassy of the Republic of South Africa
3051 Massachusetts Ave. NW, 20008
202-232-4400

SPAIN
Embassy of Spain
2375 Pennsylvania Ave. NW, 20037
202-728-2340

SRI LANKA
Embassy of the Democratic Socialist Republic of Sri Lanka
2148 Wyoming Ave. NW, 20008
202-483-4025

SUDAN
Embassy of the Republic of the Sudan
2210 Massachusetts Ave. NW, 20008
202-338-8565

SURINAME
Embassy of the Republic of Suriname
4301 Connecticut Ave. NW, 20008
202-244-7488

SWAZILAND
Embassy of the Kingdom of Swaziland
3400 International Dr. NW, 20008
202-362-6683

SWEDEN
Embassy of Sweden
1501 M St. NW, 20005
202-467-2600

SWITZERLAND
Embassy of Switzerland
2900 Cathedral Ave. NW, 20008
202-745-7900

SYRIA
Embassy of the Syrian Arab Republic
2215 Wyoming Ave. NW, 20008
202-232-6313

TANZANIA
Embassy of the United Republic of Tanzania
2139 R St. NW, 20008
202-939-6125

THAILAND
Royal Thai Embassy
1024 Wisconsin Ave. NW, 20007
202-944-3600

TOBAGO
See Trinidad and Tobago

TOGO
Embassy of the Republic of Togo
2208 Massachusetts Ave. NW, 20008
202-234-4212

TRINIDAD AND TOBAGO
Embassy of the Republic of Trinidad and Tobago
1708 Massachusetts Ave. NW, 20036
202-467-6490

TUNISIA
Embassy of Tunisia
1515 Massachusetts Ave. NW, 20005
202-862-1850

TURKEY
Embassy of the Republic of Turkey
2525 Massachusetts Ave. NW, 20008
202-518-9601

TURKMENISTAN
Embassy of Turkmenistan
2207 Massachusetts Ave. NW, 20008
202-558-1500

UGANDA
Embassy of the Republic of Uganda
5911 16th St. NW, 20011
202-726-7100

UKRAINE
Embassy of Ukraine
3350 M St. NW, 20007
202-333-0606

UNITED ARAB EMIRATES
Embassy of the United Arab Emirates
1255 22nd St. NW, 20037
202-955-7999

UNITED KINGDOM OF GREAT BRITAIN AND NORTHERN IRELAND
British Embassy
3100 Massachusetts Ave. NW, 20008
202-558-6500

URUGUAY
Embassy of Uruguay
2715 M St. NW, 20007
202-331-1313

UZBEKISTAN
Embassy of the Republic of Uzbekistan
1746 Massachusetts Ave. NW, 20036
202-887-5300

VENEZUELA
Embassy of the Republic of Venezuela
1099 30th St. NW, 20007
202-342-2214

VIETNAM
Embassy of Vietnam
1233 20th St. NW, 20036
202-861-0737

YEMEN
Embassy of the Republic of Yemen
2600 Virginia Ave. NW, 20037
202-965-4760

ZAMBIA
Embassy of the Republic of Zambia
2419 Massachusetts Ave. NW, 20008
202-265-9717

ZIMBABWE
Embassy of the Republic of Zimbabwe
1608 New Hampshire Ave. NW, 20009
202-332-7100

Washington, DC Historical Time Line

When Europeans and Africans began arriving in what is now Virginia, they met natives from three linguistic backgrounds. Most of the coastal plain was inhabited by an Algonquian empire, today collectively known as Powhatan; the southwestern coastal plain was occupied by Iroquoians; and the Piedmont was home to the Sioux. By the early 1600s, the Virginia mountains were hunting territory to many peoples and home to few.

1607 First permanent English settlement is founded at Jamestown, VA.

1608 Captain John Smith encountered the largest settlement of Native Americans in the District, the Nacotchtonk, at what is now Anacostia Park.

1662 First land patent on the future site of the District is granted.

1742 Bladensburg is established in Maryland.

1749 Alexandria is established in Virginia.

1751 Georgetown is established by Maryland Assembly.

1765 Old Stone House is built in what is Georgetown today.

1783 American Revolution ends.

1787 Constitutional Convention frames federal constitution providing for creation of a national capital site.

1788 Maryland and Virginia give land to form a federal district.

1789 The US Constitution is ratified and George Washington is elected the first US President.

1790 Congress authorizes George Washington to finalize the site for a federal territory, with stipulation that it not exceed 10 square miles in total size.

1791 George Washington announces federal site. Pierre Charles L'Enfant is appointed to design the city, and Andrew Ellicott and Benjamin Banneker survey the area.

1792 L'Enfant is fired as city planner, and the cornerstone is laid for the White House.

1793 Cornerstone of the Capitol building is laid.

1800 Congress and the rest of the Federal Government move from Philadelphia and the District becomes the nation's capital. Capitol building is still under construction.

1801 Thomas Jefferson elected President, Supreme Court arrives from Philadelphia, and Congress assumes jurisdiction over the District of Columbia.

1802 City of Washington is incorporated and Congress establishes a local governing body—a mayor and a council—for the District.

1812 War with Britain begins.

1814 British troops invade the city and burn the Capitol, White House, and other buildings. A torrential rainstorm saves the rest of the city.

1815 Treaty of Ghent, ending the War of 1812 is signed at the Octagon House, President Madison's temporary residence. Congress moves to "Brick Capitol" on grounds of current Supreme Court Building while original Capitol is rebuilt.

1816 St. John's church opens on Lafayette Square.

1824 General Lafayette visits America as guest of the nation, and park is named for him.

1835 Baltimore and Ohio Railroad reaches Washington.

1846 Residents in the portion of the Federal District south of the Potomac River succeed in having that area returned to Virginia. Smithsonian Institution is chartered by Congress.

1848 Cornerstone of the Washington Monument is laid.

1850 Chesapeake and Ohio Canal is completed. Slave trade is abolished in Washington, although slave ownership remains legal.

1855 The Smithsonian's first building, the Castle, is completed.

1861 Abraham Lincoln is inaugurated as 16th president. The War between the States begins and a network of forts is erected around the city's southern perimeter.

1862 Congress abolishes slavery in the District.

1863 President Lincoln issues the Emancipation Proclamation.

1865 Civil War ends.
President Lincoln is assassinated at Ford's Theater.

1867 Congress gives Washington residents the right to vote.

1871 Howard University is founded. Georgetown is annexed by DC. Congress creates a territorial government for the District; all local officials are appointed by the president.

1874 A panel of three commissioners, appointed by the president, administers the city; voting rights for Washington residents are stripped.

1877 Washington Post is founded.

1885 Washington Monument is dedicated.

1888 First street car is introduced in DC.

1890 Library of Congress cornerstone laid. Rock Creek Park and Potomac Park are established.

1897 Library of Congress building opens.

1907 Cornerstone is laid for Washington National Cathedral.

1908 Union Station opens.

1910 The National Commission of Fine Arts is established to oversee the development of the Capitol.

1912 First two cherry trees, gifts from Japan, are planted.

1914 Construction begins on Lincoln Memorial.

1917 America enters World War I and Washington experiences an influx of war workers.

1918 World War I ends.

1922 Lincoln Memorial is dedicated.

1924 Key Bridge opens.

1931 Hunger Marchers demonstrate during the Great Depression

1932 Franklin D. Roosevelt elected as president. Folger Shakespeare Library opens.

1935 Both the Supreme Court and the National Archives buildings are completed.

1939 Marian Anderson gives free concert on the steps of the Lincoln Memorial after the DAR refuses to allow her to perform at Constitution Hall because she is black.

1941 National Gallery of Art opens; National Airport opens. World War II begins and population again surges.

1943 Pentagon is completed and the Jefferson Memorial is dedicated.

1945 World War II ends.

1949 NATO Treaty is signed at Departmental Auditorium in the District Building.

1954 Supreme Court decision in Brown vs. Board of Education leads to desegregation of Washington's public schools.

1961 John F. Kennedy is inaugurated the 34th president. Congress ratifies the 23rd Amendment to the Constitution, giving Washington residents the right to vote in presidential, not local, elections.

1963 Civil rights leader Martin Luther King, Jr. leads March on Washington and delivers his "I Have a Dream" speech on the steps of the Lincoln Memorial. President Kennedy is assassinated in Dallas and buried at Arlington National Cemetery.

1964 Capital Beltway is completed.

1967 Congress replaces the three-commissioner District government with a mayor, an assistant commissioner and a city council, all appointed by the president.

1968 Rev. Dr. Martin Luther King, Jr. is assassinated in Memphis, TN, sparking race riots in Washington that kill several people and cause millions of dollars of property damage.

1970 District residents are given the right to elect one non-voting delegate to the House of Representatives. Anti-Vietnam War demonstrations occur on the Mall.

1971 John F. Kennedy Center for the Performing Arts opens.

1972 Break-in at the Democratic National Headquarters at the Watergate office complex leads to greatest political scandal in nation's history.

1974 As a result of the Watergate scandal, President Richard Nixon becomes the first President in US history to resign.

1975 Home rule is restored and Walter Washington is the first elected mayor of Washington, DC.

1976 US celebrates its bicentennial. Metro begins operation and the National Air and Space Museum opens.

1978 Marion Barry is elected as Mayor.

1982 Vietnam War Memorial, known as "The Wall" is built. Marion Barry is re-elected.

1984 Washington Convention Center opens.

1986 Marion Barry elected to third term as Mayor.

1990 Washington National Cathedral is completed after 73 years of construction. Citizens elect Sharon Pratt Dixon as Mayor, the first black woman elected to head a major US city.

1993 DC statehood is rejected by Congress.

1995 Pennsylvania Ave. closes to motorists between 15th and 17th Sts. to protect the White House from terrorist attacks. Congress establishes Financial Control Board to manage DC government. African American men from across the country participate in the Million Man March held on the Mall.

1996 Marion Barry is re-elected as Mayor.

1997 Franklin D. Roosevelt memorial is dedicated. The Women in Military Service Memorial opens. MCI Center opens.

1997 Anthony Williams is elected as Mayor.

1999 African American Civil War Memorial is dedicated.

B

F

G

H

I

J

M

N

R

S

V

W

Y

Restaurants, Bars and Pubs

N O T E S